Chief Constables

Chief
Constables

Bobbies, Bosses, or Bureaucrats?

Robert Reiner

OXFORD UNIVERSITY PRESS
1991

Oxford University Press, Walton Street, Oxford OX2 6DP

Oxford New York Toronto
Delhi Bombay Calcutta Madras Karachi
Petaling Java Singapore Hong Kong Tokyo
Nairobi Dar es Salaam Cape Town
Melbourne Auckland

and associated companies in
Berlin Ibadan

Oxford is a trade mark of Oxford University Press

Published in the United States
by Oxford University Press, New York

British Library Cataloguing in Publication Data
data available

Library of Congress Cataloging in Publication Data
Reiner, Robert, 1946–
   Chief constables: bobbies, bosses, or bureaucrats? | Robert Reiner.
     Includes bibliographical references and index.
   1. Police administration—England.   2. Police administration—
   Wales.   3. Police chiefs—England—Interviews.   4. Police chiefs—
   Wales—Interviews.   I. Title.
   HV8196.A3R45   1991   363.2'0941—dc20   91-11766
   ISBN 0-19-825622-1

Typeset and Printed in Great Britain by
Butler & Tanner Ltd
Frome and London

For Toby and Charlotte
—A Bar/Batmitzvah Gift

Preface

In the early days of my fieldwork for this book, I was having lunch with a well-known professor of law when the subject of my research came up. He remarked that he had found chief constables to be a rather unintelligent lot, and I must be finding the study tedious and hard going. This comment typifies the snobbish disdain with which the police in general, and their chief officers in particular, have tended to be viewed by other élites. It underlies the neglect of chief constables in the existing social science literature on élites. It also exposes the police to recurrent concern about the calibre of their leadership, such as the present flurry of calls for a new 'officer class' to be established.

In fact the data on the background and career patterns of chief constables which this study presents imply a quite different conclusion. Coming from manual working-class origins for the most part, today's chief police officers have risen to the top of the career hierarchy by dint of merit rather than social pedigree. Their success in the educational system indicates intellectual capacities which refute the canard offered by the eminent professor. The combination of street wisdom with intellectual potential is arguably the appropriate qualification for the tightrope-walking wizardry required of the modern police executive.

The chief constables I interviewed did for the most part succeed in blending the best characteristics of the traditional British bobby with the managerial skills of the efficient bureaucrat. I am grateful to them all, for their willingness to be interviewed for this research, and for their courtesy and generous hospitality during my visits to their forces. I shall not single out any individuals in order to honour the spirit of my undertaking to keep the interviews anonymous.

In the text care has been taken to prevent quotes being individually identifiable. I am sure that police readers in particular will be eager to play 'spot the chief constable'. However, my experience of their attempts to do this when I have delivered portions of this book to conference or seminar groups suggests that these attempts at identification are more likely to be wrong than right. Those who think they have been able to pin a comment to their own chief have probably got the wrong suspect.

In addition to the forty chiefs who gave me the opportunity to interview them, I have a number of debts to acknowledge. The Nuffield Foundation made this research possible by granting me one of their Social Science Research Fellowships in 1986–7, and I am most grateful for their support. Rose Jacobs and Jackie Williams of the Bristol University Law Faculty Office did a marvellous job at transcribing the interview tapes, as did Joyce Allen with processing my scribbled words. My wife Miki put up with the usual symptoms of writer's grumpiness for an unusually long time. The time would have been even longer if not for the strict disciplines imposed by the daily enquiries of my children, Toby and Charlotte, asking how many pages I had written. Thanks to them, my quill kept moving. Finally, my father and late mother's accounts of life (and death) in a murderous police state have been a source of my continuing interest in the dynamics of a benign policing system. The text was completed in September 1990, and the information given is intended to be correct as of then. I *am* aware that the Prime Minister is no longer a she.

R.R.
Law Department
London School of Economics
1 December 1990

Contents

x   *Contents*

List of Tables

Abbreviations

ACPO	Association of Chief Police Officers
CPS	Crown Prosecution Service
CRS	Compagnies Républicaines de Securité
HAC	Home Affairs Committee
HMI	Her Majesty's Inspectorate of Constabulary
JNCC	Joint Negotiating and Consultative Committee
MACP	military aid to the civil power
NRC	National Reporting Centre
PACE	Police and Criminal Evidence Act 1984
PCA	Police Complaints Authority
PCB	Police Complaints Board
PNB	Police Negotiating Board
POA	Public Order Act 1986
PSU	Police Support Unit
TIC	taken into consideration

Part I

Top of the Bill

1 Introduction
Why Study Chief Constables?

It has been said that in operational matters a Chief Constable is answerable to God, his Queen, his conscience, and to no one else. (E. St Johnston, *One Policeman's Story*, 153)

ACPO Rules is not OK.   (*New Statesman*, 23 May 1986, 3)

Chief constables are a powerful élite group of growing importance. In the last twenty years several have become prominent public figures, and their professional body, the Association of Chief Police Officers (ACPO) features regularly in debate about policing issues. In some radical conspiracy theories ACPO is the embryo of a nascent police state, the tail that 'is wagging the Home Office dog' (Campbell, 1987, 12). Chief constables have even received the ultimate accolade of heroic status: a prime-time TV series about their exploits, *The Chief*, first shown during 1990, and due to be continued in a second series in 1991. (For an interesting review by a serving chief constable see Hirst, 1990.)

What is common ground to all discussions about chief constables, whether celebratory or critical, is that they enjoy a unique degree of autonomy in how they work and the decisions they make. The next chapter will show how the case-law on the office of chief constable rests on the vaunted doctrine of constabulary independence. The two quotes which head this chapter both reflect the view of chief constables as almost omnipotent deities, although the first represents the perspective of a true believer (a former chief constable and HM Chief Inspector of Constabulary), the second that of an infidel.

Most analyses of the formation of policing policy see chief constables as absolutely central. 'The kind of policing we enjoy is determined by this small group of men whose personal attitudes are a major factor in the creation of policing styles' (McCabe, *et al.*, 1988, 134). Chief constables are, according to the dominant constitutional analysis, the prime movers of law and order policy within their areas, and collectively (through ACPO) in the country as a whole.

This makes chief constables an élite group of considerable power and significance. Fifty years ago there were over 180 chief police officers in England and Wales, and even twenty-five years ago there were over 120. The chiefs of the largest forces, notably the Metropolitan Police in London, have always been public figures of some prominence. County chief constables were always members of the local élite (Wall, 1989). But most chief constables were the heads of small borough forces, and had risen through the ranks from humble origins. They were of approximately the same status and power as police inspectors or perhaps superintendents today, and were often the creatures of their watch committees.

Two waves of amalgamations (in the late 1960s and early 1970s) have reduced the number of forces in England and Wales to forty-three. Even the smallest of these is a large and complex bureaucratic organization, employing significant resources of manpower and advanced equipment. At the start of 1990, the total strength of provincial police forces ranged from a low of 950 (Dyfed Powys) to a high of 7,089 (Greater Manchester). More than half the provincial police forces have strengths of between 1,000 and 2,000 officers, while at the other extreme there are two giant forces (with over 6,000 officers) (*Report of Her Majesty's Chief Inspector of Constabulary 1989* (London: HMSO, July 1990), app 7). The Metropolitan Police is a mega-giant, with a strength of 28,222 officers. The populations for which provincial forces are responsible range from 445,000 (Gwent) to 2,617,000 (West Midlands). Their areas range from 144,081 acres (Cleveland) to 2,679,897 acres (Dyfed Powys).

It is clear that all chief constables now command large organizations, and are responsible for policing extensive populations and large areas of the country. Their economic rewards are also considerable. Salaries range from £48,000 (plus allowances) per annum, for a small county force, to £61,029 for the largest provincial forces. Table 1.1 gives the current pay scales (as of July 1990) for provincial chief constables, and how they are distributed according to the population size of the force area.

TABLE 1.1. *The Pay and Responsibilities of Chief Constables*

Size of population in force area[b]	Chief constable's Pay[a] £	Number in this class
Less than 400,000	48,015	—
–500,000	49,230	4
–750,000	51,267	14
750,000–1,250,000	53,298	8
1,250,000–2,000,000	57,366	12
Over 2,000,000	61,029	3
TOTAL		41

[a] The scale of pay for the 41 provincial force chief constables in England and Wales is recommended by the Police Negotiating Board (PNB), and is subject to the Home Secretary's ratification. The PNB scale is related to size of population in the area, except for London. The City of London Commissioner (force population size 4,000) gets £63,105, and his Assistant Commissioner gets £49,191. The Metropolitan Police Deputy Commissioner earns £65,025 and the Assistant Commissioners get £57,366. The Commissioner's salary is set at Grade 1 civil service level, and is not decided by the PNB. This scale was agreed by the PNB in July 1990, but is not yet ratified by the Home Secretary (though this is usually seen as a formality). The full scales are given in *Police Review*, (27 July 1990), 1476–7.
[b] Population as of 30 June 1988 (given in the *Report of her Majesty's Chief Inspector of Constabulary 1989* (London: HMSO, July 1990), App. 7).

Chief constables also figure regularly in the award of honours, and a knighthood can nowadays be a routine expectation for the most successful. The proportion of chief constables with titles is actually less now than before the Second World War, however. This is because of the high social class origins of most county chiefs at that time. There is a distinct increase compared with pre-war borough chiefs (cf. Wall, 1989, 211). In 1987 Sir Philip Knights, former Chief Constable of West Midlands, became the first chief officer who had worked his way up through the ranks to be given a peerage.

In terms of power, economic class, and social status chief constables can now be considered a significant élite group. They are, however, entirely ignored in existing analyses of élites. This is probably because chief constables are unique as a powerful élite group, in that they come, as chapter 4 shows, from working-class backgrounds. This is remarkable for, as Stanworth concluded in a comprehensive review of studies of élites in Britain, 'Despite a recent broadening in the recruitment of specific elites, they remain dominated by people from privileged social backgrounds ... There has been little working class penetration of these institutional elites' (Stanworth, 1984, 261–2). These conclusions are based on a synthesis of research on the top strata in the Church, the armed forces, the judiciary, the civil service, Parliament, industry, and finance.

The police élite today differs markedly from this pattern in terms of social origin. However, they command as much power, people, prestige, and pay as other groups normally analysed in élite studies, and should be considered alongside them. There is, however, one social parallel between the police and other élites: they are all male and white. Indeed, Alison Halford, an assistant chief constable in Merseyside, and Britain's highest ranking woman police officer, recently began legal proceedings against the Home Office and her chief constable, after several unsuccessful attempts to become a deputy chief constable (*Police Review*, 15 June 1990, 118; 7 September 1990, 1752).

Chief constables are in fact an élite group about whom there is remarkably little systematic knowledge. Not only have they been left out of élite studies, but also the burgeoning research literature on policing. Police research has concentrated almost exclusively on the lowest levels of the organization. Virtually nothing is known about the life of the men at the top.[1]

The reasons for this are various. Partly it is due to a focus on the determination of street-level policing decisions, coupled with the belief that 'the police department has the special property that within it discretion increases as one moves down the hierarchy' (Wilson, 1968, 7). A lot of sociological reserach has emphasized the over-simplifications entailed by the hierarchical model of top-down management control implied in much of the police accountability debate. But if management cannot simply impose its will on police organizations, it is an equally one-sided distortion to disregard the importance of the formal policy-making levels (Reiner, 1985, 174–80).

Probably the main reasons for the research focus on the lower ranks of the police are the same as those which explain the prevailing lack of empirical research on élites throughout sociology. Access and funding are largely dependent on élite levels of organizations and thus the bulk of attention is likely to be directed to issues relevant to their problems of control, and what they need to know in order to achieve this, i.e. the activities and the culture of the lower levels. These pressures in effect often conspire to make researchers willy-nilly the 'servants of power' (Baritz, 1965). It is harder to gain access for studies of élites, because this knowledge is less useful to élites, and may even be dangerous knowledge. No doubt this accounts for some of the difficulties which were originally experienced in setting up the present research (which are outlined in Chapter 3).

Despite the high profile of a handful of chief constables, the majority remain completely unknown. During this research I have accumulated bulging files of newspaper cuttings on police superstars such as Sir Robert Mark, John Alderson, James Anderton, Sir Kenneth Newman, Sir Peter Imbert, and Geoffrey Dear. Their names and faces would be familiar, if not necessarily to the man on the Clapham omnibus, then at least to avid *Newsnight* watchers. When the *Sunday Times* magazine in 1982 published a photograph of thirty-five chief police officers, under the caption 'The Men We have to Trust', it remarked on this paradox. Although chief constables were 'some of the most powerful men in Britain ... if you saw a chief constable once in half-light, it might be difficult to pick him from the rest at an identification parade' ('The Police: A Special Inquiry', *Sunday Times* magazine, 26 Sept. 1982, 26–65).

The purpose here is to provide some basic information about this increasingly important yet uncharted élite group, the chief constables of England and Wales. What sort of people are they? From what social origins do they come, and how have they worked their ways up the police career ladder? What are their philosophies of policing, and their strategies for achieving their objectives? How do they manage their forces, and in what ways do they see themselves as accountable for the exercise of their power? How do they relate to the bodies to whom they are supposed to be accountable, in local and central government? What kind of perspective do they have on social and political matters? How do they compare with the rank-and-file police officers?

The research study on which this book is based aimed to provide some basic information on these issues, by interviewing all forty-three chief police officers in England and Wales. How this was accomplished is described more fully in Chapter 3 on the methods of the research. Before that, Chapter 2 will discuss the formal constitutional and legal powers of the office of chief constable, and how these have evolved over time. It will also describe the changing social status of those who hold the office.

Part II will analyse the social characteristics of contemporary chief constables. Chapter 4 looks at their social origins, and the orientations they brought with them into police work. Chapter 5 charts their career routes as they played the snakes and ladders of the police organization hierarchy.

The ideology of chief constables will be probed in Part III, which attempts to give the view of the world from the top of the cops. The chief constables' conceptions of the role of the police, their overall philosophies of policing and its purpose, are the subject of Chapter 6.

Chief constables' criminologies, their analyses of the problems of crime, and their strategies for dealing with them, are examined in Chapter 7. The control of public order is a particularly controversial facet of this in recent years, especially in relation to the 1984–5 miners' strike, and Chapter 8 considers chief constables' views on the problems of public order, with special emphasis on the miners' strike. Chapter 9 looks more broadly at the social and political opinions of chief constables, in particular their attitudes towards class, race, and justice.

The nub of the policing debate has been the vexed question of the accountability and control of police forces, and this is the focus of Part IV. The chief constables' views on internal management problems and their own role are presented in Chapter 10. The controversies about the external governance of police forces are looked at from the chief constables' viewpoint in Chapter 11, which considers their relationship to local police authorities, central government and the HM Inspectorate, ACPO, and the complaints system.

Part V attempts to put together the disparate views of chief constables on these topics, and see how specific individuals make sense of the world. It suggests that there are certain typical clusters of experience and perspective around the central dominant ideology of chief constables (which was the subject of Parts III and IV). These types are illustrated by case-studies of individual chief constables who approximately embody them.

Finally, Part VI summarizes the conclusions of the study, and discusses its implications for the future of chief constables. To anticipate slightly, the conclusions paradoxically undercut the starting-point and original motive for the research. This was the dominant belief that chief constables were the autonomous and powerful prime movers of policing policy. However, my conclusions suggest that although they are indeed powerful and significant, they are not as autonomous or independent as both critics and supporters of the status quo have claimed. They are not 'out of control', as the blurbs of critical books on the police are wont to declare (Hain, 1979, 1980; Scraton, 1985). They are certainly not controlled in the way that many constitutional lawyers have tended to argue they should be, that is, by local government (Lustgarten, 1986; Uglow, 1988). But the major obstacle to any sort of reform is the shadowy and secretive way in which they are controlled and organized. This work hopes to cast at least some chinks of light into this murky area.

Note

1. This is largely true abroad as well. There is a huge police research literature in North America, but hardly any empirical studies of police chiefs. There are a handful of statistical analyses of the career paths of police chiefs (O'Reilly and Dostaler, 1983; Witham, 1985; Enter, 1986). These concentrate on a range of technical administrative issues. A few use psychometric techniques to probe 'leadership styles' (Pursley, 1974; Kuykendall, 1977; Cohen, 1980; Swanson and Territo, 1982). A number of works reflect on the problems of police management and discuss alternative prescriptions for change, but are not based on systematic social research (Grosman, 1975; Geller, 1985; MacDonald, 1986; Fyfe, 1989; Loree, 1989). European discussions of police management issues are also largely prescriptive rather than empirical, e.g. Butler, 1984; Fijnaut and Visser, 1985; Bradley, Walker, and Wilkie, 1986. The extensive literature on police accountability, in North America as well as Britain, contains much information and argument about chief officers, e.g. Stenning, 1981 *a* and *b*; Hann *et al.*, 1985; Brogden, 1977, 1982; Jefferson and Grimshaw, 1984; Loveday, 1985; Lustgarten, 1986; Grimshaw and Jefferson, 1987; Baldwin, 1987; Morgan, 1987; Morgan and Swift, 1987. But none of this is based on systematic empirical research on chief officers. Autobiographies and other books by chief officers themselves are a source of insight, but not a basis for systematic knowledge. The most important are Smith, 1910; Thomson, 1922; Nott-Bower, 1926; Scott, 1954; Sillitoe, 1955; St Johnston, 1978; Mark, 1977, 1978; McNee, 1983; Alderson, 1984; Oliver, 1987. There are only two empirical studies of chiefs of police before the present one. Tardif explores the world-view of chiefs of police in Quebec, in particular their relationship with local political authorities, to which they see themselves as subordinated (Tardif, 1974). There is also a very valuable recent social history of chief constables in England and Wales from 1835 to 1985, to which I refer extensively in parts of Ch. 2 (Wall, 1989). The present work is the first to be based on comprehensive empirical research on the chief officers in a country as a whole.

2 The Office of Chief Constable: History and Powers

The office of constable has a long and chequered history, pre-dating by many centuries the modern creation of organized police forces. The orthodox account of British police history emphasizes the venerable ancestry of the police precisely as a way of anointing the contemporary force with a sacred aura distilled from the mists of antiquity. At the same time, the orthodox historians stress the depths to which the ancient office of constable had sunk by the early nineteenth century, necessitating the life-saving transfusion of professionalization instilled by Sir Robert Peel and the two Commissioners, Rowan and Mayne, to whom he entrusted the creation of his brainchild, the Metropolitan Police (Reiner, 1985, ch. 1).

The legitimating function of rooting the modern police in the ancient office of constable is to derive their origins from supposed traditions of communal self-policing. It lays the basis for the mythology of the police as 'citizens in uniform' which has played so profound a part in constitutional and legal discussions (notably the Royal Commissions of 1929 and 1960). In the same way as constables have acquired legitimacy from being seen as on a par with the ordinary citizenry, so too the powers of chief officers of police are said to derive from the basic office of constable. If the British police in general have been invested with a sacred character, then the chief constable is *primus inter deos*. As this chapter will show, the case-law concerning the office of chief constable resounds with rhetoric conferring an almost divine status on them. Just as the 'citizen in uniform' imagery disguises the growth of the legal and organizational powers which set the police aside from the citizenry, so the derivation of the constitutional independence of chief constables from the law enforcement function of ordinary constables ignores the primarily political and managerial role of chief officers. The aura of the bobby secures acceptance for the bureaucrat. In this chapter we will review the changing social and legal status of the office of chief constable.

The Office of Chief Constable before 1964

The term 'chief constable' was only applied uniformly to all (provincial) chief officers of police after the Police Act of 1919. (The Metropolitan and City of London chiefs have the title Commissioner, and hold neither the offices of 'constable' nor 'chief constable', as defined by the Police Act 1964 (cf. Lustgarten, 1986, 34). Their everyday role is, however, substantially the same as provincial chief constables, and they belong to ACPO, despite the differences in constitutional position.)[1] Prior to 1919, the term 'chief constable' was only standard in referring to county forces. In borough forces the usual term was 'head constable', although there was a variety of other nomenclature: 'superintendent', 'head officer of police', as well as 'chief constable' in a growing number of boroughs. The difference in title corresponded to differences both in formal legal position and in social status and background, between county and borough chiefs (Wall, 1989). These differences remained after the assimilation of names by the 1919 Police Act, right down to the Police Act of 1964, albeit in more attenuated form after the Second World War.

The first modern police force, the Metropolitan Police, was established by the 1829 Police Act on a pattern which was not followed for provincial forces, and remains unique. Its administration was placed in the hands of two justices (later called Commissioners in 1839; since 1856 there has only been one). The police authority to whom the Commissioner was (and remains) accountable is the Home Secretary. When in 1888 the London County Council was set up providing elected local government for London, it was specifically decided that the control of the police should remain with the Home Secretary, because of the unique national and 'imperial' functions of the Met., a decision which was the subject of much partisan controversy at the time.

When the first provincial borough forces were established, by the 1835 Municipal Corporations Act, no mention was made of chief or head constables. The new municipal corporations elected as a result of the Act were required to appoint a sufficient number of their members to constitute a watch committee (together with the mayor, appointed as a justice). The watch committee in turn was instructed to appoint a 'sufficient number of fit men' to act as constables. The watch committee had the power to appoint and dismiss the constables, and to frame regulations governing them, although the common-law powers of the office of constable were preserved.

There rapidly emerged a wide range of differences between the borough forces. The largest city forces—Manchester, Bristol, Birmingham, Liverpool—had chief or head constables who were figures of considerable power and importance in their forces and in the local community. At the other extreme, in the smallest forces, most obviously those with only one or two men, the office of chief constable was indistinguishable from that of constable, pure and simple. 'The "chief constable", in any case, held no exceptional position comparable with that of the county man: he was simply the constable who held the highest rank in the force, and his status depended on the numbers under him' (Critchley, 1978, 125).

The locus of control in the nineteenth century between borough chief constables and watch committees has been much debated of late. The standard view (found, for example, in Critchley, 1978, 131–3, and Marshall, 1965, 28–9), supported recently by Lustgarten, holds that in the nineteenth century 'the subordination of the police to elected representatives in the boroughs was part of common understanding' (Lustgarten, 1986, 39). This view has been challenged in recent years by Brogden (1982, 62) in the specific case of the Liverpool head constable, and Jefferson and Grimshaw (1984, 41–4). These authors argue that the doctrine of constabulary independence was already in being for borough chief officers, and offer a reinterpretation of some of the examples of watch committee instructions to chief officers which Critchley proposed as support for the subordination view.

The Jefferson and Grimshaw argument about the 1880 Birmingham case is an example of the rather forced nature of their attempted reinterpretation. Following clashes about the chief constable's policies concerning the prosecution of drunks and of 'improper' music-hall performances, the watch committee passed a resolution that he should not take proceedings 'likely to affect a number of ratepayers, or to provoke public comment' without first informing them of his intentions. The chief constable refused to comply unless instructed to by the Home Secretary and the justices. The Home Secretary would not intervene directly, but referred the chief constable to the Municipal Corporations Act which gave the watch committee power to make regulations 'for preventing neglect or abuse, and for rendering constables efficient in the discharge of their duties', and to dismiss any constable 'whom they shall think negligent in the discharge of his duty, or otherwise unfit for the same'. In the end, the chief constable gave way, after the council resolved that it was not desirable to retain a chief officer who was 'not subordinate to or not in harmony with' the watch committee, and threatened him with a requirement to resign.

The plain as pikestaff interpretation of this is that it demonstrates that watch committees *were* seen as empowered to give chief constables lawful orders about law enforcement priorities. Jefferson and Grimshaw's contrary reading is somewhat tenuously stretched. They claim first that the chief constable's compliance with the watch committee's directions does not mean he accepted the *idea* that he lacked independent power to decide on law enforcement. But surely the point is that, irrespective of what ideas the chief constable may or may not have entertained (and who is to know?), his ideas did not prevail. Further, they argue that all the watch committee claimed was the right to be *informed* of the chief's intentions, not to direct them. But they evidently wanted to be informed of his intentions in order to control them, to be able to insure that they were 'subordinate to' and 'in harmony with' the watch committee's views (as the council resolutions put it). I would submit that the orthodox view is correct in holding that in the nineteenth century it *was* generally accepted that watch committees *did* have the power to instruct their chief officers on law enforcement policy. The revisionist reinterpretations establish no more than the obvious limitation that watch committees could only give *lawful* orders, and that, especially in the case of experienced heads of large forces (as in Liverpool), the chief constable commanded a certain respect based on professional expertise, but that this was not necessarily deferred to.

In the counties, however, the office of chief constable was not only labelled as such from the outset, but had much of the autonomy of his present-day heirs. The County Police Act of 1839 was a permissive measure, empowering but not requiring magistrates in quarter sessions to establish forces for counties (or parts of them). From the outset the county constabularies were under greater Home Office regulation, but also more autonomous of *all* outside influences, than borough forces. The Home Secretary maintained the right to decide whether a force should be established, and to approve its size, rules, rates of pay, and the appointment of the chief constable. Guidelines for the selection of chief constables for county forces were issued by the Home Secretary Lord Normanby under the 1839 Act, and continued to be enforced until the 1919 Desbrough Committee's recommendations superseded them. But 'once in post the County Chief Constable was an autocrat over whom the justices had no power other than the ultimate sanction of dismissal ... Thus he fulfilled many of the duties which in the borough were assigned to the Watch Committee' (Critchley, 1978, 124). These included appointments, discipline, and law enforcement policy. This remained the position without substantial alteration down to the 1964 Police Act. The 1856 County and Borough Police Act, which introduced the Home Office grant and HM Inspectorate, the 1888 Local Government Act, which established Standing Joint Committees (consisting half of elected councillors and half of justices), and the 1919 Police Act which implemented the Desbrough Committee's recommendations following the police strikes, all enhanced the role of central government in regulating common basic standards. While they reduced police autonomy *vis-à-vis* central government, they did not substantially diminish the independence of the county chief from *local* electoral control.

This difference in legal status between county and borough chiefs of police was reflected in their social calibre. The county chiefs were drawn from the same landed gentry backgrounds as the justices who appointed them (and so were the elected members who formed the Standing Joint Committees together with the justices after 1888). It was this congruence of background and outlook with the local élite which made the autonomy of the county chief unproblematic (Steedman, 1984). In recent historical research on the social origins of chief constables, David Wall has noted that three-quarters of the county chiefs in office in 1905 are included in contemporary directories of élites, e.g. *Who's Who* or *Kelly's Handbook of Official and Titled Classes* (Wall, 1987, 87).[2] This was because of *who* they were rather than *what* they were (unlike the 50 per cent of present-day chiefs who also find themselves in these exalted pages). 'The inclusion of county chief constables in such directories was by virtue of their background rather than their occupation. The county chief constableship became a popular occupation for the younger sons of the landed gentry in the same way that the army and the cloth had done' (Wall, 1987, 87). This same social cachet, which integrated county chiefs with the local elite, cut them off from their men. Together with their experience as army officers this enhanced their image as autocrats.

By contrast only 5 per cent of the borough chiefs in office in 1905 feature in the élite directories, and these were usually the heads of the very large city forces, whose origins were more exalted than those of their subordinates (albeit they were usually recruited from professional rather than military careers). The majority of borough chiefs were men who had worked their way up the police ranks, and came from the same working- (or at most lower-middle-) class backgrounds as their subordinates. A common pattern was for boroughs to recruit their chiefs from the middle ranks of larger forces—usually the Met.

The Desborough Committee in 1919 examined the case for a fully professional police service with internally recruited chiefs. It recommended a movement towards this: 'No person without previous police experience should be appointed as chief constable in any force unless he possesses some exceptional qualification or experience which specially fits him for the post, or there is no other candidate from the police service who is considered sufficiently well-qualified' (para. 139). This was embodied in Regulation 9 of the rules which the 1919 Police Act empowered the Home Secretary to make governing the pay, conditions of service, and appointments of the police. But the effect of the regulation was circumvented by the county forces. They either appointed men of the traditional type with colonial police backgrounds, or former military men to assistant chief constable posts (not covered by Reg. 9) to give them the 'police experience' required. The result was that while in 1908 it was found that only three of the forty-four English county chief constables had risen through the ranks (the rest being ex-army officers or colonial policemen), by 1939 this had only increased to four of the then forty-two English county chiefs. By contrast, only fifteen of the 123 borough chiefs in 1908, and six of the 117 in 1939 had *not* risen through the ranks (Wall, 1989, ch. 2).

During and after the Second World War, the policy of only recruiting chief constables who *had* served as police throughout their careers became effective (Postwar Committee on the Reconstruction of the Police Service). However, county forces were able to stave off the full effects of this until the early 1970s, because of the legacy of the short-lived Trenchard scheme in the 1930s which provided for direct entry of (mainly middle-class) graduates to the Hendon Police College as 'officer material' with automatic promotion to inspector. 'In 1965, the Commissioner, Deputy Commissioner, four Assistant Commissioners in the Metropolitan Police, nineteen county chief constables, six borough chief constables, the Chief Inspector of the Constabulary and three of his colleagues were all trained at Hendon' (Wall, 1987, 95).

What is clear is that down to the 1964 Police Act there remained a substantial divide in legal and social status between county chief constables and their borough namesakes (with the partial exception of the largest city forces). While the latter were upwardly mobile career police officers from humble origins, the former were firmly part of the county social élite. Moreover, they were an extremely well-established part of the local élite. Usually appointed in their thirties, it was common for them to die in office after extremely long periods as chief constable.

The Surrey Constabulary, for example, was not unusual in having only two chiefs during its first eighty years: its first chief constable retired in 1899 at the age of 86, after 48 years in office, to be followed by his successor who retired in 1930 (Critchley, 1978, 142). Such longevity was matched by a few borough forces: Chester City, for example, which had only four chief constables in the whole 113 years of its existence (1836–1949), or Oxford City which also had only four chief officers from 1869 (when Charles Head, a Metropolitan inspector became its 'Superintendent') to 1968, when it was amalgamated into Thames Valley (Rose, 1979, 35–6). Evidently there would be much more scope for such chief officers to stamp a personal style of leadership upon their forces than would be usual today, and the potential for autocratic command is clear.

One final, most important aspect of the development of the office of chief constable before 1964 was the evolution of effective representative machinery. A Chief Constables Association was founded in 1896 for city and borough chiefs, and a County Chief Constables Club had existed since 1858. The present Association of Chief Police Officers was formed in 1948 by the merger of the earlier bodies. It includes deputy and assistant chiefs, the Metropolitan ranks from commander upwards, and the City of London Commissioner and Assistant Commissioner. The vehicle for these bodies to influence (and be influenced by) central government has been the Central Conference of Chief Constables, dating back to the First World War, under the chairmanship of the Home Secretary or a senior Home Office official. This meets two or three times a year. In addition there are district conferences which meet at least quarterly, also dating back to 1918. These are conduits both for the formation of a collective voice, and communication with the Home Office. (Appendix C gives a more detailed account of the history and organization of ACPO.)

The Office of Chief Constable since 1964

The statutory basis of the office of chief constable now, and of its relationship with local and central government, is the Police Act of 1964, together with the case-law this has generated. The Act largely implemented the recommendations of the 1962 *Report* of the Royal Commission on the Police, which had been established in the wake of a series of cases raising concern about the accountability of the police generally and chief officers in particular.

The Royal Commission was faced by two conflicting and cogent lines of argument in the evidence it received. The first was the view (articulated most explicitly by the Association of Municipal Corporations) that local police authorities should be (and watch committees were) able to issue instructions on policy matters to chief constables in the same way as to other local officials (but not in individual cases of law enforcement). On the other hand, several representative bodies of professional legal opinion (the Law Society, the Inns of Court Conservative and Unionist Society, and Professor E. C. S. Wade who was consulted as an expert witness) all argued for a centrally controlled force, under parliamentary supervision, on grounds both of efficiency and accountability. This view was accepted in the dissenting memorandum of Professor Goodhart. Interestingly, it was also supported by the *New Statesman*, now the champion of the ACPO/police state conspiracy theory. An article by C. H. Rolph saw the report as '22 pages by Dr. Goodhart, with a preface seven times as long by a faintly admiring syndicate of diplomats' (*New Statesman*, 8 June, 1962).

The majority of chief constables rejected the case for national control, but also reasserted the notion of constabulary independence from local control. A few chief constables (notably Eric St Johnston of Lancashire), as well as the Police Federation, went along with the arguments for nationalization, or at least regionalization. In the end, as C. H. Rolph's comments intimate, the Commission's *Report*, and the ensuing Act was a diplomatic compromise, the 'tripartite' system of control by chief officers, Home Office, and local police authorities. The latter were essentially a hybrid of the old watch and standing joint committees, consisting of two-thirds elected councillors, and one-third justices. As critics remarked at the time (notably Geoffrey Marshall) the boundaries of function, responsibility, and power between the points of the triangle were ill defined and contained the seeds of future conflict once the political and social consensus about policing broke down, as it did increasingly after the late 1960s (Marshall, 1965). There have been several excellent recent statements of the statutory position and case-law, so this can be summarized briefly (Lustgarten, 1986; Lambert, 1986, ch. 2; Leigh, 1985, ch. 1; Clayton and Tomlinson, 1987, ch. 1 and 13).

The main duty of the police authority is to maintain 'an adequate and efficient' force for its area (s. 4(1)). It is responsible for providing buildings, vehicles, and other equipment, 'as may be required for police purposes of the area' (ss. 4(3), 4(4)). Subject to the approval of the Home Secretary, it also appoints, and 'in the interests of efficiency' may dismiss, the chief constable, his deputy, and assistants (ss. 4(2), 5(1), 5(4), 6(4), 6(5)). Again with the Home Secretary's approval, the police authority determines the establishment of the force (s. 4(2)). It controls force revenue and expenditure, although it can be required to pay sums necessary to give effect to regulations issued by the Home Secretary, or a court order, or to implement statutory changes (s. 8(1), s. 8(4)). Central government meets 50 per cent (now 51 per cent) of policing costs directly, and also contributes to the local 50 (49) per cent indirectly through rate (now poll tax) support grant. The chief constable is obliged to make an annual report to the police authority, and the authority may ask for further reports on any matter connected with the policing of the area (s. 12). But the chief constable may refuse such a report if it appears to him not to be in the public interest, or not to be 'needed for the discharge of the functions of the police authority'. In the event of such disagreement, the Home Secretary decides what should be done.

This apparently substantial list of functions begins to evaporate when the allocation of powers and duties to the chief constable and the Home Secretary is considered. The role of the chief constable is described almost parenthetically in the Act. 'The police force maintained for a police area under s. 1 of this act shall be under the direction and control of the chief constable appointed under s. 4(2) of this Act' (s. 5(1)). Geoffrey Marshall argued in 1965 that this 'merely describes the existing situation' (Marshall, 1965, 98). As seen above, this meant that chief constables arguably would be obliged to follow the lawful instructions of the police authority. But Lustgarten's critique of this interpretation of the Act seems more convincing. He argues first that when establishing other local government services (e.g. Education Act 1944; Social Services Act 1970) the terminology 'direction and control' is not used to describe the function of the director. The other Acts establish a special local authority (e.g. education), or instruct the local authority to establish a special committee (e.g. social services), who are responsible for providing the service, to which end they are required to appoint a chief officer who is clearly subordinate to them. This argument by itself is indicative but not totally convincing. The main difference in the structure of the statutes is the terminology 'direction and control', the meaning of which is precisely what is at issue.

However, Lustgarten's interpretation is further supported by a consideration of the case-law. It must be stressed at once that, as is common ground between Marshall and Lustgarten, no case since the Act (and arguably none before it) *directly* has the point at issue of whether a chief constable has to follow lawful instructions from a police authority. The doctrine of 'constabulary independence' has emerged in case-law without ever being centrally at issue, through the piling on of *obiter* upon *obiter*. Of the pre-Act cases, the most often cited is *Fisher* v.

Oldham (1930) 2 KB 364. As Marshall, Lustgarten, and numerous other commentators have argued, this really only establishes that constables and police authorities do not have a master–servant relationship for the specific question of vicarious liability in tort (on which the 1964 Act in substance reverses the effect of *Fisher* by explicitly making chief constables vicariously liable for their subordinates' torts in s. 48(1) and by exposing the police fund controlled by the police authority to the obligation to pay damages). This limited decision about the absence of a specific master–servant relationship in the tort sense, however, has come to stand as authority in later cases for the broader constitutional doctrine of constabulary independence from any instructions about law enforcement methods and policy.

The most influential and often cited post-1964 Act judicial statement of the independence doctrine is that by Lord Denning in the first *ex p. Blackburn* case [1968] 2 QB 118. Mr Blackburn was seeking an order of mandamus directing the Metropolitan Commissioner to reverse a policy of not enforcing the law on gaming. The Court of Appeal (per Lord Denning, at 136) found that the police have a public duty to enforce the law, which the courts could, if necessary, compel them to perform. But within this they have a broad discretion about methods and priorities. The courts would only countermand this if it was a policy of complete non-enforcement of a law, amounting to a chief officer 'failing in his duty to enforce the law', for instance by a directive saying no one would be prosecuted for thefts worth less than one hundred pounds.

In the course of this judgment some broad rhetorical remarks were made by Lord Denning about the independence of chief constables. 'I hold it to be the duty of the Commissioner of the Police, as it is of every Chief Constable, to enforce the law of the land . . . but in all these things he is not the servant of anyone, save of the law itself. No minister of the Crown can tell him that he must or must not keep observation on this place or that; or that he must not prosecute this man or that one, nor can any police authority tell him so . . . The responsibility for law enforcement lies on him. He is answerable to the law and to the law alone' (1968 2 QB 118, at 135–6). With respect to this particular passage, Lustgarten has remarked appositely 'seldom have so many errors of law and logic been compressed into one paragraph' (1986, 64–5). He counts no fewer than six separate fallacies in Lord Denning's remarks. Whether or not he is correct, however, it is clear that the remarks are strictly *obiter* (Marshall, 1978, 58–9). The relationship between a chief officer and either a police authority or the Home Secretary was not directly at issue in this case (or any of the later Blackburn cases).

None the less, these remarks have been used as authority for later judgments in the same vein, notably by Lord Denning himself in the later CEGB case, where he cited his own earlier words to support the proposition that 'it is of the first importance that the police should decide on their own responsibility what action be taken in any particular situation' (*R. v. Chief Constable of the Devon and Cornwall Constabulary, ex p. C.E.G.B.* [1981] 3 All ER 826, at 833). In the CEGB case the Board had applied for an order of mandamus, after being prevented by protesters from carrying out a survey which they were statutorily empowered to conduct, and the chief constable had refused to take action to remove the protesters, claiming no breach of the peace had occurred or was threatened. (The chief involved puts his side of the case in Alderson, 1984.) The Court's sympathies clearly seem to have been with the Board, rather than the chief, and they found that the conduct of the protesters in unlawfully obstructing the Board's survey was itself a breach of the peace.

However, the Court of Appeal did not grant mandamus. In Lord Denning's argument, this was on the grounds of constabulary independence: 'The decision of the chief constable not to intervene in this case was a police decision with which I think the courts should not interfere' (833), citing his own remarks in *Blackburn* as authority. However, it is not clear that this view is the basis of the judgment. Lord Lawton uses another argument, with which Lord Templeman seems to concur. Lord Lawton argued that the application for mandamus 'showed a misconception of the powers of chief constables. They command their forces but they cannot give an officer under command an order to do acts which can only lawfully be done if the officer himself with reasonable cause suspects that a breach of the peace has occurred or is imminently likely to occur or an arrestable offence has been committed. In July 1981 the chief constable of Devon and Cornwall could have, and probably did, order some of his constables to watch what was going on in the field . . . but what he could not do was to give unqualified orders to his officers' (at 835). In other words, no one, whether a senior officer, police authority, or court, can order a constable to exercise a power which can only be exercised lawfully if certain factual conditions preceding it are satisfied, and this can only be ascertained by the constable on the spot (Lustgarten, 1986, 14). If this is the ground of the judgment then it too does not really establish the independence of constables from being given lawful instructions by police authorities, an issue not directly in question in any event.

The same applies to the more recent case *R. v. Oxford, ex p. Levey* (*The Times*), 1 Nov. 1986, and *Police*, Dec. 1986, 16–18). Mr Levey lost substantial amounts of jewellery in a robbery. The thieves escaped when the pursuing police car was called back by the Force control room after entering Toxteth, having informed them of this in compliance with a Force Order. The order to call off the chase was given by the control room inspector after the police car 'encountered a group of some fifty youths armed with bricks, iron bars and pieces of metal' and 'one of these youths threw a house brick at and hit PC Bark's car'. Mr Levey sought (1) a declaration that it was *ultra vires* for the chief constable to adopt a policy whereby an area was deemed to be a 'no-go' area; (2) a declaration that it was *ultra vires* for the chief constable to call off the chase when the police car entered Toxteth; (3) an order of mandamus directing the chief constable to rescind any order or decision to 'treat Toxteth or any part of the city as a 'no-go' area, which would be counter to his statutory duty.

Mr Levey failed in his action, the decision turning on the specific facts. It was found that the order to call off the chase was motivated primarily by concern for the safety of the pursuing officer. The obligation to inform the control room when entering Toxteth did not amount to a 'no-go' policy, as remarks made by some PCs to Mr Levey wrongly implied. Arguably such a policy *would* amount to the total abdication from the duty to enforce the law, with which the courts have consistently said they would interfere. The policy to inform the control room was intended to ensure that any law enforcement activities in the sensitive area of Toxteth could take full account of the current situation there. This was a matter about the appropriate *methods* for enforcing the law, a choice over which 'Chief Constables have the widest possible discretion' (per Sir John Donaldson MR). So the judgment amounts to confirmation of the view that chief constables will not be told by the courts *how* to enforce the law, provided they do not totally abdicate from their duty to do so. Once again, however, while the constabulary independence doctrine is bolstered, the relationship specifically with police authorities was not the issue.

The recent and seminally important *Northumbria* case *did* concern the powers of police authorities. However, it involved all three parties to the tripartite relation, so consideration will be postponed until after looking at the Home Secretary's powers under the 1964 Act.

The cases considered so far do establish a strong tradition of judicial support for the doctrine of 'constabulary independence'. Arguably, as Marshall claims, the statements containing this are *obiter*, at any rate as concerns the chief constable–policy authority relationship which was never directly at issue. None the less, Lustgarten is surely right that however deficient its initial basis, the doctrine of constabulary independence 'has ... embedded itself in the lore and learning of both judges and police, and it is inconceivable that, without parliamentary intervention, the courts would resile from the position they have reached' (1986, 67).

The third party to the tripartite system, the Home Secretary, has also grown in power, together with chief constables, at the expense of local police authorities, at any rate as compared with pre-1964 watch committees. The Royal Commission and the 1964 Act clearly *intended* to tilt the balance towards the centre. The history of legislation concerning police organization and accountability reflects a perennially repeated clash of rhetorics, re-emerging in the debates around the 1829, 1835, 1839, 1856, 1888, 1919, and 1964 Acts. On the one hand, there is a clear Benthamite vision of a rationally structured, bureaucratic police organization, controlled by and accountable to the centre. On the other side, there is a chorus of opposition to this, invoking fear of the trampling of hallowed British liberties by a foreign-inspired Leviathan. At each turn, the Benthamites have had much of their way, as evidenced by the very fact of the passage of new legislation. But the libertarian fears result in compromises and concessions from the clear centralist form.

Since 1964 the Benthamite vision has had undisputed sway in practice, while, paradoxically, explicit support for it has faded away to such a degree that Lustgarten can remark, 'The one point that commands near-universal agreement is that a national police force is undesirable' (1986, 177). It will, however, be argued later that to the Government a national police force is undesirable because it would make overt its *de facto* control.

The Royal Commission *Report* was clearly impressed by Professor Goodhart's centralization argument. This is most evident in the way it firmly refuted the main bulwark of the localist position: the fear of a centralist and totalitarian 'police state' (p 45–6). The reasons for rejecting the central control argument are much more tenuous and amount to no more than respect for tradition, and the importance of local ties and identity for policing. The latter point was in fact recognized by the advocates of nationalization, and various attempts to preserve local links were incorporated in their schemes for change (e.g. paras. 121, 122). The accountability argument was stressed by the advocates of centralization (e.g. the Inns of Court Conservative and Unionist Society: para. 122, p. 42) rather than the localists. The description of the benefits of local police authorities by the Commission (para. 144, para. 146) sees them not as a means of accountability but only as consultative devices, and as administrative dogsbodies. What the Commission seems to be saying is that the argument for central control is basically sound, but that it would be better to provide the means of *de facto* centralization while maintaining a semblance of local accountability, rather than to come clean on the issue. With hindsight, this does not seem too cynical an interpretation of its concluding comment on the matter, where they speak of proceeding by 'accelerating the pace at which the police service moves towards greater unity, rather than by any abrupt and radical change which might not be readily understood' (para. 150, p. 50).

The means for beefing up central control proposed by the Royal Commission were twofold. The first was the role of Home Secretary as arbiter in conflicts between police authorities and chief constables, and in sanctioning chief constable appointments. More fundamentally, the Commission intended the Home Secretary to be made statutorily responsible for the efficiency of the police throughout the country (para. 230, p. 72). This formulation was objected to successfully by the then Home Secretary during the parliamentary debates on the Bill which resulted in the 1964 Police Act, on the ground that it would give him responsibility without power (an argument which had been anticipated in Professor Goodhart's dissenting memorandum (Critchley, 1978, 286). Events since 1964 suggest, however, that the Home Secretary has ended up with power without responsibility, a well-known but rather unroyal prerogative throughout the ages. The 1964 Act specifies the general duty of the Home Secretary as being to 'exercise his powers . . . in such manner and to such extent as appears to him to be best calculated to promote the efficiency of the police' (s. 28). For this purpose he is given a formidable variety of powers: (1) to require a police authority to exercise their power under Part 1 of this Act to call upon the chief constable to retire in the interests of efficiency (s. 29(1)); (2) to require a report from a chief constable on any matter connected with the policing of any area, and to receive an annual report (s. 30); (3) the power to make grants of expenses (s. 31) and, related to this, the power to appoint the Inspectorate to monitor and advise on efficiency (s. 38); (4) the power to establish special inquiries into the policing of local areas (s. 32); (5) the power to make regulations concerning all aspects of the government, administration, and conditions of service of police forces (s. 33), and concerning standards of equipment (s. 36) (and of course the continuing practice of issuing circulars); (6) the power to provide a wide array of central services (s. 41)—a power which was to prove crucial in the 1987–8 *Northumbria* case.

Outside the sixteen very long sections (28–43) specifically detailing the Secretary of State's functions and powers, other ones crop up at odd points elsewhere in the Act. Of potentially great importance in the context of a national policing operation such as occurred during the miners' strike of 1984–5, ss. 13 and 14 on collaboration and mutual aid arrangements give the Home Secretary the clear power to direct that such agreements be made if necessary (s. 13(5)), to order a force to receive or provide reinforcements (s. 14(2)), and to arbitrate on inter-force disputes about the allocation of the financial burden of such co-operation (s. 13(3), s. 14(4)).

In the event, these powers have never been used. Instead, the most extensive mutual aid operation to date, during the 1984 miners' strike, was co-ordinated by the National Reporting Centre under the control of the President of ACPO, implicitly to the satisfaction of the Home Secretary or presumably he *would* have invoked his powers (Loveday, 1985, 131–2, 1986, 60–1; McCabe, Wallington *et al.*, 1988). The accountability implications are significant. Had the operation been directed by the Home Secretary under his Police Act powers, he would have been answerable to Parliament for their exercise. As it was, no one was.

Towards a National Force? Police Organization since 1984

Several recent developments clearly accentuate this centralizing trend already evident in the 1964 legislation itself. The statutory requirement to establish consultative arrangements in each police area, which s. 106 of the Police and Criminal Evidence Act 1984 introduced, at first sight appears an exception. But whatever the virtues of these arrangements, the form they took was uniformly shaped throughout the country by a Home Office Circular 54/1982 (Morgan, 1986; Morgan and Maggs, 1985). Paradoxically this measure to ensure local consultation is a classic illustration of the way that nominally advisory Home Office Circulars come to be interpreted as binding, and act as a major tool of centralization and homogenization.

The Local Government Act 1985, which abolished the six metropolitan county councils, considerably increased the statutory powers and the *de facto* influence of the Home Secretary (Loveday, 1991). The rate-capping powers of central government allow it to determine the budget and manpower levels of the metropolitan forces, which means the Home Secretary in effect 'now directly controls the financial resources for nearly half of the entire police strength in England and Wales' (Loveday, 1987, 211). A further consequence of the new Joint Boards which replaced the former metropolitan police authorities is to increase the likelihood of a 'hung' Board, with the magistrates thus having the last say. 'In the Metropolitan areas the tripartite structure must be viewed as little more than a legal fiction ... the 1985 Local Government Act represents the most significant and overt shift in responsibility, for the police service, from local to central government, since the passage of the 1964 Police Act' (Loveday, 1987, 211–2).

The point is underlined in the highly significant recent case of *R. v. Secretary of State for the Home Department, ex p. Northumbria Police Authority*. This concerned a Home Office Circular 40/1986 which stated that in pursuance of the Home Secretary's 1981 announcement to make available baton rounds and CS gas to chief officers of police 'for use in the last resort', it was proposed that such requirements would be met from a central store. This would extend to 'cases where a chief officer has been unable to obtain his police authority's agreement to purchase', subject to endorsement by HM Inspectorate of Constabulary. The Northumbria Police Authority sought an order of certiorari to quash the decision, on the grounds that is was outside the Home Secretary's powers under the Police Act or otherwise.

The Divisional Court upheld the circular by accepting that the Home Secretary had the power to supply equipment without the police authority's permission under the Royal Prerogative. But it rejected the view that he was also empowered to do this under s. 41 of the Police Act which permitted him to supply equipment 'for promoting the efficiency of the force. To do this when the police authority objected would be incompatible with its own responsibility for efficiency under s. 4(1) [1987] 2 WLR 988.

The Court of Appeal confirmed the Royal Prerogative argument. But it also held that the power to supply common services under s. 41, and the general requirement to use his powers so as to promote the efficiency of the police—s. 28—entitled the Home Secretary to provide such services, including riot equipment, even without the police authority's consent [1988] 2 WLR 590. What this seems to amount to is a ruling that if the local and the national government's views of 'efficiency' conflict, the Act prioritizes the interpretation of central government. In any event, this same result would be available in effect by virtue of the Royal Prerogative powers which were discovered by the Divisional Court and the Court of Appeal in this case.

The reasoning used by the Court to support its decision in the *Northumbria* case reveals several crucial facets of judicial attitudes to the accountability of the police. Interestingly these are echoed in the professional ideology of chief constables themselves, as Chapter 11 shows. First, there is a strong reaffirmation of the general principle of constabulary independence in police operations. The Divisional Court's judgment concludes with the following *obiter* remark, invoking the authority of the CEGB case. 'We would add this. The decision whether or not to use equipment supplied by the Secretary of State is for the chief constable alone to make. This court will not intervene to control the use which a chief constable makes of the resources available to him' (at 1005). Since the cited case-law clearly states that the chief constable is answerable only to the law, and not to any political authorities, for his decisions about enforcement operations, this self-abnegation by the courts appears to leave him accountable to no one.

The same strong reaffirmation of the constabulary independence doctrine is underlined by the Court of Appeal. 'There is no provision in the Act granting to the police authority any direct power to dictate to their chief constable how he is to discharge his duties either as a constable or under section 5(1) of the Act. Indeed such a provision would be so alien to the established constitutional position of the constable as to require very clear and specific statutory language' ([1988] 2 WLR at 604, per Purchas LJ). Prospective Labour Home Secretaries, pledged to achieve such a reform by new police legislation, might like to ponder this judicial warning.

Whilst operational decisions are the chief constable's alone, the supply of the wherewithal for policing is a responsibility of government. Central government's responsibility for this is paramount. This derives from the Court of Appeal's analysis of both the Royal Prerogative and the common law. Both support the view that the police are 'ultimately a Crown responsibility' (at 599). The 1964 Police Act (and previous legislation establishing local police authorities) does not dilute this in any way. 'The passing of the Act did nothing to affect the duties and powers of police constables including chief officers of police forces. In my judgement, the prerogative powers to take all reasonable steps to preserve the Queen's peace remain unaffected by the Act' (at 610, per Purchas LJ).

These conclusions are based on the Court of Appeal's reading of the relevant authorities. However, they are also justified as correct in principle. The premise of the Court's argument is that the maintenance of order is a technical exercise, and how this should be accomplished is a matter of purely neutral expertise. Added to this bracketing-off of any possible room for legitimate disagreement about methods of policing, there is the further sociological premise that whereas *local* authorities may be influenced by irrelevant ideological or political considerations, central government and chief police officers are pure creatures of reason. The court argues that:

It would be an unusual and exceptional power to give to a police authority if Parliament decreed that a constable, including a chief constable, could be ordered to carry out his duty to keep the peace in a particular manner or by using particular equipment or apparatus ... Suppose an aggressive authority ordered its constables to adopt an unnecessarily provocative approach by wielding weapons and threatening to use gas, could it be said that the constable had to obey such a command, where in his judgement the result might well be counter-productive to the faithful execution of his oath to preserve the Queen's peace? (at 604, per Purchas LJ)

However, while the danger is said to exist of 'aggressive' authorities acting in 'unnecessarily provocative' ways, the parallel problem of potentially 'aggressive' chief constables is adequately controlled by the scrutiny of HM Inspectorate of Constabulary. They ensure that the equipment requested by a chief is 'necessary and expedient'. Given this authorization by a neutral expert body, it follows that any further restrictions which the police authority seeks to impose can only be on 'ideological' or 'irrelevant' grounds:

The Secretary of State wishes to make such equipment available to police forces in cases where the chief constable of that force ... has convinced the inspectorate of police that it is appropriate ... The requirement to obtain the approval of the inspectorate ... is a reassurance that the issue of the equipment is necessary or expedient for promoting the efficiency of the police ... if the police authority's contention is correct, then by refusing on ideological or irrelevant grounds to supply equipment, which in the view of the inspectorate is necessary or expedient to promote the efficiency of the police, the authority can prejudice the performance by the chief constable of his duties. (at 606, per Purchas LJ)

The main rationale for the present constitutional position is thus the view that policing decisions can and should be determined by neutral professional expertise. Chief constables can better be relied upon to exercise this than political authorities who may be swayed by 'ideological' or 'irrelevant' considerations. Whilst this is a potent danger for local government, central government benefits from the expert advice of HM Inspectorate as a means of keeping it on the straight and narrow. The Court recognizes that as a matter of contemporary social history, political controversy about what constitutes proper policing has developed recently. This necessitates the precise spelling-out of the Royal Prerogative to keep the peace, which could be taken for granted in less troubled times. There is no ground, however, for questioning it, merely for delineating it clearly:

From time to time a need for more exact definitions arises. The present need arises from a difference of view between the Secretary of State and a police authority over what is necessary to maintain public order, a phenomenon which has been observed only in recent times. There has probably never been a comparable occasion for investigating a prerogative of keeping the peace within the realm. (at 612 per Nourse LJ)

The effects of this judgment are to make absolutely clear that the tri-partite arrangement of police governance ordained by the 1964 Police Act is not one with three clearly independent partners, as the authority's counsel had argued (at 597, per Croom-Johnson LJ), let alone three equal partners as some naïve souls might wishfully have thought. In the operational sphere the chief constable is clearly said to reign supreme. However, in the administrative and regulative functions of maintaining, providing, and equipping the police, ascertaining their requirements, and monitoring their efficiency, the role of local police authorities is entirely subordinate to and overdetermined by, central government. The Inspectorate which is relied upon to supply the neutral expertise for the proper conduct of this function is constituted as part of one leg of the tripartite structure (the Home Office) and selected by them from a second leg (the chief constables). It is hard to see where the third leg, the police authorities, is supposed to figure in this scheme of things.

In the years since the *Northumbria* case the trajectory of British police organization has been set even more evidently in a centralizing direction. During 1989 and 1990 growing national control by central government has been manifested in a variety of ways, and schemes for national or at least regional consolidation of forces have become a major topic of debate among the policing élite. The overall pattern seems to be one in which the Government wants to achieve effective central control of policing, but by proxy rather than the overt creation of a national force. Its chosen instruments for this are the HMI, ACPO, and the Met.

The cutting-edge of the thrust to greater centralization has been the Government's tightening control of the police purse-strings. Concern about 'value for money' from policing, as from all public services (although rather less stringently) was a major theme of the Thatcher Government throughout the 1980s. Home Office Circular 114 of 1983 signalled the Government's intention to make additional police resources conditional on evidence that existing resources were being used as efficently, effectively, and economically (the dreaded three Es) as possible. The even tougher Circular 106 of 1988 cast a chill over police managers and staff associations which has continued ever since. Under its strict guidelines, which require chief constables to specify the objectives which are to be met by each new post asked for, police forces throughout the country have fared disappointingly in their bids for increased strength. The alarm which has permeated policing circles at all levels is indicated by the unprecedented joint study of the threat to 'traditional policing' which was sponsored in 1989 by all three staff associations (*Operational Policing Review*, Surbiton: Joint Consultative Committee of the Police Staff Associations, 1990).

The new financial regime is not only tighter but more centralized. New powers to cap local government are being used as a means not only of restricting locally funded capital expenditure by police forces, but of inducing forces to achieve economies by standardized purchasing of equipment and centralized buying arrangements (*Police Review* 9 Mar. 1990, 472–3; 20 Apr. 1990, 786). Local accountability has been eroded, sometimes with the perverse consequence of encouraging local authorities to bid for extra resources whether these are needed or not, as the funding will largely come from central government. The Audit Commission, the independent body established by the Government to monitor local authority spending, has itself argued that:

The balance has now tilted so far towards the centre that the role of the local police authorities in the tripartite structure has been significantly diminished. Accountability is blurred and financial and management incentives are out of step ... Tight government control over local police authorities is in many areas stifling initiative and reducing the efficiency and effectiveness of local forces. Accountability suffers too, as police authorities find central government taking more and more of the key decisions. (*Footing the Bill: Financing Provincial Police Forces*, Audit Commission (1990). Quoted in *Police Review*, 22 June 1990, 1128–9).

The role of HM Inspectorate of Constabulary has been considerably enhanced in recent years as the linchpin of a more centralized co-ordination of standards and procedures. This process began in the early 1980s with the financial management initiative, and has developed apace. As Mollie Weatheritt, assistant director of the Police Foundation puts it:

Since 1983, the format and content of inspection reports have changed and inspectors have begun to work to more explicit guidelines in determining what should count as efficiency and in probing force performance ... Inspections have become more analytical and probing and the inspector's role has become not only a much more overtly proactive one but also much more closely and explicitly linked to the policy concerns of the Home Office. Since 1984, forces have been required to submit more detailed, purposefully organised information to HMIs before the latter make their formal inspections. (Weatheritt, 1986, 107–12)

In 1987, the HM Inspectorate launched a computer-based management information system, the Matrix of Police Indicators. This is 'used not only for HMIs in preparation for Inspections, but also by forces to whom the information is available on request ... Towards the end of 1989, a working group was set up ... to consider further development of the Matrix' (*Report of Her Majesty's Chief Inspector of Constabulary 1989*, London: HMSO, July 1990, 12). Inspections are evidently no longer the perfunctory affairs of police legend, but involve the collation of considerable data on a standardized basis, shaping police activity into centrally determined channels.

The scope and profile of the work of the Inspectorate is clearly extending as the Government's grip over policing has tightened. In 1988 'the continuing expansion of the role of the Inspectorate led to the creation of an additional HM Inspectorate Region, and the consequent appointment of a further HM Inspector and support staff' (*Report of Her Majesty' Chief Inspector of Constabulary 1988*, London: HMSO, July, 1989, 12). This now brings the number of Inspectorate regions to six. In late 1989, a Home Office–Treasury report appeared which aimed explicitly to enhance the role of the HMI as the vehicle of a more standardized system of resource allocation.

It is not only the number of Inspectors which has been increased. Until recently the Inspectorate was something like a House of Lords for the police. It was a place to which distinguished former chief constables could aspire after completing long and worthy operational careers, or occasionally to which less successful ones could be kicked upstairs. The change in the role of the HMI from dignified to effective has been accompanied by a change in the character of appointments to it. Several recent appointments have been relatively young chief constables, in the prime of their careers, and with the prospect of advancement in terms of operational command still ahead of them.

The most significant of these appointments has been Geoffrey Dear, who in December 1989 announced his resignation from being Chief Constable of the West Midlands to become an HMI. Mr Dear was not only the chief constable of one of the largest provincial forces, but commonly regarded as heir apparent to Sir Peter Imbert as Metropolitan Commissioner. His move to the Inspectorate was generally interpreted as a clear indication of the Home Office's concern to beef up the status and role of the Inspectorate by moving younger 'star' chief officers into it (*Police Review* 8 Dec. 1989, 2469).

Other recent developments which have enhanced the profile of the Inspectorate have included the decision for the first time to publish HMI reports, after their presentation to the Home Secretary (*Police Review*, 30 Mar. 1990). The HMI has also begun to inspect aspects of the work of the Metropolitan Police, hitherto exempt from the external inspection process (*Reports of Her Majesty's Chief Inspector of Constabulary 1988 and 1989* London: HMSO, 1989 and 1990, 13, 15).

The Home Office has also encouraged ACPO to develop a much higher profile and expand its role in recent years, as a means of enhancing the standardization and centralization of policing. (The earlier history and structure of ACPO are described in Appendix C.) ACPO first made a significant impact on public debate about policing when it established and operated the National Reporting Centre as a means of co-ordinating the massive national mutual aid policing operation during the 1984–5 miners' strike. It was widely argued then that ACPO was acting as a medium of government control of policing, or at least as a proxy for it. (This view is in fact echoed by many chief constables, who claim that ACPO's successful co-ordination of policing during the strike was an alternative to the formal nationalization of policing, as Chapter 8 shows.)

The then Home Secretary, Douglas Hurd, took up this argument at ACPO's autumn conference in 1989, when he encouraged ACPO to become the body for harmonizing policies between forces. He called on them 'to deliver effectively co-ordinated operational action.' Failing this, he implied, the present structure of local policing might be replaced by either regional forces or a single national force (*Police Review*, 13 Oct. 1989, 206–7). To deliver this enhanced function the Home Office agreed to increase funding for the ACPO secretariat, which was to become more professionalized and streamlined. It had until the 1960s been run entirely by serving chief officers, and until 1989 remained a shoestring operation managed by retired police officers. In October 1989 ACPO appointed a firm of management 'headhunters' to find a suitable candidate for the Home Office-funded post of general secretary, which was to enjoy a salary comparable with that of serving chief officers. The new secretariat would be responsible for establishing a policy analysis unit (*Police Review*, 20 Oct. 1989). Although ACPO rules required the post to be offered first to the membership, in the event a civilian was appointed, Marcia Barton, former secretary of the official side of the Police Negotiating Board (*Police*, Jan. 1990, 12).

In addition to the growth in importance in recent years of HMI and ACPO as co-ordinating bodies between the Home Office and individual chief constables, there has been a proliferation of specialist national policing units. The Met. has figured importantly in this process. The last few years have seen the formation of national or regional intelligence units to deal with a variety of issues ranging from drugs, to football hooliganism and acid house parties. In July 1989 Sir Peter Imbert delivered a much publicized Police Foundation lecture in which he advocated the establishment of a national FBI-style force to combat major crime. Speaking at the Superintendents Association Conference in September of that year, Douglas Hurd supported a modified version of that idea, a national criminal intelligence unit to combat organized crime.

The issue was debated within ACPO and the Home Office throughout 1990. It received an extensive airing at the ACPO summer conference in June 1990. A national operational CID remained controversial amongst chief constables, but the executive co-ordinator of the existing regional crime squads announced that a national criminal intelligence unit would be operational by 1991. This would integrate the work of existing units such as the National Football Intelligence Unit and regional criminal intelligence offices. It seemed that the weight of influential opinion in ACPO was swinging round to the nationalization idea, and it was widely anticipated that the new national intelligence unit would be the embryo of an eventual operational CID at national level (*Police Review*, 15 June 1990, 1180–1).

Other proposals in recent years along these lines have included a Home Office suggestion for a national air support unit, and a European drugs and organized crime unit. One of the key sources of the impetus towards centralized crime investigations units and the tighter national control of policing generally is the belief that it is an essential requirement of European integration after 1992. This was made explicit in Douglas Hurd's previously cited speech to the autumn 1989 ACPO Conference. He complained of the

apparent inability of any one agency to represent with complete authority the operational views of the police service . . . At international debates on policing issues, I have to explain that although I am the minister responsible for the police service, I am unable to make commitments on operational decisions. That causes considerable surprise. Surprise turns to incredulity when our foreign partners learn that even the representatives of chief officers are unable to deliver binding commitments on behalf of their colleagues. (*Police Review*, 13 Oct. 1989, 2056–7)

The Met. is in the forefront of advancing national developments. The advocacy of Sir Peter Imbert, the Metropolitan Commissioner, started the ball rolling for the national FBI debate. His deputy, Sir John Dellow (then ACPO president), and John Smith, Assistant Commissioner in charge of specialist operations in the Met., were prominent champions of the national CID idea at the June 1990 ACPO Conference. ACPO itself, Interpol, and the main national crime intelligence units are physically based on Scotland Yard. In August 1990 it was announced that the head of the Metropolitan Anti-Terrorist Squad, Commander Churchill-Coleman, would henceforth have responsibility for all major terrorism investigations throughout the country. The Met. is obviously a focal point for the national policing units which are likely to develop.

Another important source of the nationalization trajectory in the late 1980s was the growing debate about the quality of senior officers, their selection, and training. During 1989 a 'moral panic' about policing clearly began to spread in establishment circles, stimulated both by the bumper crop of scandals, and declining faith in the capacity of the police to control crime (Reiner, 1990*a*). The Government rapidly turned to the senior ranks of the service as convenient scapegoats. A chorus of opinion developed blaming the shortcomings of police management and calling for the creation of a new 'officer class' (Reiner, 1990*b* and *c*). This received a considerable impetus when it became known that the Prime Minister, Mrs Thatcher, was an enthusiast for the idea (*Police Review*, 9 Feb. 1990, 264–5).

Concern about the quality of police leadership has been a major source of the impetus towards centralization in recent years. In December 1988 the House of Commons Home Affairs Committee (HAC) announced an inquiry into higher police training and the Police Staff College at Bramshill. The HAC chairman John Wheeler is one of the leading exponents of greater police centralization, and has advocated a new structure of six regional forces controlled from the centre, to replace the tripartite system. It was perhaps no surprise when the HAC Report in March 1989 attributed most of the shortcomings of police leadership to lack of adequate central control leading to a deficient career structure and unco-ordinated training. 'We are not convinced that the level of co-operation within the current police organisational structure is sufficient to achieve the career development patterns to utilize police skills effectively' (HAC Report, 1989, p. xxxi. For a review of the Report see the Symposium on Higher Police Training, *The Howard Journal*, 29: 3, Aug. 1990, 199–219).

The HAC proposals recommended a number of measures to enhance the extent of rational central control over the careers and training of senior officers, such as making successful completion of the Senior Command Course at Bramshill a condition of promotion above assistant chief constable rank. The analysis of the career patterns of existing chief constables (in Chapter 5 below) suggests that most of the HAC recommendations are currently followed. Its proposals primarily involve a formal ratification of the status quo, in which the Home Office already exercises a considerable measure of control over who becomes a chief constable. The career patterns of chief constables clearly show them to be 'cosmopolitans' not 'locals' (in Robert Merton's terminology). The Police Federation's caustic portrayal of the high-flyers as 'butterfly men' is not that far off the mark (*Police*, Aug. 1989, 3–6).

The one proposal of the HAC Report which would dramatically alter the picture was its final one: 'The ACPO ranks of the police service should be established as a central service grade within the Home Office as a cadre of professional officers holding the historic office of constable but available for appointment to the developing tasks of a modern police service, both in central posts and in existing constabularies.' This clear and explicit nationalization of the senior ranks of the police was immediately rejected by the Home Office in its initial reaction to the Report (which welcomed the other recommendations). The Home Office argued that this would endanger the tripartite system where responsibility for chief officer appointments rests with police authorities.

The reality is, however, that the Home Office has the power to approve the short list of candidates interviewed by police authorities, as well as to veto the police authority's selection, according to the 1964 Police Act. It is clear that even in the period before the Second World War, the Home Office could exercise considerable influence over chief officer appointments. The memoirs of Eric St Johnston, for example, indicate how officials and the Inspectorate regarded key appointments as basically within their gift, though the final hurdle of interview by the police authority was a slight inconvenience.

On a Sunday, just after Dunkirk in June 1940, I was patrolling in Kensington when I met, by chance, Colonel Halland, formerly Commandant of Hendon Police College and by now one of Her Majesty's Inspectors of Constabulary ... Out of the blue Colonel Halland asked, 'How would you like to be Chief Constable of Oxfordshire? ... To me it was a wonderful suggestion, opening out vast possibilities. I said as much and Colonel Halland promised he would see the Commissioner the next day and broach the matter at the Home Office ... but it was not quite as straightforward as was first thought. While the Oxfordshire Standing Joint Committee and the Home Office ... were happy to accept Colonel Halland's advice, the Commissioner refused to do so ... The Oxfordshire Standing Joint Committee therefore decided to advertise the post. I applied and with five others was put on a short-list for interview. (St Johnston, 1978, 61–3)

Despite the minor set-back of having to be interviewed, St Johnston duly landed the job. St Johnston's accounts of his subsequent appointments as Chief Constable of Durham and of Lancashire (ibid. 103–5, 139–40) paint a similar picture of an old boy network of personal recommendations being the manner in which chief officers were selected. The final interview by the police authority seems to have been heavily influenced by the HM Inspectorate and Home Office view of who amongst a magic circle of potential chiefs was the next in line.

The development of a cadre of potential chief officers, and the allocation of these to particular forces, is informal and not completely certain because of the role of police authorities, which has become rather less controllable in recent years. It is this which leads chief officers to regard it as a 'lottery', and frustrates the centralists. In general, however, it has seemed to suit the Home Office better to have a system which it can heavily influence but not totally control than to make its power plain. It could be that this situation is changing as the trend towards more overt centralization gathers pace.

Apart from the HAC Report, another straw in the wind has been the saga over the appointment of the new Chief Constable of Derbyshire. This is the first time that the Home Office has openly demonstrated its control over the short-listing and appointment process. In April 1990 the Derbyshire Police Authority appointed the deputy chief constable, Mr John Weselby, as chief constable, despite the fact that the Home Office through the HMI for the area had indicated at the short-listing stage that Mr Weselby would not be approved (*Police Review*, 13 Apr. 1990, 733). The only apparent ground for this decision was the good relationship enjoyed by Mr Weselby with the police authority (*Police Review*, 20 Apr. 1990, 784–5). Despite an appeal from the police authority, the Home Office continued to veto the appointment (*Police Review*, 4 May 1990, 885). The police authority sought a judicial review of the Home Office's action, but before this could proceed Mr Weselby withdrew his candidature. The post then went to Mr John Newing, a Metropolitan Police Deputy Assistant Commissioner (*Police Review*, 18 May 1990, 990). Although there have been some previous disputes between the Home Office and police authorities about the short-listing of candidates, this was 'the first occasion on which the two sides disagreed publicly' (*Police Review*, 18 May 1990, 999).

Although not leading to public disputes, there have been difficulties in finding suitable candidates for several other chief officer posts (*Police Review*, 9 Mar. 1990, 473; 18 May 1990, 990). Anxiety about a dearth of suitable candidates is not confined to the Home Office or police authorities. In April 1990 an ACPO working party on 'Providing the

Future Chief Officers of Police' reported. It recommended a number of proposals aimed at ensuring an adequate supply of high quality senior officers, and constructing a system of national standards under the supervision of the HM Inspectorate. Prospective high-flyers would be 'starred' during their probationer training and then monitored by the Inspectorate as they moved through various stages including Home Office Extended Interviews and Bramshill course assessments (*Police Review*, 27 Apr. 1990, 832–3). Existing systems for selecting and advancing high-flyers, such as the Graduate Entry Scheme (revamped in 1989 as the Accelerated Promotion Scheme for Graduates), were held to be inadequate (*Police Review*, 11 May 1990, 936–7). From the point of view of the influential advocates of an externally recruited 'officer class', however, these reforms are likely to be dismissed as mere tinkering with a basically inadequate system. Whatever the outcome of this debate, the extent of central control over chief officer careers (already dominant as Chapter 5 shows) is going to become more prominent and overt.

Who's Boss? Police Accountability in Practice

The above review of the law in the books as well as the law in action suggests that the much vaunted tripartite structure of police governance is asymmetrical. Whenever there have been clashes between local police authorities and chief constables or central government, the former have been defeated. Where conflict has not surfaced the evidence is strong that this is because police authorities have accepted the 'professional' perspective of the chief constable (Brogden, 1977, 1982; Morgan and Swift, 1987; Chapter 11 below). This clearly unbalanced relationship between chief constables and local police authorities has been blessed by the courts as the doctrine of constabulary independence.

But what about the relationship between chief constables and central government? The courts have articulated equally the notion of constabulary independence with respect to that relationship, although it has never actually been at issue in any case. Most critical commentators also affirm the autonomy and lack of accountability of the police, the implication being that the chief constables normally prevail against central government too. However, the balance of power between chief constables and the Home Office is much harder to analyse for reasons which are illuminated by Steven Lukes's seminal analysis of the study of power.

As Lukes argues, three views of power can be distinguished. The 'one-dimensional' view focuses on 'behaviour in the making of decisions on issues over which there is an observable conflict of (subjective) interests, seen as express policy preferences,' (Lukes, 1974, 15). This is the easiest concept to test empirically. If there are overt clashes, all that needs to be done to identify power is to count who wins, and how often. The relationship between some police authorities and chief constables has been of this nature, and the chief has always been observed to win (Loveday, 1985; Okojie, 1985; McLaughlin, 1990).

The 'two-dimensional' view sees power as residing in the ability to manipulate the political agenda by preventing potential conflicts from becoming overt, through observable acts of suppression. Again, this is capable of empirical observations, although it requires some probing behind closed doors to ascertain how agendas are constructed. Research suggests that chief constables also exercize this second dimension of power *vis-à-vis* police authorities. (For example, in Chapter 11 I cite the views of many chief constables about how they try and mould police authorities to their proposals.)

The Home Office–chief constable relationship cannot be studied in terms of the above two perspectives on power. There have been no overt conflicts which can be researched from a 'one dimensional' perspective. Although there are anecdotes about behind the scenes manipulation by the Home Office (the 'two-dimensional' view)—and some are offered in Chapters 8 and 11 below—these are few, far between, and not a basis for systematic assessment. In so far as it occurs, such influence is a matter of nods, winks, and personal phone calls, largely impervious to research.

The relationship between chief constables and the Home Office can only be conceptualized in terms of what Lukes dubs the 'three-dimensional' view of power. This refers to the ability to maintain dominance by keeping potential issues from surfacing, not through overt actions (the 'two-dimensional' view), but by structural and institutional processes which avert any expressions of dissent and possibly even awareness of it. It involves the power to shape consciousness, not just to control action. This does not lend itself to empirical testing by observation of crunch cases. To the extent that 'three-dimensional' power operates effectively, there will be no crunch cases. But power may still be inferred from indirect evidence concerning the structure and operation of institutions, and the ideologies of members.

The evidence which is presented below in Parts II, III, and IV about the social characteristics and ideology of present-day chief constables suggests that we have moved towards a *de facto* national police force. It is clear from the analysis of the background and career patterns of chief constables (Part II) that they constitute a cohesive and unitary national power élite. Data on their views about accountability (Part IV) suggest that while local police authorities are regarded as at most a useful forum for discovering local opinion, the Home Office is seen as exerting power which cannot be ignored. The dominant ideology of chief constables (explored in Part III) is largely the product of the current Home Office orthodoxy, propogated by the HMI, ACPO, and Bramshill, through which most chiefs pass.

The debates currently raging about the pros and cons of greater centralization of policing concern form rather than substance. Overt nationalization would ratify and legitimate rather than transform the status quo. Whether this would enhance police accountability by making the real locus of power plain (which is why it tends to be opposed by Home Secretaries), or retard it by consolidating the marginalization of local police authorities is a moot point. Chief constables sometimes jokingly refer to themselves as the forty-three robber barons. It is unlikely that the Police Act and the case-law on constabulary independence will prove to be any more effective as barriers against encroaching central power than Magna Carta was for their feudal counterparts.

Notes

1. To complicate matters, the Metropolitan Police rank now known as 'commander' was until the 1950s called 'chief constable'. It lies between chief superintendent and deputy assistant commissioner in the Met. hierarchy, and is the lowest rank eligible for membership in the Association of Chief Police Officers. The rank originated in 1840 as 'visiting superintendent', and was subsequently known as 'district superintendent' until it became 'chief constable (Met)'.

2. Wall's 1989 thesis is a painstakingly assembled and invaluable source of information about chief constables prior to 1985. It is summarized in his 1987 article, but the thesis contains more detailed data on the social origins of chief constables, and the process by which they were appointed.

3 Assisting with Inquiries: Studying a Criminal Justice Élite

Élites need to be interviewed. The best way of finding out about people is by talking to them. It cannot guarantee the truth, especially from people well practised in the arts of discretion. But it is superior to any alternative way of discovering what they believe and do.
(Crewe, I. 'Studying Élites in Britain' 42–3)

The History of the Project

The idea of studying chief constables first occurred to me in 1980. There were a number of factors which made it an attractive and interesting project. Above all, there was the growing prominence of some chief constables as vocal and controversial public figures. Although this was before the urban riots which made policing issues absolutely central to political consciousness and debate, many commentators were already pointing to a growing politicization of the police, spearheaded by the more vocal chief constables and ACPO.[1] The accountability of the police was already becoming a central issue, with many critics arguing that the police were not adequately controlled by democratic and legal institutions.[2] This controversy was to become more intense after 1981 as several radical Labour local authorities elected in that year began to engage in conflict with their chief constables over the question of police accountability.[3] Chief constables were thus public figures of growing prominence and interest in 1980.

At the same time, a study of chief constables seemed a logical progression to plug a clear gap in the burgeoning field of police studies. In the 1960s and even more rapidly and extensively in the 1970s systematic social research on police organizations developed rapidly, first mainly in the USA, but then in Britain too.[4] However, all the research concentrated on the lower ranks of the police. Knowledge of the senior ranks was sketchy and anecdotal, a pot-pourri of chance revelation and reminiscence, titbits of scandal, and the much-publicized remarks of probably unrepresentative police superstars on the rent-a-quote circuit. This led me to conclude at the time that: 'The character of police work at the senior levels of the organisation is the greatest gap in the growing body of knowledge which social scientists have accumulated about the police ... While we have some knowledge of the social origins and previous careers of recruits, we do not have this information for senior officers' (Reiner, 1982, 165–74).

Having previously published a study of the backgrounds, careers, and occupational perspectives of the Federated ranks of the police (Reiner, 1978), it seemed a logical step to attempt to conduct similar research on the élite levels. The immediate trigger for my attempting to launch such a study was a 1979 *Newsnight* programme on which I was supposed to debate new tactics of riot control with the President of ACPO. Much to the consternation of the presenters, who were clearly hoping for some more televisual sparks of conflict, consensus broke out between us. This encouraged me to write to him seeking ACPO approval for an interview study of all forty-three chief constables then in office, aiming to ascertain their background, careers, and philosophies of policing. (The dates and precise terms of this correspondence cannot be checked now, as my file containing all the preliminary material about the research was stolen from my office shortly before I began to conduct the present interviews.)

I did not receive any reply at all from ACPO concerning my request. Instead, about six months later I received a letter from a senior official in the Home Office. This informed me that my request had been passed on to them by ACPO. After due deliberation it had been decided that my research would not be officially supported by them in any way. They did not see any value in a study compiling information about chief constables which was available to them already in their files.[5] There would also be no possibility of collecting demographic data about chief constables from these files on an anonymous basis, as I had requested as an alternative. The letter did say I was free to approach individual chief constables to seek an interview with them, but it would be for them to decide whether to grant it. The whole purpose of my research was to gain a representative picture of chief constables, and it seemed likely to me that without any official blessing the only chiefs who would respond positively would be a self-selected few. I therefore shelved the project at that time.

In 1986 I thought the moment might be right to make another attempt at the same project. Policing matters had become even more prominent and politically controversial. However, in the wake of the 1981 Scarman Report attempts were being made on a broad front to restore public confidence in policing and to professionalize the service. One aspect of this was a much greater degree of openness to outside (as well as internal) research. My 1985 book on *The Politics of the Police* had received a positive response from a number of prominent chief officers, who I hoped might therefore look more favourably on my research proposal than their 1980 counterparts had done.

During 1986 I applied successfully for a Nuffield Foundation Social Research Fellowship, to run from the autumn of that year for twelve months. I am most grateful to them not only for providing me with the time and the money to conduct the fieldwork, but for showing their trust in the project before I had been able to secure research access.

Once I had obtained the Fellowship I set about trying to mobilize support for the project in official circles. I discussed it with members of the Home Office Research and Planning Unit and Her Majesty's Inspectorate of Constabulary. Both groups were favourable to the research, so I then approached the Home Office Police Department for official permission to interview all chief constables. They replied in July 1986, implying they would support the project if ACPO did, and informing me they had already communicated this to the then president, Sir Stanley Bailey, Chief Constable of Northumbria. Sir Stanley was well known to me as a champion of police research from his participation in the series of influential seminars organized by Professor Michael Banton at Bristol University in the early 1970s (Banton, 1971, 1973, 1975). I approached him for ACPO support, and was interviewed by him and the late Harry Ross (then ACPO secretary) in September 1986.

Prior to the interview, I discussed the matter with several chief officers with whom I had a good relationship. All were keen on the idea of the research, but indicated that their own participation would be conditional on ACPO support. This underlined to me that ACPO approval was vital, and several chiefs subsequently told me in the interviews that they would not have seen me without it.

It was during this period that my research file was stolen. A number of chiefs I spoke to at the time expressed concern about it. A couple wondered whether Special Branch was involved, while some were worried about it being found and passed to the media. They tried to recall what correspondence had gone on between us, and whether its appearance in the *Guardian* would cause them any embarrassment!

The interview with Sir Stanley Bailey and Harry Ross was successful, and the proposal was approved at the ACPO Conference that year. Subsequently Harry Ross wrote a letter to all chief constables informing them that the project enjoyed the support of ACPO and the Home Office. (This is reproduced in Appendix A, together with some other relevant correspondence.) It was made clear that the participation of individual chief constables was entirely a matter for them to decide upon. However, armed with this official blessing, I began to approach the forty-three chief constables.

I decided to write to the chiefs in batches of about a dozen. In the first wave I wrote to those chief constables whom I knew and by the time I approached the second batch of twelve, I had successfully completed ten interviews. Of the twelve chiefs in the second batch, four immediately refused to be interviewed. Three communicated this to me through their secretaries over the phone, while one wrote to me attributing his refusal to a reading of my *The Politics of the Police*. 'Having now read your book (which I found very informative) and considered the request in the your letter, I regret that I am unable to accept your invitation to interview me on this occasion.' While pleased to learn that my book had an audience, I was less happy about its effect! Shortly after this, one of my first batch of chiefs, who had given me an appointment, withdrew his consent to be interviewed following a visit to the Home Office concerning some controversial public statements he had made. Sadly for me this meeting at the Home Office coincided with my scheduled interview with him, and after first postponing our interview he cancelled it altogether.

I grew alarmed about the prospects of the research at this stage, for if the rate of refusal of the second batch continued in subsequent ones I would end up with only about a 70 per cent sample. While a fairly respectable response rate, I was concerned about whether I would be systematically missing a substantial body of opinion. In the event these anxieties proved completely groundless. All the chief constables in the last two batches I approached agreed to be interviewed. I suspect that the high refusal rate in the second batch was due to these being the first group of chief constables I approached without any previous relationship to build upon. By the time I contacted the last two batches, I had already completed nearly twenty interviews. Word had evidently got around about the nature of the interviews, and it was clear that I could be seen without the chief constable's thoughts being plastered across the front page of the *Guardian* the next morning. It was my distinct impression that the later interviews were altogether more relaxed, not only because I was more fluent in handling them but because people were seeing me in the knowledge that I already had a substantial number of interviews under my belt.

After completing the thirty-eight interviews with those who agreed to see me when I first approached them, I was subsequently able to add two more interviews to achieve a final total of forty. The chief who had originally agreed to see me but then changed his mind was prevailed upon to reconsider yet again when I met him at a public lecture. He is one of the most prominent of all chiefs and I successfully argued that his participation was crucial to the project. The other change of heart was a chief I met when I attended a set of extended interviews for the Senior Command Course as an observer. He overheard me discussing the research interviews with another chief, and asked what they were about. I told him I had approached him for an interview, but his secretary had told me over the phone that he was unwilling. He maintained he had not heard of this approach, and that his secretary was probably performing her gate-keeping function with exceptional zeal. At any rate, he granted me an interview bringing the completed total to forty.

The interviews amount to a sample of 93 per cent of chief constables, a virtual census. It is possible that if I had approached the three remaining refusals, they would have changed their minds. However, they were all fairly low-profile individuals, and indeed, when one was subsequently appointed to head a controversial investigation, the newspaper reports all mentioned his retiring personality. In any event, I rested content with the forty interviews.

The Methods of the Research

All but one of the interviews were tape-recorded. One chief constable refused to be taped, and I recorded his interview in handwritten notes. This experience made me sympathetic to the chief constables' complaints about the problems of contemporaneous note-taking (one of their regularly repeated criticisms of the Police and Criminal Evidence Act). Not only was manual note-taking laborious, but it slowed down and broke up the flow of the interview.

This reluctance to be taped possibly indicates the reasons behind suspicion of me, which could also underlie the refusal to be interviewed by three of the chiefs, as well as produce distortion in other cases. The chief who would not be taped argued that no matter what the results turned out to be, there was a danger that they would damage the police image. Direct quotes tended to make them look stupid, and he explicitly referred to my earlier study *The Blue-Coated Worker* as proof of this. The statistical data would be double-edged. The media would be bound to present them in ways detrimental to the police, no matter what they were or how I presented them. It was a catch-22 situation. If, for example, it turned out that chief constables were more middle class, better educated, or otherwise advantaged compared to the general run of police recruits, the story would be of unequal opportunities for a favoured few in the police force. If, on the other hand, chiefs came from the same working-class, not highly educated, origins as most recruits did, the panic would be about whether such people were fitted to command such important positions. Finally, he argued, although I had promised not to attribute quotes to individuals, he would not be happy with his views on such controversial issues as rubber bullets going on a tape with his name on it, in case it should fall into the wrong hands, say his police authority. In sum, for all my assurances, he was worried that the results might bring the force into disrepute. Altogether, he mounted a pretty cogent case for not being taped, and I could only be thankful more of his colleagues did not adopt it.

A few others expressed hesitations about being taped, but I was able to persuade them by saying I would switch off if something came up about which they were unhappy to be taped. This only occurred twice. On one of the occasions when I was asked to switch off, the chief was not prepared to talk on tape about a dispute with the Ministry of Defence Police that he was currently involved in, about the policing of army bases. The second occasion concerned some details of an ongoing murder investigation, which the chief believed was being hindered by the PACE procedures. The common thread seems to have been the topicality of the issues. Both chiefs readily discussed apparently more controversial past events on tape.

Apart from such complete refusals to be taped on all or some issues, a few chiefs said they were not prepared to discuss in detail some matters (such as their views on police authorities) on tape because they were too negative. This, of course, itself implies clearly the nature of their views. On other occasions chiefs alluded to the presence of the tape, but were prepared to continue because of my pledge of anonymity. They would say things like: 'OK, you have a microphone on, but you're not attributing remarks', or 'I'm conscious that you've got this thing ticking over there' but 'I accept your assurance that remarks are unattributable'.

Overall, I believe that what was lost on some swings because of suspicion of the tape, was gained on the roundabouts of having smoothly flowing interviews. Whether the chiefs saw me as trustworthy, and how I was perceived, will be discussed further below. However, it is clear that ACPO support, and the guarantees of anonymity, were crucial not only for achieving a high response rate but for allowing the interviews to be taped.

The interviews lasted for an average of one and a half to two hours, and were based on a question schedule which was used in a standard way. (It is printed in Appendix B.) However, I knew the questions by heart, and did not look at the schedule unless this seemed an appropriate way to introduce a pause between questions. As far as possible I attempted to create a conversational flow.

The aim of the exercise was to give an appreciative account of the world-view of chief constables. To achieve this I allowed the chiefs to express their views as fully as possible in their own words, and although I did use probes to elicit more detail I never cut them off. The consequence was a large volume of qualitative data which was very hard to code. It involved laborious analysis of the transcribed interviews, having first coded all the responses to specific questions. However, the reasoning behind these responses had to be analysed in terms of categories which emerged only as I read the transcripts. I kept a card index of references to particular topics which arose regularly during the discussions, but were not the subject of specific questions. Examples were the miners' strike, and race relations, about which all the chiefs had much to say, but which were not specifically asked about. (The results are discussed in Chapters 8 and 9.) The replies to standard questions were analysed using SSPSS on an IBM PC.

My main concern, however, was not with quantitative analysis of replies to standard questions. I was concerned to create a picture of the chief constables' perspectives in their own words, and these are used in subsequent chapters to give a feel of their world as they see it. However, this is based on a rigorous attempt to avoid a biased sample, and indeed to achieve a census of opinion. The quantitative analysis endeavours also to indicate how prevalent particular variations of viewpoint are. Altogether I attempted to adopt the same Weberian 'action frame of reference' as I had used in *The Blue-Coated Worker*, striving to combine 'causal adequacy' with 'adequacy at the level of meaning' (Weber, 1964, 99–100; Reiner, 1978, 9–10). For this I felt interviews were an appropriate tool, for reasons indicated in the quote from Ivor Crewe which introduces this chapter.

Interviews are clearly a form of social interaction and not an invariate, neutral measuring instrument. To assess the validity of the picture I was given, it is necessary to consider how I was perceived by the chief constables. Their replies will clearly be filtered through their perception of what I knew and expected, and how far I could be trusted.

Chief Constables' Perceptions of the Researcher

During my Ph.D. research on the Federated ranks of a police force, I had generally found it an advantage to be perceived as an outsider, and moreover as a naïve student (Reiner, 1978, 15–16). This prompted many respondents to try to fill me in on the realities of policing as they saw it. The one division where a rumour had spread that I was not a bona fide student but a Home Office spy was the hardest to research.

Unfortunately the blissful advantages of naïve ignorance, waiting to be informed, were not available to me on this occasion. All the chiefs knew of and some had read my previous two books on the police. As indicated above this was the motive for at least one refusal to be interviewed. More generally, however, the reception of these publications had been broadly favourable, and helped me to get into the chief constables' offices. Once there, though, they often acted as a barrier in the interview itself. Several chiefs wished to debate, or set me straight about, points to which they objected in my books. For example, one produced the report of an internal investigation of a complaint to refute an allegation I had recycled about an incident during the 1981 riot in his area. Another took exception to a remark I made that 'one hazard of police research is the taking of mental notes while sinking under a bar as the consumption of pints mounts' (Reiner, 1985, 99). Recognizing that there is no such thing as a free interview, I duly accepted a reprimand about my allegations of alcoholism as the price of the research progressing.[6] After completing the interview I was kindly invited to lunch in the senior officers' dining-room. There I found on my left a red bottle of wine and on my right a white one! (A vivid example of the verification principle.)

While such bibulous hospitality was a rare event, almost all the chief constables I saw did welcome me with great courtesy, and I was often entertained to lunch or tea after the interview. Almost invariably the chief's driver would return me to the station afterwards, and sometimes provide an illuminating back-stairs perspective on the boss. The extent of co-operation I received was remarkable for any research, but particularly for the élite levels of what has often been characterized as a closed institution. I was especially surprised in the light of the long and arduous process of setting up access, and the many predictions from police-watchers that I would never do it.[7]

I have no doubt that in addition to the absolute *sine qua non* of ACPO approval, the pledge I gave to cite opinions anonymously and not to attribute remarks was essential to getting the chiefs to open up. That they did do so, at least in many cases, is testified to by the fact that many made statements on the tapes which would cause them considerable personal embarrassment if it were known from whom they came. The interviews are liberally peppered with comments that the respondents would dread coming out in attributable form. This encourages me to believe the picture I got was not simply a matter of public relations.

"Well, you have put me in a difficult position. [By asking whether the growth of police force size had caused management problems.] But you are not going to quote me personally, are you? [R.R.: No] Well, this has just arisen. I don't know if you know that the popular topic of conversation in this area now is ... [the possible re-organization of a number of force boundaries]."

"Are you going to write my name on this? [R.R.: No, as I said they'll all be anonymous]." (chief constable before giving his views on the question of a local police authority for the Met.)

"I wouldn't say this in the presence of——[the new chief constable of a smaller force of which the speaker had previously been chief], and certainly don't attribute this to me otherwise I will lose a friend, but I would describe this job as more difficult by a factor of six."

"Not for the record, we were forever sending our men across our borders [in mutual aid during the miners' strike] which were never charged up to my colleagues. But we must not tell the politicians that."

"The HMI is broadly speaking a cosmetic exercise—now I am being right out of order and I trust you completely—particularly when the HMI is your predecessor as a chief constable."

"None of this is attributable is it? [R.R.: Not to an individual. I'm not giving any names away.] Well, what I am going to tell you now could be a bit tricky."

All interviews are inevitably a form of reciprocal impression management. It is necessary to interpret the responses with an awareness of whom the chiefs considered their audience to be. They generally saw me as one of a growing band of at least potentially critical police-watchers whom they saw as flourishing in academe and the media. At the same time, they saw me as a social science 'expert', and this produced the somewhat apologetic tone which crept into many of the answers on social issues. This was either embarrassment at what were self-deprecatingly seen as simplistic analyses, or a sense that I was being told things I must already know.

The perception of me as one of a growing band of hostile police-watchers was frequently invoked, and underlay a clear concern for the chief constable to present himself as a reasonable, moderate 'chap'. Many comments portray me as a fully paid-up member of the anti-police brigade.

"Neighbourhood watch means honest, ordinary, nice people, the bulk of people, being a bit nosey about somebody who is up to no good in their area. And that's made out by some to be illiberal, snoopers. Well, that's bloody rubbish! The police service has to counter all this foolish thinking. With great respect, you are on the fringe, like a host of other people. It's an industry on the fringe of policing that's been generated for the last ten years ... You use terms like 'proactive' which are recent inventions by some of our, dare I say it, mock academics amongst the police."

"The police are all fair game, aren't they, from the man on the beat to the chief constable in command of the force? I mean we are the bread and butter of a great many journalists, including yourself."

"I wouldn't have been prepared to see you and certainly wouldn't have co-operated as I have if ACPO had not given you a strong recommendation. I'm not happy about most researchers. I have a good relationship with Mike Chatterton and Tank Waddington, who I know well. But I'm suspicious about most other researchers ... Generally I'm worried about the fact that there's this enormous growth of research on the police. I wonder if we're not co-operating too much. However, as ACPO gave you strong approval, I'm quite happy to talk to you."

That this was the general attitude towards my project was confirmed by a letter I was sent by a middle-management rank officer who had attended the Senior Command Course at Bramshill. They had been given a lecture on ACPO by a county force chief constable whom I had interviewed. The speaker referred to Duncan Campbell's TV programme on ACPO in his controversial series on the 'Secret Society', and the *New Statesman* article derived from it (8 May 1987)

A fairly humorous but personalised attack on D. Campbell followed, and this launched him into a long run on various 'police-watchers', e.g. the police committees in some areas ... He swiped at the GLC and the use of cash in Manchester for 'deaf lesbian' groups. We then had a general resume of variously perceived anti-police groups, *Guardian* readers ... The PSI volumes were derided, the work of the Police Foundation got a thumbs-down.

He asked: 'Anyone read Robert Reiner, author of *The Blue-Coated Worker* and ...' [pause]. Obviously can't remember, so I prompt '*The Politics of the Police* ...' 'Yes, that's it,' he continues. 'Well, he's doing some research on ACPO, and came to see me. He was surprised to find out we were all reasonable men, trying our best for our communities, and very much accountable across the board.' He then described how R. Reiner had not wanted to hear this, and wanted to find a different scenario. All of his 'everyday language' was a rejection of research, and he had obviously labelled R.R. as antagonistic to police and policing and to the audience of 36 Superintendents (most of whom won't have heard of R.R., never mind read his books) he added another 'left-wing enemy' who was coming in from the 'outside' to criticize unfairly.

Then after this 30–35 minute piling on of example after example of these antagonists to the police, he lamely finished by urging us to present a positive/optimistic front to the world, and especially to the men (on the job). I wrote this up fairly soon after the lecture, but I can't for the life of me recall whether he described you as being 'dismayed' or 'disappointed' to find that the ACPO members were 'pretty reasonable sort of people.' I think he used 'disappointed.'

Whichever it was, either adjective gives a clear indication of how he was certain that your research had presumptions and preconceptions written into its framework.

'Presumptions and preconceptions' are of course written into all research, and also into the reception of the researcher by respondents. There can be no perspective-free, absolutely objective account, but the interpretation of results requires a reflexive consideration of both sets of 'presumptions and preconceptions'. The above indicates the way I was perceived, and the problematic as the respondents saw it. Their concern was to demonstrate to me how 'reasonable' they were. This is not a manipulated false image. It is how they see themselves, but clearly they had doubts about the possibility of conveying it to me.

These suspicions about whether I was sufficiently open to accept their 'reasonableness' were expressed during the interviews themselves.

"I believe we have become more accountable. Although having read your book I'm not sure that you think we have. That is not fair."

"One thing that hasn't come out of our conversation, and let me say it's pretty important to me, is an indication of how my tiny mind works ... I think you've got the impression I'm purporting to be a one-man band, but I'm not really."

"I know you will not agree, but much violent disorder is due to TV."

"The trouble is we're bombarded by propaganda from academics like you who don't have to deal with people ... We've become too easy on things like soccer violence because we've been advised by people who've studied it."

Thus many chiefs assumed that I and most other researchers would be predisposed to reject the police viewpoint. Their concern was to convince me of their 'reasonableness', though they thought this was probably a lost cause because of my insuperable liberal academic blinkers. None the less, most expressed the view that they'd enjoyed the interview, and looked forward to reading the results. This was not because they expected a whitewash, but because of interest in the issues, tinged perhaps by narcissistic curiosity.

"I've read your book and some of your articles. They're as balanced as they could be. But I worry about the way the police are coming more and more to the centre of political debate. I wonder whether the book on chief constables that you're proposing will make things worse, whatever your intentions might be ... Well, I'll look forward to seeing the book when it comes out. What are you going to say? Are you going to say that we are forty-three bastards? What are you going to be writing about the forty-three bastards?"

Coexisting with the suspicion that I might have an anti-police axe to grind, was the perception of me as an 'expert' on society and the police. This either provoked comments that I should be able to answer my own questions, or apologies for telling me what I was presumed to know already.

"You would know better than me [that Gerald Kaufman wants to make us like the education committee]."

"You would know better than I [the problems of measuring stress]."

"As you know already [research shows we spend most of our time dealing with non-crime matters]."

"You tell me why crime is increasing. You're the scientist!"

"You know as well as I do [that some more militant police authorities wouldn't listen to sense]."

"I'm not a sociologist, so I can't really talk about social change."

Given the extent to which chiefs made comments which would have got them in some trouble had I not kept my promises of anonymity, it seems that in the interviews they did give an honest account of their views and feelings for the most part. This was certainly not always the case. One question which I believe frequently produced untruthful answers was about their future personal plans. It became apparent to me that the chiefs were often not honest to me (or themselves?) about their ambitions (but who would be?). I grew weary of being treated to poignant confessions about how a chief had neglected his family for years but planned to make up for this by retiring soon, or to long lectures on the thrill of gardening, by chief constables who then took up second careers in the Inspectorate or in a larger force.

But their pipe-dreams apart, I believe the chiefs did present an authentic account of their views on policing matters. Indeed if the views of some on such issues as race relations (discussed in Chapter 9) are cosmetic I shudder to think what the naked truth would be. Altogether I am confident that the ensuing account gives a faithful flavour of how chief constables do see the world, and the variations which exist among them.

One final caveat is important. Although I interviewed almost all the chiefs in office at the time of the fieldwork, the study is not a census of current chiefs. The rate of turnover in office is quite rapid nowadays, and in the two years since the interviewing was completed, sixteen of the forty chiefs studied have left office and been replaced. While capturing so mobile a group is like taking a still photo of a speeding bullet, the pattern of viewpoints is unlikely to have changed substantially. However, those chiefs wishing to dissociate themselves from the following can always claim that 1988 is ancient history. Researchers working to the more sedate rhythms of academe, not the fast lane of policing, are used to having their work greeted by the sanguine assurance that 'It's all different now!' So be it.

Notes

1. The politicization of the police is more fully analysed in Hall, 1979; Thompson, 1980; Kettle, 1980; Reiner, 1980.
2. Pioneering discussions of the issue of police accountability were Brogden, 1977, 1981, 1982; Cain, 1977, 1979; Hain, 1979, 1980; Bowden, 1978.
3. Case-studies of such conflicts can be found in Jefferson and Grimshaw, 1984; Loveday, 1985; McLaughlin, 1990.
4. Fuller accounts of the development of police research are Reiner 1989*b*, 1991.

5. Towards the end of my fieldwork, I came across a somewhat galling confirmation of this. My penultimate interview was with a former president of ACPO. He was keen to know some of my findings. I read him some of the data on the background and careers of chiefs, which it had taken me over a year, numerous train journeys all across England and Wales, and some £15,000 of the Nuffield Foundation's money to assemble. As I was doing this he pulled open the top drawer of his desk, and pulled out some sheets of paper from which he read out identical numbers. Unfortunately, the contents of ACPO presidents' desks are not in the public domain, so I had to expend considerable resources to reproduce them by the scenic route.

6. I understand from female colleagues that they have sometimes been made to pay a higher price, in return for an interview.

7. No doubt I was aided by the social researcher's strongest weapon, the delight people take in talking about themselves to an unfailingly rapt audience.

Part II

Who are the Chief Constables?

4 Origins and Orientations

A perennial chestnut of police debate has been the question whether police officers are distinct from the majority of the population, in terms of personality or social position. It has often been claimed by critics of the police that the nature of the work, the exercise of power and authority, is likely to attract people with authoritarian personalities. The consensus of research on this issue suggests that the police are not distinct as individual personalities, but reflect the perspectives of the social groups from which they are drawn; predominantly the lower middle and respectable working classes.[1] Some individual pieces of research have claimed to establish distinctive personality traits among the police (Colman and Gorman, 1982), but these have been subject to extensive methodological criticism, and in any event the majority of studies refute them (Cochrane and Butler, 1980; Waddington, 1982; Brown and Willis, 1985). At best therefore the studies purporting to establish that the police are drawn from distinctive personality types apply to a minority of forces.

Radical critics of the police have argued alternatively that the police draw on *socially* distinctive sections of the population, with a peculiar affinity for discipline, even if they are not psychologically distinctive as individual personalities. The orthodox view has it that 'the police of this country have never been recognized, either in law or by tradition, as a force distinct from the general body of the population' (a legend first coined by the 1929 *Report* of the Royal Commission on Police Powers and Procedures and reiterated by the *Report* of the 1962 Royal Commission on the Police, 10). This has often been challenged by radicals, who claim that the police are drawn from particularly deferential sections of the population, largely from the armed forces, and have been insulated from ordinary working experiences from an early age, facilitating the indoctrination of disciplinarian attitudes (*Labour Research*, 1975; Sedley, 1985).

However, the bulk of research on the social origins and careers of police officers does not support these allegations. In terms of social background and experience the police roughly mirror the population, with the overwhelming majority coming from skilled manual working-class or routine non-manual origins (Reiner, 1978, ch. 9, 1982). There is no evidence of insulation from outside civilian work experiences, or a preponderance of military backgrounds. Indeed, historians have shown that it has always been deliberate policy to draw the police from socially representative backgrounds, precisely to minimize alienation, and as a subtle means of social control (Critchley, 1978, 52).

However, while there has been extensive research on the social origins of the police in general, this is not true of the senior ranks. The historical discussion in Chapter 2 showed that until the Second World War, and to a lesser extent throughout the first two post-war decades (thanks to the after-effects of the Trenchard scheme), chief constables in county and major city forces were drawn directly from élite backgrounds, and, especially in the counties, military backgrounds. What have been the effects of the post-war policy of only appointing chief constables who have worked their way up through the ranks? Are chief constables today similar in origins, outlook, and experience to the rank and file? Or are there surviving patterns of differentiation?

This issue is important in two ways. First, the origins and experiences of chief constables may offer clues to the perspectives and practices they now adopt. Second, there is the question whether the myth of equal opportunity for all entrants does indeed hold good. It may not be true in reality that, as the editor of the Police Federation magazine once remarked, 'Every young policeman carries a chief constable's baton in his truncheon pocket ... Every recruit, at least in theory and regulation, starts off on the same footing' (Judge, 1972, 164).

To shed light on these issues this chapter will analyse the social origins, and the initial orientations to their police careers of chief constables. In what ways, if any, do these set them apart from the population in general, or the rest of the police force?

Social Origins and Previous Experience

Family Background

Chief constables today are predominantly children of the Depression period. The years they were born in range from 1924 to 1941, but over half of them were born between 1928 and 1932. Eighty per cent of chief constables were born during the 1930s.

Their social class backgrounds are broadly representative of the population as a whole in their generation. As Table 4.1 shows, nearly two-thirds had fathers who were in skilled manual work for most of their lives, and 70 per cent came from manual working-class origins. Almost another quarter came from routine, clerical level non-manual backgrounds. These origins thus mirror those of the police as a whole, as well as the population at large (Goldthorpe *et al.*, 1980; Halsey *et al.*, 1980, ch. 2). However, as Table 4.1 also shows, the fathers of the chief constables experienced a considerable amount of social mobility during their careers. In fact, 43 per cent of the fathers had been upwardly mobile during their working lives.

TABLE 4.1.   *Social Class Background of Chief Constables*

Registrar-General's class	Father's class during most of working life %	Father's class when son was 18 %
I	—	2.5
II	5.0	30.0
III (non-manual)	22.5	17.5
III (manual)	57.5	45.0
IV	5.0	2.5
V	7.5	2.5
n/a (military, etc.)	2.5	—
TOTAL	100.0	100.0
N = 40		

The chief constables are distinctive in this tendency towards upward social mobility in their backgrounds. They have of course themselves been conspicuously mobile in their own careers. Interestingly, their children have been even more mobile.[2] More than half of the chiefs have adult children in occupations in classes I and II of the Registrar-General's categories. In all, 70 per cent of the adult children of chief constables are in such occupations. While some of this picture of success may be distorted by the rosy spectacles of parental pride, it seems clear that a strong orientation towards upward social mobility is a marked feature of the families of chief constables. Police in general come from the upwardly mobile sections of the working class (Reiner, 1978, 158) but chief constables constitute the super-mobile.

Another way in which the family origins of chief constables deviate from the general population (but not the police as a whole) is the disproportionate number from police backgrounds. Police officers comprise less than 1 per cent of the working population. However, 15 per cent of chief constables had fathers who were policemen, and 43 per cent mentioned a police relative as an influence on them. (This roughly matches the proportion of police fathers, 14 per cent, found in a sample of the Federated ranks: Reiner, 1978, 150.) This pattern seems to be transmitted to the next generation as well. Thus 18 per cent of the chiefs have at least one child who joined the police, and there are several three-generation police families among them. (The implications will be considered below, in the section on the reasons given by chiefs for joining the police.)

Altogether, then, it seems that chief constables' social origins mirror those of the general population, and the police force as a whole. They are, however, distinctive both in the extent of social mobility found in their families, and in the tendency for policing as a career to be inherited.

The Education of Chief Constables

Chief constables have done much better in educational terms than the norm for their class of origin. This is also true of the police in general, but chief constables have in fact done much better educationally than most of their colleagues.

About 20 per cent of the children of skilled manual or lower grade non-manual workers born in the 1930s went to grammar or independent schools (Westergaard and Resler, 1975, 320; Halsey *et al.*, 1980, ch. 4). Approximately half of ordinary police officers in that generation went to grammar schools, indicating that they tended to be drawn from the educationally more successful strata of the working class. However, as Table 4.2 shows, the overwhelming majority of chief constables went to grammar schools. They are therefore drawn from a highly atypical (but sociologically much studied, cf. Jackson and Marsden, 1962; Halsey *et al.* 1980) section of the working class.

Not only have chief constables done better educationally than the norm for their class and generation in terms of the type of school they attended, but they also performed fairly well in those schools. Whereas nearly half of the police in their generation left school with no quali-

TABLE 4.2.   *The Schooling of Chief Constables*

Type of school attended by chief constable	Percentage %
Grammar	77.5
Elementary	7.5
Secondary modern	5.0
Technical	5.0
Public	5.0
TOTAL	100.0
N = 40	

fications and at the minimum leaving age, most chief constables have some educational qualifications, and stayed on at school beyond the minimum leaving age, as Table 4.3 shows. This is in line with the general pattern for grammar schools, but not for chief constables' class of origin (Halsey *et al.*, 1980).

TABLE 4.3.   *Educational Attainment of Chief Constables*

Qualification	Percentage %
None	10.0
O levels	5.0
A levels	15.0
School certificate	45.0
Degree	25.0
TOTAL	100.0

Age at which chief constables left school	Percentage %
14 or less	10.0
15	7.5
16	45.0
17	15.0
18 or more	22.5
TOTAL	100.0
N = 40	

It should be noted that of the 25 per cent of chief constables with degrees, not a single one was a graduate prior to entry into the police.

All their degrees were obtained while in police service, and half of them as a result of the Bramshill Scholarship scheme whereby a few potential high-flyers are seconded to universities by their forces. Half of the degrees held by chief constables are in law, with the other half divided into a variety of different subjects. In addition to the degree holders, another 13 per cent of chiefs hold university or other diplomas in various subjects, mainly criminology or management.

There is a clear trend towards it being the norm for chief constables to hold degrees. At the time of interviewing the chiefs, 43 per cent of their deputies had degrees, indicating that trend. Of the chief constables who have been appointed since interviewing was concluded, virtually all hold degrees, bringing the present proportion near to 50 per cent. The trend is also clear within the sample interviewed. Whereas 47 per cent of those chiefs who joined after 1955 have degrees, only 12 per cent of those joining before do. This trend is, of course, paralleled by the growing proportion of graduates entering the police during the last decade, as well as the rising proportion of graduates in the population as a whole.[3] The chief constables of tomorrow are not only likely to be graduates, but to an increasing extent likely to have entered the force as graduates.

Chief constables are thus clearly meritocrats, who have achieved considerable social advancement in part at least through educational attainment. Their exceptional levels of performance given their non-privileged social origins indicates that sum of 'IQ + effort' which Michael Young called 'merit' (Young, 1958).

Military Experience

Nearly all (90 per cent) of the chief constables have served in the armed forces. However, this does not indicate any tendency for policing to attract military types. It is purely a function of the generation to which the chiefs belong. Three-quarters of the chiefs had been in the armed forces for national service, and another 3 per cent had done war service. Only 13 per cent had done any military service beyond war or national service. Research on the police in general has shown that although most officers of the chief constables' vintage had been in the armed forces, this was because of conscription. Since the end of national service less than 10 per cent of police recruits have served in the armed forces (Reiner, 1978, 153). It seems clear that any peculiarities of police outlook there may be either in the rank and file or senior ranks, cannot be attributed to experience of military life.

What is interesting, however, is that one-fifth of chief constables were military policemen while in the armed forces. It does seem that a significant minority at any rate already indicated an affinity for policing while in military service.

Civilian Work Experience

The majority of chief constables (70 per cent) had some experience of outside employment before joining the police. (This proportion is slightly less than that for the police in general, cf. Reiner, 1978, 152.) Nor were most of these jobs casual or short-term. Forty-five per cent of chiefs had been in civilian employment for over a year, and 15 per cent for over four years. However, most entered the police in their early twenties, and almost all (85 per cent) had joined by the age of 22. It cannot be said therefore that chief constables have been insulated from experience of life outside policing. They have, however, had less outside experience than was generally true of police officers of their generation. While over a third of all police officers of the chief constables' generation joined after the age of 24 (Reiner, 1978, 153), not a single chief constable did. The chiefs thus seem to have exhibited a commitment to a police career earlier than the norm for their generation (though less so than is true for police recruits in the last three decades, which have seen increasing proportions join at the age of 19, supporting the familiar saw about policemen getting younger).

Most of the jobs done by the chiefs before entering the police were either skilled or semi-skilled manual (50 per cent), or routine non-manual (30 per cent). However, 20 per cent had attempted some form of professional or managerial civilian career before opting for the police.

Conclusion

The analysis of the social origins, education, and early work experience of chief constables suggests that they are distinctive from the general run of police officers in some ways. Coming from similar skilled manual working-class or lower middle-class origins, the chiefs seem to have outperformed other police officers educationally. They also come from families marked by a pattern of upward social mobility. To a disproportionate extent they come from police families. They also exhibited an attraction to police work relatively early on, disproportionately doing their national service in the military police, and entering somewhat earlier than the norm for their generation. In one sense then police officers do not all start equally. Some have characteristics which are associated with a greater prospect of advancement in the force. However, in another sense the data above confirm the idea of equality of opportunity. The particular characteristics associated with the chiefs, such as educational ability and performance, and an early affinity for police work, are achieved rather than ascribed attributes. They suggest that success in the race for being a chief is related to early indications of merit (though it remains debatable whether they indicate the appropriate type of merit).

Orientation to Work

Sociologists of economic life have developed the concept of an 'orientation to work', referring to 'the wants and expectations which men [sic] bring to their employment, and the interpretation which they thus give to their work' (Goldthorpe *et al.*, 1968, 184). This is seen as a key factor which 'shapes the attitudinal and behavioural patterns of their working lives as a whole.' There has been extensive elaboration, discussion, and critique of this concept subsequently (e.g. in Beynon and Blackburn, 1972; Reiner, 1978, ch.10). However, it does seem useful to identify the attractions, expectations, and images with which someone entered an occupation, as a contributing factor in the explanation of their subsequent perspectives and practices at work. They represent the initial spectacles through which work was viewed, the primary orienting grid for constituting subsequent experience.

Establishing retrospectively the initial orientation with which work was approached is of course methodologically most problematic. Differences in stated reasons for taking up a career may reflect varying reinterpretations in the light of subsequent events. Nevertheless, the way that this starting orientation to work is characterized may help understand other features of people's behaviour and attitudes to their occupation. It is with this intention that I tried to ascertain why chief constables had been drawn into policing in the first place. To minimize the risk of receiving current redefinitions of initial reasons, I encouraged the chiefs to give as much detail as possible of how they had felt at the time, in order to prompt them to relive the experience of joining.

Reasons for entering an occupation may be categorized into 'instrumental' ones, referring to the extrinsic, material aspects of a job such as pay, status, security, or career prospects, and 'non-instrumental', indicating intrinsic features of the work itself, such as the interest or the social utility of the role. Some may offer mixtures of both types of motive. (Indeed all work is to some extent instrumentally motivated in a market economy, so the difference is really one of emphasis.)

Using this categorization, it has been found that the police in general tend to have a predominantly non-instrumental orientation to their work, although the balance varies in different periods according to labour-market conditions (Reiner, 1978, 159–67). The chief constables are even more strongly characterized by non-instrumental attractions to the work than the police in general. Fifty-five per cent have solely non-instrumental reasons for joining, with another 28 per cent giving mixed reasons for having joined. There is, however, no clearly discernible difference amongst the chief constables according to their year of entry, probably because most of them joined within a few years of each other, and consequently in rather similar labour-market conditions. (Fifty-five per cent of the chief constables joined in the early 1950s, with another 20 per cent joining in the last three years of the 1940s, and a quarter in the late 1950s.)

The most common attraction of policing cited by the 55 per cent who had purely non-instrumental reasons for joining was the belief that it offered interesting, varied work, with the prospect of some excitement, and the opportunity to mix with people. This parallels the attraction of police work to the majority of recruits (Reiner, 1978, 160–1). The following quotes exemplify this pure affinity for the work itself:

"Well, I wanted to be a policemen since I was 8 years of age. It originally started because a policeman showed me across the road to school. I got to know this policeman very well and I talked to him about it, and I think, what it was, was it provided a combination I thought of an open air life with some adventure. Possibly later on when I thought about it, an opportunity to serve the community. It appealed to me."

"I was in the military police for two and a half years. It had been my ambition to go into the civil police whilst I was in grammar school, as long as I can remember . . . I certainly admired the local police in my area. I used to meet my great uncle and listen to his stories of life in the police. That whetted my appetite, so when I left school at 16 that is what I wanted to do. I tried to join the——Constabulary cadets but there were no vacancies, so I became a junior clerk with the National Coal Board, knowing that I was to be called up in less than two years . . . I had already been accepted into the——Police before the end of my national service. It was nothing to do with salary or even career prospects. I was attracted to the nature of the work that was done, pure and simply."

"The truth of the matter is that at that stage of school I knew I was going to be a policeman, I wanted to be a policeman. I knew I was heading for national service, but I didn't want to be a military policeman ... I was getting kicked about enough, and I didn't want to go kicking people about. [R.R.: Why were you so set on having a police career?] I don't know. The interest developed over a period of time. I can remember witnessing an accident and being involved with an interview, and it was at that period of time, just after I left school, that I decided I ought to be a policeman ... You know, physically large, not a particularly macho image, but I was a rugby player and people used to say 'Oh, you would make a good copper!' ... A great uncle had been a policeman, and he used to talk to me about his experiences in the old days, which were not pretty I have to tell you, but he used to chat away to me, I suppose because I was a big lad. He had had three wives, which was terribly fecund of him, and he used to always sleep with a revolver underneath his pillow, because the Fenians were coming back to get him, you know, the evil Fenians ... That engendered some kind of interest.''

"I went into the family business but I already had aspirations towards the police service. But I was below the height requirement for all but the Metropolitan Police, which I didn't want to join. However, I persisted, and after eighteen months was successful. So it was a very short time in employment outside the police service ... I suppose looking back the thing that attracted me was getting involved with people. That was the main attraction and has remained the main attraction.''

It has already been indicated above that 43 per cent of chief constables mentioned a family member as a source of influence towards a police career, and the above quotes reflect this. Fifteen per cent had police fathers and 18 per cent had children who followed them into the police. These traditional police families are a significant minority amongst those offering purely non-instrumental reasons for joining the police.

"My father was in the police service. He was a sergeant in the old—— Constabulary. I was born in a police station. I lived the first 16 years of my life in the police station. He felt that I ought to do something more than be a police officer, and felt I should go into the teaching profession ... It was twenty-four hours a day, seven days a week policing, very much the old style of doing things. There was no radio communication, no cars, my father had his own bicycle and he used to pedal round on it. My mother looked after the shop [police station] when he was out, and when my mother was out my sister looked after the shop. And when I got old enough to deal with telephone messages I would ... So having been brought up in the police environment, when I left the Royal Navy, there was no doubt in my mind that was what I wanted to do. It wasn't a sort of conscious decision of shall I or shan't I, it was just something I thought, right, I'm going to join the police force. And London had the attraction of the big city—you know, the world begins and ends in London was the philosophy in those days I suppose, so I joined the Met."

"If I tell you that my father was a senior officer in the Metropolitan Police, and finished up as a Deputy Commissioner, my grandfather had been a senior officer in the Metropolitan Police, and my great grandfather, it might give you some clue ... I had been doing national service for two years in the intelligence corps in the Army. Security to be precise, both here and in the British side of Austria ... And I suppose the thought of going back to an office occupation, having been out of doors and meeting people, didn't naturally thrill me. I was looking for something a little more varied and interesting."

"My father was a policeman and I was born in a police station, and the only thing I ever wanted to do, the only ambition I ever had, was to join the police force ... My family have got some 140 years of police service in——. My father, his two brothers both did their full times, and I had a brother who did twenty-five years as well, and now his son is in the——police ... My father was a detective sergeant, and really all I wanted to do from an early age was to join the police force and investigate crime in the same way that I had seen my father. It is difficult to put into words, but when you follow one's father's footsteps, I did see it as a very fulfilling life. The attitude of my senior masters at——Grammar School was 'what a waste of an education to go into the police!' But it did allow me to coast fairly easily through school, because at that time there were no educational requirements to go into the police."

"I came from something of a police tradition, because my father and my great uncle had been in the police, and it seemed like a good idea at the time ... I have often thought about it. It just seemed to be attractive because of the tradition. It certainly wasn't fast promotion or even high status, because the status and money and promotional opportunities now didn't exist then. I was quite well educated at grammar school by the standards of the day, and then I went into the police, which was perhaps a little unusual, given my education background, for people to do in those days."

Another significant non-instrumental attraction of the job, cited by about a third of the chief constables, was what I have elsewhere called 'the disciplined body syndrome' (Reiner, 1978, 161). This refers to the perceived attraction of a uniformed, disciplined service, with the comradeship and pride attached to this.

"I joined the Royal Scots Fusiliers, which was full of Glaswegian cut-throats, and I was delighted, after a fortnight being the only one in the entire section that could read and write, that I got transferred to the military police ... I came back, missed I suppose the camaraderie and being in a service—you're not to know the other things!—thought 'well, I'll give London a chance—bright lights and excitement for a little boy from——!' So I came down, thinking I'd give it six months and if I don't like it I shall go and do something else. I was gregarious, enjoyed company. I was 20 years old and the idea seemed quite exciting ... My father was a trade unionist who still remembered the strikes of the 1930s, and he actually disapproved of it all for a day or two."

"I had always been attracted, even from boyhood, to the police force. I remember, when I made the application to take school certificate, I told my headmaster I wanted to be a policeman, and he put on the application form 'to be a senior policeman.' He was puffing the thing for me at that stage ... It was the idea of a service which appealed, and the idea—possibly it is built into me. I like a fairly orderly existence and fairly orderly society."

"I was at grammar school when the war was on, and my one desire was to get into the war, I suppose like everybody of that age-group. I was desperately disappointed when the war ended. In fact, as far as I can recall I was in tears, because I had been accepted for the RAF. But they didn't want me because the war was over. I had been minded to study optics, but my heart was never in it. So I joined the police force as a service type of life. Optics, looking at people's eyes in a white coat, did not really appeal to me. Nine to five thing, you know. It was the service aspect of the police that did it. I had a fairly healthy respect for them, a well-ordered sort of life."

"Doing national service I had a taste for a more disciplined kind of life-style ... My father was a special constable, so I had some inkling and knowledge of what the service was like."

The majority of chief constables offered as their reasons for joining the police the purely intrinsic aspects of the job itself, along the lines of the ones quoted above. However, 28 per cent offered mixed reasons, in which intrinsic attractions were inextricably linked with more instrumental considerations of cash or career. An interdependence of motives is illustrated by these cases.

"I had an uncle who was a police officer—finished up in fact as the chief constable of——. It was partly that I suppose. It wasn't through any altruistic reasons, that I wanted to help people. It just attracted me, the uniform and the job. It's not until you get in that you realize it's not at all like what you thought, you know, the cops and robbers things, all excitement. And yet the police service is at the end of it all not all like that—it is a tremendous amount, and I like it—but a lot of it is helping people. Policemen spend a lot of their time doing good works, but I don't think you do realize before you start. I don't think that is the image that is put across at all ... And it was a secure job. In those days particularly the idea of having a job that had a pension and was secure was important. The parental influence was that you get a job and you settle in and look for the hidden things with it. It wasn't a job that was much sought after at that stage because things were beginning to boom. Festival of Britain time. And partly to me there was the lure of London, the big city."

"I did have a relationship with the police service in that my father was a serving policeman. He was a superintendent and retired shortly after I joined ... I was quite interested in the idea of farming, or teaching, but to be honest I had nothing firm in mind, no particular leanings and I was looking at a number of things. In the end I decided to go into the police service because it offered a good career. [R.R.: Did you ever anticipate reaching the heights you have done?] Yes, I did. I joined with that intention. As an Army officer I had looked around, and I thought the police service offered a good career. Obviously I had seen it throughout my childhood and thought it was likely to grow. It certainly wasn't the money that attracted me. What attracted me was the civility of the job, and seeing it through my father I appreciated that it was an interesting job. Obviously no doubt, I had instilled in me in childhood the sort of, with a small 'c', conservative views. In fact my mother was much against me going into the police service, because of the restrictions she had endured, restrictions on private life. She was absolutely against my going into the police service. But my father was for it. And I thought, you know, that it offered a reasonable career, and so I went for it."

"Whilst I was in the RAF I had to do general duty on occasions, and

one night I got talking with a man who had been in the SIB, that's
the RAF equivalent of the CID. I had always had an interest in crime
and crime investigation—it was the sort of books I used to take off
the shelf, natural reading material. And he really stimulated my
interest ... That started it off, and then I realized places at university
were difficult because this was post-war when many people were
coming back from the war all wanting to take up places at university
... I was very keen to get married, and gradually the police dawned
on me, that it would fulfil an ambition to be a detective, and another
one to ensure I got a job and a home ... My father was quite ashamed
when I told him I was going to be a policeman. My older brother
was then an accountant, my younger brother was going into the
Church, they were all into very acceptable professions, and I was
picking a plod job. It wasn't really what my father had in mind for
me."

The overwhelming majority of chief constables were drawn to the job
by intrinsic aspects of the work, albeit sometimes in combination with
material considerations. Only a small minority (18 per cent) mentioned
the purely instrumental attractions of policing. Given that policing was
not a well-paid or high status occupation when this generation of chief
constables joined, the instrumental characteristics cited are mainly
security (still a great recruiting asset for the police in the late 1940s and
early 1950s, cf. Reiner, 1978, 158–9, 162–4), and the limited alternative
career opportunities available at the time. This is illustrated by these
examples:

"I had no ambition to join the police force, other than that there
was an enormous publicity campaign at that time, and I had been
disenchanted in acquiring a further education grant. I went for an
interview and was told that my family's finances were such that they
could finance me. I said just a moment, I'm over 21 and have just
spent over five years in the RAF, and I think I am entitled to have a
grant just as long as the next guy. But I was told I was a very young
man who came out of the services and thought the world owed him
a living, which I thought was a gratuitous bloody insult, and I had
an exchange with the chairman of the board at the county hall. I got
a letter within a couple of days telling me my grant application was
refused, and there was a PS by the chairman: 'I suppose I upset you!'
And I was in a bar sitting with my ex-RAF colleagues in Leicester
Square, and there was a full-page advert in the *Evening News*, 'Join
the Metropolitan Police'. And I said 'I think I'll have a go!' And so

that's how I joined the police. I had no juvenile ambition to be a policeman, because I can remember that when I was in India a recruiting commission came out to the forces in late '46 trying to persuade people to join the police, and I didn't even give it a thought because my ambition at that moment in time was to go up to university."

"I don't think I was attracted to the police so much as that in the post-war years I was restricted to the type of work I had to do at that time, and I was keen to get away from it. The police was the opening to get away from that type of work, which was in the mining industry. It was so bloody awful! It was a contracting industry. Besides, I was 6 foot 3 inches tall, and it wasn't quite suited to my physical position. There was an influence from the family. Being a big lad, 'you ought to be able to join the police!'"

"I had to make a decision as to whether I stayed in the Army or moved to something else. And not having an old school tie, not having six O levels, making progress in certain professions was restricted to me. The public service seemed to offer the option for me of not being bound by any of those restrictions, and seemed to offer a career I would make progress in through enthusiasm and effort rather than other factors. I do feel strongly that many occupations are restricted by who you know. Many have an artificial value of what qualifications you need on paper before you can even go into it, and with the police service it seemed very open. That's what is so interesting actually, because you have people who have enormous influence but who can enter without the educational roots or social background equivalent in other institutions. I have had to serve and mix with since, people of the highest possible social background, and have mixed with people with the highest possible educational attainment. I don't think they are necessarily the prerequisites to be doing the job exceptionally effectively."

"It wasn't very romantic I'm afraid ... My departure from the RAF coincided with the Suez crisis when petrol was rationed. I'd got myself a job with a bloke called Skyways who became part of BOAC. But with the petrol rationing they couldn't now offer me the job on the date agreed ... So I was out of work, with very little money, waiting to get married ... So it was rather like one of those Kitchener advertisements. I saw a sign by——Police, and called in really out of curiosity more than anything else, to be met by a very forceful recruiting officer. Before I knew where I was he'd given me the entrance exam and a medical, and arranged an interview with the chief constable. I went along still not sure that was what I wanted to do. But I was impressed by him, and accepted by him, so I took the plunge and joined more or less by accident to be honest."

"I went into the police force purely because it was a safe career. It had a guaranteed income and I was newly married. When I first joined I was very bewildered and put off by the almost Dickensian circumstances in which I found myself. I found the whole organization very aggressive, very disciplined and Dickensian in attitude. I did not, for the first year, believe I had a career in the police service at all, but the economic climate was such that it precluded serious consideration of leaving."

With relatively few exceptions, then, chief constables approached their careers primarily attracted by intrinsic aspects of the police occupation. Only a small number of them were motivated primarily by extrinsic considerations, and these were very much the product of particular contingencies at specific periods in their lives. By contrast those who expressed an intrinsic attraction to police work often related this to deep-rooted childhood ambitions or family background.

Satisfaction with the Police Career

All the chief constables, whether initially attracted by instrumental or non-instrumental factors, expressed satisfaction with their careers in the force. There were no dissentients at all when I asked whether they were satisfied overall with their careers. However, only just over three-quarters (78 per cent) said they would join the force again if they had their lives to live over. This still expresses a high level of satisfaction, compared to most other occupations, and to other ranks in the police force. (Only 51 per cent of a sample of the Federated ranks said they would rejoin. Most professional occupations have higher satisfaction ratings as assessed by this question: Reiner, 1978, 171–3.) Despite chief constables' present levels of satisfaction with their work most have thought of leaving at some stage in their careers. At least 58 per cent remembered having considered resignation at some time. This was most commonly when in the rank of constable. Of the occasions when resignation was contemplated 51 per cent occurred when the chiefs were ordinary constables, and only 22 per cent occurred in any rank above the Federated ranks (i.e. superintendent or above).

Overall, then, the chief constables as a group express a considerable degree of satisfaction with their careers, even if these were not always smooth. The quarter who might not rejoin if they had their lives over usually attributed this to the changes in the nature of policing since their entry into the force, not to dissatisfaction with their own careers. Many expressed themselves very fortunate to have reached so far from humble origins, and to have done so in work which they found intrinsically enjoyable. But several were concerned about what they saw as a deterioration in the circumstances and content of police work, and would not rejoin if young now. Both attitudes are exemplified by these quotes:

"Strange, I enjoy coming to work, as my wife will tell you. Not to a fault, I hope. I know we tend to shield out the bad days but I can look back and say I never had any serious doubts ... I joined the service with a view to being a police officer, and I enjoyed being a constable. OK, the police pay wasn't good in those days, but I enjoyed life ... I never felt disenchanted. Perhaps I am lucky."

"I'd start all over again at the bottom if I could. I've loved every minute of it. I'd willingly start again as a constable. But the conditions are different now, the opportunities are different. I would have the chance to do the Special Course, might even graduate first. When I joined it was a much simpler structure."

"A very difficult question. I am very conscious I have given up a lot of life to do this job. I was a detective in London. Challenging and exciting though it was, I got to a stage where I was conscious I had put a lot of valuable things in life to one side. Bringing up my two daughters, they were the most affected ... Would I do it all again? I can't be honest and say I would. I am proud of what I've done. I don't think it's a waste ... But I am frustrated, and I think we as a service have lost out. I don't think we are regarded highly enough by people who make public policy."

"Be a bit daft if I wasn't satisfied with my career! I've been chief constable for ten years, I can't be but satisfied! Yes, I think I would join again ... It's an infinitely more difficult job now, on so many levels, for the lad who joins now. But of course he sees the job as it is, and certainly I'd come in now, yes."

"I've been more than satisfied, because the police has been very good to me ... I don't have any illusions of grandeur. I'm not a very clever chap. I've been very lucky, and I'd do it all over again if I had the opportunity."

The reasons for having considered resignation at earlier stages in their careers were mainly frustrations about lack of promotion, and clashes with specific supervisors at particular postings (each reason being mentioned equally often, by 58 per cent of chiefs who had considered leaving). In each case the problem was eventually resolved by a promotion or transfer, before the chief had actually resigned. Such temporary problems are illustrated by the following examples:

"I have had the odd occasion when the rain has dripped down the back of my neck and with frozen feet I have wondered ... but the only time I gave resignation anything approaching serious consideration was when I was on probation."

"As a constable I was promised a posting at a very early stage to CID by my chief constable, and the chief superintendent held me up one day and said, 'You've done very well on your probation, are you interested in the CID?' And I leapt to attention and said, 'Yes, please!' Next day I got a posting as a village bobby where there was no electricity, no running water, and in terms of career seemed to be at the end of the road. The chief and I negotiated about that, with certain promises being made if I stuck it. But half-way through I got a bit despondent, and applied for a job with Esso, and Fords, as a personnel officer. I also had a go at the colonial police. But then I heard I was going to get the CID after all and I withdrew."

"I was unhappy, very unhappy when I was deputy chief constable in——. I mean, I like the men and I enjoyed it. But I didn't get on with my boss, who I found the most objectionable man I have every worked with. I felt I had done my apprenticeship ... It did not matter because I got this job here."

Although such temporary periods of frustration were mentioned by most chief constables, they overwhelmingly expressed satisfaction with their careers. This was accentuated by their sense of achievement and a self-consciousness about their relatively privileged positions in contrast with their origins.

"I'm sitting in a rather nice position. It would be very ungracious of me to say anything but that I've enjoyed it and it's been very good to me ... I'm a lucky man, because my father hated every day he went in to that steel works to lay bricks, and never had the chance to do other things. So I am deeply grateful, and I enjoy it."

The typical view was most succinctly summed up by one chief constable, who said: 'As a chief constable you can't help but be anything other than satisfied.'

Conclusion

This chapter has analysed chief constables' social origins, approaches to work, and their degree of satisfaction with their careers. Most chief constables have come from manual working-class backgrounds, but performed far better than the norm for their class of origin. Police family backgrounds feature in the lives of a substantial minority of chief constables. Their attraction to policing was in most cases deep and to the nature of the work itself. Only a minority lacked a strong initial enthusiasm for police work. All the chief constables exude a considerable degree of satisfaction with their careers overall, and a sense of their privileged positions relative to their origins. Sources of dissatisfaction with their careers were for the most part either temporary and alleviated by promotion or transfer, or frustration at perceived inadequate treatment of the service as a whole. In short, chief constables constitute a true aristocracy of labour. Predominantly of working-class origin, their degree of moral identification with, commitment to, and satisfaction with their work is more akin to that of the established professions. The next chapter will examine the ways that chief constables have succeeded in climbing the greasy pole of the force hierarchy. What have been the paths to the top taken by today's chief constables?

Notes

1. The research is reported in Bayley and Mendelsohn, 1968, 14–30; Skolnick, 1969, 252; Reiner, 1978, 157–8; Reiner, 1985, 101–2; Brogden, Jefferson, and Walklate, 1988, ch. 2.
2. All the chief constables were married (nearly all had been married only once). Almost all of them (93 per cent) have children. The modal number of children is two (40 per cent of chiefs had two children). Nearly a quarter had either one or three children respectively, and 10 per cent had four or more. Nearly all had children over the age of 20, and only one had a child under 15 years old. They are, in sum, almost stereotypically conventional family men.
3. The trend is also paralleled in other countries. The Police Executive Research Forum surveyed a sample of 493 chiefs of police in the USA in the early 1980s. It found that just over half had at least a bachelor's degree (though the proportion varied considerably between types of force and regions of the country). The report

comments: 'These percentages are much higher than observed in earlier studies. In general, the numbers are indicative that law enforcement has been able to raise the educational level of its top officials' (Witham, 1985, 83). Interestingly, almost half of these degrees were majors in 'law enforcement/criminal justice', an option that has only recently become available in Britain in a few polytechnics and universities offering such courses.

5 The Way to the Top: Chief Constables' Career Patterns

In the previous chapter we considered the social backgrounds, and educational and work experiences, of chief constables before they entered the police force. We also looked at their reasons for joining the force. In this chapter we will analyse their careers within the force. Are there any common features which can be discerned amongst those who are successful in the competition for senior posts?

The Point of Entry

The chief constables in the sample mainly joined the police in the 1950s, with one entry in the early 1960s, and a few in the very late 1940s. This

TABLE 5.1. *Year Chief Constables Entered the Police*

Year of entry	Percentage %
1947–9	20.0
1950–4	50.0
1955–9	27.5
1962	2.5
TOTAL	100.0
N = 40	

pattern is shown in Table 5.1. As was indicated in the previous chapter, they mostly joined in their early twenties. None joined after the age of 25, even though a significant proportion (about one-third) of police recruits in the 1940s and 1950s were in their late twenties (Reiner, 1978, 153). A slightly higher proportion (93 per cent) of younger chief constables had entered by the age of 22, compared with 80 per cent of older chiefs (those aged over 55). This could indicate a trend towards a younger age of entry for chiefs. The overall pattern is shown in Table 5.2.

TABLE 5.2.   *Age at which Chief Constables Entered Police*

Age entered police	Percentage %
19	5.0
20	32.5
21	27.5
22	20.0
23	7.5
24	5.0
25	2.5
TOTAL	100.0
N = 40	

A remarkably high proportion joined the Metropolitan Police (although many of these were not Londoners). Almost one-third joined the Met., and 40 per cent of chief constables served in the Met. at some point in their career. (This proportion would almost certainly have been higher twenty or thirty years ago, as the alumni of the Trenchard scheme of the 1930s worked their way through provincial chief constable posts.) The type of force in which chief constables first served is indi-

TABLE 5.3.   *Type of Force Chief Constables Entered*

Type of force	Percentage %
County	35.0
City	32.5
Metropolitan Police	32.5
TOTAL	100.0
N = 40	

cated in Table 5.3. Within the sample there seems to be a trend away from the Metropolitan Police being the force chief constables enter. Thus 40 per cent of the older chief constables (over 55 years old) joined the Met. compared with only 20 per cent of the younger ones (under 55). However, service in the Met. at some stage in a chief constable's career is as much *de rigueur* amongst younger as older chiefs. Forty per cent of those below as well as those above 55 years of age have served in the Met. at some point.

In sum, the chief constables in the sample were predominantly recruited in the 1950s. The overwhelming majority joined in their very early twenties, on average much younger than their contemporaries. A disproportionate number entered the Metropolitan Police as their first force. The younger chief constables (under the age of 55) tended to have entered at younger ages than the older ones. The younger chiefs were also less likely than the older ones to have entered the Met., although they were no less likely to do service in it at some stage in their career.

Promotion Snakes and Ladders

The longest hurdle in the promotion stakes is the move from constable to sergeant. The years taken by chief constables to surmount this ranged from a low of four to a high of twelve. The modal period was five years, the time taken by one-quarter of the chiefs to be promoted from constable to sergeant. The average period was seven years. The years taken before promotion from constable to sergeant are given in Table

TABLE 5.4. *Years taken for Promotion from Constable to Sergeant*

Years taken	Percentage %
4–6	42.5
7–8	35.0
9–12	22.5
TOTAL	100.0
N = 40	

5.4. There is a very slight tendency for the average period spent in the rank of constable to decline. Thus the average number of years taken to get promotion to sergeant for chiefs who joined before 1955 was eight but for those joining since 1955 it has only been six. The range of years taken to get to sergeant was also lower for the younger chiefs: 4–8 instead of 5–12. One-third of the older generation chiefs took over nine years to make sergeant, but none of the younger ones did, and nearly half the younger ones were sergeants within five years.

After the first hurdle of promotion from constable to sergeant, further promotions flowed much more rapidly, though not necessarily more easily. Table 5.5 gives an account of the average length of time taken

TABLE 5.5.   *Promotions between Sergeant and Chief Constable*

Promotion	Proportion promoted within four years %	Modal time taken (years)	Average time taken (years)
Sergeant/inspector	85	2.4	3
Inspector/chief inspector	90	3	3
Chief inspector/superintendent	100	2	2
Superintendent/chief superintendent	83	2	3
Chief superintendent/assistant chief constable	100	2	2
Assistant chief constable/deputy chief constable	75	3	3
Deputy chief constable/chief constable	58	3	4
N = 40			

for each promotion between sergeant and chief constable. It is evident that after the initial hurdle of promotion from constable to sergeant, those who end up as chief constables must move fairly rapidly through the middle management ranks. This follows from the arithmetic fact that most prospective chiefs reach sergeant rank in their late twenties so they have just over twenty years to achieve seven further promotions before they reach their early fifties, after which age few chief constables are appointed. (The modal age of appointment to chief constable is 52, and the average age of appointment is 50). Thus Table 5.5 shows that over 80 per cent of chiefs spent less than four years in each rank from sergeant to assistant chief constable, and the average period in each of these ranks was two or three years. This pressure to move rapidly from rank to rank in order to stand any chance of achieving the top posts has been castigated by the Police Federation as 'the butterfly syndrome' (*Police*, Sept. 1989, 306).

Once in the chief officer ranks, however, the speed of promotion slows down slightly. Thus only three-quarters of chief constables were promoted from assistant to deputy chief constable within four years, and 42 per cent spent more than four years as deputy chiefs before being appointed chief constables. Nearly a quarter of the chiefs had to wait between six to eight years in order to get over this final hurdle before they reached the top. Clearly there is a substantial number of deputy chiefs waiting to step into the shoes of their boss, or doing the rounds of selection boards for many years. On the evidence of the above data, there is no reason for contenders to abandon all hope, however, until after eight years of futile effort.

The Butterfly Syndrome?

In its aforementioned attack on the 'butterfly syndrome' the Police Federation castigated as 'butterfly men' those who 'in their increasing pursuit of the next promotion . . . have flitted from one force to another, never settling long enough to make any impact' (*Police*, Sept. 1989, 30b). We have seen that those who become chief constables usually move fairly rapidly up the promotion ladder once they have reached the rank of sergeant. Is it also true that they 'have flitted from one force to another'?

The Home Office will not approve the appointment of a chief constable to a force if he has already served both as assistant and deputy chief constable in that same force. Thus anyone appointed chief constable will have to have worked in at least one other force previously, as a result of that rule. However, only 10 per cent of chief constables have served in only one other force prior to the one in which they are chief. Most will

TABLE 5.6. *Number of Previous Forces in which Chief Constables have Worked*

Number of previous forces	Proportion of chiefs
1	10.0
2	40.0
3	42.5
4	7.5
TOTAL	100.0
N = 40	

have worked in several forces, as Table 5.6 shows. For the overwhelming majority of chief constables the force they are currently in is their third or fourth, and for a small proportion it is their fifth. The extent to which chief constables have moved between forces in their careers is sufficient for them not to be regarded in most cases as 'locals', but as 'cosmopolitans', part of a national pool of mobile senior officers. But the extent of this lateral mobility can not fairly be described as 'flitting' from force to force.

Most chief constables have also experienced a variety of different types of force. It has already been noted that 40 per cent have served in the Metropolitan Police at some stage. Three-quarters have worked in a county force during their careers, and over two-thirds (68 per cent) have experience of a city force other than the Met. Thus the normal pattern is for chiefs to have served in three or four different forces, comprising a variety of policing environments.

Jacks of All Trades?

It is a widely believed aspect of police mythology that specialists are unlikely to reach chief constable rank, because the Home Office and police authorities look for a wide variety of work experience within the force, in particular a spell in administration. Several chief constables who had spent most of their operational careers as detectives remarked to me that they thought they were unique. As one put it, 'I think I'm the only chief constable in the country—I'm not sure, but I think I must be—with a completely detective sort of background.' Preference for all-rounders was in fact fed back in selection interviews. 'When I wanted to take the ACPO line and I went to extended interviews [for the Senior Command Course] I was faced with a lot of heavy criticism,—the fact that I was almost a one-horse chap, and really was I a complete policeman!'

It was especially widely felt that experience in administration was a *sine qua non* for the top posts. 'My career has been mostly an operational thing—primarily CID, a little in traffic. I mean, I went into headquarters for the very first time as an assistant chief constable administration. I had never been in headquarters before. That is an interesting point—there are very few of us I think like that'.

"I have worked predominantly CID. I went into CID after two and a half years on the beat, and worked right through except for a period of twelve months as a chief constable's staff officer in the rank of inspector. But after twelve months, back into CID, and I went right up to superintendent in CID. Thereafter as chief superintendent research and planning, and then staff officer to the Chief HMI. When

I returned to the force as assistant chief constable I did administration first of all, and then I did CID and general operational oversight. So it could be said I was fortunate in becoming pretty well rounded as an assistant chief constable.''

There is, then, a widely held belief among chief constables that specialists, in particular detectives, are unlikely to reach the highest rank. The preference is believed to be for all-rounders and people with extensive experience in administration. The evidence of the career patterns of current chief constables does not bear out these beliefs, however, as

TABLE 5.7.　*Career Specialization of Chief Constables*

Proportions of career in CID	Percentage %
Over half of career in CID	32.5
Even split between CID and uniform	12.5
Over half of career in uniform	55.0
TOTAL	100.0
N = 40	

Table 5.7 shows. It seems that, contrary to the widely held myth, an operational career spent predominantly in CID is not a bar to reaching the top, as about one-third of chief constables worked in CID for most of their careers. The majority, however, spent most of their time in a variety of uniform roles, but this does not indicate any bias against CID in promotion to the top because uniform patrol constitutes the overwhelming majority of police manpower.

The Centripetal Force

What does seem to be a vital ingredient of a career destined for the top is a period of attachment to a central or national policing body. There are a variety of these which seem to be equally acceptable in bringing the prospective chiefs to the attention of the Home Office and as evidence of fitness for the national policing élite. Two-thirds of chief constables spontaneously mentioned some national posting as a crucial stage in their careers (I had not in fact asked this as a question, so the proportion of chiefs with experience of such central attachments may well be considerably more than two-thirds). The postings mentioned included: attachments to HM Inspectorate of Constabulary, being on the directing or teaching staff at Bramshill, attachments to various specialist units at Scotland Yard, postings abroad such as to the EEC as representative of the British police or as an adviser in places like Hong Kong or Barbados, attachments to one of the Home Office research units, the Police National Computer, the Forensic Science Board or some other central service, or involvement in a major inquiry established by the Home Office into some policing issue.

These central attachments were generally seen as the turning-point in police careers, the experience which marked someone out for the very top ranks of the service. This was remarked upon by most of the chief constables, reflecting on their own progression.

"I became a detective inspector on the Regional Crime Squad, as a result of me having this bust-up with my detective chief super-intendent ... The jungle drums were going around the Met. about how I had fronted this man up, and I had a telephone call from another DCS who said 'I understand you've had a little bit of trouble'. And I said, 'Well, news travels fast.' He said, 'Well, how would you like to be pulled out of that lot and go into Regional Crime Squad?' I said, 'Tomorrow?' He said, 'No, Monday.' And that was it, it changed my career which really took off."

"I found my career changed dramatically because the then Com-missioner wanted somebody, an operational policeman, to be attached full-time to the Police National Computer."

One intriguing example of the role of such outside attachments to career progress is provided by a chief who said that his aspirations were raised by his successful investigation of a chief constable on corruption charges, the first time he had thought of himself as on a par with the more elevated levels of the service.

"I had no great pretensions, but in my early days as detective con-stable I was sent to investigate the chief constable of——. I stood beside him when he was sentenced to eighteen months' imprisonment. And when I came back and was promoted to sergeant the boss said to me, 'How far do you think you want to go in the service?' And I said, 'Now I think I'm beginning to have illusions that I should make inspector!'"

The experience of attachment to a national policing unit or operation is thus crucial to the career progress of those ending up as chief constables. It is important both in drawing them to the attention of national police élites, and changing their own self-perception so that they come to see themselves as potentially capable of reaching higher levels.

National Training Courses

Another crucial *rite de passage* in the development of chief constables is the Senior Command Course at Bramshill, the Police Staff College. This is intended to equip prospective chief officers with the necessary management and leadership skills for top command. Attendance at it is not, however, a formal requirement for appointment to chief constable, and the Home Affairs Committee in its recent *Inquiry Into Higher Police Training and the Role of the Police Staff College* (1989) was appalled to discover that many are elevated to ACPO rank without the benefits of having done the Senior Command Course. In the Met., for example, about one-third of those reaching ACPO rank have not been on the course. The Committee suggested therefore that successful completion of the Senior Command Course should be a requirement for all future appointments to ACPO rank.

It is almost impossible already, however, to become a chief constable without having been on the Senior Command Course, despite this not being formally compulsory. Of the forty chiefs I interviewed only two had not been on the course, in both cases because their promotion to assistant chief constable came between acceptance on the course and starting it, which precluded their entry. Ironically, one of these two chiefs was for a number of years in charge of running the extended interviews used for selecting future candidates on the Senior Command Course. Virtually all chief constables are alumni of the Senior Command Course, and the Home Affairs Committee's proposals would merely ratify the status quo in this respect.

The significance of the Senior Command Course is recognized by most chiefs. It is valued as much for its hidden curriculum as its formal content. In particular, it is appreciated as an opportunity to form or cement relationships with other future members of the national police élite, and these contacts and friendships are fondly remembered:

"I did the Senior Command Course, the Junior, and the Intermediate Command Courses before that. Almost had a permanent place at the College it seemed to me . . . My Senior Command Course was a good year, actually. Everyone who was on that course—well, one suddenly died, and one retired—but the rest have all become chief constables. Remarkable! It was a good year, or we were lucky!"

"I went down to Eastbourne for extended interview for the Senior Command Course, and sat in front of Sir James Starritt, and Mr Barratt who is now Chief HMI. If you've ever seen a pair of morticians at work on a callow youth, then that's the occasion! Of course, I do the interviews now. Bloody hard work as an assessor I can tell you! Quite frankly, going through the extended interview was the hurdle. The course itself was the icing on the cake. It is something that you have to go through, but I must say it was fairly mechanical. Thank God Ken Newman was Commandant and it was rather nice. You know you get a pretty stimulating intellectual level. I showed a paper of mine to Ken Newman and it was meant to be provocative. And Ken said it was more than provocative, it was totally untenable! But that's why you write papers isn't it?"

"I am something of a mad maverick. I did all the CID courses. I had the opportunity of going on the Junior Command Course but was unable to do so because of family commitments. I did not go on the Intermediate Command Course because of difficulties in the force at that particular time. And I did not go on the Senior Command Course. I believe——and myself are the only ones who haven't been. I created a little history there. Because I'd been appointed assistant chief constable, and after my appointment came the selection date for the Senior Command Course. And when I went down to Eastbourne I was told I couldn't participate as I was already ACC, and was sent home. They then invited me to go back and face another board, but I took advice on this from my then chief constable and decided it was a no-win situation, so I missed out on it . . . The Home Office circular as it then was precluded assistant chief constables going on the Senior Command Course . . . and as a result of me they amended it and made it clear that under no circumstances could anybody go on the course unless they'd gone through the extended interview."

"I remember coming back on the train from Eastbourne, after Extended Interview, with a little chap from the Met. called Newman. He was a sort of community association affairs man and I was a detective. We met on the Course again. He got on by merit, and I was somebody's blue-eyed boy!"

In addition to the Senior Command Course which is virtually *de rigueur* for prospective chief constables, most (73 per cent) have also been on the Intermediate Command Course at Bramshill. Only one-third of the chiefs have been on the College's Junior Command Course, however. The Special Course was established in 1962 as a vehicle for training prospective high-flyers selected from the ranks of constables by the same extended interview method as is used for the Senior Command Course. It is too new for most of the present-day chiefs to have benefited from it. Fifteen per cent of all chief constables have been on it. However, 50 per cent of those chiefs who joined the police after 1955 have been on it, indicating its future significance as an element in the formation of chief constables. Similarly, none of the older chief constables were able to take advantage of the Bramshill Scholarship scheme (introduced in 1966) whereby a few promising young offices are seconded to take university degrees. However, this will clearly become an important staging post en route to the top in future. Forty-two per cent of those chiefs who joined the police since 1955 have in fact been Bramshill Scholars.

Another significant national training experience in the lives of future chief constables is the Royal College of Defence Studies course. This is a highly prestigious and selective, invitation-only course offered to prospective leaders of the armed forces and a few senior police officers every year. John Stalker is one of its best-known alumni, and he describes its significance well in his memoirs (Stalker, 1988, 19–21). Ten per cent of current chiefs have been on it, and these select few are conscious of its status as a breeding-ground for high-flyers.

"I came here as deputy chief constable. It was a curious appointment in some ways in that when they asked for applicants for the post of deputy chief constable they made it clear on the application form that actually they would be considering the successful applicant for the job of chief constable when the Chief Constable retired in nine months' time. And that is how it happened. I was actually at the Royal College of Defence Studies at the time, which is a twelve-month course. You will find there have been several chief constables who have been there. It is the top course basically for military, and for senior civil servants. It is an international course. There are about sixty students a year, from most countries. And every year they second on to it normally two policemen. I had a letter which said I am allowed to put rcds in small, lower-case letters, at the end of my name, but I haven't done it ... Anyway, I applied for the job here as deputy while I was at the College, got the job, was appointed here in December when the Royal College of Defence Studies finished. Then I was reinterviewed for the chief constable's job the following April and got the job."

"I was ACC Ops. when I was invited, if my police authority agreed, to go to the Royal College of Defence Studies, Seaford House. I had this phone call: 'Oh, this is somebody who is speaking on behalf of the Home Secretary. We have two questions for you. Would you like to go to the Royal College of Defence Studies, and would you like time to think about it?' And I said, 'One, yes, and two, no.' And that was the end of the conversation. I went off to RCDS for a year. Quite the most outstanding experience, that I don't think will ever be exceeded in my life. It was so stimulating, the quality of people that were there ... Have you been there? [R.R.: No ... but a number of your colleagues have talked about it.] The working day basically is 10.30 to 1.00, for one input each day by a visiting lecturer. Nothing is done in-house by the RCDS except for some afternoon seminars ... For example, the first six weeks you do the super-powers. I remember we were doing Nixon's foreign policy in '66/'67, so they would fly in a guy, first class, who was his adviser. He would give you an hour's talk, an hour's questions, have lunch and go home. It was that quality! We went to industry, the three services, did a tour of Africa, Tunisia, Nigeria, the Ivory Coast, Kenya."

It is evident from these accounts, and the analysis of career patterns, that national attachments and national training courses are the crucial rites of passage in the formation of a national police élite. Through them potential high-flyers from the forty-three different forces are welded into an increasingly cohesive unitary élite. The identity of the future chiefs is transformed, and they begin to think of themselves as destined for the top. Their reference group becomes the others who have been through similar experiences rather than their immediate colleagues in their local forces.

The Appointment to Chief Constable

Most chief constables are appointed in their early fifties. The youngest age at which a chief constable was appointed was 42, the oldest was 56. The average age at which they were appointed was 50. The full distribution of ages of appointment is shown in Table 5.8.

On average they have been in office for six years, with the range running from one to twelve years in post. The majority have been in office for under five years, as Table 5.9 shows. The longevity of nineteenth-century chief constables is evidently not matched by their present-day counterparts.

TABLE 5.8. *Age of Chief Constable when Appointed*

Age appointed chief constable	Percentage %
42	2.5
44	5.0
45	5.0
46	10.0
48	7.5
49	15.0
50	12.5
51	12.5
52	17.5
53	5.0
54	5.0
56	2.5
TOTAL	100.0
N = 40	

TABLE 5.9. *Chief Constable's Years in Office*

Years in office	Percentage %
1–5	62.5
6–10	20.0
11–12	17.5
TOTAL	100.0
N = 40	

Most chief constables were deputies in another force at the time of their appointment. Just over a quarter were promoted to chief constable from being deputy chief constable in the same force. A few came from being chief constable in another, smaller force, from being ACPO rank in the Metropolitan Police, or from some other senior police position, such as Commandant or Deputy Commandant of the Police Staff College at Bramshill. The full pattern of positions from which chief constables are appointed is shown in Table 5.10.

It seems to be widely felt that incumbent deputy chief constables are at an advantage with police authorities, other things being equal, when it comes to replacing a chief. However, many incumbent deputies are precluded from appointment by the rule that all three ACPO ranks

T ABLE 5.10.   *Position of Chief Constable when Appointed to Current Force*

Position	Percentage %
Deputy chief constable, another force	52.5
Deputy chief constable, same force	27.5
ACPO rank in Metropolitan Police	7.5
Chief constable, another force	7.5
Other	5.0
T OTAL	100.0
N = 40	

cannot be filled by the same person in the same force. This accounts for some strategic lateral mobility by deputy chiefs who have been assistant chiefs in a particular force. They move sideways in the rank of deputy chief constable in order to be in post as deputy in another force when a vacancy for chief there is imminent.

"I like the system which operates. It destroys nepotism to a certain extent. You can't do the three ACPO ranks in the same force. So if you're ACC in one force you're stuck, you've got to go. If you become a deputy you can't stay there, it's best to get up when you can and go as deputy elsewhere. [R.R.: So, it's best to move as a deputy?] If you look at it purely in career terms it is."

"I was thrown in at the deep end as a deputy, because I'd been deputy two weeks in——when my then Chief Constable dies suddenly. So all at once there I was eighteen months into ACPO rank and I was acting chief constable, which the Home Office agreed to, and the police authority were very happy for me to do it. But I was barred from chief constable by the arrangements—you cannot fill all three positions in the same force."

"After the RCDS I went back to——and was made deputy. At the time I was applying for other deputy's posts. I mean, I wanted to get away because of the three-post rule."

The demographic characteristics associated with becoming a chief constable thus appear to be primarily a willingness to move between ranks and forces, sufficiently rapid progress up the intermediate ranks to be in ACPO rank by the late forties in age or earlier, and success in gaining a national policing assignment and a place on the Senior Command

Course. These are the steps leading to the national police élite. But what are the strategic ploys for achieving the right moves? Some have already been encountered, such as timely lateral transfer as deputy chief constable in order to circumvent the three-post rule. The next section will present some more tactics in the ACPO rat-race.

Tips For the Top

Only two of the forty chief constables I interviewed admitted to me that they had joined with the ambition of becoming chief constable. This openly careerist outlook must be well known to their colleagues, because they were also identified by several others. In both cases they planned their careers carefully throughout, but even the calculatedly ambitious recognize the need for an element of good fortune:

> "I go back and visit old friends from time to time, and I met one at a dinner a few weeks ago. He knew me very well when I was on probation. He said, 'Well, one thing about you ... you knew where you wanted to go.' And I said, 'Oh, did I really?' And he said 'Yes, you used to sit there and pore over your books and say one day I am going to be chief constable' ... I didn't ever trust chief constable was within my grasp because it seems so fragile, it's not a very structured form of appointment. You depend on the support of a local police authority to appoint you to ACPO rank. Therefore, although I believed in my own ability, I felt there was a lot more fair wind and fate to it than just pure professionalism. But I knew I would like to get there."

The majority claimed they did not start off with any lofty ambitions, and were prompted to lift their sights only after some early success or encouragement:

> "I come from a working-class background, and never anticipated I'd reach high rank. There are about two people in this country, and they may not be honest with you and I won't tell you who they are, who avowed right from the start that they would be chief constable ... I believe you just look for the next job, and then you pinch yourself and say, 'Well, what the hell am I doing up here?'"

> "I was on duty at the training school about 1961 when I was still a constable. And I can remember the inspector left his hat in the cupboard one night, and I tried his hat on. And I thought, 'I wonder

if I'll ever be an inspector!' So it certainly never occurred to me to be more. I think if you ask most of my colleagues honestly, your expectations rise as you rise through the job. You talk to people, and they think inspector or chief inspector was about really the limit of their aim. Because in those days a chief constable or inspector was like God, and getting that far was a good effort. And that was at a time when there were a lot more chief constables, there must have been about 150 of them."

The overwhelming majority of chief constables did not aim for the heights early on in their careers. Their aspirations were the product of moving up the promotion ladder, and the gradual realization of what might be possible. Success in getting a chief constable's job is partly dependent on the vagaries of which posts come up when a candidate is in the window of opportunity in terms of age and rank, and is also subject to the whims of particular police authorities even if the interview short list is reached. Many chiefs described this as a lottery, and were highly critical of the element of chance involved which could frustrate an able candidate or elevate an unworthy one.

"It's all right if there just happens to be a vacancy for a good chief superintendent to become an assistant chief constable. But you cannot, as we stand, say, pick somebody who has applied to be deputy chief constable in a big police force and say this chap should instead go off and be a chief constable getting used to dealing with police authorities in a small one. And then he'll really be the man for one of the big metropolitan forces. The whole chain is impracticable without central career planning. You find you've got short lists of people going round the circuit. A small job will be advertised one day, and the best man going round the circuit will get it. Then a big job will be advertised, and the man who came second for the small job will get the big one. It's a lottery."

"Did I ever imagine myself in the chief constable's chair? One of the problems of ACPO rank is it's a bit of a lottery in terms of how and where the vacancies occur. I saw myself entirely as an operational man. I wasn't interested in assistant chief constable admin. or personnel or whatever. I was fortunate; the first application I made was to——, and it was operational, and I got it. But it's a big factor, how and when the vacancies occur, and where you happen to be at that point in time, because one's only a contender for a limited period of time."

Pasteur once remarked that fortune favours the mind that is prepared. While there is evidently an element of good fortune in being in the running for ACPO ranks at the right time, chief constables are well aware of the deployment of appropriate tactics to ensure one comes to be appropriately placed. These are necessary if not sufficient ingredients of success. The tactical lateral move to deputy chief in a force about to lose its chief has already been mentioned. The following is an especially calculated example of it.

"My then chief,——, who is now in HMI, said to me if you want to apply for jobs you will have my full support ... So then a job for deputy chief came up in——. And I was looking more at who I could work with, and there was a chap there called——who seemed a pleasant chap. I'd met him at conferences, and he seemed fairly professional. So I applied for the job as deputy there, was lucky and got it ... None of this is attributable is it? [R.R.: Not to an individual. I'm not giving names away.] Well, what I'm going to tell you now could be a bit sticky. I was there for six months when Mr——comes in and says I'm going to retire early. I think the police authority quite honestly appointed me with that in mind. But I couldn't dream of being promoted after only being a deputy for seven months. You have to be two years a deputy before you could be chief constable. It's not written down, but it's Home Office policy. So a friend of mine, known to me for years, was persuaded to apply, but I felt it was a good job he could do, and I could be with him as deputy ... Then two years later he came in to my office and said you ought to apply for the job as deputy chief constable in——. And I said, 'Go wee in your best hat. I'm not going to——!' What do I want to go as deputy for anyway, sideways move! So he walked out, knowing me well enough that I'd go after him and say, 'What's it all about?' And, in point of fact, what had happened was the then incumbent deputy here applied for a job as chief in his old force and got it. And my predecessor Mr——was getting ready to retire and leave it to the crown prince! So there was a discussion at whatever level saying we want a substitute deputy who is ready to become a chief, really to sit here while the present chief gives him twelve months. That's how it was put to me. It being very fragile, I said, 'What are the guarantees?' 'Ninety-nine point five per cent. And the point five per cent is the good men and true on the police authority who, if you worshipped at the wrong chapel, or a local man got into the fray, or whatever, take against you.' So I sat and agonized about it with my family, and we came over on a dull dreary February day to look, but still decided we would come ... When the short list was up, I went for long walks thinking, 'Christ! Where do I go if I don't get the job! There's nowhere to go!' You can imagine. But the rest is history. I was appointed chief.''

This anecdote illustrates not only the kind of tactical lateral mobility involved in becoming a chief constable. It also demonstrates that the Home Office, the HM Inspectorate, and incumbent chief constables co-operate in developing a covert substitute for the overt central career planning of which they bemoan the absence. It may work with only 99 per cent certainty, and depend on some wily machinations, but the game of musical chairs played by prospective chief constables is not the completely unco-ordinated lottery that it is represented as. Steps are sometimes taken to rig the game which might shame a mafia casino, but the facade of local police authority selection keeps this under wraps.

From the point of view of the individual, getting to the top also demands assiduous career planning. One part of this is trying to acquire the right profile of relevant experiences on your curriculum vitae. This is a juggling act because it is a tricky balance between training and education on the one hand, and operational experience on the other, and must be got right. The career histories of successful chiefs show the value of degrees and central attachments, but, on the other hand, at the wrong time these can remove prospective chiefs from being in the running for crucial promotions.

"As a result of going to Bramshill on the Special Course I was offered the opportunity under the scholarship scheme to go to university. I was then 30, in fact the second oldest person on that Special Course. And I realized that time was running out. If I spent three years at university, and then had to come back and reinstate myself in the police force, at least four years had gone during which I could have been made inspector. I took the gamble that if I worked hard I'd be able to make another rank in that time. So I went ahead that way. Others with me, who were younger, did it a different way.''

Others had the educational route closed off for them:

"I was nominated for a Bramshill Scholarship but my old chief constable wouldn't let me go. He thought my career interests would be better served if I stayed on. [R.R.: What were you wanting to study?] Perhaps that's what put him off! Politics and government!''

In any event, getting the academic–practical mix right is a key element in constructing the best c.v. for moving to the top. So is combining different types of work experience into the right package. It has already been shown above that being a career detective is not a bar to promotion to senior levels. It is, however, advisable to develop a varied career profile:

> "I went into CID as a detective constable when I was only 22. And I remained there all the way through as detective sergeant, detective inspector, detective chief inspector, until I was 36, for fourteen years. I then applied for a place on the Senior Command Course and was told by the interview board really that I had to have more service in uniform. So I moved sideways as a uniformed chief inspector for a bit. I never went back into CID. Each of my promotions since was as a result of going on a central attachment."

> "I was accepted as an instructor [in the training school] but I had to go for an interview before a panel. And there must have been sixteen people asking questions. The first was, 'What are you doing here, son. After four and a half year's service how can you possibly be an instructor?' Well, it pulled me up by my bootstraps to think there were people up there thinking I was too young and inexperienced, when in fact I thought I was pretty good."

Having acquired the appropriate career profile, with education and experience, specialist expertise, and an all-round perspective, balanced into the right recipe, the next step is to 'throw your hat in the ring'. The would-be chief must make it known that he is interested in joining the charmed circle, and get on to the Home Office's list of approved prospective chief constables, by trying for some jobs he does not necessarily want or expect to get:

> "You were expected to apply for everything. If you didn't you got blackballed. So you looked in the *Police Review* and thought 'God! I wonder what's going to be in this week!' I mean I applied to——[a south-east England force]. I couldn't afford a house there no more than fly! You had to get your hat in the ring and leave it there, you couldn't be choosy, that's what one was told, if you were on the circuit. Once you got a ticket that you were acceptable, you got a ticket and you went in the pool. Then the police authorities decided. But first you threw your hat into the ring to see if you got short-listed. Once you got short-listed you knew you had a clean bill of health. Because, as you know, Home Office don't short-list some, or

they say, 'These could not be confirmed in their appointment.' So the first thing you wanted to do as an eager beaver was to find out whether you had a clean bill of health. You thought you had, from the very veiled discussions you had on the Senior Command Course, so you just stuck your hat in the ring and thought 'Christ!' And once you did that it was no looking back. You popped in for everything that came up."

"I came down here a deputy. I was on the circuit, so I came down here."

"I was going for a number of them [ACC posts] all the time. Well obviously, once I'd done about two years in the rank of chief superintendent then I was off again. So I was going from 1970 to 1971 to interviews for ACC."

A key factor in the big breakthrough is patronage. It is not only what you have done or what you know but who you know, as several beneficiaries of the system pointed out.

"In my early days as a a young officer the belief was that you only became a sergeant by the dint of about fifteen to seventeen years' experience. John McKay came to the force in 1959 and had a belief in young men. I was qualified and was very pleased to be promoted within six years, which was quite fast at that time ... This took me into the chief constable's office, which seems to be, when one looks back, one of those places that people's careers get moulded. People like Bob Mark, Frank Cavanagh, Bert Laugharne, James Anderton, Peter White, and others all worked in these sorts of environments. My assistant here——, was there as a cadet when I was a sergeant. I stayed for a spell as sergeant there in administration, having never administered in my life, which somebody seemed to think was a way forward ... Then I did a spell back at headquarters as inspector, staff officer to the chief constable."

"When I came back from the Junior Command Course I was staff officer to the chief constable ... and I later served him as an ACC. I think, for some reason best known to him, he seemed to take a shine to me or pick me out as somebody who may have the potential. He was an extremely hard man to work for, hours upon hours upon hours, and he demanded perfection, no less. But he was a man from the old Trenchard scheme, who talked to you when you worked close to him, about standards, about manners. He talked about caring for people, and it takes a lot of time to do the job the way he saw it. I was doing a tremendous number of jobs at that time, quite incredible actually. I was his staff officer, running capital building projects, complaints against the police. I was honorary secretary of the Voluntary Fund, I was doing firearms and shotguns, and an application for reorganization and an increase in strength of the Constabulary ... It said in the local headlines that I went from detective constable to chief inspector in four years ... 'Rise nothing short of meteoric'."

"I was on the RCDS when I was persuaded to apply for deputy chief constable in——where——was chief. He had been Commandant of the Police College when I was on the Senior Command Course, and against my better judgement I did apply. I thought, this is ridiculous, how can they appoint me when I'm away? But anyway, the police authority on his advice did appoint me deputy, and later I was appointed chief in succession to him."

To those chief constables who do not see themselves as having achieved the pinnacle of their careers, but aspire to move to bigger forces as chiefs, or to the HM Inspectorate, the same sort of tactics must be deployed for these further steps up. However, especial delicacy is required before applying for another chief constable's post for failure would weaken one's authority as a chief. The Inspectorate is also a delicate matter, because it is not a position that is applied for, but where choices 'emerge'.

"I've left it too late to move on from here. You know the nature of the game. You throw your hat into the ring and everything else. They've brought the retirement age down now to 55 and I'm 51. So I suspect if I was going to move, how do you define it, upwards—I mean, the Liverpools, the Manchesters, the West Midlands, and so on, it's too late. I shall have to be quite happy to stay in here and mature."

"My mind goes back to the place where I spent the majority of my years——. It is a fine force with very high traditions. If——, who is a great personal friend of mine, left soon I would think seriously about applying. But I would only do so with certain indications, I wouldn't want to go as a substantive chief and be totally rebuffed. I wouldn't mind losing to another chief, but I wouldn't want to go and be totally rebuffed. But the thing that would condition me more than anything as to whether I would apply would be the colour and stance of the police authority. I don't ever want to be in a command position where I've got to fight two battles."

"If HMI came along, yes I would be quite happy to take it, because that is the top job one can aspire to."

"Really once you get to chief constable there are only two things left that I could look at logically now. One is to look for command of a bigger force because there is obviously a bigger challenge and slight financial advantage to doing that. And I suppose the other thing is the Inspectorate—towards the back-end of your service you might be lucky enough to be asked to join them ... If the chief constable job of——became available, having been the deputy there I might look at that, and it's not too far. But much would depend on my age, health, and general circumstances, as to whether I'd apply. As you know, you don't apply for the Inspectorate. You get called to better things!"

It may be of interest that all three of the last-quoted chiefs did in fact get the various posts towards which they expressed aspirations. This suggests that ambition and careful career planning, aided by successful 'networking' and making sure one is the name that emerges for vacancies one does not apply for, can play a significant part in the competition for a chief constable or similar post. Of all the bits of career advice I received from these successful climbers possibly the most useful was the following succint if cynical tip for the top: 'I've been a lucky chap, able to move about fairly frequently and bury my sins and mistakes.' Or as the Police Federation might put it, 'Butterflies rule, OK.'

The First To ...

One final aspect of the race to the top which has not been addressed yet is possibly the most elusive yet vital. How is the first promotion hurdle surmounted in time to be in a position to compete effectively for further promotions, and how is attention drawn to specific candidates to allow them in to the charmed circle of national attachments and courses?

During my analysis of the interviews I was struck by the number of times chief constables would tell me, 'I was the first to do such and such', or 'I was the youngest promotion in the country at that time'. I kept a card index on all these 'first to ...' references. Nearly all the chief constables made remarks of this type, and some made a dozen or more such claims to fame.

This alerted me to two key aspects of the progress to chief constable. The first is that most chief constables had some very early successes in their careers which led to promotion to sergeant and/or transfer to a specialist unit, more rapidly than the norm for their generation. Second, they were able to build on this momentum to make further innovations, drawing them to the attention of the powers that be who determine the career paths of senior officers: the Home Office, HM Inspectorate, and the most prominent chief constables. While some of this early success is attributed (by the recipients themselves) to luck, it must also be related to an ability to make and take opportunities. This is plausible in the light of the way that chief constables stand out from their colleagues in terms not only of educational achievement, but an orientation towards policing based on intrinsic attraction to the work, and a police family background which would sensitize them to the prerequisites of successful performance in the organization. All this can be capitalized upon by the career tactics outlined earlier, as growing ambition feeds on success in a mutually reinforcing spiral. The 'first to ...' file suggests that chief constables are innovators rather than adaptors, even if this seems somewhat paradoxical an attribute of those at the top of a conservative organization concerned with order. The paradox that runs through the interviews is of a contrast between broadly conservative social views and the need to innovate to get ahead, coupled with and fuelled by a sense of personal confidence and efficacy which is bolstered by the constitutional doctrine of constabulary independence, an important part of chief constables' professional ideology.

Police officers are generally not shrinking violets and chief police officers even less so. Many of the longer serving chiefs have almost turned independence into a cult of personality. Indeed, they are regularly referred to by their colleagues in their own and other forces as 'personalities'. This is not only a product of the vaunted autonomy of the office of chief constable. It is a consequence of the fact that chief constables are the successful few in a competitive system where being 'the first to ...' reach particular ranks or introduce innovations is the key to achievement.

This pattern is evident in chief constables' discussions of their first promotion or transfer:

"When I joined, for anybody to be promoted under twelve or fifteen years' service was unheard of. My aim was CID, and I got on to that with three years' service, which was a bit unheard of in those days. And suddenly out of the blue I was promoted out of CID, which again was probably the first one in——."

"I was the youngest detective inspector to have been appointed in—— at that time."

"I was promoted sergeant with six years' service. One of the youngest promotions in those days."

"I was promoted sergeant after nine years as a constable, which was good going in a force of that size. I was looked upon as rather a youngster to make the rank of sergeant."

"After eighteen months in the force I was extremely fortunate. There was a vacancy as an aide to CID. I applied for it and got it, and had a very good run of detective work, which resulted in lots of commendations. Whenever we turned the corner there was always something happening! So when I was appointed to CID I only just had three years in, and the normal in those days was in the order of six or seven years. So nobody would speak to me when I went to my first station, because they thought I had friends in high places! It was so unusual. But it was a combination of things—a single man, hours in the day were of no moment to me, and I worked morning, noon, and night, and was happy doing anything. It's a reflection if you like, if you work hard your rewards will come. They certainly did as far as I was concerned."

This 'first to ...' syndrome is manifest in many directions other than early promotion or specialization. It appears in the training and education sphere. Some were on the first Special Course at Bramshill, one was the youngest ever on the Senior Command Course, or the most junior in rank to have gone on it. They were among the first Bramshill Scholars, or amongst the first in their forces to go on particular courses. They were early members of particular legendary units ('I was in A 10 from Day One') or operations ('I went into the CID as a detective inspector engaged with what were known as the "carbon-copy" murders'). Above all, they were responsible for a host of strategic and organizational innovations in all ranks during their progress up the hierarchy. Several claimed that their forces had initiated various strategies associated with Sir Kenneth Newman's tenure as Metropolitan Commissioner before he had taken them up. Others claimed to be the first to introduce the idea of a force video journal as a means of communication of policy to the rank and file, to establish the type of internal consultation arrangements which the 1978 Edmund-Davies Report recommended, to pioneer lay visitors schemes, to introduce plastic bullets or CS gas, to develop a computer for major crime investigations, to experiment with tape recording of interviews, to introduce specialist training for fraud investigations. There were few chief officers who did not lay claim to some organizational or operational innovation they had pioneered.

A few had so prolific a list of inventions that they could claim to be the police Edisons. The following string of 'first to ...' claims is an example of these:

"I was appointed to the CID within nine months of joining the police. That's related to the hierarchy that prevailed at the time, and there may have been a patronage factor. I remember my then divisional chief of CID was a well-known figure, a man of some legend as it turned out ... He saw something in me, and I was a CID officer within nine months! ... I went to the Yard as a first-class sergeant. And I remember arriving and someone saying, 'Who do you know to arrive here?' People that went to the Yard in those days were selected or privileged people, it wasn't a normal posting. There had been some degree of in-house selection as to whether you had the calibre to do the job. You were selected to deal with the more difficult type of inquiry. Most of your inquiries were mastered by the Director of Public Prosecutions. It wasn't the mundane crime complaint ... I'm going to claim something here. Much of what's reflected in the Edmund-Davies Report was in being here anyway. So a lot of Edmund-Davies's recommendations is a template from what prevailed here ... I quickly set up what I called consultative groups within the force. I had to break through a lot of sound barriers ... We pursued the concept of planned policing two and a half years ago, and it's really taken off. It's up and down the country now ... We have the 'Chief Constable's Sayings': that's disseminated, and then each division and subdivision draw up their aims according to the environment in which they're working, but they mustn't go outside the force ... We introduced a system here first where any officer could come and see me without declaring why. They don't come and see me too often I must say, and when they do it's on personal issues rather than professional ... I was the first force to introduce a complaints subcommittee of the authority—well, when I say I, it was at my suggestion—and I used to give them access to complaints files. Now that's become the norm. So we can claim one or two firsts."

Although most chief constables do not claim as many 'first to ...' achievements, they do characteristically state a record of early promotions, training, operational, and organizational accomplishments leading to their being singled out for advancement to the national police élite. The pattern is then confirmed by a string of innovations when in office.

The quote above also illustrates a common tendency to identify organizational accomplishments with personal achievements. 'Le force, c'est moi' seems to be a motto, with frequent use of what can be called the royal singular: 'my' force, 'my' authority, 'my' city/county, 'my' crime rate, and so on.

Conclusion

The analysis of chief constables' career patterns and tactics for advancement indicates a number of ways in which they are set apart from their less successful colleagues. These may derive from the background differences found in the previous chapter.

Chief constables tended to enter the police younger than others in their generation. They were disproportionately likely to enter the Metropolitan Police, or to have served there at some point in their careers. They moved rapidly up the promotion ladder, the longest gap being promotion to sergeant, though this was achieved earlier than the norm on average. Thereafter there was normally an average of only three years or less between promotions. They have usually moved between several different forces on the way up. They are usually not specialists, but a substantial minority have had CID careers. As they move up they increasingly become parts of a national police élite, with attachments to a central policing body, and experience of national training courses being almost essential. They are usually appointed at around the age of 50, and most have been in office for under five years. Most are appointed while deputy chief constable in another force. However, there is a feeling that incumbent deputies ('crown princes') are favoured if they do not fall foul of the 'three-force' rule.

Few chiefs had lofty aspirations when they joined. But their ambitions are fuelled by early success. Various tactics for advancement were identified: well-timed lateral transfers, careful curriculum vitae planning to balance the desired sorts of experience, 'throwing your hat in the ring', and being willing to try for jobs you do not really want to get on 'the circuit', acquiring powerful patrons, and moving fast enough to avoid the flak for failures. Underlying the whole career pattern of the successful there is the blend of luck, effort, drive, and self-confidence which I labelled 'the first to ...' syndrome. It is the sense of having, and deserving, a place in the sun.

This section of the book has tried to describe and analyse the chief constables' social background, approach to work, and career patterns. In the next part we will consider their philosophies of policing and social ideologies. We will move from who chief constables are to what they think.

Part III

The Ideology of Chief Constables

6 Philosophies of Policing and the Police Role

During the late 1970s and 1980s, as policing has become more and more embroiled in controversy and conflict, the police have been driven increasingly to reflect upon their fundamental mission. As the practice of policing increasingly was forced into the 'fire brigade' mould, so a variety of arguments developed about whether and how what was widely regarded as the traditional British style of policing by consent could be resuscitated in the face of modern pressures. In the late 1970s the 'community policing' philosophy of John Alderson, then the chief Constable of Devon and Cornwall, represented a much-debated attempt to articulate an appropriate contemporary variant of what was believed to be the British tradition (Alderson and Stead, 1973; Brown and Howes, 1975; Alderson, 1979, 1984). As Alderson's public advocacy of his views increased, so his stock with his colleagues seemed to plummet. After his controversial evidence to the 1981 Scarman inquiry into the Brixton disorders (Scarman, 1981) he became virtually *persona non grata* with his fellow chief officers and he resigned the following year.

However, his views carried great weight with Lord Scarman, and the Report's recommendations owed much to Alderson's ideas. For some years after the Report was published Scarmania prevailed in senior police circles, and his writings acquired virtually the status of holy writ. Although in private many police officers at all levels expressed considerable reservations, indeed resentment, about Scarman's analysis, explicit and open criticism was politically unacceptable (Benyon 1984*a*). Many influential chief officers, notably Sir Kenneth Newman as Metropolitan Commissioner, attempted to introduce new policing strategies in the spirit of Scarman (Reiner, 1985, ch. 7). These in fact fell in with a world-wide movement of experimentation with 'community policing' ideas (Skolnick and Bayley, 1986, 1988*a*, 1988*b*), although the term itself was not used much in the British context except to refer to John Alderson's work. The essence of these strategies is the notion that crime control cannot be handled by the police alone, but depends upon close co-operation and involvement with the public. Specific tactics associated with this strategy include a multi-agency approach to social control, neighbourhood watch, consultative committees, lay station visitors, crime prevention panels, victim support schemes, and enhancement of the Special Constabulary. Altogether they comprise a conception of policing as a much broader enterprise than the traditional functions of patrol and investigation, with the police having a responsibility for dealing with wider causes of crime and disorder, not just responding after the event or seeking to prevent or deter offences by maintaining a uniformed presence.

Previous research has shown repeatedly that the rank and file of the police tend to be critical of these new approaches, regarding them as distractions from the core police tasks of crime-fighting and detection (Reiner, 1985, 76–7, 133). They dismiss the broader service conception of policing as 'bullshit' (Reiss, 1971, 42) or 'codswobble' (Reiner, 1978, 213–17). A recent survey of a national representative sample of 1,226 police officers (which was coupled with a census of the ACPO ranks) confirmed that the rank and file remain wedded to a 'strong' approach to policing, and dismiss broader community-oriented philosophies as 'soft' (*Operational Policing Review 1990*, sect. 6) Thus the sample as a whole felt that 'responding to emergencies and detection and arrest of offenders were the highest priorities ... strong traditional policing is the most effective means of Policing ... crime prevention, community liaison and other "soft" policing approaches are not favoured' (*ibid.* 21). However, the census of ACPO ranks implied that there is quite strong support for many aspects of the community approach among them, which is opposed lower down the hierarchy. While 81 per cent of the whole sample regarded detection and arrest of offenders as one of the three most important police tasks, only 64 per cent of ACPO ranks did. Nearly three-quarters (72 per cent) of all ranks saw 'work with local council departments such as housing to plan crime prevention' as one of the three least important police jobs, but only 53 per cent of ACPO ranks did. Forty-three per cent of the non-ACPO ranks saw 'work with local schools' as one of the three least important tasks, yet only a few of the ACPO ranks did. By contrast, 45 per cent of ACPO ranks saw setting up 'squads for serious crime' as one of the three least important tasks, but few of the non-ACPO ranks did (*ibid.* 10–11). Overall, the ACPO ranks seemed to place a relatively greater value than the other ranks on community-related activities such as liaison with schools or ethnic minorities, while placing less emphasis on 'law and order' approaches to the control of crime (*ibid.* 14–15). It is noteworthy that these differences in attitude are a function of rank, not age or generation. 'Age is clearly not correlated with rank in respect of these issues. An increase in rank is likely to lead to a more favourable disposition towards soft policing whereas an increase in age without rank will tend the other way' (*ibid.* 14). Indeed the 'toughest' views of all were those of older police officers who remained in the lower ranks.

My survey of the views of chief constables was concerned to ascertain their policing philosophies, raising a similar set of issues to the *Operational Policing Review*. However, I attempted to probe the reasoning behind the beliefs of the chief constables by open-ended interviewing. The *Operational Policing Review* research utilized a postal questionnaire and does not offer any account of the ways that opinions are formed, justified, or related to each other. This chapter will consider the chief constables' conceptions of the policing role in general, and the next chapter will look more specifically at their views on crime and public order.

What's it all about, Alfie?

Chief constables tend to espouse a broad view of the police role. They see the police as concerned with the wider social aspects of crime, and not just as specialists in the detection and prevention of crime and the control of disorder. Of the chief constables I interviewed, 50 per cent inclined towards this wider conception, with only 13 per cent indicating the narrower approach. However, 35 per cent claimed to stand in the middle. This seemed often to be a coded way of espousing a narrow view without explicitly disavowing the validity of the broad conception which was generally acknowledged to be the Home Office flavour of the decade in the wake of Scarman. Thus there was as much criticism of the broader, Scarman-type initiatives amongst the middle-roaders as was articulated by the few who overtly championed the narrower function. In short, the prevailing philosophy of the police role amongst chief constables is a form of Scarmanism. Dissent from this is expressed as a 'middle' view, with whole-hearted explicit questioning being very rare.

The characteristic 'wide' account of the police function is illustrated below:

"I have a broad view of our role. The police are part of a very complicated mechanism in our society. They cannot to a large degree influence education, although we should try a bit harder to influence the purveyors of education. I don't think they can influence to any large degree the family unit. I don't think they can or should influence morals, that is one area of the arena that we should stay well out of in the police, in terms of public utterances, and that goes contrary to Jim, but that's a passionate view he holds. My general philosophy has been for a number of years to say to my customers, help us to help you. Now that is done by a process of communicating with the public, humanizing the whole organization, and saying to people, look, this service is very much a secret service, incestuous, intro-spective, and I don't think it should be. Back in my days as super-intendent in——, I held a public meeting in the Town Hall and said come along and listen to us and tell me about your gripes. That is the stand we should take. There is an enforcement problem, but the kernel of it all is creating confidence in the public that they feel able to go about their business in the Queen's Peace ... You, the public, all have a responsibility and a partnership to make society a better place in which to live. You can't leave that to me totally. Policing by consent is no longer enough. It has got to be policing by co-operation, a partnership."

"The boundaries of policing are ill-defined and that's a happy cir-cumstance. That enables me, for example, to put a sergeant and two constables working full-time in——[inner-city ghetto] with a brief to get on and get involved with young people ... Youth club work, the sergeant playing ping-pong, he was very good at it. He got into the crypt at——with black Rastafarians. A difficult and dangerous job, but he was very successful at it. It put forward a police image which was other than a repressive one. We opened up a centre and ran it as a drop-in centre for ball players. Social services would use it to get in touch with black kids who were heading for trouble. So I run with the full view of policing. The police is actually a unique organization in that it's got highly skilled people dedicated to peace-keeping. I take the view that where society has problems it's the role of the police to try and ease society through those problems, and to create conditions where change and evolution can take place. The flexibility we have enables every chief constable to really set his own boundaries, so that the police job can grow and change according to the stress in any community."

"I'm very much towards the broad view of having some responsibility for removing or helping to remove some of the social causes of crime. I certainly don't subscribe to the narrow view that we are only here about investigation of crime. Yes, that's one part of my job quite clearly, but our range of roles is much wider than that. It's geared towards the other extreme ... I am firmly of the view that starting from the base step that we cannot do our job without community acceptance and community participation, it necessarily follows that we have got to be very involved with the community. We have got to allow the community to participate in a lot of what we do, decision-making and so on and so forth. It follows necessarily that we get involved in a lot that will contribute towards social causes of crime."

"The old objects of police remain pretty valid and good as set out in 1829. But we have got to work a lot harder these days on a whole wider range of issues. I very much agree with the Metropolitan Commissioner's views on a sort of contract with the public and with other agencies. So I see it as police having prime responsibility for prevention and detection of crime, preservation of public order. But in order to achieve that I think we have to perform a whole lot of other social-type functions, enlisting the help of the public and other agencies."

"If you read the Royal Commission on the Police in 1960 you will find in the Final Report that we have seven areas of obligations. Unfortunately it is my experience, and I speak having served thirty-five years, that that definition isn't sufficiently broad to meet the views of Joe Public. If you seek to police a county such as this there is no set model to police it from. I have a concept of a patrolling officer, a community police officer, patrolling his small village or township, and he provides a sense of support or familiarity which gives confidence to the public. I empathize with that notion very warmly. To a large degree it is possible that in the rural areas that model works very well. . . . Obviously in a larger city that role becomes increasingly complicated. But the role of the police is or should be the type of support I have identified. It should be one of encouragement, on my part, certainly, and I hope of my officers, towards a sense of citizenship ... I mean by that, why do kids break into schools and burn them down? What causes a terrible vandalism feeling in shire counties or elsewhere? Can you educate kids through essay and art competitions and school visits to perceive the consequences of what we do? And can you encourage them towards this notion of citizenship and sense of responsibility? ... I use the consultative committees, the mayoral office, a vast chain of historical connections, and informal networks, where I speak kindly to parents or whatever in an encouragement sense."

The regular use of the word 'community' by those espousing the broad view of the police role suggests an affinity with the community policing philosophy of John Alderson. Clearly his ideas have been very influential, as transmitted by Scarman and others. But, as mentioned above, association with his views is disavowed by almost every chief constable. Great efforts are made to distinguish their philosophies from his, even (or especially) when they sound similar.

A slight majority (55 per cent) of chief constables did declare some sort of belief in community policing. But nearly as many (45 per cent) argued it was a meaningless expression. The views of the latter were often grounded in a rejection of John Alderson's beliefs, but most of the former also strove to distance themselves from his arguments. Virtually the unanimous view of chief constables, whether they thought community policing a useful phrase or not, was that it was old wine in a new bottle. The standard view was that it referred to the traditional practices of British policing, although they then divided almost evenly into those who thought it a useful label and those who saw it as obfuscatory. Typical of those espousing the label are the following:

"What it means to me is having a good relationship with the community, an understanding of what the community is about, and some perception of what the community think the police should do about it. In fact we had a very interesting TV programme produced here last year on what the producer believed was the community policeman. The producer rang me one day and said, 'I'm fed up reading about the police in high profile, and knocking of the officers. My belief is that there is still somewhere with the old-fashioned policeman of the type that used to kick my backside as a young lad.' He said, 'Have you got one?' I said, 'Yes, we have a number of them.' ... So we found him a man at a parish out in——Division called Bob who was there for fifteen years. And he made a marvellous human interest documentary about the village policeman. This was a man related to the village and its surrounds, who was part of them and yet had to stand apart from them in a sense. He had an understanding of what the village was about, the need for that tranquillity, and to sort of ensure that strangers coming into the ground were clocked and identified. I know it can mean all things to all men, community policing, but I think the policeman is in the community, and it is that ability to get an interface between the two. That's what policing is all about."

"I have followed the whole thrust of the movement towards community policing, it's part of my objectives. But in a rural county like this, apart from the exploding areas in——and——, my big cities, that kind of policing in the rural areas is what's been going on for years and years. Community policing. Now we've tried to redefine it in the sense of city policing by getting officers in permanent positions and giving them responsibilities for areas. I agree fully with the concept that community policing is a good thing in that sense. An officer known working his area, is respected in that area. The difficulty is that sometimes we don't have enough manpower to make it meaningful. My critics say to me: 'You keep talking about community policing but we never see a community officer because you're always picking them up and taking them away to do the other things.' And they're quite right . . . The priority is the community policing, though. I've just been given twenty extra men. I asked for forty, the Home Office allowed me twenty. I'm putting them all into the biggest ethnic group area of——for community policing."

"It's the approach to policing that puts value on having policemen who can stay on a minute, can be flexible, get to know the community. That's the basic building brick that I would look for in any policing style that calls itself community police. It's the business of getting close and staying close to the community that's being policed. The community beat officer is the basic building block, but you can't keep him in isolation and say that's community policing, now shall we get on with bashing them. The trend should run through the organization."

Those who objected to the term 'community policing' did so because they saw it as merely a new label for old-style policing, or because it was seen as prioritizing a 'soft' approach which can only be realized in a few idyllic places but which implied an ideal that made most policing seem lacking.

"Community policing has become an unfortunate phrase. It produces the flat hat–round hat syndrome, doesn't it. You put your Panda policemen out with their flat hats and they dealt with all the 999 calls, used to come screaming round the corner and deal with trouble.

Whereas your community PC used to be on the patch and he was seen very much as a man who was there to do all the social work on that beat, and not particularly get involved in law enforcement. That was one of the problems the Panda scheme created. So if you have the all-singing, all-dancing policeman you do away with that. Community policing is an unfortunate expression. I believe we are all policemen, trying to serve the community, and it doesn't matter whether it's me as chief constable or whether it's the guy walking on one of his beats, we're all trying to achieve the same thing. Community policing—I personally believe it's become an unfortunate expression used by politicians and political rhetoric, and frankly it means nothing to me."

"It's become a hackneyed phrase where you are a community police-man and therefore you are a good guy, and leave all the rubbishy work to all the bad guys. It is seen as something delightfully simplistic whereas it is not. I would expect the policemen—and I have many of them—in country areas that police villages to police with a degree of understanding, sensitivity. But if people step over the line then they breach the law, and they are dealt with in accordance with the law. That's the reality of the situation. But the unfortunate image is that the community policeman is the guy who is the avuncular bobby who stands with his size 12 boots, smiles at everybody, and pats little kids on the head, and is completely ineffective in law enforcement terms. Because if you are going to have a community, that presupposes that that community is a fine, good, upstanding, law-abiding community. If it is then that makes the job of the policeman much easier, but if it isn't he can't shirk from his responsibility because he happens to be looking after the community."

"It doesn't mean a damn thing. It's just one of those terms you use which are recent inventions by some of our, dare I say it, mock academics—'community'. It's not an identifiable group. The com-munity of——shire, which is the family we look after, is a very all-embracing cross-section. Last night I spent a lot of time with a group of men who are on a murder inquiry in part of our inner cities. A lot of public sector housing. To talk about that group as a community rather builds a notion of a nice cosy group of people who love each other and get on. But nothing could be farther from the truth. That's a fictional development."

Both those who accept and those who reject the utility of 'community policing' as a concept, tried to dissociate themselves from John Alderson's philosophy. This is as true of the believer quoted first below, as of the non-believer cited afterwards.

"To me community policing doesn't just conjure up the Alderson syndrome which of course causes so much publicity. To me it means regular policing by the same officers of a particular area and getting to know that area intimately and giving the public the opportunity to get to know them. That is my version of community policing, and we practise it in this force."

"I think that it's a bit of a gimmick. I know John Alderson well, . . . and we had long discussions. Where John Alderson went wrong— and it's the greatest fear of my life, I geared a lot of my management to combatting the Alderson syndrome—is that Alderson had some wonderful ideas. He started them and preached them, but they weren't happening that well in the force. He had the ideas, but they were never sold then to the force. So what I call the Alderson syndrome is that if I have ideas up here of what I want and ought to do, I want to make sure they're communicated down there."

There was only one chief constable who not only was prepared to support Alderson's views explicitly, but recognized the irony that the current orthodoxy derived from someone who was now treated as a pariah figure.

"I am very much influenced by John Alderson, thus I certainly believe—I think I'm quoting fairly accurately—we have a duty to activate the good as well as to deal with the bad. So much of police resources are now ploughed into the social end of the balance . . . our involvement with schools, the realization that crime isn't the sole problem of the police, that is all a fairly modern concept pioneered by Alderson largely. But I am also realistic and practical enough to believe the best lesson in crime prevention is locking up a villain . . . There's no doubt that we've all been influenced by him, and you know the tragedy is that John Alderson is eventually outside the pale, although his ideas hold in every headquarters throughout the country . . . I see community policing in its more specialist form as part of the common goal. For me it was never a cosmetic exercise which it might have been at one stage for John. Community policing as Alderson later developed it is more than traditional policing. In recognizing the proactive element and inter-agency co-operation, these concepts weren't part of traditional policing. But I believe that every so-called community policeman first and foremost is a policeman and has a job to do to enforce the law, and equally every officer who is not a community policeman, a response officer in other words, also has a duty to the community ... He went beyond this, but certainly one of the fundamental criticisms of Alderson, accusations indeed, was that he was in fact inventing the wheel.''

The dominant philosophy of the police role among chief constables is thus a broad community-oriented one, which has it roots in the ideas of John Alderson, though this influence is usually denied, and the term 'community policing' often dismissed. As already indicated, however, a minority (13 per cent) argued for a narrow definition of the police role, while 35 per cent did so in a coded way, championing a 'middle' road which rested on a critique of the broader conceptions.

"We have the primary functions of maintaining law and order, public tranquillity on the streets, that's tremendously important. You can maybe sometimes prevent problems on the streets by becoming involved in the sort of social side of the community. We have to police on the basis of society's acceptance."

"I'm towards the narrow end ... Our prime object is a peaceful law-abiding community. We are charged basically with the enforcement of the law, and we try and do that through a variety of avenues. Our main function is to try and prevent offences happening if we can. When they do happen then we have the responsibility to try and detect those who are responsible. Linked to that you can't ignore totally what is causing crime to happen. But we don't really have a great deal of power or resources at our disposal to try and do something about the causes of crime in society. We can try and highlight and sometimes remove, by dealing with other agencies, when things are happening which are—to use a silly phrase—a running sore. Say, certain activities which attract people to come and commit nuisances late at night ... But there is a limit to what the police can do because we haven't the means or power to tackle the root causes of what breeds crime. Our crime prevention activities is really the police presence on the streets."

Paradoxically the most explicit advocacy of a narrow approach came from a chief officer who had pioneered the broad approach which has become the dominant orthodoxy. His experience of this had led him to query views with which he was strongly associated in the public mind.

"These days I find myself ambivalent on that issue actually. I am exercised by the frustration that abounds because we are aiming too few resources at too high a demand level. I wonder whether we are focusing our energies correctly. There has been an evolutionary movement over the years to try and warm up the hinterland of policing by community relations, and there has been a development of thinking, a more problem-oriented style. And that has been quite resource intensive. Any number of people needed to task the Home Beat configuration. We found ourselves in conflict with other agencies because you get difficult issues of confidentiality and issues of whether police are straining beyond their mandate and that sort of thing. I must say I have toyed with the idea of late of whether we should focus ourselves more directly on our acknowledged function of policing. I don't mean in a pure law enforcement sense. There is an argument for saying that if only we, as a management team, could so inculcate various principles and so on in our men that they perform the job absolutely within the law and in impeccable fashion, then, if that ideal could be achieved, there would be less need for the public relations activity. Because the various community initiatives which police leaders take are very often to repair damage done by inefficient policemen, by unthinking policemen. I construct a scenario where you spend much more time than we do now indoctrinating constables with a proper appreciation for the role that they have in a society like ours, a democratic society. So you really get them to internalize as a personal value the essential requirement that they carry out their job in the way which is consistent with the kind of society we want to live in. Now, that would take much longer in training then we do now . . . It all depends on how you define the police mandate. As you know, I have attempted a restatement of those objectives . . . but I suspect that attempt has not really succeeded. It needs a more subtle definition somehow. It has something to do with achieving a situation where neighbourhood institutions are able to work with that degree of freedom from interruption that they produce a harmonious state of affairs in the locality. Now that still requires you to work in quite tight co-operation with other services. But if you were doing that within the confines of a much more strictly defined police role, so it wasn't trespassing on roles commonly thought to belong to other agencies, the whole thing would be much easier. I am wavering about the line of thinking I had before, where it was to do with depositing responsibility on the police for problem analysis and mobilizing other agencies. One runs into all kinds of political difficulties when you define the police role in a broad way, and these troubled me."

While only a handful inclined to the narrow view, and, as the above case implies, these could be for quite paradoxical reasons, a substantial minority (35 per cent) argued for a 'middle' road as a coded way of espousing a traditional law enforcement road. The following quotes indicated clearly that the 'middle' was often a code for a specific 'law and order' conception.

"I'm in the middle position. The problem is that the police service are trying to be all thing to all people. And in so doing we're probably failing miserably. I mustn't be quoted on this personally, but you've got people like the probation service, social service, education department, prison service, whose concern it is to take care of offenders, or to educate a child so he doesn't attain anti-social behaviour. Now the police have tried to get in on the act, and have been encouraged to do so. But there isn't a longstop behind the police. If we fail to catch the wrongdoer, there's nobody else sweeping up behind us. We haven't placed as much emphasis on catching and detection as we should have done. I blow the other way. Where we have failed is that we fail miserably in trying to prevent crime."

"I'm somewhere in the middle to be honest. There's a growing realization that the police alone can't sort out all the problems of society. The public at large are accepting that they have to do their bit. If you look at the sheer arithmetic of the equation there are 2,000 policemen in this force area and over a million inhabitants, which means there is one of us to every 500 of them ... The opportunity effectively to do anything, when the odds are so enormous, without public co-operation wouldn't exist. That is probably what is meant by the policing by consent about which we hear so much. If the public were geared and organized to do something that we chose them not to do, there is little effectively we could do to stop that, so we have to try and get them on our side. But I don't agree with theories put forward by some eminent police officers about the commitment to public affairs. I'm all for involving the force within the community and if you look at our organization we have a very strong set-up in that regard. But I feel honestly, and perhaps it is only a gut reaction, that what the public most like us to do is to uphold the law. If for whatever reason we are seen not to prosecute people who commit offences we lose an awful lot of ground."

"I'm certainly not either extreme, which makes me sound terribly ambivalent. You can look at it in a philosophical way and lie back and muse about an almost idealistic view of society. The goody-goody policeman, the little white God principle, you put him up there and he goes out and polices. But what you've got to realize you are dealing with, even in a county like this, you are dealing with a complex group of people. Society is complex and we do have ethnic minorities and all sorts of competing groups. The notion that the police are a cohesive force is nonsense. So you are dealing with an almost impossibly constantly moving dynamic situation. There is no point in trying to get a single philosophical thrust ... It is a simplistic notion that we are law enforcement officers ... A lot of police officers have a broader social service view. But you also have those who use that view to give them an excuse to be uniform-carriers, and don't actually perform a social service at all."

"I don't see the police service as having a right to dictate the pace of society. We have always got to be chasing the problems. Our role is wider than simply investigating crime and arresting people ... We all believed not many years ago that we could put the world right in that very simplistic fashion. But it dawned on us over the past decade that this wasn't all our role. There is now the reverse danger of forgetting or overlooking that central part of our function in the new enthusiasm for the more ancillary roles."

The dominant view of the police role held by chief constables is now a broad, community-oriented one. However, this is being rethought by some of its pioneer champions. There is also a more cautious or conservative substantial minority who believe the enthusiasm for wider approaches has gone too far. They seek to restrain it by espousing a 'middle' ground.

The broad philosophy is evidently one which many chief constables did not hold earlier in their careers. It is unlikely, for example, that those who spent most of their operational lives as detectives would have held it then. Many chiefs were in fact aware of how their views had broadened as they reached ACPO rank and came to appreciate the larger perspective on the police role.

"I was blinkered and I accept that now. I try and tell other people who are, if you like, following the same path of specialisms, that nobody was a keener detective in the sense that I believed what I was doing was the most important job in the police service, that without the CID the whole job would collapse, that we were doing the major thing that the public wanted us to do. It wasn't till I came out of it that I realized it was just one part of the whole policing problem. So, yes, my views have changed quite considerably."

"My views have changed every time I've moved up in rank. For the simple reason that he who doesn't change is incapable of policing this modern world. If you're unable to change I don't believe you're adaptable and therefore able to provide this very wide role of management."

Thus some recognized that chief constables tended to adopt a broader view of the police function as they moved up the police hierarchy because this was more congruent with the role of manager of a complex organization. It was also pointed out by many of those who rejected the broad view, as well as some of those who accepted it, that there was government pressure in this direction since the Scarman Report. The broad view had become the favoured line of the Home Office, the Inspectorate, and Bramshill. This was as important, at least in making it the current orthodoxy of chief constable philosophy, as was any elective affinity it might have with the position of being a senior management executive.

"I am not so sure whether our view has changed. I think rather we have been overtaken by events. In the sense now that the Government has issued its classic circular on crime prevention, and suggested that chief executives have this role to play in the county. Indeed the chief executive in this area chaired the multi-agency crime prevention committee on which I am represented by the superintendent of the community relations department. I could argue that has usurped the unique function of the police in leading on crime prevention. On the other hand I welcome it in the sense that it demonstrates that other people are prepared to accept they have a role in crime prevention. This is the fundamental change. No longer is it left for the police to take all the initiatives."

"The whole multi-discipline approach, if you like, to crime in the county, and the developments that came of Scarman. We took it on board . . . And Scarman's consultation committees. But I know certain areas where they said 'Well, we're not having those; we don't need them. We're a law-abiding area, we have no ethnic minorities. This is a nonsense—we are ignoring it!' And so they do. We put them in here although I didn't think I needed them, and they are working quite well."

The broader, post-Scarmanist philosophy has thus only become the dominant outlook among chief constables with some pressure from the centre. Many chief constables, especially in the county forces, deeply resented this. Over half of them still simmer with resentment at what they see as a package of reforms and a philosophy that was quite unnecessary or inappropriate for their areas, but was foisted uniformly on the country because of the problems of a few big city forces.

"We over-reacted to some extent following Scarman. In some areas perhaps sufficient hasn't been done but on the whole we have over-reacted to Scarman's attitude. We always over-react as a service. Crime prevention comes along and we over-react, pour resources into that sort of project. And then it became slightly unfashionable again after a short time, we take a few men out again, and so get it in proper perspective."

"I believe, because we have been grasping for a solution to a problem, we have listened and taken on board too much of that general philosophy following Scarman. There are occasions when you've got to have hard, positive policing ... One of the things that really disturbs me about policing is the advice and circulars that come from the Home Office, like the stream of circulars following from Scarman, recommending new forms of consultation and so, essentially, softly, softly or community policing ... In this county the relationship overall between police and public still remains good. So we can afford to get away with forms of police practice which would no longer be acceptable anywhere else. For example, my CID got intelligence of impending copy-cat rioting in 1985, information that there would be rioting on Saturday afternoon and evening, sparked off by some ring leaders throwing bricks at shop windows. What my detectives did was go to the pubs where these people were drinking on the Friday night, haul out the leaders and give them a stern warning that if they set foot in town on the Saturday they would be arrested immediately. Now this was beyond the limits of police power. It is the sort of thing that, if it had been done in Liverpool or any other major city, any sensitive area, would have led immediately to an enormous row between the local police authority or other bodies and the police. But here it was simply accepted and seen as good practice, and they averted a copy-cat riot as a result. So the kind of advice about consultation and so on that is appropriate in the big cities is not appropriate here."

"There are police officers who are consulted rather regularly—the same ones—but I don't know that Lord Scarman was really talking about provincial-style policing. I don't think he was. You see, the Metropolitan Police, and not many will admit this to you, had almost a perverted delight in the fact that they were completely outside politics, they had nothing to do with local politicians, nothing to do with the town hall. That just wasn't their problem. We didn't work that way in the counties. As a detective inspector I used to attend rural district council meetings to talk about crime problems, way back, twenty years ago. We'd always done it, for goodness knows how long. So I don't think Scarman's Report was really levelled at counties. We were separate from something that was happening in the Met."

"Well, it's all right Lord Scarman pontificating, making his recommendations, about consultative committees, maintaining tranquillity, and so on ... It's a very difficult area and I don't see any sort of simple answers short of saying we will enforce the law. It's a matter of, at the end of the day, fine judgement in the way we have to go. It's more of a problem, if you like, for my contemporaries that are in the deprived urban areas than it is here ... If you allow things to deteriorate to where people imagine they can with impunity break the law then we really are on a slippery slope, aren't we? That's something we have to be very mindful of, and it's very easy I suppose for Lord Scarman to make all these points."

"Lord Scarman hit on beautifully written reports if I may say so. But the preservation of public tranquillity can't be achieved by failing to enforce the law, because if they are mugging, using drugs, or whatever, they will bring the law into disrepute and therefore there will be a breach of public tranquillity whichever way you go. Whereas there may be times when a police officer is wiser not to act, for his own personal safety, there are times when the police service has got to say 'Now!' Can I cite an example? Shortly after Lord Scarman reported I was deputy here, and there was an illegal drinking den operating, run by a West Indian gentleman, in one of my towns. We knew about it and so he was visited and told not to do it ... 'knock it on the head!' We also knew because of the other experiences, the Black and White Café and those things, that almost inevitably a group of people up there would have caused difficulty. But there came a time when we had to deal with it, and having been given the warnings and opportunity to rectify, he didn't, so we conducted a properly policed raid with everybody there. Because to allow him to flout the law would be counter-productive, you have to face it. But the point inside the Scarman Report, that was quite valid, was that to deliberately question people on fishing expeditions can be counter-productive, or to go out of your way to pursue a defendant without good cause. And that has happened a lot in the urban areas, certainly in the Metropolitan Police—they have over-exercised their authority and created flash-points.''

"One of the problems of the Scarman Report was that in my view he did his homework well in the areas where he did it, but not enough in the counties. It's a pity he didn't come to some areas like this. You can list most of the forces in this country as counties where the consultation in fact works well on an informal basis. Now in fact we had to set up these formal committees, immediately start making platforms for them. A bloody question mark whether they're necessary! Nobody's satisfied!''

This view, that the Scarman-derived community-oriented approaches were unnecessarily or inappropriately foisted on the country, is predominant amongst the county chiefs, but this does not mean they reject his basic approach. As we have seen, most chiefs *do* accept the broader view, but the county ones tend to resent what they see as pressure to do what they were already doing, and to adopt over-formalized styles of operation which did not suit their areas. However, the chiefs in the larger, city forces (those where Lord Scarman had done his 'homework' as the last quote put it) were pleased with the extent of influence their views had had on it.

"I happened to talk to Lord Scarman a great deal before he wrote his Report. I'm not for one minute saying he adopted my views, but I know we're at one on these issues. The sort of point he was making on the difference between law enforcement and social tranquillity. What it means is just being sure-footed! ... The problem is largely lack of communication within the police where the message gets twisted and the perception at the bottom is of a no-go area, a policy which inclines towards going soft.''

"The Scarman balance has been expressed in an oversimplified way by many. I understood at the time exactly what Lord Scarman was saying, and quite honestly in my own evidence to Lord Scarman's inquiry I referred to the need to be mindful how you actually operate and deploy your forces in highly sensitive inner cities where tensions run high. Indeed Lord Scarman was kind enough to quote entirely, word for word, exactly what I said on this point and it formed the basis of his own notion of the balance ... in the normal course of policing the community. But that has been extended by commentators much too far. Lord Scarman never intended that—no matter how tense an area might be, no matter how difficult problems were, no matter how high the risk of consequential public disorder—the police had not to do what had to be done. That should not influence police officers not to do their job when manifestly the choice is not theirs to make. We operate here on the very simple basis that we police not just sensitively but sensibly."

The majority of the sample (75 per cent) did agree with Lord Scarman's basic analysis of the problem of balancing public tranquillity and law enforcement. However, the county chiefs argued for the most part that traditional British policing always had been based on this. The proper use of discretion was the key to achieving the right balance, and this had never been a problem in most parts of the country. They resented the imposition on them of devices which aimed to revive this tradition in the cities where the exercise of discretion to maintain the tranquillity–law enforcement balance had become problematic. However, while sharing Scarman's concept of the need to balance the value of law enforcement against that of public tranquillity, just over half (53 per cent of chiefs) believed this could lead to the creation of 'no-go' areas, as the Scarman approach might inhibit the younger constables. Only one-third of the chiefs felt this was not a problem because they were able to communicate an appropriate sense of discretion to their force. The danger of Scarmanism leading to 'no-go' areas was explained in ways illustrated in the following quotes:

"There isn't a problem in this force. But for instance in——shire, we had riots there, five shops were burned down. I was right in the middle of it as deputy chief constable at the time. Policemen are becoming so wary of criticism that we do things wrong. We wouldn't deny for one moment that there are warts on our organization. But we are now continually criticized. Scarman started this in a way. Officers are now becoming wary of doing anything that starts trouble. I think the other side, the criminals, know this, and they know if they start trouble *en masse* and then criticize the police they are going to get some public support. I was listening to the radio this morning, where a vicar from St Paul's was saying this. Yes, he was on the radio this morning, saying that the police have the wrong approach in our area. They go in and deal with crime! Now if you just leave people alone, let them smoke their pot and take their drugs, it's OK. And young PCs who hear this find it very difficult where to draw the line. I'd agree with Lord Scarman that if you arrest someone in possession of drugs and they get fined £100, but as a result of that arrest you cause a riot and £2 million worth of damage, it makes sense to back off. But the other side recognizes this. We've reached a position where if a group of individuals go down the high street smashing shops and looting at night they're going to get arrested. They'll start a riot, the majority fighting the police. The others go along and loot and, in the case of London, actually murdered families under cover of other great troubles."

"If you were doing your interviews in the canteen with the sharp end, what they'd say, very promptly to you, was we haven't got it right. They see themselves threatened by the new approaches. They think we've moved too far the other way. I feel rather glib sitting here saying there is a balance which can be found—not no-go areas, but policemen working somewhere in the middle. I tell my people they're very lucky. They still have a public here generally that likes them. They've never worked in an area where the hate is bouncing off the walls at them as they walk on their beats. I tell them to treasure it and work at it ... There are problems we all recognize here, the ethnic minority city areas. I've got some in——and I've seen little problems at the bottom, seed corns that are ready. But on the whole it's not a problem in this area, unlike the Met."

"I think no-go areas are now a danger. It needn't have been, quite honestly. The police service was probably at fault over the last two decades, as we were trying to grow accustomed to the imposition upon the country of a huge ethnic minority, of doing our level best to make sure things went well. And in so doing, not imposing the law in relation to those communities in quite the same way that we would have with the indigenous population. That probably created many of the problems that now exist. Had our reaction to the ethnic minority been along strict non-partisan lines from Day One, had we policed them in the way that we are in the habit of policing indigenous populations right from the outset, then I don't think that problems that now are very real and exist would have arisen. Now, fortunately in the area I am responsible for, we don't have the problems that many inner-city areas have. But we do have areas with quite large, in the sense of 8,000–10,000 people, ethnic populations. We try very hard indeed not to treat them differently to anyone else. Sometimes we get a backlash. Not from the people with whom we are dealing, from the ethnic populations, because they don't see us doing anything different with them to what we are doing with the indigenous populations. But because they are aware of the kind of activities they are indulging in, which we won't countenance, being committed elsewhere for reasons which it was a mistake to allow ... At the time

of the riots you will have read the disquiet of the policemen on the
ground who, I'm sorry to say, were anxious, and could foresee what
was going to happen long before their commanders. They attributed
it to the fact that they were not allowed to police those areas in the
way that they were policing every other area.''

While most chief constables did feel there was a problem that Scarman-
type approaches may create no-go areas, most also felt this was not in
principle different from the difficulties police officers had always had in
exercising discretion. Tuning the antennae of police officers to use
discretion 'sensibly' was widely felt to be the adequate answer, though
this was more complicated in a multicultural society with different
norms of acceptable behaviour.

"I don't honestly believe what Scarman said in itself may cause too
much of a problem. The great problem with the police service is the
communications problem ... There is nothing wrong, is there, if you
see a crime committed and you normally go in and know you can
arrest and take the person to a police station. But if you were in a
coloured area such as St Pauls and you see an incident committed
and you know who did it—you don't go in at 4 in the afternoon when
the Black and White Café is heaving, you wait until 7 a.m. next
morning and knock on his door and pick him up and take him in.
The end result is virtually the same. Ken Oxford, Ron Broome, Jim
Anderton, they're facing this each and every day. But the problem is
communication: explaining to policemen that philosophy. In modern
policing now you expect an awful lot from your policemen, they have
to exercise their judgements on a day-to-day basis, changing their
style from one environment to another.''

"The prevention of no-go areas is a must. It must be your highest
priority that you don't have areas where the law doesn't attain ... But
you do have gradings of behaviours which you are prepared to accept.
I used to brief officers for football matches ... 'Now, look, you're
going to have a phalanx of supporters from X, if they tell you to piss
off, just accept it ... as long as they're not terrorizing other people.'
Now, if you put them in the middle of the town tomorrow night and
a chap was told to go on his way, and he said, piss off, he'd not do it
twice, he'd get nicked. I wouldn't be foolish enough to raid a house
in St Pauls if I thought I was going to start a riot. The way to do it
is to go in at 7 a.m. and nick whoever is in there ... If somebody's
got 10 lb. of heroin in a house, and I'm going to need 500 bobbies to
get in there on a Friday night and I can't guarantee I can hold it, I've

got to find some other way. There's always this trade-off. The great thing at the end of the day is discretion. Discretion is vital in the way we police."

"Scarman doesn't have to lead to no-go areas, but it can do. What a policeman has to do, whether he is a constable on the beat or a chief constable, is to assess, in the inner fraction of a second flat, what is the position on the street. Somebody has knifed somebody and just walked round the corner—well, tranquillity goes down the drain. You go and have a look and that's the end of it. If you start a riot, that's hard luck. You're not going to let him get away with it ... The inspector has to do similar with his own men, so he can assess if they're OK for jobs or not—'For God's sake don't let Charlie do it, he won't be any good!' ... some laws create special difficulties and enforcing them is very likely to cause a riot. But if you don't there's danger you end up with different laws in different parts of the county ... I see the police service as the go-between between the desire of the courts and Parliament to say that's the law and the multi-coloured leaders of a community which will change within twelve months. Now, there's a problem with AIDS. The law won't be able to catch up and it's up to me in the police service to try and monitor it so I don't make any mistakes. Cannabis is illegal—it's no good saying it's legal in one place. But we can't get too simplistic. You can make a law here that all clubs will close at midnight and probably get away with it. Try that in Manchester and there'll be blood on the streets. Parliament only has to cope with it once every few years, so they say cannabis is illegal, but we have to enforce it ... There is a need to take account of local needs, provided you don't fall into the trap— and this is the responsibility of the chief constable—of pandering to tiny minority groups. We are trying to save the whole community ... You've got to know what is going on, identify how great feelings are, whether someone's just making a loud noise, or whether it's a justified noise or a powerful noise."

In conclusion, then, the dominant philosophy of policing expressed by chief constables is a broad community-oriented one deriving from the influence of Scarman. However, a substantial minority of chiefs, especially in the counties, see policing in narrower law enforcement terms. They particularly resent the imposition of formalized solutions to problems of community relations which they see as non-existent in their areas, the sins of the cities being visited upon them. While most share the view that public tranquillity is of paramount value, they do not see this as new but the tradition in their areas. Pursued in trouble-some spots this philosophy carries dangers of creating no-go areas, especially if different standards are used for different ethnic groups, which some see as an implicit message. The solution is the wise use of traditional police discretion. But tuning up the antennae of young constables is more problematic in today's multicultural society, with the attendant increase in deviance and disorder that is seen to occur. Chief constables' analyses of the general problems of crime and public order will be looked at in the next chapter.

7 Chief Constables' Criminology: Crime, Causation, and Control

Chief constables' views on crime, public disorder, and how they should be controlled are evidently a central aspect of their professional ideology. These are the core tasks of the police in public opinion as well as in the perspectives of all chief constables, whether they adopt a broad or narrow view about how best the police can perform their function. This chapter will consider how chief constables analyse the issues of crime and disorder, how they think the police can best deal with them, and the impact of recent legislative changes, notably the Police and Criminal Evidence Act 1984 (PACE), the Crown Prosecution Service (CPS), established by the Prosecution of Offences Act 1986, and the Public Order Act 1986.

The Problem of Crime

Almost all chief constables believed that crime was now a greater problem than when they had joined the police. This was claimed by 83 per cent of them, with only 7 per cent arguing crime was not a greater problem (the other 10 per cent were undecided).

The main basis for this belief was the chief constable's own experience. When I asked them what evidence they had to support their view that crime was a greater problem, 43 per cent referred purely to their own experience. Only 28 per cent supported their argument solely by pointing to the criminal statistics.[1] Another 28 per cent referred to both the statistics and their personal experience to back up their opinion.

The majority of chief constables expressed considerable scepticism about the validity of criminal statistics as a measure of the extent of crime. They articulated all the warnings about their interpretation which form the traditional fodder for criminology lectures on the pitfalls of the official crime statistics. This seems to be something of a new departure, for a decade ago chief constables appeared regularly to buttress demands for more resources with references to the rising crime figures. Like the Government, which introduced the recent record quarterly crime rate increase with a long cautionary note about the problems of statistical interpretation, chief constables now regularly recycle what were regarded as the views of radical criminologists in the 1970s. It is more likely to be the new 'left realists' in criminology or Labour Party spokespersons who emphasize statistical increases in crime.[2] Those who have been in control of institutions with a responsibility for controlling crime paradoxically seek to play down the significance of official statistics. What appeared in the 1970s to be a left–right split on the importance of official statistics, now appears to be an outsider–insider split. Incumbent governments or officials are inclined to stress the pitfalls of the dark figure of crime, while opposition parties are prone to moral panic (Reiner and Cross, 1991, introd.).

The following accounts illustrate the characteristic view that the problem of crime has worsened, and how this is backed up by personal experience rather than statistics:

"Crime is undoubtedly a greater problem now. [R.R.: On what evidence do you base that?] Well, when I was a young PC walking the streets of——[a large city] in 1956, which isn't so long ago, if we had a robbery we had to inform the then chief constable, day or night. Robberies were literally unknown. In fact, I remember after a few years being called to a scene somewhere, a drunk had been knocked down, his wallet taken, and it was treated with great concern, a high-ranking CID officer dealt with it. I wouldn't like to say how often that happens in this county now. For instance, over the last weekend we've had a family held up in their house whilst their house was robbed and all the valuables taken, their children were threatened with violence by three hooded men. We had another girl attacked in the street that night, she was lucky to get away with just having her purse stolen, and that's just last Saturday and Sunday. And two police officers had their noses broken. In those thirty years things have changed so drastically. I was in the CID for a long time, but then became a uniformed chief superintendent. And when I went out in a Panda car with PCs in the division in which I was working I was amazed, having been away from that work for so long. When I was a constable everyone wanted to get out and get into CID. One went out and looked for crime, it was very difficult to find a case to deal with. In fact CID officers would come along and take it away from you, if you had something good. Any crime was dealt with by CID. It's changed now. When I went out with an officer in a car instead of patrolling they went from incident to incident dealing with crimes. I was amazed how many crimes they dealt with in eight hours. That is how it is now, fire-brigade policing. Not to mention the public order problems, football violence, and so on."

"Oh gosh, yes! Oh, there's not the slightest doubt that crime's a greater problem. [R.R.: What leads you to say that?] Well, just my own personal experience. I mean the sheer volume of crime. The sheer nastiness of the violence that you face is far greater now than it ever was when I joined. This may sound a contradiction, but when I joined there was almost a camaraderie, I mean I've actually been on the floor with a couple of dock labourers trying to kick the hell out of me. They've been suitably arrested and taken to the police station and charged, and they've apologized and asked to shake my hand in the morning, and said it was the beer, I'm sorry about that. I don't think that happens these days. The violence you get these days is far nastier. Far more people are ready to turn, not only challenge the police officer, but resort to violence against them. Look at the statistics of assault on the police. It's partly the judicial system. In my early days there was a retired Indian Army colonel on the Bench. His phrase was, 'How dare you assault one of *my* officers!'— and it was invariably a prison sentence. And, as I say, there was almost a sort of—not brotherly love—but a comradeship in adversity with the villains. The following morning they were saying sorry. But, particularly among the youngsters now, you find this degree of resentment as well as violence. You certainly find it amongst the coloured community, of that there's no doubt. My son is a police officer, and he served in Moss Side, Manchester. He went to university, got a degree, but he always wanted to join the police service. I'd always told him to wait until after his degree, when you've got some other string to your bow, so he waited and got a good degree, a 2.1. I know we're all biased about our own children, but I believe he's a very good all-rounder, sportsman, physically tremendously fit, worked in summer schools with children from all over the world, and has an ease of communication. Talked to him about the problems of Moss Side. He came back in his first three months and said, 'I can't understand it, Dad. I can't even get close to them. The first thing they do when I appear in my uniform is spit at my feet. I can't talk to them, there's no dialogue.' They won't talk to him, to them he's a pig. He finds the coloured people he has to deal with are infinitely more difficult. Someone drew a knife on him the other day, and his colleague was stabbed three times. He only got a small stab in his hand. They were arresting somebody—he's in plain clothes at the moment—who tried to sell him a packet of cannabis. It's an example of the way in which the violence is escalating.''

"Crime's a larger problem, that's beyond doubt. It's a bigger problem in that the standards have fallen, standards of behaviour amongst criminals. There's a greater disregard for the sanctity of the person, that's the greatest move I've seen. People are prepared to rape and indecently assault and attack and wound and beat and push and shove and abuse people. Without seemingly having any shame or regard for the fact that those people may be affected for the rest of their lives. I've seen some terrible cases. I remember one woman in——[large city] who has never been to bed without her clothes on since the day she was raped, that sort of thing. There's this piratical attitude of violating the property. Even if you think somebody's there you'll take the chance, and it might involve violence ... So, yes, crime has got larger, worse. There's a lot less respect for the person and the property.''

These quotes illustrate the typical views of chief constables, that crime has got worse, not only quantitatively but qualitatively, and the way that this is usually backed up by reference to personal experience rather than statistics. Some combine both experiential and statistical evidence to support their conclusions:

"Well, certainly, any glimpse of the statistics will tend to support the contention that crime's worse. I think there's far more violent crime. I'm really concerned about violence, and violence particularly in this area towards police officers. It's easy to romanticize about this or fantasize, but whereas in my day when you went to a domestic dispute, a pub turning out or whatever, the mere presence of the uniform was sufficient, these days the presence of the uniform is an invitation for it to be attacked. The cases of my officers getting beaten, kicked, for no good reason whatever! You stop a car, for example, because you think it's stolen. And five or six yobs come over from the nearest pub and attack you for stopping the car. That's happening here now. It's a very worrying trend.''

Although some chief constables based their conclusions on rising crime on the statistics, at least in part, the main source of their views was personal experience. Most seemed very cautious of the pitfalls of interpreting criminal statistics. They were aware that part at least of the increased level of recorded crime could be due to an increase in public reporting. One cause of this was a change in public attitudes:

"It is easier to report crime. The increase in figures that you find in rapes will probably come from women's readiness much more to come forward these days because they think they will get a more sympathetic hearing. There's a reservoir of unreported crime. Crime statistics have been almost a well-kept secret for many years ... Statistics are not a reliable record of what is happening within society."

Reporting of property offences (which constitute the bulk of the crime statistics) had increased also because of the spread of insurance:

"More crime is being revealed now than forty years ago ... You hear about the tip of the iceberg, well, there's more of the bloody iceberg being revealed now. People now have a greater property responsibility or involvement, insurance and so on. They are persuaded or invited to report more crime now whereas before they didn't. There's still many unrevealed facets. People don't report motor vehicle crime because they're going to lose their no-claims bonus. Crime is an enormous problem—it was ever there, but wasn't revealed."

The rise in criminal statistics was itself a source of further reporting, as it fuelled greater sensitivity about and fear of crime. Fear of crime becomes a major problem in itself which needs tackling, but it is an uphill battle because of the media highlighting of crime:

"There is a greater public awareness about crime and we have become in certain respects rather too efficient, because we record everything and figures go up, and the dear old media publishes these stark figures. They really mean very little but you are continually being bombarded by questions about crime. I don't want to lessen the seriousness of people committing offences but in reality the emphasis is too great. Fifty per cent of offences are very minor indeed. These crime statistics we produce do not portray the real problem. They give everything the same kind of credence—you get a cross for one murder and you get a cross for stealing a bottle of milk."

"Ever since I came here I've been trying to convince my colleagues and others that the so-called crime wave only exists in statistics. There's a letter we send out most years to senior citizens that explains things like the fear of crime. In this county there are one and three quarter million people. Do you realise that there are only fourteen people actually injured as a result of burglars smashing into their homes? It's due to the general ramshackle method you use for recording the crime rate. I remember in 1963 when the rate of indictable crime shattered the first million barrier. Horrifying headlines! But most people don't even know what an indictable crime is—it's a mixed bag of threat. The bulk of crime doesn't actually threaten the average citizen, only those operating in a particular environment, drugs, woundings. Let me quote again this letter to senior citizens. One piece of intelligence we put in there was to tell them that ten times the number of people who are injured in their homes by crime are hurt because of some idiocy over driving, including being hit by golf clubs, umbrellas, handbags, civil servants' suitcases, and briefcases. Yet the fear comes from the small number! I've never been able to persuade them. I got one of those letters in a very bold hand from the Isle of Wight telling me: 'Round objects! Don't you read your local newspaper!'"

In addition to increases in reporting offences, the statistics were inconsistent due to changes over time in police recording practices. Sometimes these were due to technical changes: new counting rules, or recording procedures and facilities, for example.

"A factor is the computerizations of criminal records. We've now got a criminal information system, and all the crimes are input into the computer—the computer doesn't lie or forget, and once it's in it's in. In the old days the memory of the detective might mean that he forgot to put in a larceny of a handbag, or put it in as property lost. We've become more rigid so crimes can't be cuffed."

"Statistics don't give us the true answer. One of the best examples was that in 1972 we set an arbitrary limit and the Home Office said we would record for the purpose of criminal statistics criminal damage worth £20 or more. Well, if we were trying to keep the statistics level criminal damage would now be £120–30 or more, but we're still recording £20 offences. There's a very simple example of how crime figures change dramatically. You can't come to conclusions on the numbers game."

Another type of reason for the police to record proportionately more offences is the organizational interest of police forces. At some points in time boosting statistics may be seen as an effective weapon in the competition for resources. The context was changing now because crime had risen despite manpower increases. This had stimulated the turn to the broader policing philosophy described in the last chapter.

"We were tempted and used the excuse of being under strength and bombarded by crime when we were clearly under establishment. We said when we got up to establishment we'd be able to deal with it. But there's now the realization we couldn't stem the rise of crime. It's gone up continually, and we've been doing what we thought was everything to prevent it and it hasn't worked. So we've got to look for help. And I say in this county what better way to help than to join the Neighbourhood Watch or Special Constabulary."

Thus the statistics are seen as a dubious basis for policy, and reliance is placed instead on the lessons of experience. However, on this basis a small minority (7 per cent) of chiefs do not feel crime is a greater problem, or are not certain. Their views are illustrated below:

"I don't frankly see crime as a greater problem now, no. I think crime has changed over my period of time. There's more tendency to violence. I see criminals being cleverer, and being better defended, so it's become more difficult for the police to do their job ... But I don't see crime in itself being a greater problem. I've always been around in areas where there's been a fairly high incidence of crime similar to the types we get now. But the criminals are getting a bit more difficult to nail than they used to be."

However, whether there actually was more crime being committed, or just more being reported, there was an increase in the police workload:

"We don't know whether there is more people committing crime or whether more crime is being reported. These things are never totally measurable. But the volume of crime that is reported is clearly a problem for the police, because you have to endeavour to try and investigate all reported crime. That obviously means that as crime goes up and your resources stay flat your officers are having to spend less time on certain types of crimes. It's a management choice."

Explanations of Crime

The overwhelming majority of chief constables, then, do see crime as a much greater problem than when they joined, believing it has increased in quantity and worsened in quality. How do they explain this trend? The predominant criminological theory articulated by chief constables is a conservative variety of 'control' theory.[3] Rising crime (and disorder) are seen as functions of the declining influence and hold of moral and social controls. Almost all the chiefs explained increasing crime in such terms, though several other theories were put forward in addition. The most commonly articulated theme was of an erosion of moral standards resulting from a cultural climate of permissiveness. This was attributed primarily to a failure or an unwillingness to do their job on the part of the key institutions of informal social control.

"I don't want to moralize too much but I do think the attitude of the public has changed. I wonder to what extent the fact that mothers have gone out to work has lessened the influence on the upbringing of children. I take the view that fathers don't have anything like the influence mothers have got. Traditionally the father's at work and the mother's at home. The process of change started in the war and has carried on since. More and more women go out to work now than did during the wartime I'm sure. Attitudes have changed. Pornography, for example. There have been changes in the acceptability of sexual behaviour, if you like. A softening of rigid laws which led to rigid behaviour being the accepted level. What might have gone on behind the scenes is another matter. Overtly these things have changed."

"The nature of society has changed fairly substantially in my time. The mobility, freedom, and so on. I came from a small town in Scotland where, God help you, if your father was arrested for being drunk or something, it put disgrace on the family for forty years because everybody lived in the town. That whole structure has broken down, even more so in the big cities. There is no corrective influence coming from the community. People don't know each other so well, so there's no reaction ... All that sort of thing has mitigated against any sort of community crime control."

"Let us start with the nuclear family which is now really perhaps not the normal thing. If I go to a school and talk I've got to be careful ... because many of the audience will be from single-parent families ... A father or parent who drifts in and out of their relationships ...

That sort of social change damages stability. The increase in the working life of women dramatically has changed society. [R.R.: How has that increased the crime problem?] A youngster growing up from a single-parent home which I believe is less stable, really is, therefore, more likely to get involved in crime. You can see that on many of the large estates. For example,——is an area where a lot of single-parent families live and there are, I believe, a lot of social stresses beginning to emerge. I think the working housewife is not at home when the kids come home, and is busy and tired, and perhaps hasn't time for socializing with these young barbarians. Not youth, but barbarians— they've been called that from time immemorial. So I think the influence of the home is less and the Church has decayed. The influence of the schools has dramatically changed. I'm horrified when I go to some schools. I come from an old-fashioned grammar school where one respected the teachers and you wore uniforms. You offered respect and there was a pattern and discipline in school. Now I go in and it looks like chaos and disorder ... That must have an impact on young people who will grow into people who are criminals over the next decade.''

''All the changes in social attitudes, the attitudes of parents, of schools. It's been terrible to see how the teaching profession has lost so much respect from kids, parents, and the rest. As an outside observer, I don't think they've had the support of governments, but equally they've got to build themselves from within.''

''There's no shame in conviction anymore. There is no chastisement or approbation by society. Most of that stems from the fact that if I stood in an audience, as I often do, and say black and white and shades of grey, how many of you would evade or avoid the tax man if you could, they have a little snigger. Or how many of you would say, if you're given a parking ticket, 'Why don't you go and catch the bloody robbers?' Now that's living by double standards. You either want a good society and you live by the sword or you don't. Standards generally have fallen: the demise of the family unit, and education has fallen away abysmally. I used to lead the civics team into school back in the late 1960s, and I used to spend 90 per cent of my time in the staff room talking about standards to teachers, not talking to the kids. They were trying to defend falling standards—my subjective view of course. But I think they were wrong.''

''I suppose a lot of policemen would react by saying, maybe from the sixties onwards, a lot of attention was given to the importance of freedom and self-expression. Some may suggest, that may have generated the troubles we are now experiencing. Freedom, which then led, it seemed to me, in some way, to a deeper concern for the criminal than for the victim. One wonders about balances.''

''I take myself back to the village I was born in. The very thought of someone going to a court was a sanction in itself. It was sort of talked about—oh, he's been taken away by the brass buttons, I think was the phrase used, unless I lapse into Geordie which I could do if you want. So there were sanctions, neighbours' sanctions. Those sanctions have disappeared. They've been watered away and replaced by some muddled thinking about what is illiberal, because we've started emphasizing rights against responsibility.''

John Maynard Keynes remarked many years ago that 'Practical men, who believe themselves to be quite free from intellectual influences, are usually the slaves of some defunct economist.' In this case it would appear that chief constables' criminologies echo the analyses of various defunct and not-so-defunct criminological theories. The prime perspective is a conservative variant of 'control' theory, as outlined above, attributing rising crime to an erosion of the efficacy of informal social controls in the neighbourhood, family, and schools. This is usually traced back to the 1960s (à la Norman Tebbit) or beyond that, to the Second World War. Intriguingly, it is often suggested that 'shame' constitutes the mediating variable linking informal control processes to the inhibition of crime, as the last three quotes in particular indicate. This is uncannily reminiscent of the brilliant recent attempt to synthesize some leading criminological theories using 'shame' as the integrating concept (Braithwaite, 1989).

This is the dominant explanation favoured by chief constables, but by no means the only one. Classical and neo-classical criminology also make a prominent appearance,[4] in the form of complaints that the severity of sanctions imposed by the courts has declined, and increasing crime is the consequence. This argument is sometimes a version of the previous one, when the link between supposedly declining sanctions and rising crime is seen to reside in a symbolic process: reduced sanctions signify less 'shame' is attached to offending. More usually, however, the claim is more straightforwardly classical—the deterrent sting of sentencing has been lessened, making crime more attractive, or the incapacitation period of incarceration shorter.

''The changes in sentencing! We used to say the thought of being caught was always a deterrent. If you look down over the years it used to be, if you got caught, you had a pretty good certainty of being quite vigorously punished. Look at the punishments in 1950 when I joined, where you could still get fourteen days with hard labour, which was probably the best example of a short, sharp shock. Whereas today, unless it happens to be serious, you're going to get either a conditional discharge or a suspended sentence at the worst. So the chances of being punished for crime these days first time round are far less than they used to be.''

"The regurgitation of the criminal is now a big fact. Prison, you see, is less. We put a lot of resource into catching a good thief, or a good rapist on many occasions. We put enormous resource into that. And then you go into the judiciary system, and the judge in his wisdom says you will go to prison for five years. But what you find is that, if you look at your prison releases, within two and a half years they're back in circulation again. And it's very few leopards that actually change their spots. So you've got them setting up somewhere else, and you put enormous resource into catching the same one. I find that particularly true now in the sophisticated burglary type of things, and particularly the sex offences.''

As in classical theory generally, it is not only lower severity of punishment which is regarded as a cause of increased crime, but reduced certainty of punishment. Clear-up rates have fallen (chief constables' explanations of this will be considered below, but recent legal changes such as PACE figure large in them) and this decreases the risks of committing crime:

"Crime is a bigger problem now. One of our problems has been the Police and Criminal Evidence Act, which is doing undoubtedly what all chief constables knew would happen. Elements of it, we said, would have the effect of increasing our crime level but reducing our detection rate. The likelihood of detection is less and therefore more people take the opportunity to commit crime.''

Another factor mentioned by several chief constables was the increase in opportunities for crime in contemporary affluent and materialistic consumer societies. In line with the 'situational crime prevention' analysis developed by various researchers in the Home Office Research and Planning Unit this is seen as increasing the possibilities for casual opportunist offences:[5]

"Over 90 per cent of crime is property crime, and the opportunities to commit crime have never been greater than they are now. You've got so many young people with cash in their pockets and that wasn't the case thirty years ago. And there's all sorts of attractive things, like your tape recorder here, all kinds of things which weren't around thirty years ago. And the common car—I mean, a third of all crime is related to the motor car. When I joined the police there wasn't one single person on my station who owned a motor car, and, you might find it hard to believe, but in my subdivision they didn't have a police car. They had one motor bike, that's all, and there was great excitement when we were issued with our first Ford Popular. The opportunities to commit crime have increased enormously. Standards have changed with it. As living standards have increased by access to material goods, at the same time other standards have declined, so you have one pulling against the other. Inevitably there's been an increase in crime."

One common perspective on the growth of criminal opportunities in a consumer society was to link material advance with moral deterioration as twin aspects of modernization, as the above quote does. In other accounts it was connected to the rise in unemployment, in particular youth unemployment. Many chief constables did perceive unemployment to be linked to crime. However, the link was not seen as lying in pressures towards crime which were generated by unemployment leading to deprivation, whether absolute or relative.[6] The nexus between unemployment and crime was interpreted within the moral framework that constitutes the dominant perspective of chief constables. Unemployment was a factor in crime because the devil makes work for idle hands. It creates the opportunity for unemployed youths to take advantage of the opportunities for crime generated by a more affluent society. Thus the chief constables' criminology steers clear of any radical discourse about the social roots of crime which would be fundamentally critical of government policy. Nevertheless, recognizing an unemployment–crime link is implicitly to criticize government policy for failing to maintain full employment. However, this connection tends to be attenuated by its place in a deeper moralistic discourse, in which all causes of crime are interlinked as symptoms of modernity at an overarching metaphysical level beyond policy control:

"I believe that we're an agency dealing with symptoms. There's a big disease somewhere that we can't cure. I'll try and do my best on the edges, continue to deal with the symptoms. But the disease is what really wants tackling, and this is where there's got to be a massive political will ... There's a lot of idle hands and a lot of stuff to be taken. A lot of crime is an idle hands syndrome ... We do live in a different society. I don't think the permissive society is simply words. We've got into a situation where people are more likely to say, yes, it's all right, it doesn't matter, than they ever did before, so there's a lot of crime down to that. I worry about that."

"We live in a materialistic society, with more things to steal these days. We didn't have videos and microwave ovens and things that this, and there weren't cheque books and credit cards a few years back. There was not the number of vehicles and things left in vehicles to steal. So the fact is, we have become more materialistic, more affluent as a society, over the last few years. That might enhance the attitude of those who have and those that don't: so envy creeps in, if I can't get it by fair means I'll get it by foul. The old saying, the devil makes work for idle hands. I don't think that because a man is employed one day and unemployed the next changes an honest man into a dishonest man. I don't think that happens. But if somebody has a propensity to be dishonest and he has got more time on his hands, he's likely to be more active in a dishonest way."

A final facet of the explanation of increasing crime provided by some chief constables was the development of a multiracial society, the influx of black people and foreigners. This will be considered in more detail in Chapter 9, when we look at chief constables' views on race. However, it fits into the dominant overall perspective on crime in that the growth of an ethnically heterogeneous society was seen as a factor in the break-down of traditional morality. This was partly because black people were seen as more recalcitrant to traditional authority and morality by some chief constables, a theme indicated in some of the earlier quotes in this chapter. But, more generally, they were seen as new, foreign, as an aspect of that overall modernity which links all the disparate criminogenic developments in the contemporary world. County chief constables in particular seemed to dread the encroachment of a crime-ridden modern culture, hitherto confined to metropolitan areas, but which was creeping into theirs. Black people were the visible symbol of this danger:

"When I talk to our training courses the point I always make is a very simplistic view. We have a responsibility here in counties like this. They set up a datum, a norm from which others can see how far they have drifted. There is a loyalty and an integrity in this part of the world which is way above any other I have ever experienced.

Well, it's changing rapidly, frighteningly. In the last year we had an 11 per cent increase in crimes, it's going to be one of the highest in the country. When I came to this county ten years ago it was quite unique in every respect. We never followed crime patterns that were occurring in other parts of the country. But now we are following national trends. They happen contemporaneously in this part of the world. We have had a massive road-building scheme, the southern part of the county has opened up tremendously in the past few years— three, four years. As recently as that, if we had a serious crime we could virtually lock this county up. But now the crime is committed and the villain is gone before the crime is discovered. We have a fairly volatile town in——where rising 7 per cent—which comes as a surprise to many people—rising 7 per cent of the population literally is black. We have a black and white problem there. Fights. And when we meet the leaders, the minority group leaders, it's quite amazing. It is a marvellous exercise in restraint when they make outrageous statements. They complain bitterly about harassment and what have you, and what happens, really, is they're telling you what's happening in other parts of the world. How they perceive things is the thing that matters. We have terribly unrestful weekends, not because of anything that's happened here, but Mrs Groce in London can affect the attitude of your black people. We have had our problems here, not in geographical areas as such, but so far as premises are concerned— certain pubs used by certain groups for drug taking, and taken over if you like by blacks. So we have experienced it in a small way."

In sum, the dominant criminology amongst chief constables is a conservative formulation of control theory. Crime is seen as a worsening problem, not, primarily, on the basis of statistical increases, but qualitative changes perceived by personal experience. The cause of it is seen as a fundamental moral pathology in the culture of modernity, primarily due to the failure of informal institutions of social control, the family, Church, and education. Formal institutions of control, notably the courts and legislature, have also weakened authority by reducing the severity and certainty of punishment. This is as much a symbolic problem of undermining moral standards as an instrumental one of reducing deterrence. A more secular set of material factors are also adduced: more opportunities for crime, increasing unemployment. However, these tend to be interpreted as criminogenic because they fit within the broader pattern of erosion of moral controls. The key theme is this master trend of modernity undermining morality. The influx of black people is seen to symbolize this to many, especially in the county forces, who fear the changes this brings.

The characteristic criminology of chief constables is congruent with the dominant broad community-oriented conception of the police role which was outlined in the previous chapter. If the sources of crime lie primarily in wider communal changes, they must be addressed at that level. Chief constables eschew a pure 'law and order' approach to their duties in crime control, in about the same proportions as they espouse the broader conception of the police role. As already argued, the pattern might well have been different a decade ago. But the 'law and order' solution tends not to be favoured because chiefs are well aware that it appears to have been tried and failed. A minority argue, however, as Shaw did about Christianity, that the problem with the 'law and order' approach is that it has never really been tried.

Police and Crime Control

The general view, amongst chief constables now, is that the 'law and order' package, increasing police numbers and powers, is not the key to controlling crime. A majority of chief constables do not believe that a rise in police strength would improve their performance in dealing with crime, although a substantial minority does. When I asked the chiefs whether they agreed with the conclusion of Home Office Research and Planning Unit studies which called into question the view that increasing police strength would reduce crime,[7] 48 per cent agreed, but 35 per cent disagreed (with 17 per cent unsure). This cannot be attributed to deference to the authority of the Home Office. When I later asked the chiefs whether getting 500 new recruits would do much to improve their crime control performance, a bare majority (55 per cent) said it would, but a sizeable minority (45 per cent) said no. This substantial proportion of chief constables who deny a straightforward relationship between police numbers, crime, and clear-up rates are not contradicting their regular requests for more manpower. They usually argued that although there is no direct and immediate relationship between police and crime levels, the broader community-oriented strategies they favour are if anything more labour intensive than reactive policing. Contrary to what a fiscally parsimonious government might claim, community crime prevention should not be interpreted as policing on the cheap. It was also commonly argued that even if police numbers were not a solution to crime, a visible police presence did help allay the fear of crime and boosted public confidence. The following quotes represent the characteristic viewpoint:

"It's a great dilemma for Government. They've increased substantially the number of police officers. I'm not talking about this Government only, but Governments over the years since I've been in. When I joined the service, there were about 60,000 police officers. There are 120,000 or something now. The primary duty of the police is to prevent public disorder. If I wanted to make inroads into my crime figures, I would need an enormous number of people for police officers on a preventative role. I really would, and it just wouldn't be justified. The problem of crime is too often put solely on the doorstep of the police. We have possibly the least possible effect on crime when you look at the whole community. It sounds a bit trite, but it starts in the home."

"We must always be challenging old ideas about policing. The deterrent effect of the constable alone patrolling on his beat is probably limited to a certain extent. The argument is he will only come across a burglary once in every thirty years. What he does is to create a condition in the mind of those who are looking for these things, where patrolling is done sensibly: 'I don't know whether this cop's going to come around the corner.' Quite apart from the argument of whether he can actually individually prevent crime is the other argument about the sense of order that he brings into society. If you draw your curtains and see a constable walking his beat you feel more secure. If you see three there you worry!"

"There is no simple correlation between giving me more manpower and I will reduce your crime. In fact, I don't even tell my police authority when I'm asking for manpower that I will decrease crime. I fully accept that these mysterious engines that are driving crime upwards will not be altered by that. But I have a much more pragmatic reason for wanting policemen. The demands on the police service from all the other functions, not just the huge investigation of crime, all the other things we're taking on, is eating into our manpower. We cannot make a simple police presence on the ground in many areas. The sheer perception of seeing policemen, however valid it is in the reduction of crime, is very important in the perception of people. If the country actually said we want to tackle crime, we're actually prepared to double the police budget—I know the Conservatives increased it, but if they doubled it again—they might get an effect.

I'm too realistic, I realize that that is not likely to happen. It's financially and politically impossible.''

"To make any impact the numbers of police have to be so significant that no society will afford them. By the end of the next financial year I'll have 2,259. To make a real impact I reckon I'd have to have about 20,000. But you couldn't afford it. I accept that you can't stop crime by constantly pouring policemen at it. But what you do do if you can, you raise the level of your presence on the streets, you do reassure people. It's this question of the fear of crime . . . We've got to try and persuade society, if we can, to do much more for itself. Apart from anything else, policemen are so bloody expensive these days.''

"The present level of police officers is of paramount importance, not in terms of reducing crime, but in terms of providing reassurance and other services to the community . . . Now our numbers are so restricted, and with all the pressures on us, we're having to work more in the reactive way. The amount of resources we have for what I call 'investment policing'—in the schools, other educational establishments, in other areas of the community—where acting as catalyst we might have some positive influence for the long-term reduction of crime. That's where we ought to be investing more numbers, in investment policing.''

A substantial minority (just over one-third) of the chiefs did not accept the Home Office questioning of the police numbers–crime control link. They would welcome increasing police numbers as a direct contribution to controlling crime.

"An increase in manpower would have a considerable impact on our town crime, there's no doubt about that. Because our burglary rate is going through the roof; we had a 33 per cent increase last year. Not serious burglaries—opportunist crimes, detectable crimes. There's no doubt about that. A criminal has got to get to a crime and he's got to get from the crime. Very few crimes are solved, detected at the scene. Our best opportunity of discovering the criminal is catching him on the way to the crime. It's very often the case that if we've got men out on the ground he can be caught coming from the crime. We're not doing that because the men aren't there, they're too heavily committed. Being a large rural county we're very thinly spread. We have no reserve of men to do the unusual. It's terribly difficult to gather a posse.''

Police Powers and Crime Control

Most chief constables were equally sceptical about the other part of the 'law and order' package, increasing the legal powers of the police. This is certainly a difference from a decade ago, when chief constables' evidence to the Royal Commission on Criminal Procedure (which reported in 1981) was decisive in producing recommendations for extensions of police powers.[8] Chief constables' current views were undoubtedly based on the recognition that the subsequent Police and Criminal Evidence Act (PACE) of 1984 had given them much of what they had wished.[9] Their opinions were also tempered by the realization that extended powers were likely to be balanced by new safeguards, and the general perception that the safeguards of PACE had resulted in a net inhibition of police methods for investigating and clearing up crime.

The overwhelming majority (95 per cent) of chief constables said that there were no new legal powers which the police needed now in order to improve their ability to control crime. However, the majority (70 per cent) also felt that the 1984 Police and Criminal Evidence Act (PACE) had been detrimental to crime control. This did not mean they were seeking its repeal, which was accepted as not politically feasible. It meant, rather, that detectives in particular had to adjust to a new set of procedures and constraints, which at least in a period of painful transition, was inhibiting their effectiveness.

"There are no new powers we need which spring to mind. Some of the problems we used to have have been overcome by the Police and Criminal Evidence Act, and the Public Order Act. There were certain areas in the public order field which I was very unhappy about but most of those loopholes have been plugged, for example I've always felt strongly that there ought to be a requirement to give notice of marches and that's now in the Act ... But the safeguards in PACE will be proved, I think, to slow down the detection rate considerably. They will inhibit in many ways the pursuit to the bitter end of some crime. The general principles of PACE are like the old Judges' Rules, but some of the small print is a problem. Take a case where it's become extremely difficult: multi-arrests. We recently had a case involving the murder of a Hell's Angel. We had to arrest thirty-five people, who've remained in custody ever since. I had my DI (detective inspector) who should have been the main man doing the investigation in court all day and every day, sort of going for the extra remands. Custody officers, when they get that number of people in, it slows the system down. The contemporaneous notes that are now expected slow down the work of detectives. That's the biggest change in police thinking—ask any detective. I wrote this morning for my Annual Report that in the fullness of time the Police and Criminal Evidence Act and the Crown Prosecution Service will be seen to have been in the interests of all of us, and I think that's true. But at the moment they slow down the effectiveness of police work in many ways— because the balance has gone much further than we expected, not necessarily more than is desirable, but it's going to set us back. And really the only people that benefit by it are the guilty.''

It was also generally perceived that an increase in police powers might be counter-productive from the point of the view of the wider, community co-operation approach to crime control which most chiefs espoused:

"The powers we have are pretty well adequate. One wants a police service which is acceptable to the great general public, and yet which has sufficient powers to carry out its work of enforcement. Now I think those powers are there. I wouldn't go along with people who would say, 'Yes, we should lock them away for ever!', or anything like that. That's not the way of a caring society. The powers are adequate, though there are difficulties, checks and balances. The PACE safeguards had some negative impact. It's early days yet, but criminals are not so willing as they used to be to admit other offences they may have committed which formerly would have been taken into consideration (TIC). Our detections dropped 5 per cent last year and that's pretty well because our TICs dropped that amount. It may be because they're getting legal advice earlier, or they too have studied the Act. Lots of policemen have been inhibited because of the paperwork demanded by the Act. In my early days as a policeman there was a large problem of drunkenness—it seems the country was going downhill rapidly. And there emanated from central government a form which, if my memory serves me, was four foolscap sides. And every time a policeman had to arrest a drunk he had to fill this form in. Now that solved the problem of drunkenness overnight, because policemen stopped making arrests. It's the same now. Before PACE a policeman would use his instinct, his nose he developed over the years, and arrest on suspicion on the flimsiest of grounds—but more often than not that arrest turned out to be a good one. There were some that didn't, one accepts that mistakes were made and will continue to be made because we're all human. Now a policeman looks more closely at his suspicions before taking that final step. So yes, it has been inhibiting.''

"We shouldn't have more legal powers. Not really. We have to accept we live in a world where we're not the only occupants, there are other people's considerations to take into account. There are things which would help that would be so punitive the population at large wouldn't find them acceptable. Therefore any benefit you might get by that added power would be lost because we'd lose the confidence of the people.''

The majority view (held by 70 per cent) of the chief constables was that PACE was detrimental to crime control. A major source of this was seen to lie in the inhibiting effect of the safeguards on police practices which had previously been successful in producing clear-ups. The increase in police powers was apparent rather than real because it merely confirmed formally what had hitherto been covert practice, while the safeguards were a new departure, a bureaucratic nightmare of encumbrances restricting police effectiveness:

"By creating another set of rules and regulations and requirements for us to follow you're going to clog us up in bureaucracy. The courtroom argument is whether we play by the rules—whether the chap's guilty is just another side issue ... The powers just regularize what was already police practice. I mean, in this county we had no distinct stop and search power. People were regularly stopped, searched, and arrested, but that put us in a weak position to argue our case. What we were really saying was, 'OK, let's have this stop and search power so that the policeman and the citizen know exactly where they stand.' We weren't arguing for new powers, we were arguing to rationalize what we were actually doing. But then the whole thing got into a ridiculous situation. Not only telling us that under certain circumstances we had to be able to justify when we could stop and search, but it also went on to give us a code of practice about how we were to do it. This is nonsense! In many scenarios that occur daily we haven't got the power to take a man's hat off! It's Alice in Wonderland! So a lot of things that came in PACE I was totally opposed to, and made my voice heard through the channels. The problem was, at the time, we were dealing with the Royal Commission, which was a forerunner to PACE—we at ACPO hadn't got our act together. We didn't argue on evidence, we argued on anecdote. We should have argued that PACE demanded an in-depth evaluation of our laws on evidence—in this day and age they're nonsense. The protection of a suspect has swung around quite dramatically from the days when the Judges' Rules said there should be a right of silence. We ought to take off the shelf the 1972 11th Report of the Criminal Law Revision Committee which had some sensible things to say about abolishing the right of silence. My hobby horse is that Parliament is overweighted by lawyers, so they kicked that Report into touch, and because of that the Royal Commission saw there wasn't enough mileage to bring it back.''

"There's been a marked drop in the detection rate, and you're talking really about the effects of PACE. What really does society want of us? Having been a practical detective for most of my years I know. You sometimes get a bit of information that somebody did something. And it's no more than that, no more evidence to show. Pre-PACE you may well be satisfied in your own mind that that man has been at it. So it's a question of interrogation. This is the sort of difficult area you get into—when you talk about interrogation. People obviously imagine all sorts of things happening, from rubber truncheons to bright lights and all the rest of it. Really it's not like that at all, but there are certain things that make a person more amenable to interrogation. If you put him in the detention room with three or four hours to consult with himself, it may well be that when you go and ask him questions he'll tell you. Now, at the end of the day, what does society want? Do you want your detective officers to be interrogators and detective officers, or on the other hand do you want the Marquess of Queensberry rules all the way along, and everything looks fine? I'm not suggesting that when a police officer used to have a person in the station there was anything improper. But if he had reasonable grounds for investigating he did ... That's all gone now. It's an emotive subject. It creates in people's minds all sorts of potential for unlawful things, Dick Tracy and all the rest of it. But I consider my force to be a large number of very good chaps, as honest as the day is long, who in the course of their investigation of crime have worked on bits and pieces of lawful knowledge. These days, before or when you arrest someone, they have access to a solicitor. Time without number the solicitors say, 'Don't answer any questions.' So you're waiting until such time you've got sufficient evidence to arrest; you're waiting for the results of forensic evidence. And the forensic science service is creaking at the seams. So really you're muzzling the police in terms of crime detection. The counter-argument is, of course, you know, civil liberties are going to go out the window because you'll lock us all up and throw the key away, and the rest of it. It's a matter, at the end of the day, of have you got confidence in the police service to stay within the law and do their job effectively and efficiently. Tape recording has helped us work quite effectively—produced straight pleas of guilty, cut out all the nonsense of allegations of verbals."

"The community itself has to decide the balance between the liberty of the subject and the benefits of living in basically a crime-free society. You pay a price whichever way you shift that balance. If you want a totally efficient police service you can have one if you're prepared to pay the price and have no liberty at all. Rights and responsibilities are a bit out of sync at the moment. There's too much emphasis on rights and not sufficient on responsibilities. The right of silence ought to be looked at ... With all the problems of the stop and search approach, the law-abiding citizen has nothing to fear from a policeman saying, you know, 'What are you doing about at 2 or 3 o'clock in the morning, and why are you carrying a case?' The criminal has everything to worry about that happening! PACE says the officer has to have some reasonable grounds he can articulate, and that will reduce the number of policemen prepared to look into what might appear not quite right. That will jeopardize quite a few detections. What happens is the policeman is out on his own, he senses, and that's about as strong as you can put it, that circumstances are not quite right. If it's a stranger and it's an area where there have been a few house burglaries, he'd like to check him. But unless he can really say that chap was linked to the crime, something that gives him reasonable ground, then he can't do anything. Whereas, before PACE, in my younger days, you'd be more inclined to stop him and try and establish some rapport. Now you need more than that if you're going to comply with the law."

"PACE certainly initially inhibited officers from doing stops in the street, and there are signs this may carry on. It certainly inhibited the spontaneous road checks we used to do, that I'd been brought up on in the Met. I mean, the number of crime arrests I've had from, at 3 a.m. in the morning, just sealing off a route that was known to be a rat-run for the local villains. That produced all sorts of arrests and clear-ups. Now we can't do that anymore. The main point about PACE is it's affected the upper end of the criminal market, which was always my fear—the 4 or 5 per cent that you really need to keep in the cells for a long time because you're struggling. You know what they've done, but you're struggling to get evidence, forensic and so on. If you've got grounds for keeping them in, PACE lets you, but the problem is you've got to reveal your case if you go to the magistrates for an order for further detention. We deal with London villains here, they come down all the time to break into our nice stockbroker houses. And what you find is they just sit tight and say nothing, absolutely nothing, until they know you've got to take them to court. They wait to see the strength of the case. And their solicitor prepares the defence on the basis of what they know you know, and frankly we don't know a lot at that stage. I'm being a bit tongue in cheek. Obviously one has to be aware of the safeguards which are there for the individual. But when you're dealing with squads like the Regional Crime Squad, your drugs people, they really need time, and they don't want to reveal their hand because it defeats the object of raiding houses for forensic and so on. It's that top end of the market, that we previously kept in for twenty-four hours plus, that's creating a problem."

"Could you please switch the tape off? [Field notes]: There's a murder case now with two child victims here. Before PACE we'd be able to round up suspects and hold them for questioning without any timetable pressure. Now this major crime will probably not be cleared up."

Thus the majority view was that PACE had undermined police effectiveness by limiting police discretion, and subjecting police practice to a burdensome bureaucratic panoply of procedures, rules, and regulations. A substantial minority (nearly one-third) of chiefs did see it as potentially valuable, however. This was mainly because it forced police practice into more professional channels. Policing by plan had to replace policing by hunch. A related benefit was that police evidence would be more trusted as it had been gathered within the constraints of a rational set of procedures.

"Some forces produce statistics that say, since the introduction of PACE, the number of people put before the court has reduced dramatically as a result of the restrictions placed upon us ... We've not found it in my force area. We police are a fairly conservative body. So when contemporaneous notes were first brought in by PACE, it was, 'Oh dear, me! This is going to curse us!' And yet it really strengthened the police case immeasurably. The same with tape-recording, despite the criticisms about suspects taking the scenic route to the station."

"My people are trying to convince me at the moment that I'm losing the detection rate because of PACE—police are losing the initiative and so on. I'm saying that these are the safeguards that are built in by Parliament. If Parliament feel there should be such safeguards then we've to live with it, so let's not start mucking about and trying to moan about it. Tape-recorded interviews, I think, are the best thing in the world, because I hated the conflicts about the old voluntary statements, the old verbals business. I hated it because it was unprofessional. If you can't do your business within X number of hours and you've got to have him released, OK. I've tried over a number of years to break down the old city principle of lock 'em up, incarcerate them, and so on. And when you come back to it the best way is the old county principle that you're better off with a report for summons unless you've got to lock him up for his own safety or the community's. If we've got to have some more safeguards, fine, though I'm one of those people who thought we were doing bloody nicely, thank you very much. If people did their jobs properly."

"With the initial introduction of PACE there was a dramatic fall in the number of crimes detected. That's now starting to improve. There were so many fundamental changes and policemen have to become accustomed to them, get used to operating with them. Contemporaneous taking of notes of interviews was imposed by PACE, but we had done it on this force for serious crime for several years. It has its disadvantages. You can imagine the seasoned interrogator, the frustration he must feel because he has to interrupt the flow of the interview at a critical time, and perhaps lose the thing that was just about to emerge. But the credit side is that contemporaneous notes are rarely challenged in court. Whereas previously a detective's summary of perhaps a four- or five- hour interrogation might only cover a couple of pages of typescript and would lead to all sorts of allegations about what had gone on in that length of time, or was something favourable to the defendant omitted. My force and others were horrified at the thought of tape-recording of interviews. Now they welcome it with open arms. So PACE, despite all its faults, has been imposed on us, but has made us far more professional in our approach. We have to work harder to get other evidence rather than relying simply on what we could get the defendant to confess to."

"PACE is going to change our way of doing the job because we're going to see more surveillance of criminals, particularly the professionals. Over the next few years there'll be a tendency, particularly in the professional criminal field, to see more telephone-tapping— we'll see ourselves going more the American way. Because we've got to compile much more evidence, particularly about the very serious criminals, before we take them to a police station or speak to them ... The detection rate will fall because, with PACE now, all the pressure is to get people into police stations and get them out again, so we're not spending enough time talking to them to find out what they've done in the past. Much of the detection rate in the past was TICs and that's going to come down. It could get very easily abused, when you get a thing like Kent, which was very unfortunate. There is the contemporaneous notes problem, but it's being overcome by taping which detectives take to like wildfire. The right to silence and access to solicitors, with the detention limits, mean our frequent customers know they'll be released if they keep silent. But on the whole it forces us to a more professional approach."

One of the ways PACE was seen as detrimental to crime control was by inhibiting stop and search on the streets. Most chief constables regarded stop and search as a useful police tactic. However, the majority (73 per cent) felt that it would be wrong to target particular social groups for stop and search on the grounds that they are more likely to commit crimes as recorded by official statistics. This would not constitute the basis for reasonable suspicion under PACE, and is specifically precluded by the Code of Practice on stop and search. Nevertheless 18 per cent of chiefs thought this could be a useful tactic, and another 9 per cent felt it could be, but recognized arguments against as well.

The conventional view that stop and search, targeted against specific groups believed to be more prone to offending, would be counter-productive is exemplified below:

"Stop and search is a necessary power. But targeting it against particular groups would cause difficulties. If you reflect back to the
1960s, when we were in the drug scene, and all those with long hair
and jeans were stopped, it caused a great outcry, didn't it?"

"What groups are you going to target? What does a thief look like?
There are hunches. But then, you see, the chap who's walking along
with his rolled umbrella and his bowler hat and his briefcase will turn
out to be a thief, but he's taken the trouble to sort of disguise it."

The more ambivalent view taken by 9 per cent of chiefs is illustrated by this case:

"In the short term it would have a significant improvement. If you
have firm information that a particular group are committing crime,
quite clearly, if you target them, then you're going to clear up more

crime. And if the sentence of the court is such, it would take them out of circulation. So you're going to prevent them as individuals from committing such a crime. That has to be balanced against the importance of not seriously alienating people that needn't be alienated. So targeting has a part to play but has to be seen to be done in a way that is aware of the adverse effects of such a policy.''

The view that targeting was definitely useful, put by 18 per cent, is illustrated by these quotes:

"It's difficult to target precisely. What happens is the policeman, out on his own, senses that circumstances don't look right ... If you've got an area where there is a high proportion of ethnic minorities you're going to get a high proportion of those stopped and checked. I don't think there is any way you can avoid that. It's totally wrong to pick on a man because he is black, yellow, or pink, just because of that colour without any attending circumstances. But if you've got an area where you know there are a lot of street robberies, or an area where you know you've got black offenders involved in house-breaking, then clearly there's nothing racially discriminating if you start to say, 'Well, we're looking for people who are black because the descriptions we're being given are black', any more than it's discriminating if the offenders are male as opposed to female, then you don't pick on women you pick on men. The trouble is, it's perceptions, it's not how the ethnic minority see it. We shall have got rid of the racial aggravation in this country when the ethnic people stop saying you're picking on me, or you stopped me for speeding not because I was speeding but because I am black. It's an easy answer from their point of view to make, you know, 'I'm not stopped because I am committing an offence, but because I am black.'''

"Stop and search is a power that county policemen still use very, very sparingly, as I find by looking at my returns ... I know men don't walk around with masks on and swag written on a bag, but there's still, sometimes, that feeling that you want to search somebody. If there's a group moving around committing offences, like the peace convoy, all right, you bring all your people around it and pay it all the attention. But it can be oppressive if you detail people to have a hit rate on a small section, like the late chief constable of Manchester, years ago, did: 'I don't like homosexuals so we're going to sit in lavatories.' You know, well, that's too much.''

"If there was any group that, in our intelligence, I mean confirmed and assessed intelligence, that that was a group who are out to disturb the queen's peace, yes, they should be targeted and dealt with fairly but none the less firmly. Whether they were black or whatever. That's our task. That's what the community pays us to do, and I think they would rightly give us a kick up the backside if we just left them to go because someone might feel it's illiberal to target them . . . We have an area in——where there are actually more coloured people than in St Paul's in Bristol. But I feel confidence there, that we have the community, if you can call it that, we have it right on our side. And we've proved that by going in, when in 1985 they were having trouble in Handsworth, we had some intelligence that people were buying excessive quantities of petrol. We went into the community at grass-roots level, told the people what we thought was happening, and now we are going to search to find this. We would like you to help but we don't want you getting in the way. We're fortunate in this particular area, of course, that most of those who come into the area from outside are property-owning people. They're buying their houses, they've got a vested interest in the place being stable and prosperous. We went in, put out this special team, targeting, finding out where this petrol was. It turned out that with the full help of the community we didn't have to make any arrests, although we made a lot of visits to homes and caused a lot of disturbance. It turned up with some of the local coloureds. The policeman's biggest weapon is inconvenience, not arresting people. Some people call it harassing. But there is no way we could do our job without occasionally having to inconvenience people. If it's just to stop them and ask questions, that's an incon-venience. Anyway, it turned out to be a group of—I was going to say punters, but they were not really punters. They were, rather, a low-level group of coloureds from Brighton, Birmingham, and Bristol who were running a few girls, prostitutes. And it so happened that both ourselves and the local community were doing a lot to get rid of the girls on the streets and the punters. This was so successful that they were having to take their girls to places along the coast for them to work. That's why they were buying the petrol, so they could store a can in the back of their cars, drive down, and bring their girls back. It was as innocent as that—well, if you can call that innocent—it wasn't sinister. We were able to convince the community and consequently there was no trouble about harassment.''

All chief constables recognized that clear-up rates for crimes reported to the police had generally fallen over time. However, the overwhelming majority (83 per cent) felt this was not the fault of the police in any way. Some of the reasons given for the clear-up rate decline have already been noted, such as the alleged impact of PACE. However, in addition to adducing reasons for a fall in the clear-up rate which pointed to constraints placed on the police, most chief constables challenged the validity of clear-up rates as an index of police performance. One line of argument adduced here has already been encountered: the fact that the recorded number of crimes has risen independently of increases in the occurrence of crime, because of tighter control of police recording procedures. More crimes being recorded would increase the denominator of the clear-up rate and thus reduce the rate, other things being equal. A similar point was that the numerator of the rate, the number of clear-ups, was itself a dubious measure. Questionable procedures had been used in the past to boost this, such as prison write-offs and pressure on suspects to admit offences to be taken into consideration (TICs). Tighter regulation of police interviewing and recording practices restricted these possibilities, and had the effect of cutting clear-up rates.

"You've got to look very carefully at the system of recording the clear-up. The ability to manipulate them is constantly there. Criminals used to ask for some crimes to be TIC'd in court. They now say, 'Hang on, that'll make me look worse. I'll end up in prison'. Some forces have detectives go along to prisoners after sentence and say, 'Well, come on, we can talk.' And get write-offs that way. But there's a significant new effort to stop it. Our systems are getting more refined, much more accurately reflect the situation. You also need to look carefully at the crime figures. I won't malign any force, but attempted burglary could be put down as broken glass. So you reduce the crime rate and still clear up the same number, and your detection rate rises! Our TICs have halved so our clear-up rates will fall. The detectives work just as hard, they're just as effective, but the apparent detection rate has gone down."

"You've got to look at statistics frankly. I know—no, let me say I suspect—that not everyone does their crime statistics as they should do. Certain discrepancies stand out to me even today between forces that would not bear close scrutiny. Crime statistics often in years gone past were not done with the thoroughness they are now, and probably were flattering. The statistics are far more professionally presented now than they used to be.'"

A related point about the problematic nature of clear-up rates, as indices of police effectiveness in relation to crime, was made by most chiefs. If crime rates rise then clear-up rates will fall, other things being equal, even if each police officer works with the same effectiveness, because they are confronting an increased workload. A better measure would be clear-ups per police officer, or, better still, arrests per officer (which would not be sensitive to variations in TICs or prison write-offs). On this measure most forces have improved their effectiveness in dealing with crime, despite the handicaps imposed on them by PACE and other restraints on practices which proved effective in the past.

"Clear-ups per police officer have not fallen, though the percentage of crimes detected has fallen. But that's because the number of crimes recorded is going up and up. It looks, because the detection rate has dropped, that you are in fact less effective than last year. You may be in terms of preventing crime. But we're detecting and identifying more offenders with the same resources. And that's despite the constraints that have been placed on the police in the manner in which they do things."

"The increase in crime is much greater than the increase in resources to investigate crime, so a smaller proportion is cleared up. I think, too, that police officers are no longer prepared to take legal risks. Years ago, we took risks arresting people and detaining them and hoping to get a statement out of them. You took a risk because you knew they were the ones though you couldn't have produced evidence. Now the calibre of officers prepared to take such risks has reduced. First of all, officers are more educated, why should they stick their necks out and risk getting them chopped off? In the past the old policeman was prepared to take a gamble and a risk to try and ensure justice, to try and find the perpetrator of an offence, and reassure victims and local people. Now we're not prepared to stick our necks out... But we're still successful with the serious crime that comes along, armed robberies, murders. They're mainly domestic, but there's the odd difficult murder. We have to devote so much resources on the more serious crime, we're hardly looking at the minor crime. It's the minor crime that keeps going up, as people get more telephones, and insurance."

"Stop and search played a part in the deterrent mechanism of preventing crime. And that's one reason why the detection rate is going down, because we do less since PACE. The terrible problem about stop and search is that it's seen to be a way we attack black youngsters. I know they see it that way, but I think we should do much more... Another problem is that TICs are a big proportion of detected offences, and they're going down because of PACE. But the number of *arrests* hasn't gone down, just the number of detections through TICs out of those arrests.''

Most chief constables did not regard the fall in clear-up rates as a criticism of police effectiveness, questioning their validity, and/or attributing their decline to constraints placed on the police.[10] However, a small minority did accept that those who live by the statistics should die by them. It was disingenuous to start questioning the validity of statistics when they were detrimental to your image if you accepted them when they were favourable. This view was more common amongst the small number of chiefs whose forces had not experienced a decline in clear-up rates.

"In my force area, my crime clear-up rate has been maintained fairly well. I don't say that with a sense of complacency. They're a measure like any other. People who've got a very poor clear-up rate would say it's an inexact measure, which it is. But there's a slightly defensive element there. I mean, they would point with some sense of achievement if their clear-up rate was what it is in my force. If it happened to fall dramatically, I'd probably take the line that it was a very imprecise measure!''

An institutional change which, like PACE, had its roots in the Royal Commission on Criminal Procedure, was the establishment of the Crown Prosecution Service (CPS) by the Prosecution of Offences Act 1986.[11] A substantial minority (38 per cent) did not think the CPS should have been set up, and another 19 per cent had mixed feelings about it. However, 43 per cent did agree with its establishment, although many of these expressed considerable reservations about the actual working of the new system. It is hardly surprising that there should be substantial questioning of the independent prosecution system since it removes what was hitherto an important responsibility of the police. None the less more chief constables (but not a majority) agreed in principle with the idea of independent prosecution, than rejected it. The Operational Policing Review's national survey revealed that the majority off all ranks of the police service (65 per cent) felt the CPS had reduced police effectiveness. This negative view of the CPS was most pronounced amongst detectives (71 per cent), and least amongst probationers (37 per cent) who presumably had no direct experience of the old system. Amongst ACPO rank officers the survey found that 53 per cent believed the CPS had resulted in a decrease in police effectiveness and only 16 per cent thought it had increased it (*Operational Policing Review* Section 6, 1990, 16–17).

The main objections put by chief constables were that the CPS was centralized and insensitive to local opinion, that it was an expensive but underfunded bureaucratic encumbrance, that less cases would be prosecuted which was demoralizing for victims as well as arresting officers, and that the very creation of the CPS was a token of lack of confidence in the police. These views are encapsulated below:

"I am totally and utterly opposed to it. Without a shadow of a doubt. There are various reasons. The first is that—and this is the fundamental point—the change is an indication that the public don't trust the police. It wouldn't have been introduced if it wasn't that the public—by this I mean the small group of people who influence legislators—had decided that the police weren't being sufficiently objective to leave it with us. The danger is that if you remove trust from people they behave less responsibly... If the public in this country signify too frequently a lack of trust in the police, then the police will be less responsible. There's another important aspect. A police officer is answerable to the public for the enforcement of the law. If you take away his ultimate sanction, which is to place a person before the courts, then you are giving him the responsibility without the weapons to carry it out. If he then deals with disorders on the streets on Friday night at eleven o'clock with an eye to a solicitor on Monday morning at ten o'clock, who is going to decide what happens, then you are denying that officer the weapon to deal with the disorders which society holds him accountable for, and that is fundamentally wrong. The third aspect is that it has always been a principle in this country that prosecutions in principle in this country have always been taken after two considerations. One is the legal aspects, and throughout my whole service this has always been done on the advice of lawyers. The second is what the Director of Public Prosecutions or Attorney-General calls 'the public interest.' Now, the police service is very much of the people and part of the people. They have tremendous links with the community ... and are responsible for what happens on the streets. So they have a very firm feel for what is in the public interest. The original proposals for a Crown Prosecution Service were on the basis that there would be a police authority-type organization to assist them. That would have lessened the disadvantages, but has never been introduced. You now have a group of people, who have gone from school to university to chambers to nice cosy city offices, where they'll decide what's in the public interest without having any understanding at all of the things they're dealing with. They've never been into a doss house or a prostitute's place or what have you. They just have no grasp of the world in which the people in the cases they're dealing with live. They're the least well equipped to judge the public interest."

"It's ill conceived in a number of points. One is the apparent belief that in the police all we did was toss a coin and decide whether the case went to court or not. There was a lot of effort went into making reasonable judgements, not only on the evidence that was available but also on the public need to prosecute. The vast majority of cases had a legal eye cast over them anyway. So the argument that unworthy prosecutions will now cease is not so. What really worries me, is that the decision not to prosecute will be made not on the public good but in terms of budgetary constraints. If there are not enough solicitors to deal with cases, then the threshold at which cases go from prosecution to non-prosecution will be raised. I don't think a lawyer understands the effect that sort of policy will have on the public we serve. First of all, I don't think the public see a separation. It will still be seen as a police prosecution as we started it, so a bad prosecution will still be our fault, no matter how much we say that the police never even prosecuted. Also, I don't think they appreciate that the differences in prosecution policy across the country weren't a bad thing. They may reflect what the community is willing to accept. So if somebody sets up an obscene bookshop in the centre of Soho they are unlikely to attract the attention of law enforcement. You set them up here and they would—the public would be saying to the chief constable, what the hell are you doing about it! We don't want that sort of thing here! And I've got to respond to that. Scarman tells me so! But the policy now is that that level of pornography will not be prosecuted, it's in the public interest that it's obtainable in London. I think you've got to have differences, by the individual chief constables developing their own prosecution policy that matches up with public expectations. . . The man who eventually pulls the strings that matter will be the Attorney-General. And we've seen more examples in recent years, with the Attorney-General developing a political stance or being accused of adopting one. And that brings prosecution decisions into the political arena. When the chief constable had it, he took all the brickbats but at least he wasn't accused of being political—not too often anyway! The CPS has been a vote of no confidence in our performance. It said, 'Police service, you've not done well enough! We now have to tell you not only what the law is but how to implement it.' That was seen as a vote of no confidence by many, and that's why I'm frustrated."

Many chief constables accepted the establishment of the CPS, however, as a *fait accompli*. They were still concerned about aspects of its implementation, notably underfunding, and the possibility of a higher threshold for prosecution. This would inhibit the police in practice, but had to be put up with:

"It's the will of Parliament, and I'm sufficiently well disciplined to accept it until Parliament changes its mind. We'll carry it out to the best of my ability. I said to my senior officers that they'll have to be very, very careful and much more professional in future in the preparation of files. Because, whereas under the old system it was a police mind that was directed to the facts of a case, now it is a legal mind, a legally trained mind. The police mind would more probably see a need for action. For instance, in some cases of non-accidental injury to children, which is very emotive at the moment. There are times when a case conference in which we take a leading part as policemen, along with social services, probation, teachers, and other things, will recommend proceedings against parent or parents. Not because we like to see parents punished, but because this gives the court an opportunity to place some sort of supervision on the child. A policeman making that sort of decision will see it because of his background. The Crown prosecution may not because of his legal background... Sometimes a prosecution can be used to draw attention to a particular problem. One often gets the case, or used to, where people who were involved in some public disorder of a minor nature were brought before the courts purely to show cause why they should not be bound over to keep the peace. That was a most useful provision. They'd not done anything terribly wrong, but they went to court and were warned, and told you are now bound over to keep the peace. This was a very useful curb... One always had to be careful not to be grossly unfair and put some poor person to the trouble and expense of defending themselves against a case which really hadn't a chance of success. But the CPS will be concerned only with the chances of winning."

Some chief constables warmed to the CPS more positively, however. They accepted that it was right in principle to separate police and prosecution decisions. They also saw potential benefits for the police in such a separation, which might enhance public trust. Justice may have been done before, but not seen to be done. In practice, though, the system might not realize its potential due to underfunding:

"I'm very happy with the CPS. I've always considered it to be undesirable from the point of view of stressing the impartiality of the prosecution system for police to be involved in the level we were. I say that, after many years of being very actively involved in the prosecution process, being the man who made the decisions on whether to prosecute or not. But from a public acceptance point of view this is the only way forward."

"I approve of the separation of investigative procedures from the prosecution procedures. What I bitterly resent is the inadequacy of central government in founding a service and expecting it to take on board the responsibility, and then manifestly failing to fund it. I've just left a meeting with the new Director of Public Prosecutions who took office today. What a charming man he is! I'm talking on the issue of the CPS to the ACPO Conference next week. I have an awful lot more to say which I'll only say within the confines of the four walls of the ACPO Conference. I don't think there's any merit in broadcasting ACPO's views. All it will do is create a lack of public confidence in the judicial system, therefore I think it's important that what I have to say is for the ears of my colleagues only—and the senior Home Office officials who'll be there, unpalatable as it will be to them no doubt. But they're trying to run it on the cheap. If they're not careful about the implications of what they're doing, it will have very serious repercussions at the lower end of the scale, for public tranquillity and public honesty."

Personal Involvement in Criminal Investigation

Controlling crime is evidently one of the central policy issues which concern chief constables. However, this is primarily at a level of overall responsibility for the efforts of their force in this direction. As we have seen, most chiefs believe this is best tackled as a broad, community-oriented effort, rather than by police patrol and law enforcement alone. It follows that chief constables' own direct involvement in specific cases is small. Thus the overwhelming majority of chiefs (80 per cent) said they would never get directly involved in a criminal investigation of a specific case themselves. The remaining 20 per cent could either conceive of, or were able to cite experiences of, cases where they might become involved personally. These would, however, be exceptional, and would usually have a national dimension.

The majority of chiefs not only said they would not get directly involved in specific cases, but felt this would be wrong. Too close personal involvement by the chief would undetermine the morale of the investigating team, and create the possibility of uncomfortable conflicts if disciplinary issues arose. There was also the danger that the chief might be remote from the current realities of street policing. For most chiefs the only sort of investigation they could envisage becoming directly involved in would be a major scandal in another force which they might be called upon to deal with, or a terrorist incident with a high public profile.

"I'd only get directly involved if I was asked to go to another force by the Inspectorate or the Home Office to take up an inquiry. I did the Birmingham bombings inquiry... to investigate how those Irishmen came to be beaten up and all the rest of it. But I don't get involved in cases in my own force. I merely see myself in an advisory role. After any major crime or inquiry that's been running a couple of days I go along. Mainly on a rations and manpower rather than belt and braces sort of basis. When I became an assistant chief constable a very senior commander in the Met. told me that when I got into ACPO rank my job was supervisory and advisory, and not to get involved. Needless to say, I didn't follow that advice. And there was a particularly nasty murder of a girl who was strangled. We had a very, very senior detective chief superintendent in charge of it. And I went along on the first day and started asking things. He was very polite about it but he said, 'Whose case is this?' So I take an interest and go along, but stay out of it because that really undermines the authority of the man in charge. I've learned my lesson. I go along purely as a morale booster and to check they've got sufficient men, accommodation—a welfare rations sort of approach."

"You should distance yourself from particular cases because you're formulating policy. Also if you get involved in any investigation and it goes wrong, you're the disciplinary authority, and it can cause quite serious problems. My predecessor learned that to his cost. A chap called——was raping people in the southern end of the county and committing all sorts of unpleasant acts. The chief was so close to the inquiry and what was happening, that when two officers had to be disciplined he couldn't deal with it."

"I wouldn't go out and say, 'Right, I'm taking charge of this investigation.' But I might be inadvertently involved. The hardest job when I was assistant chief constable was to nail myself to the chair when we got a good murder. In fact, we've had several very interesting murders here. I've gone out after thirty-six to forty-eight hours because I have a professional interest, and it allows me to look at our professionalism. I think also the people on the ground—not the detective superintendent or chief superintendent in charge of it, he may think why in hell doesn't he get out of the way and let me get on with the job—they're pleased to know I've a professional interest and am keen for their efforts to succeed ... I came home one night and there was a big fight on in one of the small towns we were passing through. We couldn't drive past it anyways because it was all out in the road. My driver and I got out and started getting involved, trying to break it up. Actually I said to the driver, 'Come on. We've got to do something about this.' And I got out and found he was still in the car. Quite sensibly, he'd used the radio to get back-up resources. It shows how out of touch I was! We pulled these people apart and there was a bit of finger-wagging, telling them in no uncertain terms there would be trouble, people would find themselves arrested, if they continued. As it was they did continue, and when the other resources arrived they were taken into custody. I was asked to go along and give evidence, but they all pleaded guilty. I think the message got across—'You know, the chap who came in and sorted you out initially was the chief constable. It may not be the best bloke to attack in court.'"

The most common sort of investigation chief constables would get directly involved in, was a major allegation against officers in another force. Several chiefs were currently engaged in such cases where they had been appointed investigating officer.

"Look at me now, I've got a team of officers, three superintendents, four inspectors, and a back-up team, and I'm having a terrible job with this inquiry [for the Home Office]. The same with any other chief officer who gets a deep inquiry into a serious complaint ... I'm under the supervision of the Police Complaints Authority."

One-fifth of the chiefs did believe in taking a more direct involvement in cases:

"I don't get involved in normal criminal investigations, but possibly disciplinary ones. But any chief constable worth his salt—I've got to get involved sometimes. It's no good just being the leadership man and the man who goes to dinners and meets Prince Charles. For example, I had my finger on the murder of——[a police sergeant whose murder was headline news], all the way down the line. We concluded that——in Ireland killed Sergeant——and tried to kill Constable——. We got so close to them ... but the courts wouldn't give them up. I don't get heavily involved like knocking on doors and so on ... But I go to every incident room, not just for morale boosting—because I happen to have been involved in one or two cases before, and I like to think I can help. My detective specialism is balanced by my team. My deputy's one of the best administrators around, and he balances me off ... I went out there Saturday night myself at midnight, on the streets of——, where the young policemen are frightened to death to go out when the night clubs turn out. They need to go in twos ... I stopped a fellow myself a fortnight ago urinating down the street, 11 o'clock at night. And he said, 'Who the hell do you think you are?' I said I'm a police officer. He said, 'Well, I'm sorry.' And I said, 'Well, I think you ought to be.' He said, 'Well, can I say something before you go, Mr?' I said, 'Yes.' He said, 'Why don't you tell those buggers up at the town hall that if they keep the public urinal open after six o'clock at night, I wouldn't need to do this.' Now you might laugh at that, but he did have a point!"

"Well, I did go over to help one of my colleagues, one of my officers, the other day, and arrested somebody in the middle of——. The press of course thought that was great. I got more kudos for that than anything else I've ever done. There was a smash and grab at a jewellers, with five youngsters. I was coming back from a function with my driver, and we pulled up at this crossroads. And three lads came hurtling round the corner. A police car rushed round and an officer jumped out and grabbed two of them. There was a hell of a fight going on. We got out and helped him with the two he'd caught... The press thought it was terrific. I'd certainly get involved. I mean, I regard myself very much as a police officer. But the chances of it happening are few and far between. If there was an investigation I was aware had political overtones, whether in the sense that a local politician or VIP was involved or some other aspect, and I was anxious that it went right, I would keep myself informed of developments but never take a direct role. Though as chief constable in——I did get involved in several arrests. The radio is on in the car, and if they are looking for a red Ford Fiesta, number ABC 123, I'm as much on the look-out. I'd take a great delight if I happened to come across it!"

"Let me make it perfectly clear to you, I'm a police officer. So yes, I do get involved. The evening before last a neighbour of mine reported a very suspicious incident to me, which potentially involved a suspect, a mugger and burglar in one, hiding in a van in the fields. I went to that van, and if he'd been inside I would have arrested him. I am just as much a policeman as anybody else. If I use the example of, say, the big disturbance at the Sikh Temple in——eighteen months ago. I personally went to that and I was involved in negotiations, and I dissuaded people from breaking the law. That's my job."

The different responses to the question of direct involvement in cases clearly reflects the bureaucrat–bobby tension in the role of chief constable, which will be elaborated in Chapters 10 and 12. The majority, sometimes with reluctance, see their role primarily in bureaucratic terms. They will get involved in cases only in a supportive, resource-providing capacity, or if the cases involve checking the heads of other police force bureaucracies, or have some other national dimension. But a substantial minority see themselves as bobbies wearing chief constable uniforms, and relish the chance to get directly involved. In general, however, chief constables' involvement in the control of crime is at a strategic level, and is mainly inclined towards a wider community co-operation policy for achieving this.

Notes

1. For a lucid and comprehensive discussion of the problems in the interpretation of crime statistics see Bottomley and Pease, 1986.
2. An example of this 'new left realist' criminology is Kinsey, Lea, and Young, 1986.
3. For a discussion of 'control' theories in criminology see Hirschi, 1969; Box, 1981, 1983; Downes and Rock, 1988; Braithwaite, 1989.
4. Succinct critiques of 'classical' theory in criminology can be found in Taylor, Walton, and Young, 1973; Vold and Bernard, 1986; and Roshier, 1989.
5. For a discussion of this perspective see Clarke and Mayhew, 1980; Clarke, 1983; Bottoms, 1990.
6. The evidence about the relationship between unemployment and crime, and theoretical explanations of it, are reviewed in Box, 1987.
7. For examples see Clarke and Hough, 1980, and Heal *et al.*, 1985.
8. See Royal Commission on Criminal Procedure *Report*, 1981; Leigh, 1981; Reiner,

1981; Hillyard, 1981; Zander, 1981, 1982; McBarnet, 1981; Baldwin and Kinsey, 1982, for discussions of the recommendations from a variety of perspectives.

9. Useful accounts of the Act itself are found in Zander, 1990; Freeman, 1985, Bevan and Lidstone, 1985. PACE has generated an extensive critical and research literature. For samples see Baxter and Koffman, 1985; Benyon and Bourn, 1986; Irving and McKenzie, 1989; McKenzie, Morgan, and Reiner, 1990; Dixon *et al.*, 1990; Sanders *et al.*, 1989.

10. Most criminologists would also question the clear-up rate as a sound measure of police performance (e.g. Bottomley and Pease, 1986).

11. For discussions see Sanders, 1987, 1988; Hall Williams, 1988.

8 The Problem of Order

Public order was the most dramatic and prominent policing issue of the 1980s. Many commentators have emphasized both the extent of disorder in British historical experience and the perennial respectable fears it has engendered (Pearson, 1983; Benyon, 1985). However, the urban riots of 1980, 1981, and 1985, and the violence of clashes during industrial disputes, notably the 1984–5 miners' strike and outside the Murdoch press headquarters in Wapping during 1986, are without parallel in recent British experience. What is beyond debate is the profound shock which these events caused to the police. The 1981 riots and the ensuing Scarman Report were the catalyst for a climate of reorientation and reform which set the parameters of police policy during the 1980s. The trauma engendered by the miners' strike has been compared by one commentator to the Vietnam War's effect on the American armed forces (Graef, 1989).

In this light it is hardly surprising that the overwhelming majority (95 per cent) of chief constables said that the control of public disorder was now more difficult for the police than when they joined. Ninety per cent felt public disorder had increased in both frequency and seriousness. Unlike crime in general, there are no official statistics which could support this view, apart from trends in the rate of public order offences. However, these primarily refer to everyday, small-scale activities, which may have escalated, but were not the heart of the matter. The basis of the chief constables' concern was the few large-scale, sensational events already referred to. It was their experience of a qualitative sharpening of disorder which underlay their pessimistic assessment. However, there was also concern, especially amongst county chiefs, about the perceived increase in smaller-scale disorder, 'slow rioting', which was seen as an escalating and alarming phenomenon. During 1987–8 this developed into a 'moral panic' about rural 'lager louts' stimulated by an ACPO Report which was highlighted in the media. (Subsequent Home Office research has questioned the ACPO interpretation, cf. Tuck, 1989.) The concern remains a real one to chief constables, however. (A cynical interpretation would be that riots mean resources, and the county chiefs felt left out of the act.) Many chief constables were well aware of the arguments of Geoffrey Pearson and others about the long history of fears about disorder (Pearson, 1983). They were convinced, none the less, that the problem was worse now, on the basis of their own experience of an aggravating quality of disorder, epitomized by a supposedly greater readiness of people to resist violently the authority of the police. This general perception of an increasing problem of disorder is illustrated below:

"One can detect a totally different atmosphere. I mean, taking the micro-situation of a PC going to a pub disturbance. I could recall when even a diminutive chap like me could be called and people would freeze and everything would stop. Now the likelihood is that they would all turn on the police and assault him."

"After a long period of time where we had fairly reasonable behaviour by people involved in industrial disputes, there is now a greater chance of industrial disputes becoming more disorderly. There are elements that are going to use those tranquil moments to cause disorder. Wapping was a fine example of that. In 1981, following the Brixton, Toxteth, Moss Side riots, no matter what the surveys of attitudes to TV say, I'm quite convinced we had copy-cat behaviour elsewhere. This county was no different. There were outbreaks on a particular weekend. We have had to give aid over to——shire when they've had difficulties. We've had to give aid during the miners' strike, though we've not had to go down to Wapping. Our specific problem, that's arisen of late, has been in the more remote places where you would not expect an outbreak. You might have them attacking the natives of——[small town], as happened just before Christmas when they were having a do on there, a quite legitimate party. And suddenly a lot from——[small town in next county] descended on the place. It was mayhem. We had to get reinforcements into quite a remote area. And about four or five days later we had, over in a village called——, people come down from——[large town in adjacent county]. They'd had a quarrel the weekend before, and there is an outbreak of disorder. Now getting people to these kinds of spontaneous incidents is a problem. There is a willingness to use quite significant violence by people not connected with the area. Something that didn't happen before. In a quiet county like this, I last year got 250–60 police officers assaulted out of an operational strength of less than 1,200. Some of them are quite trivial, some of them, quite honestly, I would not have charged with assault when I was a young police officer. It may be a sort of self-protection by the officer in some cases because he fears being complained about. But that doesn't lessen the fact that about 100 or so are quite serious assaults where injury is being caused.''

"It depends how far you go back into the past. If you were to go back into the middle of the last century, thank goodness I live now and not then. If you were to go back ten, twenty years, yes, it is far more violent. When I was doing my early policing, if I whispered gently into a fellow's ear, 'You hit me and you know what's happening to you', he knew how the courts would treat him, how society would react to such violence. That was often sufficient to save me getting a thumping. Now the policeman in the same situation would get thumped first.''

"Disorder is a bigger problem. There's a greater willingness, by the groups of people who gather, to stand fast then ever there was before. The problem was caused less than 20 years ago. Nobody knows this better than I do, with very great respect. Think in terms of Friday and Saturday nights. Public order in mining villages is like bedlam, and always has been like bedlam. But you know that you despatched a couple of cars, or even, in a small mining village, the local constable went off on his bike, and, as soon as he arrived, they run, they're off. The big difference nowadays is that they'll stand and fight. And if anybody gets picked up they'll try and rescue them, even to the extent of besieging police stations. This is the great public order problem.''

"I look back on the days of the beginning of football hooliganism. We were then being bombarded by propaganda—from academics mostly, who didn't have to go and deal with these people—that we should allow these young people to let off steam on a Saturday afternoon on the terraces. 'It may look nasty to you, but it's part of the subculture. They like to go back to their home town and show a black eye that they got in a fight.' Well, here we are, something like 70 deaths later on! ... Disorder is much worse. Not just the real serious public disorder where we move into the riot stage. The disorder that occurs every Friday and Saturday night is much more serious, more violent, more difficult to contain and disperse. Whereas, before, a couple of policemen could talk people into going away, now, if prisoners are taken, you get the people arrested for the initial disorder and others for assaulting the police trying to get them released."

The causes of this increasing problem of disorder are seen as lying in the same breakdown of moral authority to which rising crime was attributed. Crime and disorder are part of a package deal, the monstrous progeny of moral decay and permissiveness. They interact with the material progress of an affluent society, which provides alcohol to allay whatever inhibitions have slipped through the blandishments of permissiveness, better communications to fan the fashion of copy-cat disorder, and transport to speed the disorderly more rapidly to unpredictable locations. The affluent society brings material affluence but moral squalor. The police, as the visible symbols of the older moral authority, become the nub of a greater recalcitrance to control and discipline, and attract violence rather than deterring it. There is also a growth of politically motivated disorder, planned and organized.

"The people that indulge in public disorder apply a strategy in pursuing their aims more so than they did before. Public disorder in my younger day was very spontaneous. There wasn't a master plan. I'm not contributing to the conspiracy theory, but it does invite certain political activists, who will enjoin the initiatives in the main. The miners' strike is a perfect example. You've got to be alert to the possibility of public disorder, it has a greater place in the priority of things now. Your intelligence-gathering has to be sharper, to recognize the possibilities of something developing into public disorder. With the gymnastics of the city government here holding public meetings, all of them are a vehicle for disorder."

"Disorder is more frequent, more serious, and more confused. The primary thing in which it has become different is that people's attitudes towards being well behaved have somehow changed. There are less inhibitions among people to express themselves in a vigorous and violent way. There is a restlessness about, certainly in this community. Our county, the rolling hills which you came down through—we hear a deal about inner-city problems, but there's a small version of the same problem in almost every hamlet or town in this area. We've had policewomen attacked at night on their own. We've had an attempted rape of a policewoman in uniform, an unthinkable thing. We've even had in our cathedral city,——, that ancient Domesday town, restless youngsters who invade the precinct.

And weave a fear, yes, fear, unease in people's minds, when they dress unconventionally, act unconventionally. I mean they go walk around with their life-saving apparatus on, their earphones and ghetto blasters, and they expect the policemen to solve that misbehaviour! Well, he's not an environmental officer, he doesn't even have that power. At one time he could say to a youngster, 'Cut it out!' But now you get a lot of lip back from the youngster, and the youngster goes home and complains to his mum. That officer will get a super-intendent on his back, for a complaint against the police.''

''The scale and nature of public disorder has changed. I know in past history we've been through cycles of very serious disorder ... We've seen in recent years cars being overturned and set on fire. We saw most unexpected savagery in St Pauls. So it's become more violent, increased in scale, increased in sensitivity politically. It's a much too complicated social phenomenon for me to even attempt to explain, except I think if you try to pin it down to race or unemployment you're being much too narrow. There are much more subtle factors ... A challenge to authority. Questioning of authority comes at a much earlier stage now. It's fine provided you have the built-in self-discipline to live with. But, even in driving behaviour, we're much more aggressive. We're becoming a much more aggressive society in every way.''

''It's changed for a variety of reasons. One is that violence, without any doubt, is much more pervasive in the media ... In news pro-grammes twenty years ago the same message would be conveyed without the gratuitous demonstrations of violence. There's no doubt that the senses are deadened by continual exposure to something. And if you go into a video shop and see the nature of the videos that can be borrowed—they play on people's basic animal instincts of sex and violence. The media do it because they make more money out of it ... People used to enjoy cock-baiting and dog-fighting. The viciousness below the surface in human beings is a lot closer than people would wish to admit.''

In response to this escalation of disorder and violence directed against them, the police have had to respond with tougher, more co-ordinated and militaristic methods of control. Chief constables are aware of the dangers of this. It becomes part of a ratchet of levels of force spiralling upwards. However, chiefs feel this path was forced upon them. They are unanimous in believing that the more forceful methods of riot control developed by the police were purely reactive and inevitable, given the greater problems of disorder they faced. The traditional British police philosophy of 'winning by appearing to lose' remains paramount. But the level of force that constituted a 'minimum force' response has been pushed upwards reluctantly but necessarily.

The police story of how they have been forced, step by step, down a road they did not want to follow is indicated by these accounts:

"I would like to take issue with some of the things that you have written on this. In some of the things I have seen in your writing you develop a sort of scenario where the police have been tooling up, to use John Alderson's phrase, tooling up. I just can't see it that way. I describe it like this. You can identify various milestones along the way. Probably the first significant milestone was 1976, the time of the first Notting Hill riot, following the Carnival. We saw the terrifying spectacle of policemen having to pick up dustbin lids to defend themselves against really quite a furious barrage of bottles and stones. Really, as a reaction to that, the police thought, well, we'd better have shields. And I can remember the training which was given at the time, which was very, very definite in indoctrinating constables in the notion that these were for defence only, they were not to be regarded as offensive tools but just to protect them. That was drilled into them, and actually it has left us with a legacy of a mental attitude which is quite inconvenient now in many ways, the defensive mentality. And then was the first time they were actually deployed, in 1977 in Lewisham, in I think a good cause. Then we go to 1980 and again we have this in Bristol, the unedifying spectacle of constables virtually leaving the centre of the place undefended. Much to the discontent of traders and so on. And there was a lot of agonized thinking. This great preoccupation to retain the traditional image, the introduction of reinforced ordinary policemen's helmets, and a little more beefing-up in training. And then, of course, 1981 was the trauma of petrol bombs. As a defensive reaction to that, the introduction of flame-proof overalls and all the rest of it. You may not have intended this, but the impression has been given by you that the police had a conscious policy of tooling up. Whereas in fact it has always been a reluctant, incremental reaction to a developing situation ... Beefing up of mutual aid and the raising of our own capability was put in very strict juxtaposition with an intensification of our efforts in reducing the conditions which produce riot. The analysis was that, really, the many problem estates are the seed-beds of trouble, and therefore we had to develop a sensible strategy in relation to estate policing ... The thinking has always been dual in character:

you have the capability to deal with violence when it breaks out, but work like mad to stop it happening. You've got to run these two things in tandem, because it must be a matter of some criticism of the police if they can't protect people against arson, rape, and looting."

"It has occurred because we have responded to violent situations. It must be Notting Hill that sparked all this off, 1976. Because if you go back to the Grosvenor Square riots, they were the first major test of my career. I don't want to go back to riots of a long time ago—1919, when the soldiers were called out, and that sort of thing. But looking back at the last thirty years in which I have served, we had the Grosvenor Square issue where, on the Continent, CS gas was being used and baton-charging, and all that sort of thing. And somehow the Met. police held Grosvenor Square, albeit there were problems with it. And in Red Lion Square, albeit that somebody was killed, it was still nothing much to worry about. But you started moving into an industrial dispute area and this certainly became very, very violent. 1972, Saltley, was the first major defeat for the police for a long, long time. We had to respond to violence. Street violence. The odd thing is, in 1959 they never got reported—we had race riots in Nottingham and, if you read the history of the police, there's nothing said about it at all. But the race riots in St Anne's in Nottingham quickly subsided, they didn't lead us to react to violence because it wasn't necessary, it went away. The recent riots are totally different. They're not blacks versus whites. Also there are industrial disputes. And somebody has decided they will have a go at the police for whatever motives. The police feel it's their job to uphold law and order and I'm sure that's right. There's nothing terribly new in what the police have done in trying to control industrial disputes. If you go back to the 1920s . . . my father was arrested for assault for throwing a brick at police officers at a colliery dispute. And to bring it up to date, my son, who is now a policeman, had a brick thrown at him at the same coalpit during the miners' strike! But the level and scale of violence now has been such that we've just had to respond. It might seem pretty heavy-handed to some people but it was inevitable."

"It's not a good thing for the public to see their police officers in a visor, with a big truncheon and shield. Not a good thing, it doesn't do the image of the police service any good. Indeed I was on the General Purposes Committee of ACPO during the time of the riots, and we strenuously resisted bringing in these NATO-type helmets. Our first step was to have a reinforced helmet, to keep the image of the constable. That didn't last very long, and we were forced down the line of being more sophisticated. It's quite terrifying when you see fifty officers advancing with shields and visors, but it was a necessary step."

"The way in my early days we policed things like the Lord Mayor's show was much less professional, a bit amateurish really. What you did have was a nice orderly crowd, whether it was the Coronation or whatever, you didn't have threats of extremism and terrorism in those days. The clever, the shrewd, the man with wise police experience was told to go to a certain point in the street where the procession passed. Even in those early days, '47, '48, '49, we had the Jewish and Mosleyite row going on in the East End. But you could stand as a police officer and humour the crowd. You could bring the children to the front so there wouldn't be too much pushing and you chatted to them. Most events really, 95 per cent are the sightseers and 5 per cent are the sights. Now, if you can regulate that 95 per cent in a friendly affable way, you don't need a machine-gun, like they believe they need in Northern Ireland with their soldiers. Because the average member of the public, when Mr Bobby says, 'Stand there!' or 'Hold back!', he does just that. There's no physical contact ... There's this unthinking view which you've proposed about the militaristic drift. Yes, some of the developments in the early days in '68 in Grosvenor Square, blokes like Ken Newman, we all saw there had to be a change. Because the static role of the police officer had to match the more mobile role of the disorderlies. I don't mean by that just the processions. This was the days of Tariq Ali, the student revolution as it was called. It came over from France with, what was the German's name, Danny the Red ... [R.R.: Cohn-Bendit] Something like that. It was quite obvious that we were exposing police officers to health and safety risks. It happened in 1974 with the miners' strike. There's legislation to provide protective clothing for workers. Now the police officer's work-place is the street. Nobody complains about him having a motor-cycle crash helmet. But some of them, the unthinking, take exception to him having a safety helmet. I mean, as a young bobby, I had a safety helmet. It was designed that if somebody hit me on the head it would give me some protection. But it was overlooked that instead of hitting me on the head, they just tipped the helmet, and I would be ass over tit on the ground and my head would be bare! The police service has been pushed, not willingly gone, down this road. Every step has been reluctantly taken to respond to the escalating problem and also the escalating risk. Take the miners' strike—the year 1974—we were having problems in Essex,

Birmingham, Leicester, and other places. We took injuries, quite substantial injuries, to police officers. Take the recent miners' dispute. Again substantial casualties were taken by the police."

The development of a more co-ordinated, tougher, and more militaristic style of public order policing is viewed by chief constables as a purely defensive reaction to the escalation of violence which they have encountered. During the miners' strike of 1984–5, it was revealed as a result of the trials of miners on riot charges that the new strategy had been formally laid out in a secret document, the ACPO Tactical Options Manual, developed in the early 1980s, apparently on the model of colonial policing (Northam, 1988). The strategy in the Manual, and the secrecy with which it was shrouded (which attracted criticism from the Police Federation), was defended in similar terms as a necessary reaction.

"The Tactical Options Manual really only provides police commanders with a set of options to be more effective and efficient when dealing with disorder, without unnecessary use of force and wastage of resources. In other words, to try and put some science if you like into the business of crowd control. Basically that's what the manual is all about. How to control people who are in mass and might be gathering together with violent purpose. It not only deals with violence but peaceful demonstrations as well. The options of crowd control are equally good for a peaceful demonstration or march as they are for a violent one. It's about the science of controlling people. How to defuse a situation to try and reduce the possibility of violence. A lot of people misunderstood what the Tactical Options Manual was about. They saw it mainly as a catalogue of tactics for the police to get involved in a very much more positive role than they normally are, working in concert with shields, supports by horses or dogs, possibly supported by the use of CS or baton rounds. [R.R.: Given that there has been misunderstanding of it, would it have been better to introduce it with some consultation with police authorities or Parliament?] No! It's got nothing to do with police authorities at all. It's an operational matter ... The difficulty of informing anybody about what's in the Manual, the moment you start making it public, you reduce its effectiveness. I mean Army Joe is hardly going to discuss his tactics before he goes to war! Really, we would be crazy to come open. [R.R.: Some of it has been made public in the court cases ...] Well, they haven't actually been made public. What happened was that a certain disclosure was ordered in open court to lawyers, they made a few notes. But the actual sections were never made public. [R.R.: Weren't some sections read in the House of Commons and lodged in the library there?] No. There's a lot of mythology about this. None of the Tactical Options Manual as written has ever been made public. But, as a result of the Orgreave trial at Sheffield, certain of the principles in one or two of the sections have become known, but not in the precise form they are in the Manual necessarily. They claim they are lodged in the House of Commons library but I know nothing about them ... I don't know on whose authority they could be there. You see, it's not a Home Office document. It's a document produced by our association (ACPO). It's confidential for our own use, and the use of the police service. It was basically written to provide material for the training manuals. That's its main function. It's also a guide for those who have to plan for public order situations.''

Within the array of public order methods, one of the most contested has been the use of plastic bullets. The controversies about the Home Office decision to provide these for training purposes to those forces whose police authorities would not allow their purchase, and which led to the case involving the Northumbria Police Authority, have been described in Chapter 2. The great majority (78 per cent) of chief constables said they would be prepared, if necessary, to use plastic bullets in a riot situation. Only 13 per cent said they would not, with another 9 per cent undecided. All but one of the chiefs said they would be prepared to use plastic bullets even against the opposition of their police authority, if, in their view, the situation demanded it. (This point will be developed further in Chapter 10 on accountability.) The following are typical of the arguments used in support of the majority view:

"One response would be to wring one's hands in anguish and say how awful. The reality is you've got to respond. You've got a vicious circle. There's not a lot the police can do about it unless society changes ... I'd have to look at the real threat. If people were going to die, I'd have to say, 'Yes, use them.' [R.R.: What would you do if the chair of your police authority said you should not use baton rounds?] I'd say, 'Thanks for your advice', and carry on. Remember, we've real bullets not just baton rounds. It's a sad stage to go through, but there doesn't seem to be anything at the moment between a piece of wood and bullets. You need something in between, and, sadly, baton rounds give you another option."

"I'd have no alternative. My primary duties are to save lives. If baton rounds are the only way, the incident can't be cleared by any other means, then if they turn around and say, 'Sod those people in that building', then I'll turn around and say, 'Sod you! I'm going to use them.' [R.R.: What if the chair of your police authority told you he didn't approve of the use of baton rounds?] I'd agree with him that I don't either, but if people are dying I've got to use them."

The minority who would not use plastic bullets were not mainly the more liberally minded chiefs. Paradoxically the few objections came from those who saw plastic bullets (and other riot control hardware) as a sign of police weakness, the inability to control disorder by traditional face-to-face methods. This could be called the macho objection to plastic bullets. Real men don't need baton rounds.

"It depends on the nature of the guy who is overviewing it really. You've got to get your strategies right. You can have basic ground rules, but you've got to be more covert than overt, and you've got to have greater mobility . . . I've certainly learned my lesson here. You've got to have a tactic to meet the worst, but you don't indulge in a form of militarism. That would be counter-productive. And this is what riles me about the Metropolitan Police at the moment. They're going down a paramilitary line, and I'm a bit worried that it might explode because they've got the wherewithal to deal with the worst: armoured vehicles, plastic bullets, CS gas, they're really pursuing them. [R.R.: But most forces are equipped like that now.] Yes, but you keep it under wraps. You don't make a lot of noise about it . . . My fear is it could happen. Given another Tottenham situation I think they'll be using the plastic bullets sooner now than later . . . If you've got your tactics and strategy right you can clear crowds without the use of baton rounds . . . I'm a firm believer that it's all very well for some chief officers to make noises, but they've never had to make that decision. It's not an easy decision to make. I lean very heavily on my colleague in Northern Ireland, that if he could withdraw the baton round concept he would do it. It's too simplistic. If you'd got your strategies and tactics right, had enough mobility—I mean, our big problem in '81 here was we got into a siege mentality. It was almost like *samurai*, the old concept of battle, where you drew up lines and shot at each other . . . When they had the trouble at Handsworth and at Tottenham, we had similar trouble here. But it was all over in nine hours because we had mobility. We made it unattractive for people to gather together . . . If your intelligence is right, if your understanding of geography is right, if your divisional commanders are well trained and know precisely where the trouble spots are—because, let's face it, these people always act the same. There are certain spots where you know they're going to make a stand, so you make it unattractive for them. You clear it, very quickly. You have shock troops go in quickly. The fact of life is that some innocent people are likely to get hurt as a consequence, but I think the end justifies the means really. But you can avoid using baton rounds."

However, the majority view was that the more militaristic forms of riot control could not now be avoided. The traditional philosophy of relying on manpower alone imposed too high a burden on the personnel involved, and officers nowadays could not be expected to become cannon fodder:

"It is a duty and responsibility of me and the senior officers of this force to equip officers, to give them the training, so that they can weld themselves together into units when it is absolutely necessary for the public good to preserve tranquillity, and for your own protection. If you don't protect them, you can't go back to the business of the 1960s and early 1970s, where you've got to be seen to lose sometimes to win. That might have been a reasonable sort of philosophy at that time when it was a completely pacific period apart from one or two minor excursions. The atmosphere's changed completely. Violence has increased incredibly, so you've got to give your officers the protection they deserve ... The police are not responsible for notching up the next ratchet, what we do is try to prevent the ratchet actually happening in the first place. We don't solve anything by public order methods, I'm quite convinced of that. There are other things we have got to address, that society has to address in the community—deprivation, alienation, racism ... We won't solve these social problems with public order equipment. But we are facing the reality that public order happenings will go on, you will have more outbreaks in the difficult areas ... We would always start with traditional policing methods, but in the end you have to respond. Once missiles start coming in you can't say to the officers, 'Well, be brave chaps! Just lie down when a brick hits you and bleed comfortably and don't yell too much!' You've got to face it. If you actually get into the situation of losing as at Saltley, they get the impression that by using violence they will inevitably win. They thought they had at Tottenham, 'We were winners on the day, we gave the fuzz a good hiding.' It's a very dangerous notion. We have to have sufficient well-trained men actually in the end to curb it. Which we can do now, touch wood!''

One possible solution to the problems faced by the police, in having to maintain the bifurcated role of routine everyday policing as well as a capacity to deal with extreme public disorder, is the creation of a specialized 'third force', intermediate between police and army, geared specifically to riot control. This has been proposed by numerous influential commentators (Morris, 1985), and seems to have a fair amount of rank-and-file support. The Operational Policing Review found that 28 per cent of the police sample supported the third-force concept, though 60 per cent were against, and 12 per cent undecided. However, they found that ACPO ranks were more hostile to the idea, with 84 per cent against and only 12 per cent in favour (*Operational Policing Review*, 5: 6 (1990), 18). Of the forty chief constables I interviewed not a single one supported the third-force concept. (All were against it apart from one who was undecided.) The basic objections were that it would be hard to construct an adequate form of accountability for such a body, that it would be too expensive to keep a body in permanent readiness for what were still only sporadic outbreaks of serious disorder, and that since such a body was specifically organized for coercion it would inflame and exacerbate trouble. While most chief constables recognized the problems faced by their officers in adjusting between extremely different kinds of policing situations, they felt that experience suggested they were capable of doing this adequately. A third force was thus unnecessary, wasteful, and counter-productive.

"If you'd asked me five years ago, I'd have said yes ... I thought we were getting to the stage where it is so difficult to expect a young policeman to change his spots, from being a community-style policeman to being in defensive riot gear. You're confusing the poor guy. We found enough of that problem on the miners' strike. But I've changed my mind and I don't mind admitting I've done so. We have got to try to the bitter end to stop the pendulum ... I'm not sending my men out in strength now. I think that in itself is the beginning of the end. We get twos, and they want to be in threes, and my people put to me the business of marauding vans, which I don't mind. But I've said that the key part of this business is jolly Joey and settling things down ... The chap on his own is much more likely to get away with jolly Joey. But if there is a serious public disorder job you can very quickly swing that in.

"One of the great strengths of our set-up is that the chap who is today forming part of a PSU (Police Support Unit),[1] to deal with some violent situation, is the chap who tomorrow will be parading the high street, or in our case his village. That officer's policing philosophy will be largely influenced by his general role and he will not see himself as the great storm-trooper. A third force, and I've had the chance to see it actually working in France, the whole ethos of that force is to deal with a violent situation. It breeds a reaction in that man, no matter how well trained he is, to react violently himself. Our men are restrained a great deal by their normal policing function."

"A third force, completely separate from the ordinary police, raises very complex constitutional issues as to who controls the force and to whom it is accountable. It runs right across all our present assumptions about constitutional questions. At the moment if you want a higher level of capability in the police then you think in terms of military aid to the civil power (MACP) ... If I want MACP my first step would be to speak to the Home Secretary and say, 'Look, I can't handle this, we need a higher level of force.' He then speaks to the Secretary of State for Defence and you get the constitutional conventions about the relationship between the police and the Army. The police in the lead, giving the Army a specific task. Now, where would a third force stand in that constitutional context? ... A policeman is faced with the very salutary thought that he has to exist in this community afterwards, and that conditions what he does. A third force would have none of these inhibitions when it's brought in. I don't mind admitting I created my concept of a third force, and just created it within the police. That is the establishing of eight territorial support groups, which can be brought together to a unit of just 1,000 men. But the concept has been conceived responsibly. We're taking great care of the selection of these men, psychological profiling, and we make every effort to exclude the cowboy mentality ... We're very meticulous in the training to tell them that they're not some kind of CRS third force, but a body of people who are meant to be very versatile in their activities. They can be switched from plain clothes, targeting, surveillance, to within an hour being riot-equipped public order people, indoctrinated very strongly with ideas of minimal force. That is a better option because, unlike an independent third force, it's deployed in line with public police thinking."

All chief constables believed that they had been forced to develop more robust means of dealing with disorder. However, as with their views on crime, legal powers were seen as only a small part of the matter, a minor weapon in the police armoury at best. Only a bare majority (53 per cent) thought that the reformulation and strengthening of police powers in the Public Order Act 1986 (POA) would help the police.[2] A sizeable minority (40 per cent) felt it would not help and 7 per cent were undecided.

The majority who welcomed the POA saw it as a desirable reformulation of police powers in the public order field, which also gave the police some specific new powers to deal with situations which had hitherto proved problematic. In particular, the new offences of disorderly conduct and criminal trespass which the Act introduced were considered helpful, as were the enhanced powers to regulate marches and meetings:

"I hope the Act will help. Otherwise I've wasted the past two years of my life! I spent a lot of time working with the Home Office advising them of the police aspects, trying to come up with what I thought was a balance. This was to try and ensure that the police were not given draconian powers, to avoid pushing the police into the centre of political confrontations so that they would be seen as government tools, and as far as I possibly could retain a sort of historical balance that we now have and not let the National Union of Mineworkers' dispute push us into something that would change the nature of our relationship with the public. At the same time, what I also tried to do was to allow the police to intervene at an earlier stage in public disorder, so that by using disorderly conduct—say, for example, you have a football match and you have someone who is obviously going to generate violence—then you can at any rate go in and say you have to stop that. And then if he carried on you take him quickly away from the scene. This will prevent him generating violent confrontation which would require use of the other sections. So I hoped in that way to give the police more discretion, and to try if I could to prevent the policeman having to bluff . . . The problem is the public call the police to deal with molestation and when they get there there is nothing they can do so there is a tendency for the policeman to try and bluff his way out, 'Clear off or else!' Once upon a time, perhaps in the 1930s when we were a more law-abiding society, that would have been accepted. The policeman's word would have been taken as an authoritative one and he might well have cleared off. Now this is not likely to happen, and the policeman finds himself pushed into a position of having to do something. And this has resulted in unnecessary confrontations where the policeman's bluff has been called and he hasn't really had the legal powers to actually deal with it. By producing a piece of legislation that actually did allow policemen to intervene to maintain the quality of life I hope that we have actually solved the problem.''

"Certainly the new offence disorderly conduct will broaden our ability to deal with the bottom end of the scale. It will be helpful to have advance notice of processions and that sort of thing. That has always been a problem for us, and it will impose a discipline hopefully on some of the groups. I'm uncomfortable about the injection at the last minute of what really is criminal trespass. I argued against it and see that as a problem. But in general terms, the codification of the thing, the clarification of riot, unlawful assembly, I see as an advantage, helping us rather than hindering.''

While the majority of chiefs welcomed the Act in general, nearly half adopted a form of legal scepticism. They felt that legal powers were, at most, of marginal significance for police practice in this area:

"It helps clarify certain aspects of public order law. I don't think it will make a great deal of difference in reality because if people are going to riot or come out and demonstrate they're going to come out and riot or demonstrate irrespective of what the law says. I mean the common law has been pretty able to cope with most situations over the years. Whilst this gives a few more powers and does tidy up a few loose ends, if people choose not to comply with those powers then the situation will be exactly the same. The problem is not defects in the law. A Saturday night disturbance even, where you've got a dozen people involved and two or three policemen together, is a very confused situation even then. It is unlikely that the officers will all see exactly the same things, and that is used by the defence to try and discredit the prosecution ... Riot is not an easy offence to prove and you are not likely to get evidence which is totally consistent.''

"The Public Order Bill is laying out the rules of engagement with greater definity and less argument now. There are parts of the Bill that you ought to know we are not too happy about, we've got some misgivings. You see, a lot of these things sound very attractive on paper or whatever but can create a lot of legal tangles. The lawyers are going to have a field day. Somebody said 'Let's start by killing all the lawyers.' Who was it? Richard III? But no, it rationalizes the rules of engagement a bit more, but it's not going to go through with great ease because people see their fundamental democratic rights being eroded. A phrase that's used with glib frequency, but they don't really understand that those democratic rights were never really there in the first place anyway.''

Those who were undecided also expressed explicit scepticism about the capacity of law to resolve fundamental problems of policing and politics:

> "I think it's a bit of 'suck it and see'. There are tools there that can be useful, but it might take us into more political controversy which we are always trying to avoid. I've had examples of this when I was ACC in——. The firemen were on strike, and wanted to march on the busiest Saturday in December through the town up a one-way road against the flow of traffic. I wrote to them on behalf of the chief constable and said it was against our advice because it would not only cause tremendous disruption—which was probably what they were after—but might cause the breach of the peace in people who were frustrated in doing what they always do that Saturday of the year. They wrote to the chairman of the highways who gave them written permission to do it. I wasn't in a position to do anything other than to keep talking. Eventually I persuaded them they wouldn't be able to do it physically, it would break up their march and the buses that come down here would clog up the whole highway, and they'd spill out and so would be defeating their purpose and be broken up. And members could well get clobbered. So on that ground I managed to get them to change the route. It would be nice to have a law which said, 'I don't care what you, the chairman of the highway authority, think, as the chief constable I am saying no and these are my reasons!' But people would be out to dent that."

The Miners' Strike

As has already been mentioned, the 1984–5 miners' strike was a profoundly traumatic experience for police officers at all levels. The prolonged dispute witnessed scenes of violent conflict between pickets and police which were without parallel in recent British experience. They had certainly never occurred before in the television era, and their regular depiction on news bulletins stoked the heat of controversy. The massive nation-wide policing operation, co-ordinated by ACPO through the National Reporting Centre at Scotland Yard, led to accusations that a national police force had effectively been created. Altogether the police appeared to many to have become direct tools of government policy. The strike represented a high point in party political conflict about policing.[3] Although I asked no questions directly about the strike, almost all the chief constables volunteered their interpretations, often at great length.

The generally accepted view was that the strike had profoundly damaged police–public relations, although it was hoped that the lost ground would be recovered in time. It had also changed the image of the police in an unfortunate direction by regular public exposure of police in riot-control paraphernalia.

"The miners' strike was a big set-back to the image of the police as classless. We were seen once again in the Tonypandy role, or back to Peterloo, or even worse. That we were agents of the State. I don't think we were all entirely insensitive to it. I made a big play about this during the strike, where I applied the law as fairly as I could. That is one of the reasons why I avoided the omnibus charges like riot because they are very draconian. They bring up notions about the judge in red robes and being deported. The Tolpuddle Martyrs. I tried very hard to police it with empathy, a great deal of patience. Perhaps too much patience. I know very well I was criticized for perhaps being a little moderate. [R.R.: Who criticized you?] Well, the comment was put about, I couldn't put a name to it. But I know there was a suggestion ... I wouldn't like to have dealt with South Yorkshire. It was a dreadful thing to any chief to have to face. I know we didn't issue universal stop policies but we were firm and made it clear we wouldn't tolerate breaches of the law. On either side of me I had forces with a very firm line, but also their mining communities gave a very clear indication where they stood. I stood in the half-way house. But, as the chief constable, finally you must stand alone."

"The miners' strike did more harm for police–public relations than many people would be prepared to admit to. For all sorts of reasons, but the principal one is that people got used day after day for almost a year to scenes of police officers in riot gear armed with truncheons facing the people. They saw police officers being injured, they saw police officers inflicting injuries and it's commonplace now. As a result my fear is that the whole perception of police–public relations has changed in people's minds. What only a few short years ago would have been regarded as totally unacceptable behaviour is now tolerated. Even in a lovely quiet area like mine ... There would have been heavy criticism in years gone by if we'd gone into a football ground wearing safety helmets and carrying shields. Now nobody comments because they say, 'Oh yeah! We got used to seeing this.'"

Several chief constables pointed out that they had considerably ambivalent feelings during the strike. Given their working-class backgrounds, they had identified with the plight of the striking miners. Unfortunately, the latter had been led astray by militant, politically motivated leaders. The police had been forced to turn against people with whom they had sympathy in order to protect the rule of law:

"Being a Welshman originally, one has got some difficulties in the miners' strike, I have to tell you that ... My father was a miner ... you've got to realize my background. My uncle was a miner. My father had to go as a butty boy till he broke away from it and bettered himself considerably. Consequently his—although it doesn't really matter—his politics, he was a socialist ... I felt sympathetic towards the miners' cause. I didn't feel a great deal of confidence in who was appointed by Mrs T. to go and ruin the mineworkers' industry. And I felt sympathetic to them because what was happening was not in their best interests ... I'm not saying I'm a socialist, don't get me wrong, I never indulge in politics. But what I'm saying is the whole thing was handled badly. I mean by the then chairman of the National Coal Board (NCB). The things he said about the police, you've only got to go back: 'A couple of lame-brained American cops could have sorted it out in two minutes.' Didn't appeal to me at all! McGregor is an old man and wouldn't have been able to destroy the strike without the police. It's a very difficult topic to talk about, the miners' strike. You see, Scargill launched himself—he didn't act in a demo-cratic way in the interests of the miners. He brought the strike on in the first place. Nottingham weren't supporting him, and in an anti-democratic way he spread the strike. And the only way he could do it was within the worst manifestation of this very, very hard-Left Militant Tendency attitude which prevails in Manchester, Mersey-side, and everywhere else, where they use intimidation ... The reason the police became embroiled in it was because he sent his insurgents into Nottinghamshire who had voted to work, to try and stop them from working. Now the police went, once Charles McLachlan [then the chief constable of Nottinghamshire] had called in for support. He got support because they were behaving in a reprehensible way, using violence towards other mineworkers going about their business. From there on in—talk about ratchets—it escalated and escalated. But at the end of the day the police ruined the flying pickets. A phenomenon which came with the Shrewsbury thing [the building workers' dispute of 1974], where you've got this flying picket—go in, damage, do all that kind of thing, and clear off. Which is not on at all! I mean, picketing and trade disputes in themselves are at common law illegal. They are only legalized by certain amounts of legislation which allow you to picket in certain ways. But the basis of actually stopping anybody going about his own business in his own legitimate way, is illegal in common law, the British law, that was the basic theory.''

The role conflict experienced in the miners' strike, given their social origins, was acute for some chief constables and their families.

"My other lad, who's got two degrees, also joined the police. His probation was at Orgreave. They threw bricks at him in my home village, and there was a riot. His wife just said: 'You leave the police or I leave you.' So he left the police.''

Despite their realization of the damage done to the police image, and their ambivalence about the issues in the strike itself, almost all the chiefs regarded the police operation as justified and necessary law enforcement. Contrary to the accusations made against them, especially by the Left and the Labour Party, the police had acted as impartial upholders of order. As such they had the invidious role of being 'piggy in the middle', attacked by all sides.

"I see the police service very much in peacetime as one of the strong pillars of democracy, trying to ensure that society doesn't become destabilized, so that the democratic process can work through the democratic process. The classic example was the miners' dispute. Unpalatable as it was for me to commit my resources to activity outside the county. That really brought home to me that we were there to make sure that government—and it wouldn't have mattered which government—a government properly elected, was not brought down, or a country's base ruined because of a group of people who wanted to bring about their way by unlawful means. This moves the police role out of straightforward simplistic stopping crime, to showing the strength of the police service as a pillar of society in the law. In practice, though, some of the things that we did, I must admit, we went to the boundary of the law. The Dartford Tunnel issue. We went right to the boundaries of the law and probably went beyond the spirit of the law. We never really knew what went on at that check-point. If people were just being advised to turn round and they then interpreted that as, 'I was told to turn round'—then we may not have transgressed, just giving advice ... Now as far as the National Reporting Centre, again so much political mischief has been made out of this! A quite sensible arrangement under the mutual aid section in the Police Act. Probably the mistake we made was siting it in London, but that was just for convenience's sake. You know, it does become the centre of communications. And usually the Met. can push somebody out of their office and create a space. So it was set up there. But you know, I had regular discussions with my police authority members here and made everything very plain to them ... Several times I was asked to provide by the NRC and I said no. My requirements within the force were much greater at that moment in time, and no one could direct me. The pressure was that you've got to look at the time when perhaps you yourself might need mutual aid. And the fact that you had turned down a request might be remembered ... It's knock for knock. We were regarded by many people as the proper organization to deal with this particular national problem, and therefore we had to come together to deal with it."

"The miners' strike could have been ended a damn sight quicker than it was. We were left in the middle for far too long ... The speech by Gerald Kaufman [then Labour's Shadow Home Secretary] when the miners' strike was on frankly made me feel ill ... condemning the police as an invading army, bully boys, etc. It was really a vitriolic attack ... I expressed the view during the miners' strike that we were left in the middle in a sort of criminal law situation that should have been resolved civilly."

The charge about which the chief constables clearly felt most sensitive was that the National Reporting Centre (NRC), operated by ACPO as a co-ordinating mechanism for allocating mutual aid between forces, had in fact been an embryonic national force, controlled by the Government.[4] Many chiefs emphasized that the NRC had merely acted as a clearing-house for registering forces' need for aid and the availability of support units in other forces. No compulsion was involved, and no government pressure, although the Home Office was briefed regularly about developments. Chief constables were perfectly free to refuse requested resources, and did so when their own local needs were thought to be paramount. A common claim was that the success of the voluntary mutual aid operation had prevented the establishment of a national force. A national police force would have had to be created by the Government, had the chiefs not been able to co-operate spontaneously. Centralized co-ordination was the price of the survival of local policing, according to the orthodox view:

"If we had failed on the miners' strike we would have been regionalized within two years, and then become a national force ... Mutual aid was not requested by the Home Office. I declined to supply more than six PSUs [Police Support Units] during the miners' strike because I couldn't police the county. There are other forces that I felt could stand a larger share. I might be wrong, but I did refuse. Twice I refused to supply the numbers they wanted.''

"There was no suggestion of us [the NRC] telling people what they would send. It was a question of going and almost, cap in hand, begging them. There was no direct operational responsibility by the president [of ACPO] through NRC. You've got to look back at the history of how that grew. Because what used to happen originally was we based it on regions. And we found that the chappie—usually one of the senior chief constables—took the job if there was trouble, he would co-ordinate mutual aid in the region. But some regions were well off and some weren't, so we had to go over on a national basis. We did have chief constables in the NUM dispute who, for very good reasons sometimes, were reluctant to send officers. In some instances we aided by sending men to them, and knocking them off the supply list altogether. But most forces sent to others at some time. For instance, right in the middle of the NUM dispute, Sussex had a problem with a party conference, and Nottinghamshire ended up sending to them. And when the Met. was in the state opening of Parliament, right in the middle of the dispute, the Met. went off the list for provisional officers ... So it was a facilitative rather than operational role for the ACPO president as head of the NRC.''

"The miners' strike showed the need for uniformity and a united approach. It's for ACPO to ensure that the uniformity is there from a voluntary participation, rather than bring about a national police force. The great fear, of course, is that a national police force would become too politically motivated. If we can get our efficiency from agreement between the forty-three forces—as I like to think we do—the miners' strike indicated how we could go forward together, and I ran the NRC for a time. Provided we can continue on these lines the need for a national police force will fade. The need for a national police force was pushed back by the way we responded to the miners' strike.''

While showing that there was no need for a national police force, the strike also demonstrated to many chiefs the potential dangers of local authority control. Had police authorities been empowered to give operational instructions, many would have disrupted the proper impartial policing of the strike for partisan political reasons or parochial local motives:

"Following the 1981 disorders, up and down the country, every chief constable has seen the light and the mutual aid system has been refined. A force like mine has a commitment to produce so many PSUs in the event of national disorder so I have to have a certain percentage of my officers trained in public disorder ... Generally speaking, apart from the weekend flashpoints, all this training would not be totally necessary to this county. Our rate-payers feel aggrieved, and they did feel aggrieved in the NUM dispute of course. Because we just had two or three pits with problems. Most of our men were going outside the county ... Ordinary, traditional policing goes out the window, particularly with young men, they tend to adopt the gung-ho, altogether lads, over the top approach, and we're against that in——shire ... In the NUM dispute I know, as indeed many other chief constables know, that if our police committees had had their way no policeman would have left——shire. And this would have been true up and down the country ... And you and I have views about the NUM dispute, but it would have ended up that the country would have been in a dreadful state ... Because in the main the committees make political decisions, they've got to be hung out to dry on ideology. Decisions that are influenced by the areas they are serving, which are not necessarily in the best interests of the country as a whole. Plus the fact, and this goes without saying, that they are not professional in the way they look at policing."

The general view was that the miners' strike had been policed in a nationally co-ordinated way by the separate police forces, facilitated by the NRC under ACPO's direction. This was reluctantly done by the police as the only way to satisfy their professional law enforcement obligations. It had averted rather than precipitated the formation of a national police force. The operation had not been directed by the Government but was a voluntary police initiative of a non-partisan kind. Forces were not compelled to participate more than they wished.

One significant exception to the national co-ordinated policing operation was freely admitted to by several chiefs. This underlines its voluntary nature, while at the same time it implies the conditional nature of the 'spontaneous' police co-operation. The Government clearly kept an anxious eye on developments and was inclined to intervene if arrangements did not appear satisfactory. One significant opting-out from the NRC operation occurred in Wales. At the outset of the dispute the chief constables of the four Welsh forces (most of whom were in fact Englishmen) agreed that it was desirable to keep the dispute Welsh. Using 'foreign' English police to control Welsh pickets would have exacerbated tensions and proved counter-productive. They also resolved to forgo the use of specialized riot equipment, even at the risk of suffering heavier police casualties in the short run. This example of the 'winning by appearing to lose' philosophy received the approval of the Welsh local police authorities, but was viewed with suspicion by the NRC and the Police Federation. The example demonstrates that forces could resist central direction, but that there was pressure for them not to do so:

"Right at the beginning of the dispute, the four Welsh chief constables got together at my instigation because I felt that we had to do something here that wasn't going to be done anywhere else. We had to keep the thing Welsh. I've been here long enough to realize that was important. That if we started importing English policemen to Wales it would be a rallying call and would cause us immense problems. So you have to give us credit for being a bit cunning about that. And at no time during the dispute did we use anybody other than our own people. Had I had to bring them in I would have used the other people on the streets and not on the pickets ... Right at the beginning of the dispute I thought we had a number of responsibilities and discussed them with my chairman, a Labour Party chairman. First of all we have the responsibility in law to ensure that any man who wishes to withdraw his labour and to picket can do so, and I'll defend that to the last inch. But I also have a responsibility to ensure that people who wish to go to work can do so peacefully. In addition I have the responsibility to ensure the dispute does not impinge on any other organization through threats or intimidation, who are likely to lose their jobs ... [R.R.: The steel workers?] Yes. And so, during the steel strike we were enemy No. 1, to them during the coal strike we were the greatest thing since sliced bread. So everything that we did I told the committee about, but they didn't want to know! They sat on the fence, because they were not in favour of the strike. The miners weren't generally, but they came out to support their union ... It was a very lonely time for us because we were never quite sure whether we were doing it right or wrong ... On one occasion we had to climb into the bloody awful riot gear, because we were really under such severe attack. But we had a deliberate policy of not using that as well, and that went well with my local politicians of course ... When the National Council For Civil Liberties came here to talk to my authority they pressed hard about why the force did not allow the pickets to talk to the men on the buses. One of my young members from the mining community said, 'If you'd done that here there would have been a bloody riot, so it was a sensible decision on the part of the police' ... Because of the philosophies that we policed it with, it didn't get out of hand, it wasn't a *cause célèbre* ... because we policed in Wales with Welshmen who understood the animal they were policing. We were able to cool it a lot of the time, that's the art of being a good policeman ... We had to use our support groups for short periods, but the local policemen could grumble and blame them ... They say 'We're not like that, we're the lovely ones.' That's being the cunning policeman."

"To start with, much to the annoyance of the National Reporting Centre in London, the Welsh forces treated it as a Welsh coalfield problem as opposed to a national or local one. We had to be as flexible within Wales, as mobile as the pickets were ... It was touch and go whether we called in aid from elsewhere, but had we done so it would have been an immortality I don't particularly want. Because in the valleys they still talk of 1912, 1926, Tonypandy, and all that went with it, as if it were yesterday. So I think we succeeded by not calling in the English police or the London police. In this force we had 132 officers injured but we did not resort to riot gear of any kind. We policed it throughout in our own gear. Right from the word 'go', here we were masters of the propaganda war—whatever the NUM did, we trumped it one way or the other ... We were forever sending our men across the borders. Not for the record—we were never charged up by my colleagues by the way—but we must not tell the politicians that! The trouble is we live in an age where no publicity equals no problems equals no extra resources! ... Once you've committed your police authority to finance a CRS-type squad or called in officers from elsewhere, the temptation to use those resources to justify your original decision to call them in is great. Not for the record, I think that may have happened with some of my colleagues in the miners' dispute ... I had the Federation in about the police injuries. I said, 'Look, this is what we are dealing with, I don't want to call men in. These are my problems. Yes, I deplore the fact that police were injured, but, long term, it's better.' We had this discussion round the table, and they went along with it, they accepted."

However, while the official version of events, which denies any central pressure to conform to the national policing operation, was maintained by all chiefs during the recorded interviews, it is clear that such interventions did occur in fact. For the most part, the extent of spontaneous co-ordination was sufficient to pre-empt any central direction. The above quotes themselves indicate, however, that the NRC was unhappy about the Welsh opting out of its activities. Presumably, had things got out of hand, it might have brought some pressure to bear. Beyond the Welsh example of independence, I was told anecdotes outside the formal recorded interview which confirmed the existence of overt central pressure when voluntarism did not produce the required goods.

It was rumoured that at least one chief constable had resigned prematurely because of feeling Home Office opprobrium as a result of less than whole-hearted co-operation with the NRC, and consequently that there were no further career prospects for him in the police. One chief officer related in my presence a story concerning another nationally prominent chief constable telephoning chief officers in adjacent forces to tell them that if they failed to mount road-blocks in their areas to stop pickets reaching pits in his area, he would send his own men across the county line to do it himself. The following is a reconstruction (noted immediately after the event) of an off-the-record example of direct Government intervention offered to me by one chief constable after the formal interview had ended:

"During the miners' strike, Sir——[a senior Home Office civil servant] attended a meeting of chief constables with a personal message from the Prime Minister. She was convinced that a secret communist cell around Scargill was orchestrating the strike in order to bring down the country. The fact that the police could not prove this conspiracy existed was because of the weakness of our intelligence-gathering. She wanted us to set up a secret Public Order Intelligence Unit, to infiltrate and monitor groups and activities which threatened order. This could be separate from Special Branch or CID, though formed from their personnel. To my surprise and horror, instead of telling her that was rubbish, my senior colleagues all agreed to do it. It's been set up in London, I believe, but I've been frozen out because I showed my shock. [R.R.: I thought Special Branch already did monitor such groups for this purpose.] No. It only looks at subversive groups and activities. This was to look at legitimate groups like the NUM, to gather intelligence re public order."

Altogether, it seems clear from the recorded comments, as well as those offered outside the formal interviews, that the miners' strike did represent a high point in the national co-ordination of policing public order—although similar developments had occurred in earlier industrial disputes (Morgan, 1987). The absence of sustained government direction, and perhaps the creation of an overt national police force, was averted by the coincidence of the policing operation organized by ACPO with the Government's wishes. What is clear beyond doubt is the complete transformation of police public order capacity during the 1980s.''

Notes

1. Police Support Units (PSUs) are the molecules of the mutual aid system as it has been refined since 1974 to provide a means for rapidly mobilizing support for forces under pressure. Each PSU comprises 23 officers (an inspector, 2 sergeants, and 20 constables) who are trained for public order duties, but normally do routine policing at local level. They can be readily mobilized when necessary to provide aid in areas where problems develop. For fuller accounts of changes in public order methods, and the debates about these, see Jefferson, 1987, 1990; Waddington, 1987, 1988, 1991; Northam, 1988; McCabe *et al.*, 1988.
2. The Public Order Act is described and assessed from different standpoints in Smith, 1987; Sherr, 1989.
3. Detailed accounts of the policing of the strike, and the debates this gave rise to, can be found in Fine and Millar, 1985; Scraton and Thomas, 1985; McCabe, Wallington *et al.*, 1988. The policing operation is compared to previous industrial disputes in Geary, 1985, and Morgan, 1987. The effect on the rank-and-file police is conveyed vividly by Graef, 1989.
4. A cogent case for this view is mounted in Loveday, 1986.

9 The Social Philosophy of Chief Constables

The characteristic social philosophy of chief constables has already been implied in their analyses of increasing crime and disorder. The majority (especially of county chiefs) share an ideal conception of a harmonious, morally integrated society with a stable and accepted structure of authority. This is widely, although not universally, assumed to have been the reality in earlier times, at any rate in the areas they police. But these traditional rural idylls are seen as being threatened by the cosmopolitan and permissive culture of modernity which is spreading out from metropolitan pockets to engulf the whole society. The result is general upward pressure on rates of crime and disorder, and an aggravation of policing problems. In this chapter, I will examine more closely the chief constables' views on society outside the police, as the context within which they see the police operating.

The following account sets up the model of a harmonious, integrated, orderly society which most chief constables seem to hold as an ideal benchmark for assessing social trends:

"We have a responsibility here in counties like this. They set up a datum, a norm, from which others can see how far they have drifted. There is a loyalty and an integrity in this part of the world which is way above any other I have experienced ... Policemen here differ in style. It's still a very personalized county. They know very well that should they upset people it's going to get back to senior people much more quickly than in an impersonal environment ... In a right-wing county ... it is still a case of poets and peasants, you know. I mean, in this county now people are still very confused whether they should invite the local sergeant into the kitchen for a mug of tea or into the drawing-room for a gin and tonic, still have to wrestle with that one ... There is still a very distinct class barrier in a shire county. But on top of that we have a much more cosmopolitan society. Whereas, before, one occasionally saw among a number of churches perhaps one Roman Catholic church, now you see not only the odd synagogue, but now even here in——you find mosques, temples, and people. It's very sad to see them not integrating hardly at all ... In a county like this you will find deference paid to the rank of a person, I mean socially."

The common (though not universal) social benchmark was this idealized rural haven of a society which was harmonious, despite social inequalities, because all knew and accepted the social order and their place within it. This was becoming threatened by the development of divisions in society based on attributes other than a shared sense of rank. The result was confusion and conflict, rootless cosmopolitanism where no one knew or accepted their place in the scheme of things. Policing itself suffered as a consequence, becoming less personal in style and more a business of bureaucratic regulation.

Social Harmony and Social Divisions

Almost half the chief constables (48 per cent) believed that Britain was no longer the harmonious society it once had a reputation for being. Only 38 per cent thought it still was a fundamentally harmonious society. Another 7 per cent felt it was not possible to come to any overall conclusion: some aspects were still harmonious, others not. Finally, 7 per cent challenged the premiss that Britain ever had been a harmonious society; this was at best a myth based on little knowledge of British history.

The most common view was that Britain was no longer as harmonious as it had been. To those who held this view, this was usually a matter for regret.

"Looking back and remembering a more stable society thirty years ago, there wasn't the heightened public disorder problems as at present, there wasn't unemployment. There wasn't the materialism there is today. When I first got married and moved into my first house, the front room and one bedroom were empty and unoccupied for the first three years. We decided not to buy things unless we could afford them. That's not just my native Scottish heritage coming out! It was the basic canniness of people of that generation. Now today, in any walk of life, young people seem to want all the materialistic things whether they can pay for them or not. That has a bearing on people's dissatisfaction levels.''

"There is a whole range of changes in the fabric of society which has contributed towards different attitudes towards the police and authority. Totally different attitudes to family life, towards religion. The attitude of educationalists. When I went to school in Wiltshire I went in a very structured environment. I wasn't taught to think of great wider issues. I was taught arithmetic, and when I went up into grammar school I had two periods of history. Now that's all changed, and with it the general attitude to authority. When I was a PC in uniform walking along the Strand, the presence of the uniform was enough to carry me through the vast majority of situations. Nowadays, that doesn't apply. It was partly that, after a major world war, people went away and came back with a different attitude. I suppose the biggest thing was when they invented the Pill and that changed our morality. People have obviously been taught to think for themselves and have a wider perspective. Far greater than I ever did, and I had a very good grammar school education to the age of 18. But it was very narrow ... Generally our relationships with young people are much more taut and tense than they ever were. Certainly the ethnic minorities present special problems, there's no doubt about that. There's a different understanding. And between the young ethnics and the older ethnics there's a bit of a gap as well ... A lot of things in society have changed for the worse. When I was a young detective in the East End of London there were a lot of problems— poverty, and everything. But there was a closeness about the communities. Little Johnny was here, and your mum and dad were there, your grandmother was around the corner. All that sort of thing. Nowadays, we've got a much more mobile sort of society. A lot of our problems are caused because in our development areas most of the people have come up from London into a totally alien environment. There isn't the cohesiveness within the villages. A lot more single parents. A lot more youngsters in difficulties.''

"It has been a harmonious society. But the big change in my lifetime, especially in policing terms, was the influx of the coloured population back in the 1960s. That was one of the fundamental changes I've seen. The other fundamental change is that we've become a more affluent society. What I would have regarded as the working class, of which I was one when I joined the police, that working class has now become very, very blurred. There is much more money around for people to do their own thing."

The social changes which have eroded the harmonious and stable structure of authority are not all undesirable. Freedom and affluence are benefits even to the police, although they make the task of policing harder:

"There's more mobility, a better based education which gives people a better knowledge of their rights. This is not wrong, in fact it is correct. But it makes it difficult for us in the transition period. The younger officers don't see the problem, but the older ones do ... Society has changed so much. You get people living here from all over the world. We've got a different mix, and it's a difficult absorption process."

"Disorder is a penalty we have to pay for the balancing out of society—there are not quite such distinct financial classes as there used to be ... The disharmony is arising not because there is still a broad span of class in society, but because those that are most disadvantaged are more readily identifiable. And they do somehow have the ability to organise themselves to make themselves heard, and that creates conflict. There is a way of life now that you must be in conflict. If you are in the middle of the road you are regarded as a wet or naïve. Sitting on the fence is regarded as an unacceptable place to be. To walk in the middle of the road is somehow the most dangerous, and people are less willing to do that in the political spectrum, so we have a conflict situation. That worries me. But I do believe there is not the economic or opportunity divide there was within society in my days as a boy. For me to have got to university would have been a tremendous achievement, bearing in mind I came from a large family, had only got matric. from school, and hadn't got the background that I could wave as part of my credentials. I could do it today, I am damn sure I could, without any difficulty."

"The people you recruit today have grown up in a more liberal background. We are all conditioned by the society in which we live, and there has been a tremendous liberalization. I've always been an independent minded sort of person, and my liberal attitudes in these areas was sort of finished off at university, the time of the riots in the sixties. People have now thought about the job more, there's more genuine concern for the public ... People generally are more questioning, more liberal minded, more concerned with the individual, better informed about individual freedoms than ever they were. And therefore we continually have to justify the actions we take. As much as it might annoy us when certain individuals from the Left start to get on our backs, we *should* be asked questions and be in a position to answer ... It's a difficult period we have to go through but I am sufficiently optimistic that gradually it will get better. You know, there's a lot of talk about racial hatred and the like. But the prejudiced people are the people who are my father's generation or my generation. There isn't the prejudice amongst the youngsters that have been brought up in a multicultural and multi-coloured society. It's gradually breaking down. I have only to make any remark at all at home, and I am questioned by my 14-year-old daughter. Whether it should be feminist or racial or whatever it may be. It is good for me to have that questioning. It is becoming clear that youngsters accept colour in a different way to us. We will see ourselves through, but it will get worse before it gets better."

The most frequent image held by chief constables is thus of a society which is less harmonious than it used to be, although not all think this is unequivocally undesirable, whatever difficulties it may cause the police. However, just over a third (38 per cent) felt British society was still basically harmonious. Limited pockets of tension had been highlighted by the media and others, but predominantly it is still a stable social order as it used to be:

"The fact that communications are so much better makes society appear to be less harmonious than it was because the little local problems which always occurred now get national media attention where before they didn't. I can remember in my early days police vehicles being stolen, but that was purely a matter of local interest. The media nationally were not interested. So one gets an impression of less harmony when that is not the case. The experience in this county is that generally here is a society which lives quite harmoniously. There are bursts and bubbles here and there, neighbours fall out because of raised feelings sometimes, but this has always been the case. I happen to live in a village where I rub shoulders with farm workers, solicitors, gamekeepers, poachers, licensees, parsons, and we get along very nicely, thank you. I don't think there are any social divisions. We live together as a community. The alleged divide between unemployed and employed exists but nevertheless in society they tend to rub shoulders and get along together. As far as ethnic minorities are concerned we in this county do not have that problem to a great degree. The greater part of our ethnic minority population is centred on——. There I've been to meetings of ethnic minorities. I've been to a service in a Sikh Temple. We get on famously. Occasionally there's a bubble, but it's always resolved without a great deal of fuss because there's understanding.''

"There are a lot of divisions. We're multicultural and that doesn't make for harmony. You've got to keep trying and trying to do your best to bring everybody together. We've been more successful than we often give ourselves credit for. There are divisions: people who are working and people who aren't. People who are black and people who are white. I think there are people who are brown, and all the rest of it. I think it's multicultural. But having said that, I take the view that unless you're very careful you look at it with a jaundiced eye. You can say what a bloody awful place this is, and it's not really. Where else in the world would you want to live but England anyway! Where else in England would you want to live but this super county! It's a good county to live in. Perhaps I'm a bit spoiled through being here.''

A sizeable minority of chiefs felt that Britain remained a harmonious society. The common perception of increasing conflict was rooted in an ahistorical ignorance of the extent of disharmony and disorder in the past:

"I have very grave doubts as to whether it was ever particularly harmonious. One has to bear in mind that, to a large extent, we conceive history through middle-class and upper-class eyes. Therefore I think it is possible we are getting a view which is not actually true. If one actually reads books looking at different strata of society one does not get the same impression. I'm very doubtful indeed whether there was ever this sort of Golden Age. Unless one looks at the very brief period from the early twenties, when one looks to see how the General Strike was conducted and is greatly surprised to see how non-violent it was. There may just have been a short period when for some reason Britain was slightly less turbulent in some ways than other countries.''

Chief constables are divided on the question whether Britain is less harmonious than it was. However, they all recognize the existence of social divisions today. The majority (75 per cent) see these divisions as increasing. One-fifth do not think social divisions are becoming greater, while 5 per cent think they are in some ways and not in others. I asked chief constables to name what they saw as the main social divisions in Britain today, and these are shown in Table 9.1. (The question was open ended, and the categories used are the chief constables' spontaneous offerings.)

TABLE 9.1.   *Main Social Divisions Perceived by Chief Constables*

Type of division	Percentage mentioning it first %	Percentage mentioning it second %	Percentage mentioning it third %	Percentage mentioning it at all %
Race	30.0	25.0	7.5	62.5
Youth/age	5.0	5.0	0	10.0
Unemployed/employed	20.0	2.5	5.0	27.5
Class: haves/have nots	32.5	10.0	2.5	45.0
North/South	10.0	17.5	7.5	35.0
n/a	2.5	40.0	77.5	
TOTAL N = 40	100.0	100.0	100.0	

Table 9.1 shows that broadly economic divisions are perceived as the most salient by chief constables. A larger proportion mention class or the division between 'haves' and 'have nots' first than any other division: 32.5 per cent. In addition, 20 per cent mention another basically economic division (unemployment–employment) first. However, overall, the most often mentioned division was race. This was mentioned by 62.5 per cent of chief constables altogether and mentioned first by 30 per cent. The North–South divide was also mentioned by over a third of chief constables, but mentioned first by one-tenth. The only other division mentioned, young–old, was given by less than one-tenth overall.

The following quote is typical of the majority who cite economic divisions as the main ones:

"The obvious one is the working population and the unemployed. That is quite clear, although in my view there isn't the gross poverty in a county like this that there is perhaps in the inner-city areas where you have greater social divisions of poverty and wealth, deprived, haves and have nots. I think it's the haves and have nots which is the greatest division, but I don't think it's apparent here, because I think whatever anybody says about this government or the social service structure I don't think people are badly off. Their needs and wants are on a far higher level now. You know, if you have no television set you're starving."

Inequality and Justice

Although economic divisions were frequently cited as the most important in society, they were not usually seen as having much direct relevance for policing and law enforcement specifically. I asked the chief constables whether they thought the old adage 'one law for the rich and one law for the poor' still held true. Hardly surprisingly, just over two-thirds (67 per cent) did not. However one-quarter (25 per cent) thought it did, while another 8 per cent felt it was still true in some ways. The predominant denial of any influence of economic factors over the application of the law is illustrated by these quotes. The majority clearly feel that class discrimination is a thing of the past:

"I think there used to be one law for the rich and one for the poor. I was brought up in a rural community, and I certainly would have believed that to be the case before I joined this organization. When I first came here nine years ago I had a belief it might have been the case by certain things that were said about what had happened previously. The then chief constable made it very clear. He was a Geordie and a very blunt-spoken man. He said there was not one law for the rich and one for the poor, there was just one law. And I can tell you a tale in confidence to support that. A certain very titled man in the community had a force radio in his possession which had been allowed to him by the former chief constable, so that his security man could contact our control and say all was well. His personal assistant was a retired chief superintendent. The then chief constable got to know about this and rang this fellow and said, 'You get that radio back! There is no right for anyone except police officers to have a police radio.' The man in question eventually came and asked to see the chief constable, and the chief constable said I'll deal with this myself. I saw the chief constable immediately afterwards, and he said, 'I had a chat with that man.' He said he felt as though he had been a little boy who has had his hands slapped. He'd said, in fairness to him, he recognized my simple sort of philosophy: that if he has one of our radios the little lady in the corner shop has an equal entitlement when she asked for one, and that's just not on. It was back within a week, and the same man donated two police dogs to us within the month. I've faced the same situation once with a large multinational organization. And I said, 'From now on you can afford to buy it; there's no private right into our network. It's coming back!' In the past, in the old county environments, there probably was the old landed gentry, and the local squires seemed to think they were above the law. Certainly in my time here there have been a number of people who've been falling foul of the law, Members of Parliament and others who tried to make that point. They eventually realized that the only point they can make is to the magistrates! They're wasting their breath on either me or any of my senior officers."

"I don't think there's any truth in it now because I don't think there are any rich or any poor. There might be modestly at the end, but there isn't the split there has been formerly. Because being poor is relative. And how anybody in the future will ever be able to become rich in this society I am not sure. There will always be some who have less than others, but I'm not sure I would describe it as rich or poor."

"When I first joined the squire was very inviolate as he came home drunk as a lord in his car. He got put to bed, and nobody stopped him or if they did they took him home. That does not apply any more. It doesn't matter what your caste or creed is, if you transgress the law then you get dealt with."

"I think not. I am sure that so far as police are concerned, and that is all I am concerned with, that declaration of office that we make weighs heavily on all of us. I don't think there are too many members of the police service that frequently or readily depart from that undertaking they have given, 'without fear or favour'. That may not be so in the eyes of the received. But that I suppose is about social standards, and standards of behaviour as accepted between groups. And if you are of a group which has a different standard of behaviour compared to other groups then quite naturally you will attract the attention of the police more, and therefore be prone to thinking that it's bias."

The last quote shows that this is something of a sacred cow response. Accepting that policing is sensitive to class factors, *per se*, is to acknowledge malpractice. So recognition of a relationship between class and law enforcement usually did not amount to an acceptance of bias against the poor. The third of the chiefs who recognized that there may be 'one law for the rich and one for the poor' usually saw this as occurring primarily because of the actions of other legal actors, not the police:

"There isn't bias in policing terms, because there's a greater anonymity about issues like fixed penalties, wardens, radar. They are non-selective. The class system does not intrude in those sorts of processes. Nor does the debate on drugs, because a deb coming out with a bit of hashish, you know, is still an offence. The law about drugs is fairly well applied firmly. The distinction is that if you can still pay for the best legal advice you have a better chance of acquittal. Therefore, that criticism I would direct more to our legal system."

"The rich can afford better services, that's the essence of it. I don't think the rich get better policed within a county. I haven't got more policemen in the richer areas than the poor. In fact my policemen are all over the areas where the problems are! Which are the council estates and so on. So, in a sense we apply more attention to them, but it tends to lead to those persons."

"A rich man can afford better legal advice and representation when he comes before a court. And if one can afford someone to represent you on £30,000 for one court case you're better off than with some very intelligent and good local solicitor on legal aid. But I honestly don't believe that a poor man who commits an offence is going to be dealt with in any way diffently to a rich man. The days have long since gone when the Lord of the Manor committed a motoring offence and it was forgotten about, but the poor chap down the road who didn't have lights on his bike was prosecuted."

Inequality before the law did not only arise from the economics of legal representation. It was also structurally easier for the rich to commit offences without being detected, and they were also more likely to commit offences, such as serious frauds, which were harder and more expensive to detect. Thus the police were more likely to deal with poor offenders, but this arose from the political economy of detectability, not direct bias. The police themselves were either classless, or biased against the wealthy.

"There are the privileges of class in the sense that offences committed anonymously in the privacy of a room, or even a private party, are harder to detect. There are advantages in social class in that sense. But the police service has come through fairly well on what I call its classless image recently. I mean, if I took you into that far conference room you'll see the past chief constables' portraits—Colonel So-and-So, chief constable 1856."

"In the enforcement of the law generally there's no difference at all.

But there's a lot of people who break the law and go unpunished because they are quite sophisticated in the way they break the law, such as the people fiddling income tax, fraud, that sort of thing. They are able to cover their tracks and they're not as obviously criminal as some. But if you're talking about the general criminal law such as stealing or motoring offences, there's absolutely no difference."

"We are always going to have the greatest difficulty with people who are challenging authority generally, and who feel disadvantaged, however rightly or wrongly, and who are going through their maturing years. That's a fact of life ... It is much easier to fiddle a few thousand on the Stock Exchange or on your income tax than it is to steal a pint of milk, so it's true to an extent there's one law for the rich and one for the poor. It is equally true to say that going to court is very expensive, so money can assist in justice. That's something that is class related. There are a lot of villains who have done very well out of having a lot of money and bent lawyers. But I believe quite strongly, as far as the general public and normal policing is concerned, it's irrelevant. Of course people don't have equal chances in life, in the fundamental structure of society. It depends very much on where they're brought up, what their parents' expectations are, what nursery schools there are, all sorts of factors. Life's never been fair."

A small minority of chiefs were prepared to admit that class and social position might affect law enforcement even more directly:

"In a county like this you will find deference paid to the rank of a person, socially. That is one thing, when you come to a county like this, you have to wrestle with, you've got to decide very quickly whether you're going to be your own man. There's an awful lot of hypocrisy about it. Let me quote you a recent example. We had information about two public schools quite near here. The boys in the sixth forms were going to have a go at each other in quite a nasty way. They were tooling themselves up. We got to know this and were able to intervene before anything happened. And the ringleader of one group was identified, and it was going to be a nasty affair. I mean, we were talking about hatchets in people. We got hold of this lad and made an appointment to see his parents. His father is a member of the county council, and also a member of my police authority. And when an inspector went along to see him simply to tell him what happened, he was duty bound to report it, the inspector said, 'I think it would be as well really if I saw you in your son's presence.' And he said, 'You are not seeing my son. I am a county councillor, a member of your police authority, and under no circumstances are you going to speak to my son.' This sort of thing happens often. Now that has a tremendous effect on policemen in the lower ranks, you know. Oh, yes! And another, confidentially between you and I. A person of this town who's a magistrate member of the police authority, rather pompously is all the time seen without a licence on his motor-car. Another person became a magistrate, and his one desire was to sack that magistrate! Although I have served for thirty-seven years that sort of thing still rocks me."

"I have to accept as a professional policeman and chief constable that there are groups within society who are more likely to be dogged by the police than others. It's not a division between rich and poor as such. Everybody stands equal in the eyes of a policeman basically. But, you see, I suppose the classic is that if you get a couple of youngsters driving a Ford Cortina late at night they are more likely to be stopped than a couple of 30 years olds driving a BMW. Because a policeman's judgement is that a couple of teenagers in a Cortina— the Cortina is fair game for stealing—a couple of tearaways are likely to steal a Cortina, so that's why they get stopped. Equally if you drive through my ground with long hair and a bedroll on the back seat in June, July, or August you're more likely to get stopped and searched for drugs than if you came down in your present appearance. On a motorbike or whatever else, with a bedroll and rucksack, you would be. So it's not what you call rich or poor, but I do think policemen target people on their perception of who commits a particular type of crime."

A majority of chiefs, then, do not admit that there is any difference in the law for rich or poor. A minority, however, do accept that such variations do exist. This is because of the ability of money to purchase legal representation, or the impersonal structural biases of the system. A few also acknowledge the occurrence of biased enforcement by the police and other agencies.

Race

Lord Scarman, in his seminal report on the Brixton disorders, portrayed racial prejudice and discrimination within the police as an occasional rank-and-file aberration, not an institutionalized phenomenon. He specifically denied that it occurred 'knowingly, as a matter of policy', and exonerated the 'integrity and impartiality of the senior direction of the force' (Scarman, 1981, paras. 2.22 and 4.62). Since then the conventional wisdom of liberal police reform has been premised on the assumption that racism is a 'canteen culture' phenomenon, and that senior ranks are concerned to eradicate it, albeit with less than complete success. However, little is actually known about the views of chief officers on questions of race, apart from occasional public pronouncements.

My interviews did not directly ask any explicit questions on race or ethnic relations. We saw above, however, that race was spontaneously mentioned more often than any other social division when chief constables were asked to name the main divisions they perceived (see Table 9.1). In addition, all the interviews spontaneously referred to racial questions at some points. Overall, these volunteered comments do not endorse the standard view that prejudice is predominantly a problem confined to the rank and file. A number of the chiefs, especially the younger, better educated chiefs and those in the metropolitan areas, did discuss questions of race without invoking negative stereotypes of ethnic minorities. However, most of the chief constables, especially in the county forces, did invoke such negative images.

The standard view was to regard the presence of black people, or sometimes 'foreigners' more generally, as problematic for the police. This much was a standard perception, and in one sense no more or less than an obvious truth for policing in the 1980s. What made the approach to this problem one that can fairly be called prejudiced is the casting of the issues in terms which made the characteristics of black people, or their presence in itself, the cause of the difficulties. Those chiefs with more experience of racial tensions tended not to do this. They saw white prejudice, or social discrimination experienced by black people, as at least part of the equation. However, a majority of chiefs short-circuited such reasoning to identify blackness *per se* with problems. As has already been indicated in Chapters 7 and 8 on crime and disorder, and earlier in this chapter, ethnic minorities were seen as the symbols and sometimes the spearheads of that turbulent spirit of modernity which was disrupting traditional British harmony and morality. As such their very appearance was dreaded by the chiefs of many rural forces. This was illustrated by the story told to me by the driver of one county chief. The previous week he had been driving the chief along when they spotted a black man (described as 'coloured') walking down the road. The chief had said to the driver: 'Hello! What's that? Give us a few more of those and we'll have problems here.' Not only were ethnic

minorities often regarded as a source of crime and disorder, they also
tended to be seen as instigators rather than victims of racism.

"When one looks at the incidents that you've got, where was it, in
West Yorkshire recently, with a 90 per cent Asian element in schools
and the parents wanting to take the white children away because their
education was suffering. When you look at the riots of Handsworth,
all these sorts of things are pointers to a degree of divisiveness. If you
felt that society was integrating and becoming multiracial that would
be fine. But what one sees up and down the country are pockets of
ethnic groups and minorities, not necessarily black, becoming far
more vociferous about their rights."

"The danger of no-go areas is heightened where there is a considerable
ethnic minority and all that follows from that ... Every weekend the
coloured youths and others come up to the city centre, have their
night out, and at 1.00 or 2.00 in the morning they go back, in groups
of twenty or thirty, and they start smashing cars on the way back, as
they are inclined to do ... Fortunately these groups are quite small.
You've got the advantage here that the coloured community are quite
identifiable, we know the people we're dealing with."

"I have an incredible public here, it is sparsely populated. A stranger
sticks out like a sore thumb. If a black man appeared it would be the
source of, you know, excitement. So I'm very lucky in that respect
... We are a fragmented society. A lot of it stems from social
conditions, be they jobs or housing. Sadly some of it stems from
increasingly subversive and skilled elements in our society, who whip
up work for the idle devils' minds. Some of the greatest problems
that we face in that fragmentation inevitably are ethnic minorities. I
have never yet succeeded in getting an ounce of movement on the
ground from a Rastafarian in any argument or debate. I would not
get him to move one iota. He believes Ganja is right. It's part of his
religion. He doesn't know where bloody Ethiopia is from his socks,
but you know! That sort of thing worries me. There is no room to
talk to people rationally. It's not a problem here. Society here is not
fragmented at all, it's very cohesive. It's not the most comfortable
place to live if you're unemployed, but people here are still generally
kinder. A form of community spirit."

"As far as blacks are concerned, I suppose they would argue that
they're picked on. But in a particular area, if the officers are happy
that it is the greater likelihood that a particular colour, race, or dress
is more likely to be carrying drugs, or dangerous implements, one

must expect those people to be stopped more than others. It's just a fact of life ... These are not new problems. The Jewish community in London and various other immigrant groups had problems but you can grow through those in generations. But I'm not sure the colour problem can be grown through. I mean, white Jews and Hungarians and Poles can be assimilated within a prejudiced society— and let's make no doubt about it, we are a prejudiced society—because of their looks. They are no longer fairly apparent. But it's a problem we're going to have for many years. It's all worse because of the deprived situation within the inner cities where these people tend to congregate or reside ... Yes, there are racial attacks. But they are what I call a football hooligan type of thing, and they're given a label 'race' because colours are involved. We had one here last Saturday night: six coloureds against six whites. If they'd been Coventry supporters and Liverpool supporters, it would have been the same sort of thing. I think there is much more racial hatred from coloureds for whites ... The basis of racial hatred in many ways is a threat, when one sees a different race as a threat. I don't think these white youths see the West Indians as a threat. They see the Indians as more of a threat, in terms of education. And they have that facility for making money and pulling themselves out of the community to live a prosperous life. It's a pity there can't be a great sort of assimilation within the population. Because if you go to places like Norfolk and some places like that you don't see coloured people. And places here where we've got them there's not much of a problem because nobody sees them as a threat. It's something I won't be able to solve."

"Where the difficulty arises today, is what different sections of the community see as acceptable. Within the black communities some things are acceptable which the white section of the community see as crucial. And you can take it outside the field of drugs, and you will even see it in reverse. The black communities not only want racial discrimination, racially biased offences, to be more strictly dealt with, they want the law tightened even more, where the white section may not. It poses for police a particular problem as piggy in the middle ... In our large cities there are far more worrying divisions, like the growth of the black community with the problems that is creating."

"There was a time in the 1950s, after promotion to sergeant, there was a very interesting advertisement in the *Police Review* for inspectors in the Solomon Islands, and I was tempted to have a go at that. But then my wife took a book out of the local library. It wasn't a new book by any means, it had probably been in existence for some fifteen to twenty years, but nevertheless it talked of cannibalism still being rife in the Solomon Islands ... So that put me off ... Last week some West Indians, being a boisterous lot, decided to start a party at 5 in the afternoon. And they'd gone out and bought crates of ale and got steadily more drunk until about 3 in the morning. The party was still going strong, and the neighbours were complaining about the reggae, the loud reggae music, and the noise ... And a young policeman had to go there with very little experience. Well, how could he deal with that situation where offences were taking place? There was noise, the need to calm the neighbours, and he had a difficult position. If he intervened and made any arrests, for example, for violation of the licensing laws, then he would be accused of being a racist. If he did nothing then he would be accused of neglecting his duty by the neighbours. How do you train people to deal with these sort of incidents?"

Similar perceptions of black people as especially prone to cause trouble were offered by some chiefs in the more urban areas with substantial ethnic minority populations. However, it was rarer amongst them.

"As ACC I had responsibility for community relations. I used to attend meetings when the sort of general antagonism we see expressed now was beginning to emerge. But then you could even go to meetings with black members of the community who didn't have a great deal of antagonism ... Now if you're a black and you look and see another black who's arrested he'll shout for help, particularly if there's a group of you. You'll go and help him. That's the sort of conditioning that's been applied. He's not culpable, because it's police harassment taking place ... It's a self-evident fact that if I want to address a group of black youths, I find it difficult to find one. They really only exist out there. How you communicate with them is the problem because you can't gather them together, because they are fluid individuals—they just happen to come together at a particular time as a group of black youths. Unfortunately, they want to think the worse. If there's something that goes wrong it's our fault basically. I don't know what we're going to do except have a black youth union. Terrible! ... Colour is now emerging as the major important social division. There's no indication in any of the areas I'm aware of that new members of the community are distributing themselves amongst the older members of the community. I think the ghetto mentality is still there. Within my force there are areas where a particular problem is emerging. In one of the poorer quarters of the cities there is conflict on the basis of they're getting more than us, and the division is one of colour."

The more usual attitude amongst chief constables in metropolitan areas was one which recognized the problems of discrimination suffered by black people. They were also aware that the apparent relationship between blacks and crime was misleading. The political economy of housing in a discriminatory society forced black people to live in areas which suffered from high crime rates, but they were not responsible for these high rates. This was a prime example of the ecological fallacy. In so far as young black people were disproportionately involved in some kinds of offending this was the product of deprivation not an intrinsic relationship between race and crime.

"There's a lot of emotive nonsense talked about this. More black males get into the criminal justice system. But a similar argument was talked about years ago, that more Irish immigrants were prosecuted in——. Well, that was a fact of life because there were more Irish immigrants there. In certain areas here there are more blacks committing crime, because it's within the community in which they live. You'd be surprised if there were a lot of Irishmen committing crime there, because there aren't any there. Remember the big debate that went on about the suspected person law, 'sus'? I did some analytical statistical research which showed up contrary to the commonly held belief that more blacks were subject to the vagaries of the sus law than whites that it was untrue. We showed—and people will say 'Ah! He's bound to say that'—but if you accept the honesty of the enterprise, the number of blacks arrested per white was 1 to 12, 1 to 15, something like that. [R.R.: That's obviously at odds with the Home Office research in London.] I know, I question the Home Office research, its methodology and validity. It may be true for London."

Similar views are also expressed by some of the younger chief constables in county forces, though this Scarman-inspired perspective on racial issues is less common amongst county than urban chiefs.

"Young black males only create crime in some areas because they're the deprived. It's not blackness *per se* . . . We recently arrested twenty West Indians for street-trading in drugs in a cosmopolitan estate in a deprived area, with very volatile people. To go in and arrest them in one go would lead to a riot. Therefore we set up discreet cameras to film all the drug transactions. So early one morning we mounted a clean efficient operation to arrest them. Putting tranquillity first doesn't undermine law enforcement. It's a question of *how* it's done."

The majority of chief constables, however, regarded black people as in themselves the source of problems for policing, rather than this being a consequence of the discrimination they experienced. This was a facet of what is undoubtedly a broadly conservative social philosophy shared by most chief constables, and which has been outlined above. However, it does not follow that chief constables are necessarily Conservative supporters in party political terms.

Party Politics

There is a strong inclination amongst chief constables to declare that they are apolitical. This is more than just a denial that political considerations affect their work decisions. It was rather a frequently expressed suspicion about politics as such. The adjective 'political' is commonly used as in itself a pejorative term, as in the following examples:

> "My problem is the authority's main concern these days is their own local political challenges . . . It's turned itself into a forum for mediocre party political debate."
> "My own experience has been very good in the sense that I've not been involved in police authorities which have been overwhelmingly political. There's been a more balanced approach."

At times it seems that chief constables are not content merely to keep politics out of policing, but wish to take politics out of politics. Political considerations are regularly contrasted with rational ones, as if political attitudes cannot be motivated by reasons. The common refrain is of the commitment of the police to political neutrality, that is to the centre, to moderation, to goodwill, and good sense. Partisan politics disrupt the sway of reason and common sense. (These views will be explored further in Chapter 11 on accountability.)

Some chiefs are aware that their attitudes may appear Conservative inclined. They none the less affirm their commitment to neutrality rather than partisanship. It is the polarization of politics which has made conservatism appear to be partisan rather than a consensual norm.

"Now I'm being asked to speak about policing problems and law and order, as a chief constable. If somebody wandered into the room not knowing who I was they might think I was the next Conservative candidate for the constituency. I find that worrying, because I don't want to be that. I want law and order to be an issue which there is a general consensus about politically. We shouldn't be seen to be in one camp or the other. That used to be how it was."

Having experienced problems in a previous research project when I attempted to ask questions about police officers' political beliefs (Reiner, 1978, 11 and app. 3), I avoided doing the same this time. I did not ask the chief constables how they voted (or indeed whether they voted— one distinguished former chief officer is on record as not having voted since taking office because police 'must be men and women of the middle'—McNee, 1979). However, I did ask them whether they felt it made any difference to the police which party was in power. The majority (57 per cent) thought it did not. Just over a quarter (28 per cent) did believe it made a difference, and another 15 per cent thought it could do.

The majority view is really an affirmation of the belief in strict police neutrality. However, many of those who said it made no difference did perceive Labour as more hostile in ideology to the police. It was believed, though, that such anti-police views would be toned down if the Labour Party was actually in office, as it had always moderated its views when in government in the past.

"It's never made a difference so far which party is in power. Of course, different political parties will have different ideas on how to handle various problems. But I'm here to serve the Queen, and therefore whatever political party is legally elected. And I've had no troubles serving under Labour or the Conservatives. And I hope that will never come about. Many police officers have been rather worried about some comments made by Labour politicians in recent years. But it never happened before ... They tend to tone down in office."

However, many chief constables who felt that on the basis of past experience it made no difference to the police which party was in power, wondered whether this would be the case in future. They worried that Labour was more under the control of extremists than it used to be, and that even its mainstream leaders supported commitments to give police authorities control over policing policy. (This latter proposal caused general alarm to the chiefs, as will be seen in Chapter 11 on accountability.)

However, most felt it was the duty of the police to accept the will of an elected government, even if they disagreed with it. They deplored the 1984 speech made by Les Curtis, former chairman of the Police Federation, when he wondered whether the police could continue to give equally loyal service to a Labour as to a Conservative Government (*Guardian*, 4 Oct. 1984, 5; 6 Oct. 1984, 14). However, one-fifth of the chiefs echoed these sentiments, and said they would resign if a Labour Government came to power and attempted to change the constitutional position of the police. The standard view that the policies of an elected government had to be accepted, even if they were unpalatable to the police, is illustrated by these examples.

"I don't think it makes any difference at all which party is in power. That was a grossly irresponsible remark by a rather stupid and ignorant man. We are here to serve the people, to carry out the laws made by Parliament. And who happens to be in power is totally irrelevant. It's very arguable as to which party makes life easiest for us, anyway. It might surprise some people. I think most police officers would say policing is easier under a Labour Government than it is under a Conservative Government. We get more resources under Labour than under the Conservatives. The Labour Party often have a greater understanding of the nature of our work. They are not patronising. The nature of government policy is different when each of the parties is in power, fundamentally different, and policing is easier when the Labour Party is in power."

"It was quite wrong for him [the Federation chairman] to make that remark. If you were one of my officers saying that I'd have to discipline you. It's a quite astounding statement against the police. It should not matter which party is in power. If you don't like it, get out."

A minority of chiefs (20 per cent) took that to its conclusion—they said they would resign if Labour came to office and implemented its policies on police authorities (giving them the power to control police policies). While the majority of chiefs thought Labour would prove as friendly in office as it had done in the past, a substantial minority (28 per cent) felt this to be too sanguine, and feared the worst. Another 15 per cent were uncertain but concerned. (These views may well have changed in the two years since interviewing was carried out, as Labour has made clear efforts to repair its bridges with the police, while the

Conservatives have ended their honeymoon period with the police, cf. Reiner, 1990a; Rawlings, 1991.) The deep suspicion of Labour's plans which was expressed by these chiefs is illustrated by the following remarks:

"My experience so far is that when we've had a Socialist government, materially, in bricks and mortar, cars, uniforms, things of that sort, we've done all right, but on pay we've done badly. When we have a Conservative Government, morale has lifted. Because we are then not only given better pay and conditions, but we are given support in the House. People actually speak up for us ... Now what worries me—I don't know if I've read too many books!—if we get a Socialist Government, would the moderates be able to control the extremists? I have reservations about whether they would. Therefore I think we might as a police service suffer in terms of morale, in terms of constraints on our activities which I don't think are necessary—there's enough there now! We would only destabilize society, which some people under that movement would be only too happy to see."

"If their new act is going to say that the power actually lies with the police authority to direct the chief constables, and that's Parliament's wish, then what I shall probably do is resign, without being too dramatic, because it would be impossible to work with. I don't think the record of the British police deserves to be treated like that, I think we've been much more responsible. And I would hope that when the time comes, even if a Labour Government gets in, they would think very carefully about their manifesto, think very carefully about what they're doing."

"It's a political thing. Whenever we get the next Labour Government, at that time we'll produce a look-see at how the police are organized. While we stay with Margaret things will remain as the status quo ... In my experience it hasn't made a hell of a lot of difference which party was in power. Thank God, the party in opposition always changes and becomes responsible in office. But some of the things that are being articulated now—I could not be a chief constable whereby I go to my police authority and they tell me the policy I'm going to adopt. My conscience wouldn't let me do it, and I'd rather retire and resign. Putting it in a nutshell, if we got too much of a leftist view of how you police I'd prefer not to be part of it. [R.R.: You see the leftist view as worse than the Right for the police?] Or too much extreme Right. But I think fortunately we as the police can counterbalance the extreme Right much more than we can counterbalance the extreme Left. If that makes sense to you. [R.R.: Is that always true, or just at the present time?] I couldn't say if it's always true. We could have a scenario where an extreme right-wing government gives a directive to the police when there's a dock strike to appear at the dockside armed, to ensure the people work. Now I would not be a party to that, and as a chief constable would say, 'No, I'm not going to do it.' But the Left now, you see, would by Act of Parliament say there would be nothing wrong, if the people wishes it that way, if the style of our policing was taken out of our hands and put into the hands of politicians. You could argue that's what they're elected for. To me that would be an anathema as a professional policeman, and I could not be a party to that. But on the wind of change you've people growing up who accept those systems for what they are. Someone else will follow me. Just that I could not agree with them."

"It's difficult when you get the many outrageous statements that are made by politicians. Particularly during the miners' strike about Jack-booted fascists . . . But I was appointed deputy chief constable in 1976 in——[a large city force], by a socialist administration. I found them to be the finest group of people I could wish to meet. They were, and I'm not being disrespectful in any way, they were sort of cloth caps, good working man, feet on the ground, supporters of the police. They were fine people, and I had a marvellous rapport with them. We had wonderful equipment, everything was fine. But in——[county force] where the blood is blue there was a tendency to be more demanding in terms of desire to control. There is now a much higher profile from the present government of the day. Your great problem comes in trying to imagine what sort of government there could be in opposition to this one. If I had a government that followed the lines of the group of people who appointed me in 1976, I'd work for them without any worries whatsoever. I could work for the present administration, generally speaking, without any worries. I'm not awfully sure how we would be going in terms of an extreme left wing."

"I would guess that, listening to the posturing of the so-called opposition party at the moment, they're going to repeal every bloody bit of legislation that's been put on the statute book in the last few years . . . We're like army commanders or civil servants, the bellyaching stops once Parliament has decreed that they are the Parliament. You either go along, or you get out if you feel strongly about it. You get out . . . I've known many Home Secretaries of varying political persuasions. I can only think of one who was bloody useless."

"The Labour Party document spelled out what they mean when they say accountability. It's control. I think that's wrong for UK Ltd."

It is clear that there is widespread concern amongst chief constables about the possibility of a Labour Government implementing proposals to subject police policy to police authorities. While most think these commitments would be modified if Labour was actually elected, a substantial minority believed it was unwise to extrapolate from past experience of this as the party's fundamental character had changed. Some believed they would be forced to resign if Labour took office and implemented its policies on the police. Concern about Labour's ideology was, however, attenuated by the widely held perception that Labour was better for the police in material terms, at both local and national level. The Conservatives were seen to be hostile to public expenditure generally and much tighter with the purse strings, even for so favoured a part of the public sector as the police.

"My philosophy is to be apolitical. But let me say straightaway that I think the police service has always done better under a Labour Government than a Conservative Government. If you go over our pay rises and our capital building projects and our establishment increases, my experience is you've always done better with a Labour than a Conservative Government. It's almost obvious because a Labour Government is for capital growth and public sector growth and a Conservative Government is against it."

"We are always better off under Labour Governments. You know, they love to call us names and challenge us and all the rest of it. But I've worked for quite an extreme left-wing authority when I was in——, there were communist card-carrying members, one senior officer of the county council was a known activist. Perhaps it's because they're such good spenders that our slice of the cake is sufficient for all we want and a little more. I never had to fight for equipment and things that I have to fight for now, in a right-wing county. Because there is a tradition of low rates, low pay. It's still a case of poets and peasants ... But they are miserly and mean in this county, compared with Jim Anderton and my colleagues in these difficult areas, who are far better off than I for resources. Every statistic will prove that."

In sum, the chief constables tend to be ambivalent in their views on which party is better for the police. Labour is perceived to be economically preferable but ideologically hostile. However, most chiefs thought the ideology would be muted with the prospect of power. No doubt they feel vindicated by developments over the last couple of years.

During the late 1970s and early 1980s there was a marked tendency for chief constables to become more prominent and apparently partisan, in their public interventions in media and political debate (Reiner, 1985, 73–6). However, most chiefs now question the wisdom of this, and see it as a threat to their desired images as apolitical. No doubt this was influenced by the difficult position James Anderton, the most outspoken of chief constables, encountered during the period of the research as a result of his controversial speeches on AIDS and other topics, which attracted considerable debate and criticism (McLaughlin, 1990). The overwhelming majority (70 per cent) of chief constables thought that the high public profile adopted by some chiefs had caused problems for the public by undermining their apolitical image. Only 28 per cent felt it was not a problem. The consensus is clearly that chief constables must be wary of developing too high a public profile and endangering their professional standing:

"It's a dangerous development like every development that is taken to extremes. It depends why you do it. I'd take a high profile if I believed the cause justifies it in a particular case, but with great reluctance. My colleagues who don't have the same reluctance—the numbers who have sought a higher profile have been small—I think they've been the less intelligent and far-sighted chiefs. That's a very emotional and subjective comment!"

"I'm very sceptical about the motives of the press. When Jim Anderton was newly appointed, they treated him very well at first, encouraged him and stimulated him as they have done with every spokesman, and then exposed him and chopped him! They did it with other people who are inadequate in the public field, Jim Jardine [former Police Federation chairman] for instance ... Although it is attractive to get a higher public profile, you should avoid speaking out on general issues away from your own responsibilities. There are inherent dangers in it."

"We should stay out of a public stance on moral values. I have my own private views but we should stay out of it in terms of morality, in terms of public utterances. That goes contrary to Jim, but that's a passionate view he holds ... I believe a chief constable should only be seen to give forth publicly on those matters that are within his professional purview. I don't think he should be an opinion-maker."

"If I want a television camera here I can get it at the drop of a hat—

if I think this afternoon there is some issue of vital importance, good people out there. But if I make some statement, by definition I will be attacking the Government or in support of them, saying the right thing for one set of politicians and the wrong for another ... When Robert Mark opened the door to the media in 1972, with his Dimbleby lecture, it was a modern, forward-looking concept. Except that we are not all Robert Marks! He had a particular skill which he used to great effect. Some would say too great an effect! I don't believe in secrecy but you can have too great a degree of openness. What I do believe in is professional mystique."

"The unfortunate thing was we went through a time when people were vying with each other to be the media image. Hopefully now we're past that period. If there is genuine public concern about an issue it makes sense to appear on your local television and nip in the bud any misconceptions. But when you get on to these 'Question Time' type things you can get into all sorts of difficult areas if you're not careful."

"I don't like to be in the public limelight. I am basically on the shy side and shirk unnecessary television interviews. I will do them when I have to as a matter of duty, but don't enjoy them and would never volunteer ... There are now directives anyway. I'd refuse the interviews some of my contemporaries have done which involve their personal lives. I'm not in the public entertainment business. I'm here to look after the normal people of the county to the best of my ability. I don't think they're interested in whether I ride a horse or shoot ... I don't like the public profile some chief constables now follow. I think it raises fears in people's minds, which may not be based on a lot of evidence, but has implications which affect us all."

Those chiefs who did not think the higher public profile adopted by chief constables recently was a problem, argued that it was necessary to have the police perspective put forcefully and effectively in public debate. This had not been done sufficiently vigorously in the past.

"It did have dangers when Robert Mark started it, and Alderson and so forth followed on. But there is a place for us to speak up. We should not be the silent service and keep our head down and say nothing. It is right that we are heard in political debate, the problems we are facing, the responsibilities placed upon us."

"We have a responsibility to be persuasive and influential on important issues. A silent chief constable is no use to the public or to local politicians, because they're not sure what he's thinking. I'm probably very well known locally for my views, which is right because I police this county. I'm not well known nationally for my views because I've not been involved much in national publicity, though it can always change. [Ironically this chief constable, within days of the interview, became engulfed in a *cause célèbre* which was headline news for many months.] Mind you, if chief constables are trying to influence the Home Office rather than the public, then publicity may be overdone."

"I occasionally get concerned when I see some of the performances, if that's the right word, of some of my colleagues. I've made it perfectly plain to them, they give the appearance of walking on water, and that's not good for the police service. But we, senior police officers, made a Conference decision about this in 1983, particularly with the potential public disorder situation. There's a no man's land where, in the past, we as a service took a reticent view ... didn't do enough to counter some of the adverse things. The lie is half-way round the world—as it was described by Jim Callaghan—before the truth gets its boots off. We've got to be prepared to get our boots on a bit earlier and use the media for that purpose."

"I'm out almost every night of the week, because when I get invitations to speak to the mothers' union, it's just as important as the faculty of law of the university. I do it because I like it and people like me to do it and want me to do it. When I don't get the invitations it's time for me to retire ... But I operate on low profile. It's not my business to pontificate. I'm not speaking against Jim now, because I tell him what I'm telling you. And I defended him in private on Friday night very vociferously in a very important arena on a much more difficult issue. [This was a reference to an inquiry into a major *cause célèbre*.] But Jim is Jim!"

"There's no problem provided the points made are not themselves politically controversial. Certain things needed to be said. I admire the people who stood up and said them because they drew attention to the ills of society, which required at least thinking about if not curing."

There is a clear difference of opinions here. Most chiefs are wary of intervention in public debate beyond matters in which they are directly involved professionally. A significant minority, however, welcomed the vigorous presentation of a police perspective by some chief constables in recent times.

Altogether, chief constables tend towards a conservative social philosophy. The ideal is a stable order and firm structure of authority, in which all people know and accept their place in the hierarchy. This is perceived as threatened by the advent of a less deferential, more permissive, rootless cosmopolitanism. While this is itself a political perspective in the broad sense, chief constables are wary of political conflict and yearn for a bygone consensus. They worry about the advent of a Labour Government pledged to change the constitutional position of the police, but only a few would not be able to accept it if it happened. Despite holding strongly felt beliefs about morality and society, most are cautious about the extent to which it is appropriate for chief constables to press their views in public debate. The media are like a Pandora's box, liable to destroy those who meddle.

Part IV

The Control of Police Forces

10 Bosses in Blue:
Chief Constables and Police
Management

The job of chief constable has changed dramatically in the last quarter of a century, as was described in Chapter 2. Police forces have grown from being predominantly small units primarily oriented to local communities, into huge bureaucratic organizations, serving large areas with far less local identity. The rank and file of police forces, represented by the Police Federation, have become more vocal and assertive (Reiner, 1978). The change which has occurred in the management role of chief constable is analogous to moving from running a corner shop to managing a local branch of Sainsbury's. In addition, the generation of chief constables studied here is the first to have been selected entirely from people who were recruited as constables with no special avenues to the top. At the same time, the environment they police has become far more turbulent (as has been explored in Part III).

The result is that the job of being a chief constable has become incomparably more complex and burdensome. In this chapter we shall consider the chief constables' own analyses of their role as the top police managers. Most are well aware of the awesome change in the scope of the task:

"If your man who commanded the force in 1935 came back today to the same force, he couldn't do the current chief constable's job. They were different styles of forces, a different style of command. It was a more personal style of relationship—policing was not in any way as professional as it is today. In many counties it was much more localized, and so, therefore, its function was to keep people happy. I'm not belittling it. They did a tremendous job at the time. Hendon did a hell of a lot of good for the police service, though that doesn't mean we need another Hendon today."

"The changing role of people like myself is particularly marked at the present time. It's fairly obvious that most of my predecessors have only been concerned with the smooth running of their organization and its performance. What is now required of a chief constable is a very wide remit. Not only of considerable financial acumen—and I mean that—but a great knowledge of computerization and many other issues. In essence what it is really about is being a manager of many resources and an organization directed towards many objectives ... With very close financial pressures and constraint and pressure on local authorities, the role of chief constable is being forced by financial pressures, never mind constitutional pressures, into the forefront of public life."

"You can think back over the years where there were forces where the chief constables were hardly heard of, let alone seen, and the force was probably run by a deputy. The chief popped in and saw things were all right, and that was it. Those day are gone absolutely."

"My own standard, without seeming arrogant, is essentially a six-day week. I don't care whether it's an eight-hour day or a twelve-hour day! When I joined there were 147 police forces, and 147 chiefs, to deal with the same discipline, management, police authorities, and with deputies and often assistants as nowadays. If you look at what we've taken on in terms of the work-load, we've got too much on our plate. It gives support to this notion that chiefs are enormously powerful people with vast reservoirs of resources to command, with monstrous legal powers. It feeds the rumour."

"It's much more difficult now compared with running a force of 150 officers or even 600 officers. How can you compare that with nearly 3,000 including civilians? It is much more complex, a greater responsibility. Some of the old chief constables would find it very difficult to settle back into their seats if they were to reappear, with the span of responsibility. A lovely story, Eric St Johnston told me. He was appointed chief constable for Oxford City when he was 28. And the chief constable he took over from said to him: 'Now St Johnston, don't get any of these new ideas and start coming to the office after lunch!' So that sums up the concept of the 1930s, which is not relevant, I can assure you, to the 1990s." [The full story can be found in St Johnston, 1978, 69; the force in question was in fact the county force of Oxfordshire, not the Oxford City Police.]

The changes in the demands placed upon the chief constable's role were widely recognized. However, there were substantial variations in how these were responded to. It has already been shown in Chapter 7 that a substantial minority of chiefs still see their role as bobbies rather than bureaucrats and try to retain as much of a direct operational involvement as possible. On the other hand, there is a minority at the other extreme, who embrace the bureaucratic role wholeheartedly and are happy to see themselves as managers of large and complex organizations with essentially similar tasks as those of all managers. Most chiefs, however, experience and attempt to cope with a tension between the two roles. They recognize the pressures driving them in the bureaucratic direction but hanker after the policing role as well, and try to distance themselves from a purely managerial conception of their function.

Examples of the chiefs who still try to keep alive the 'bobbying' aspect of their role were given in Chapter 7. However, the following sum it up quintessentially:

"I have a closer interest in day-to-day affairs than perhaps some of my colleagues. It's my natural instinct. If one is worth one's salt, we are all tutor constables in a sense ... It was a nice mix, when I first became a chief constable, of being a manager and a commander. I am hardly ever a commander now. I'm a manager. I mean I could be an insurance officer or bank clerk really. Most people join the police service for the reason I joined, sort of an active life, mixing with people. But the fun goes out of the police life when you get to the rank of, say, chief constable or superintendent. You stop meeting with people."

"I believe we are all policemen, that we are all trying to service the community. It doesn't matter whether it's me as chief constable or whether it's the guy walking on one of his beats. We're all trying to achieve the same thing."

"When you look at the policeman's oath ... I am a policeman the same as the constable on the beat. My primary duty is prevention and detection of crime, and the preservation of life and property."

On the other hand, one-fifth of chief constables saw their role primarily as managers. To them managing the police organization was basically like managing any complex organization. They espoused the role of bureaucrats rather than bobbies, and revelled in the language of management theory.[1]

> "The role has changed completely. In the past chief constables would take a much more intense or direct part in investigations and operations. Now a chief constable is like any other manager. I visited a cheese and yoghurt factory today. I felt the managers could step into my job, and vice versa, even though cheese and yoghurt are not at all like police and crime."

> "It's the same in any big organization. Your demands outstrip your resources, and you try to match the two together as you are best able. That's the job of the chief constable."

> "I do very sincerely believe that I am the chairman of a public company and I have 8,000 people working for me, but more importantly I have a shareholding of two and a quarter million. Those shareholders are the most important thing to me ... I am concerned with dealing at the end of the year with my statement to our shareholders about all our work."

> "The growth in size of forces has made the chief constable's job much more of a financial manager, managing his resources. It's caused the problem to be financial control, disposition of your resources, management problems such as staff appraisal, staff assessment, and management, getting policy down to all levels of the organization, and indeed sucking up information from all corners ... I developed a strategy for policing, to make this organization effective ... I have worked hard on trying to introduce a system emanating from a policy statement that I write each year, setting goals for this force, and local subdivisions set their own local objectives, and I involved constables in that so it is a bottom-up process ... When I was about a year and a half into this the Home Office issued their famous Circular 114 of '83 which they quote at you, but that clearly was pointing people towards management strategy, setting objectives and goals. But we were into it before then ... It's similar to Sir Kenneth Newman, because I like some of his ideas, although I have to say to you I think it's an over-academic approach."

> "I see myself much more like the managing director, and leave the people who are more expert at crime detection to it ... Things like the Audit Commission, Home Office Circular 114 of '83, liaison committees out on subdivisions, consultative committees, much closer financial scrutiny—not for dishonesty, but what we're doing with our money, money cost effectiveness. They're now trying to

change an organization, from one which was totally concerned about the operational job, to saying that when you get to a certain level you've really got to stop thinking like an operational police officer. You've now got to become managers.''

The majority of chief constables recognized the changes in their role but regarded them with ambivalence and some regret. Their heart remained in bobbying but they accepted that in reality their present role was primarily pure management.

"The enormity of a chief constable's job under the broad umbrella of administration precludes him from getting involved in investigation ... Something has got to give ... You might administer it but not get involved *per se* ... It depends on the enormity of the crime really ... I very much have an overview. You remember——: the death in policy custody. I then took over virtually the administration of it, but the actual day-to-day investigation was done by a senior police officer on my direction. There was almost a daily reportage of where they'd gone so far, and what they intended.''

"I only deal with cases if the Home Secretary asks for a chief to investigate something. I am unfortunately mostly an administrator. I always liked crime investigation.''

All chief constables recognize that their role has become primarily that of a manager, albeit most regard this with some nostalgic regret for their days as operational police officers. Given that they are now senior managers, what do they regard as their prime tasks, and what style do they adopt as managers?

The Problems of Police Management

I asked the chief constables to identify what were the main management problems facing them. The results are shown in Table 10.1. (The question was open ended, so the range of issues selected was determined by the chiefs.)

It is clear from Table 10.1 that most chief constables regard financial pressures as their most significant management problem ('Getting blood out of a stone', as one put it.) After that, the problem of internal communications within police forces ranked next, and was clearly seen as an important problem by many chiefs. This was linked to another issue seen as important by several: the growth in size of police forces.

TABLE 10.1.   *Chief Constable's Main Management Problems*

Management problem	Percentage mentioning it first %	Percentage mentioning it second %	Percentage mentioning it third %	Percentage mentioning it at all %
Finance/budgeting	57.5	2.5	—	60.00
Growth in size of forces	10.0	10.0	—	20.0
Internal communications	27.5	10.0	2.5	40.0
Growing central control	—	7.5	2.5	10.0
Balancing conflicting pressures	5.0	27.5	—	32.5
n/a	—	42.5	95.0	
TOTAL	100.0	100.0	100.0	
N = 40				

I also asked about this issue directly, and the overwhelming majority (78 per cent) of chief constables did feel that the growth in size of police forces had made the job of managing them much harder, although 20 per cent did not think it had. The other significant management problems mentioned were the increasing pressure on the police from central government (cited by 10 per cent), and the difficulty of juggling conflicting demands from different audiences: different sections of the public, the law, members of the force, ACPO, local and central government (mentioned by nearly one-third).

The job of financial management was now regarded as the most pressing task facing chief constables, especially since the Government's Financial Management Initiative, promulgated by Circular 114 of 1983. It was recognized by all that this had become the key role of police managers, but this was resented by many.

"My main management problem is obviously financial. I'm sure everybody says that. I do spend far more time now dealing with finance. When I first joined the——force and went around headquarters it was a sergeant in the Finance Section who drafted the estimates. And the estimates seemed to go through and back again to us by the next day. They sent the finances over to the county treasurer, he got it into the draft budget. There didn't seem to be any problem. But now it just seems to be endlessly going on and on at headquarters."

After financial matters, the next most significant problem was personnel management and communications, which the growth in size of forces had clearly exacerbated. As seen from the chief constable's chair the problem was how to keep tabs on and influence what was going on on the ground in a large complex bureaucracy, where the crucial points of service delivery were dispersed over a wide area on the streets:

"We here, sat in our ivory towers, don't know about it. Traditionally the county policeman has grown up with this discretion. The mark of a good or bad policeman is knowing precisely when to jump in, when to pedal or walk slowly so he didn't reach the scene before the offender got away. I am quite content to go along with this. One of the main things is to get policemen with common sense, a balanced man, and he knows—the hackles on the back of his neck tells him when he's got to be careful ... I was thinking recently about the number of crime reports I see. OK, I know I had 39,000 crimes last year, but how many crime reports did I see? I can't remember if I saw one! When we had the rape business, you know, the Thames Valley TV film about how they dealt with the rape victim. I then sent for all the rape files and read them in depth, and asked a number of questions. But that would only be twelve or fourteen. If something happens then I'll send for it. But now I generally do not see any crime files."

The chief constable's role in relation to operational policing is usually a kind of management by numbers. At best he sets up suitable systems, and most crucially recruits the right individuals for work that is highly discretionary. It is then up to these individuals to paint in the right colours to complete the picture properly, and the chief can only control this tangentially. The chief would expect to be directly involved only in the most serious operations and the major administrative issues, especially the bottom-line budgeting decisions.

"The management of the police force is much less personal than when I joined. I joined a relatively small force, just under 200 men, and the chief constable would know every man ... It was a much more personal touch in the sense that the chief officers would know everybody and would be making decisions without the same level of bureaucracy that we have at the moment. There wouldn't be the sophisticated staff appraisal systems and promotion selection systems that perhaps there are today. Some forces even then were quite big, so they would have had them ... You have to look at the papers that come across your desk and if it is sensitive or difficult or a policy matter then clearly it is something that you've got to deal with, or give it to one of your immediate senior officers. If it is basically an operational matter which comes over the desk then it goes down to the divisional or subdivisional level with appropriate directions to deal with it. Where I am concerned, there are two elements as to what I do. There is the running of a fairly large organization with all the attendant problems that anybody has whatever the organization— using the resources you've got, controlling them, managing the budget and your manpower. And then there is the object of why the organization exists, to try and make the level of service that you provide in a community the highest level you can achieve, the deter- mination of which things you feel need priority. These are decisions in many respects which are not uncommon in any organization. I wouldn't turn anything away but odd things come to my table where I would refer it to so-and-so to do. Occasionally you get things too late, particularly for forward planning. Officers can go too far along the line before coming to you for a decision and then you can feel a bit inhibited because he has gone two steps too far—for example, recently, in the preparation of the capital programme. It came to me later than I would have hoped. I was close to being presented with a *fait accompli*. Items of the capital expenditure programme put in the wrong year as to what I want with my overall strategy ... Oper- ationally of course you can't know everything and people down below have to make judgements as to what they feel all the way up the line. I need to know about the more serious crime that is happening in the county, and even minor crimes where it is causing considerable apprehension in the community. Because I might want to shift resources to try and do something about it. But sometimes the chap has to make a judgement, and you can't always kick his backside because he makes mistakes occasionally. So you're very much in their hands in any force, particularly in a place like this county with its geographical area. Communications are quite a problem, and a lot of policing is local. It's very thinly spread, and it takes time to get to you. Obviously if there was a murder in the county I'd know within about half an hour of it being reported. But sometimes things you need to know don't get to you. People below, you give them the discretion, the authority to make decisions, but occasionally it mis- fires."

Despite the difficulties of keeping tabs on what went on in a large dispersed organization this was part of the chief constable's job. It was a mark of failure if the chief did not know of major issues and developments.

"When John Alderson shredded his Special Branch files a few years back, because he'd just discovered what was on them! ... I had to say, 'Well, if a general has been there six years and didn't know what files were kept, I would have sacked him as chief constable."

Too Big for Their Boots? The Size of Police Forces

We have seen that most chief constables thought the growth in size of police forces had caused significant management problems. The general view was that the expansion of forces had brought about a qualitative change in the character of police management. It had moved from a personal style of face-to-face relations to a more formal bureaucratic approach. Most chiefs regretted this. It cut them off from the practicalities of policing, and reduced the sense of identification with a particular locality. The chiefs of the smaller forces strove to retain what they saw as the 'family' flavour of the older forces. The chiefs of the larger forces struggled to develop artificial surrogates for the personal touch. Some took these points to their logical conclusion and argued that the largest metropolitan forces were unmanageable and should be split up.

"Your personal contact has dissipated. I speak to old chief constables of borough forces and they knew everybody and everything. You could manage about 700 or 800 people and know their peccadilloes, know their families, know all about them. A force like this which is about 4,800, I can't possibly know them. Some you know more than most because you rub shoulders with them in the social intercourse which goes on: rugby teams, football teams. But as to actual prowess as a policeman you don't know him, not really. That behoves your management communication has got to be as sharp as possible. The problem in a hierarchical organization will ever be getting information down and up. You can issue orders and policies but you can't force them to read it, can you? In the time I've been chief constable I've issued a dozen personal memoranda, that's about all, on the belief that if I ration it they'll read it out of sheer curiosity. 'What's the old bastard writing to us about now?' ... We introduced a system here where any officer can come and see me without declaring why. That's always a break-point for middle management. Now he's reluctant to stop the good idea guy because he knows that guy can come right to me. They don't come often I must say, and when they do it's very personal rather than professional issues."

"I honestly feel a small force suits my style and philosophy of policing. I've been all my service a practical police officer, and I do still like to be involved. It's surprising in a small force how you can actually be involved. The miners' dispute, for example, gave me an opportunity—National Front marches, things like that crop up. Then I have the opportunity to be much closer to my officers, get to know them individually, which I wouldn't in a bigger force ... The bigger the force, the harder it is. I can get my philosophy, my policy, and objectives document which I prepared recently, down to a fairly low level. We are the only force without a journal which circulates to all offices, but we have a video journal, which goes right down to every officer who sees that every six weeks. All the legislation, everything comes out on video. They see it at different times in their stations. Individuals go in when they want but checks are made that they all see it ... I'm forever speaking at local functions, it's all reported in the local paper. It's possible to police in a conurbation and not even know what the man at the top is thinking. That is not so easy in this force ... We all live in——shire. We all understand, identify with the area, and the people can identify with us. That isn't necessarily so— I mean how many people live in Brixton today ... I don't know if you know the fact that the district councillors in——have got together and recommended that the——police force be split up into three ... I believe, yes, that forces can get too big ... The biggest problems and most serious complaints have always proved to come from the bigger conurbations. This suggests to me that the control is far better in a small one—not that I think this is an optimum size for a force. I think the right size is about 1,700 or 1,800."

"In this force, because I'm still small, I can still know most of the people, and I can run it as a family as opposed to a force. I still believe the personal qualities are very, very important. If your style of management becomes very *laissez-faire*, so that you acknowledge that everything that goes on in society generally ought to go on in your police force, then the personal qualities of your officers will go down-hill very, very quickly. So you see, we still know of every breakdown of marriage, we still work hard so that the policeman in society is seen to be upholding the law of standards. We can't do much about it, but we make an awful lot of noises so that the policeman feels very uncomfortable while that sort of situation is going on ... In my view there is an optimum size to command a police force really effectively from the top. I would hate to be a Ken Newman trying to manage that elephant that he's got there. In a smaller force you can influence from top to bottom very quickly, and have an enormous influence on what goes on from day to day. What's the optimum size? I would guess around the 2,000 mark. Once you go bigger than that your management style has got to be adjusted to cope with it. It would be very difficult to be a chief constable, on the style of management I've got, in Avon and Somerset which is 3,000, let alone something like the West Midlands. For instance, I will sit down and talk about an individual murder, as I have this morning. I've been talking to the detective superintendent for about half an hour. I would doubt if Jim Anderton would to that, because he gets too many murders ... I look at what's been going on with the Moors murder case, I would guess that's handled between ACC and chief superintendent, head of CID. When they see Mr Anderton, it's to say, 'You ought to know so that we can dig up the moors next week.' ... But start right down at the bottom end. How many chief policemen do you know that go and visit in hospital? I go and visit all of mine if they go into hospital. So I have a style of management which is local, a welfare conscious style. I've got time to send—my staff prepare for me—letters to officers who are injured on duty or are long-term sick, three weeks or more. I write a letter to them saying how sorry we are and all the rest of it. So I can have a very personal involvement. I do the rounds and go to a Special Constabulary parade once a year, and make a special survey, so they see me as a person. When the hippy problem is down here I'll go and visit them. The other day things were really popping. And I go down there every day. And they see me in the top high-profile chief's role. So I'm not only the figure-head. Now you take Geoffrey Dear. Half his force probably only see his photographs in the newspaper, so his influence on the force would be more on the PR side, which is for public consumption. As opposed to my style of direct involvement. My deputy and I can spend many hours talking about what's going on in the force. Whereas if you get too big, and especially if you get national commitments as well like Jim Anderton has at the present time, you have to pass so many things to the deputy [John Stalker]. Now I don't decry delegation, but it depends to what extent you are really the controller, or just chairman of the board."

"People say this is a family force—1,000 of us of all ranks. We're small enough to know each other and have radio contact with each other, and be able to speak informally. I don't think there are any problems that are allowed to fester ... I do not favour large police forces, in fact I think they are a disaster. The chief constable of West Midlands went on public record as saying he had no control over his force, which I think was sad. It has caused problems. It seemed overnight we had these amalgamations and we had the formation of some very large police forces. It means that the contact or under-standing a chief constable can have within his force, or with local politicians, the local officers or various councils, must be minimum. Take Thames Valley—three counties there, I don't know how many district councils. He can't really know what's happening. All that happens is that's devolved to various people—superintendents who are very much in charge."

This critique of large police forces is not a sour grapes reaction of small force chiefs. It was in fact especially prevalent amongst chiefs in the larger forces. Thus 93 per cent of chiefs of the large forces (3,000 officers or more) felt the growth in size had created problems, compared with 68 per cent of chiefs in forces with less than 3,000 officers. A clear majority of all chiefs believe large is not beautiful, but this was particularly true of those with experience of big forces.

The minority view was that large forces had advantages which out-weighed the disadvantages. These were said to be certain economies of scale, such as the possibility of having more specialist squads and the capacity to assemble rapidly a large body of officers if these were needed in an emergency. There were better career structures for the officers, and there was more scope for using advanced technology. It was also felt that a plethora of small forces could suffer from the opposite problem to the large force's lack of local identity: too much variation in policing policy between areas.

"There are benefits in the logistics of large forces. You can get 1,000 men on a Saturday night like that if you wanted it. If you wanted a detective superintendent 5.00 on Friday night for a serious inves-tigation, you could find one very quickly. There has to be a minimum optimum level that is economically viable. If we go back to the old days of little boroughs and 300 policemen, there was so much duplicity of effort. If you go back to the old style of watch committees and that localized policing—there is a difficulty in trying to do what you wanted to do for the benefit of the whole. It might be seen in one little area that one thing is good and in the next little borough it's not good. At least there is a greater degree of consistency."

"I think it's made it easier, depending on what your starting-base was. The small borough forces which I had really have gone, and we should never move back to that stage. I would say the region of 1,000 to 3,000 men is the sort of range of a good, manageable sized force. It's much better to have those resources to deal and divert to your major problems."

"A police force basically needs to be large enough (*a*) to be able to provide the specialist resources, and (*b*) to offer a decent career structure for the people in it, and (*c*) to be able to provide enough inherent ballast to be able to cope with serious emergencies. So managing a very small force—the smallest I've worked in had about 1,700—that was on the sort of bottom edge of viability. Fundamentally a police force needs to be not much less than 1,700. If you get up to too many thousand things start to get a bit cumbersome. I think the Metropolitan Police certainly is much too large."

Consultation

Since the Report of the Edmund-Davies Committee (Home Office, 1978), which followed the unrest in police forces in 1977 over pay and conditions (Reiner, 1978, 34–45, 273–6), it has become mandatory for chief constables to establish joint negotiating and consultative committees in which the Police Federation is represented. These are intended to allow the rank and file a say in the formulation of police policies. Facilities for consulting rank-and-file views had in fact existed before in many forces, but this more participative structure of management became mandatory after Edmund-Davies.

I asked chief constables whether consultation with the rank and file about policy, along the lines of the Edmund-Davies recommendations, was desirable, and whether it had caused any problems for the management of police forces. Consultation was almost universally felt to be desirable (95 per cent of chiefs said it was). The great majority (75 per cent) also said it had not caused any problems for management, although a minority (amounting to a quarter) said it had caused some. The majority view that a participative management style, based on a strong degree of consultation, was not only desirable but more effective, is illustrated below:

"It doesn't cause me any problems. I can only speak from my own experience as chief constable here. It is a healthy situation that the Federation members know if they have a problem. One of the current ones ongoing is this apprehension about AIDS and Hepatitis B. Take that as an example. When Hepatitis B was first seen to be a serious problem I offered the people in the drug squad and at risk a course of injections at about £70 each, and no one wanted it. Then suddenly in a wide sphere they get apprehensions, came back hot foot and said, 'Boss, can you change your mind and do something about it?' Now there is an open door here—my door. Although I encourage them not to come knocking at my door first. Not because I don't want to see them but because I believe there is a proper chain of consultation. And problems in this force are first resolved, if at all possible, at divisional level. If they cannot resolve it there, or there are matters of a general nature across the force, they come to the assistant chief constable of administration. If it's a discipline aspect, they go to the deputy. If they can't resolve them, they have a right of audience with me at any time, just by arranging an appointment. And they do from time to time. They come in and have a chat about a variety of things. And we can talk also, of course, quite informally under the Edmund-Davies style with a joint negotiation and consultative committee. In fact, we are due to meet tomorrow on common ground, and they will put up matters they think of concern. Or I'll put them up. And I've tried to involve them on all working parties. One of the major working parties we had when I became chief. I looked around and thought we need now to set a template for the future, with regard to organizational and personal needs for resources for the future. It hadn't been done in the light of the formation of the force ten years previously. Very little resource addition, only forty odd officers, with the population growing, crime trends, and problems with race, etc., etc. So we decided then to set up two working groups. One was to look at civilianization. The Audit Commission came in and told us there were fifty posts, police jobs, going to be thrown out and civilianized. Of course, the Federation's initial reaction to that was, 'We don't like it!' We put them on the working party, and said, 'Well, you go and look elsewhere.' And they came back and said, 'Well, boss, we still don't like it, but we are convinced there is no alternative. To make the best use of resources you've got to go down the road of bringing in police officers where professional skills are involved, otherwise bring in civilians at half the cost.' They've been on that working party, and every working party we've got on at present: one on career development and appraisals, on health and stress. They don't only feel they are involved, but in fact we are prepared to listen to their viewpoint. They recognize at the end of the day that, if we don't like their viewpoint, then it cannot be sustained. We agree to disagree. At the end of the day the chief constable manages the organization. But it is far better to manage it with the acquiescence of their support ... I wouldn't want to shout it too loudly but I draw up what I believe are the policies for the next year after consultation with the senior officers of the force, and chief superintendents right down to grass-roots level."

"It creates challenges for police management, but I believe in consultation. I believe you get the Police Federation you deserve. You must encourage people to be responsible. I have a policy meeting about once a fortnight, and the Police Federation and Super-intendents' Association get their papers and come in and sit and debate. If you like, that's part of my training, and they clearly understand. Certainly they're made to play a part in the decision-making process, but I have a decision to make, because I have to account for it. They can say how awful it is, but that's the decision. We were all part and parcel of that decision. There are some police managers who would say: 'What's it got to do with them!' It's fairly easy to say, 'Do as you're bloody told!' But we sit around a table and decide, if at all possible, together. It suits my style better to take people along with me."

"I believe the only way for the police force to move forward and be effective is to change our management style dramatically, to a consultative and participating style. You've got to seek the widest possible consensus to the policies you're developing. At the end of the day it's down to the men on the ground, so you've got to let them own the action. They must be responsible for the development at local level of the tactics that are necessary to achieve that overall policy. That requires a much more precise management style than the old authoritarian one, and a much more careful assessment of where you put resources ... Here we have six autonomous areas commanded by superintendents. I refer to them as mini-chief constables. The tactics they each employ to address a policy could be different. If you work at this consultation–participative style it can be very, very effective in defusing a lot of this lack of understanding ... Management is all about persuading others about how they work towards an aim. I watched the chairman of ICI on television the other night giving an interview on management. I was very pleased that someone who runs a multinational company should be talking the same language as I was talking in the police organization. I believe in taking the involvement of the rank and file to the limit. They're involved in all the policy-making. They certainly sit down with me when we finalize the policy statement that is issued ... I've changed the management style of this force totally round from the authoritarian hierarchical system to a very consultative, public-spirited style, and I am satisfied with it. That's a very pompous statement, but you should go and ask others who have to work with me. All the indications are that it's proved useful."

"Without wishing to identify anybody, my predecessor didn't want change. He was utterly opposed to any sort of change, and was quite happy for the ship to go along in a particular way. I felt there had to be a different approach. I was conscious of two thrusts really. The first of those thrusts was the fact that the Home Office had highlighted, quite rightly in my view, that we had to make a better use of resources. Second, I was convinced that we had a system of management here by backside kicking in a chain, or a ladder. That you managed by, you know, if the guy was doing something wrong, you kicked him. And everybody kicked everybody else. Any decision that was made by a constable had to be ratified and reviewed by a sergeant, then an inspector, and so on right up the chain. I was getting files on my desk that had been to everyone, the world and his wife, and there was no decision to be made. It was not management, it was supervision, and we had to get away from that. I was concerned, going around the divisions, that the people weren't feeling fulfilled. That sergeants were feeling that inspectors were sitting on their shoulders and so on. They were all chewing over the same stuff all the time. There was far too much influence coming from headquarters. And you've got to stimulate the activity out there. So with that main thought behind us, we got together a really good management team. And I didn't say, 'Here is the structure we're going to do!' I'm not for this mechanistic system which Kenneth Newman is noted for. I like organic change, evolutionary change: people have got to understand it. You've got to build in flexibility, sew the sort of skeleton to let people put the flesh on it, because as long as the skeleton is a particular size and shape you can at least control it."

"Much of what's reflected in Edmund-Davies was in being here anyway, so a lot of Edmund-Davies is a template from what prevailed here. We've always had consultation, that was brought about when I came here. My predecessor would keep the Federation happy at any price, to the erosion of good order and discipline if I might say so.

So we restructured it very quickly. I had one or two hiccups, then set up what I called consultative groups within the force. I've always been a great believer of staff management dialogue. I had to break through a lot of sound barriers, policing here being what it was. It was very rigid, a 'you should know your place' sort of situation. My middle management took no great delight in having to discuss certain issues with staff representatives. My experience is that the staff representatives will go so far with you, but when it comes to making a decision, they say, 'But that's your problem, chief, not mine.' I think it's an advantage frankly, because you keep them informed, but what you're doing—and you might say I'm being a little devious here—you're giving them a status. Whereas if your staff representatives are sent for by the chief in an unstructured way, and he says, 'Look, I ought to tell you this is what we're going to do. I'm just marking your cards to dispel the rumour factor.' Then they are going to go back to their organization and want to know who the chief has taken into his confidence. I think there's a status factor. Let's face it, they're their representatives. You probably may not care for them because they seem to have been a pocket of under-achievers. Human nature being what it is ... We here have a consultative committee that meets with the deputy on a wide range of domestic issues, and we have various out-groups that deal with such domestic issues as uniforms and canteen, which are dealt with outside that committee. They deal with the nuts and bolts of it and come up with propositions. But in the broad policies of operational policing and administration we seek out their points of view."

It is evident that the majority of chiefs not only see consultation as desirable in principle, but as a useful tool for controlling the organization in practice, through the creation of consensus, and containment of conflict. Despite this, a minority of chiefs regarded the new pressure to consult as problematic.

"We have a very good relationship with our staff associations. But we have over-reacted. We went overboard on the idea of consultation. I mean, in this force, I shudder as a rate-payer occasionally, to think I've got a full-time Federation secretary to look after the members of my force, or this force, and to deal with the problems they have. Now if anybody is grossly underworked it is he really. We have a joint liaison committee, which hasn't met for three years because we iron everything out at grass roots. We met on the two occasions previously as a matter of course, because we thought we should have a meeting, so for two years we met slavishly. It was an over-reaction. What has happened now, I think management is sorting itself out from a period of soft management of industry. It's happening outside, after a period of very soft management, giving in, giving in. To some extent this has happened in the police service too."

"I think they should be used. I have Federation representatives on all working parties, and I set up working parties to look at any change in procedure or policy ... I accept they have an important part to play. But my senior officers, my chief superintendents, have been concerned at the way I meet the Federation on our JNCC [Joint Negotiating and Consultative Committee]. Because the Super-intendents' Association representatives reported back to them that I was discussing with the Federation matters that I should first have discussed with them. They thought that in fact the JNCC was acquir-ing a higher status than the senior officers' conference. My view is that it is consultative. It doesn't decide, but I want to know the views of the chaps who have got to carry it out. It's as simple as that. I have to appease. OK, I obviously tend to senior officers' views. But the JNCC certainly considers all matters of importance."

In addition to the few chief constables who had reservations about the legitimacy or utility of consultations as such, there were some whose reservations concerned whether the Police Federation was an appropriate vehicle for this:

"Until you said the words 'Police Federation' I would have responded that I tried to involve everybody in the management of this force, right from the bottom to the top, because out of the mouths of babes come some things, you know. The Federation I always acknowledge, but sometimes I just go and tell them what I'm going to do. Because, quite frankly, I don't think they've got the knowledge or training or professionalism to contribute to the sorts of things I consider. Where I do feel they have a role to play is if it's going to affect the men's lives. I worry sometimes about the Federation, that it's losing its way in the role that it is performing in the service. I just read the résumé of their Blackpool Conference, and they are talking even now about getting another shilling out of the job, and restoring another rest day. I think sometimes their decisions of what they go for doesn't represent the rank and file of their membership who are pretty apathetic anyway and don't care. I think sometimes they pursue causes which, if they're not careful, they're going to alienate all the good will in the Association of County Councils, the Association of Municipal Authorities. Sadly, some of the time chief constables and I think the Federation—I am talking about Surbiton now, headquarters—the Federation ought to stand back and take a look at itself. Look again at the law which put it into being. What it was put into being for was 'the welfare and efficiency of the individual'. So often you will hear men *en passant* saying, 'Well, it's a load of bloody nonsense. I don't know why they asked for that. We don't need that!' But I do consult at all levels. I don't do it slavishly. I'm not prepared to sit here and say I consult on every turn. I know the things that I want to do, and if I feel they have a contribution to make they can come and make it, they're very welcome. If I feel I'm going to do it and it's not going to be changed, I'll say that. I'm not going to go through the motions, to posture for the sake of it. I am very lucky, I have a very good Federation."

Police Federation

The above reservations about the role of the Federation in consultation were symptomatic of a more general hostility to the Police Federation on the part of one-third of the chiefs. In fact, virtually all the chiefs were hostile to the concept of police unionism. With only one exception, they opposed the idea of making the Police Federation an independent trade union like some Continental police have, without the fetters imposed by the Police Acts of 1919 and 1964. (The exception argued they were already like a trade union so it would make no difference.) The general opposition was rooted in a sense of the special characteristics of the police as an occupation which preclude full union powers. This conception is in fact shared by most of the Federated ranks themselves (Reiner, 1978, ch.5). The following is characteristic:

"I believe the set-up that we got here is good for the British police service. If we went into a trade-union type posture, where you'd be bound to have affiliation with the TUC, you would then get analogies drawn between the shopfloor worker and the policeman. Having read Huw Beynon's book, *Working for Ford*, they are automatons in human form, who go there and get paid a good screw to be bored out of their minds, and think that's blagging the trade unions. That attitude would start to pervade the service, and the whole good will and community spirit that policemen do so well would be dissipated."

Those chiefs who had reservations about the Federation felt it already had too much of the power and attitudes of a trade union, and its campaigning activities could impugn the image of impartiality in the police service. Many distinguished between their own local representatives, who were seen as acceptable, and the militancy which was regarded as emanating from the Federation headquarters at Surbiton. A few felt, however, that their own representatives had been contaminated by the spirit of militancy:

"We did an exercise on the allowances some officers got, and as a result of that exercise saved about several thousand pounds. Which created all sorts of problems for us because they said, 'You are taking away a perk.' There was a tremendous kickback. Because I think the Federation, union, or whatever, is in the game of winning Brownie points, not losing Brownie points. But I'm afraid my Federation lost an awful lot. I have got a secretary who is fairly articulate. Well, he writes a lot of letters, he took a degree at the university about two or three years ago. My predecessor had refused to allow him time off to go to university. Anyway, there have been lots of problems there. At the end of the day it is all to do with who manages, the right to govern. Normal Federation has got a role to play in terms of putting its members' viewpoint in a way that is acceptable, through the JNCC."

"There's a desire for a union amongst some Federation officials, but there isn't the support in the rank and file. The only time it emerges is when they feel they are being suppressed in pay terms ... The Federation don't tend to raise things in terms of efficiency. They're not forward-looking, they don't see it as their role to improve the management of the police force ... If you come along and talk to my Federation they would be happy about the ambience here, pleased about the relationships which exist. There might be one force where there was a distinctly bad odour between the chief constable and the Federation, and that would be one out of forty-three. You go to Surbiton and talk to the Federation there, and all you'll hear about is the bad case!"

"The Federation concept is right. The criticism I have is now they're tending to become a trade union, with a local trade-union office here. I've said to my people, 'Look, for God's sake, if you don't agree with those people there at Surbiton, say you don't agree with them! You're not bound to do what they're telling you to do!' For instance, at a disciplinary hearing, the Federation are officially saying, 'Don't say anything.' I say: 'Listen! That's absolutely bloody stupid advice, because the policeman has got a perfectly good explanation for what's happened. And even if he hasn't, if he's done something wrong or made a mistake, why the hell can't he say so! And we can go to the complainants and say sorry.' But you're getting from the Federation, 'Say nothing!' That's where I fall out with them. They're tending nowadays to be much more like a trade union. They want a professional wage with a trade-union mentality.''

"I had a little bit of a problem last June with the Police Federation. Or with some individuals rather than the Federation as a collection of individuals. The Federation are involved in every one of our policy-making bodies. Not, obviously, my policy advisory group, but all those down from it. In addition we have the JNCC. They come and see the chairman and secretary, or me, or the ACC admin., preliminary to the JNCC. We have a very good rapport. The difficulty is we're trying to create a sounding-board on each subdivision, of constables, just a few representatives of what is going on. And the Federation resent that, they see that as usurping their particular function. But the Federation rep on each division tends to represent his own view because he hasn't the capacity to get round to everybody. Now this is in the melting-pot. The difficulty in our hierarchical organization has been that top management is cloistered. Perhaps the inspectors would have had a say, and they're part of the Federation, but it's always been us and them. You tell us what to do and we will go and do it. I will now listen to them, take it into account. I can't do everything because there is no common thread. There's disagreement whether they should wear blue shirts or white shirts, helmets or caps, Nato pullovers or tunics. Whether they should have cars or bikes, response policing or community policing. So you listen to them all, and then explain why you're going to do certain things. That's the toughest thing, explaining to the Federation. We've just had elections, and the new group of people in the Federation are more intelligent, open, and understand more. Not that they reflect my views—they question me quite fiercely. But they listen rather than just representing a kind of dogma and duel-based view of what I should be doing ... God forbid they should ever become an independent union! I remember one particular chief constable, when I was regional secretary of ACPO, resigned at the publication of Edmund-Davies, because he couldn't actually bring himself to listen to members of the Federation. 'I couldn't bear them coming in and telling me what they think!' And he went. He was well over his time, but that was the trigger. It was a bigger change for chief constables

than you will ever perceive ... And what happens now is the whole
Police Federation get carried away into the political field.''

Police Discipline

These attitudes of hostility to consultation and representation are symptomatic of a deeper regret felt by some chief constables about the
passing of the more autocratic and militaristic discipline which used to
characterize police forces. Concern about the relaxation of discipline
was in fact more widespread than the anxieties of a minority about
participative management styles. Just over half of chief constables (53
per cent) thought the relaxation of discipline caused management problems. A third of chiefs did not feel it was a problem, while 7 per cent
believed that there had not actually been any relaxation of standards of
discipline.

The majority view, that there had been a decline in discipline standards, and this was a cause for concern, is illustrated below. It was a
perspective that was characteristic of, though not confined to, older
county chiefs.

"As an old-fashioned policeman, because of my length of service, I
do cringe a little when I see policemen walking around without hats
on. In fact I was in London yesterday and saw the Met. officers at a
scene. A policeman and policewoman without hats had just walked
back to the car and got in. They could easily have put their hats on
when they left the car. Longish hair, OK, yes, it makes me cringe a
little, but I don't get enraged about it, and rush out force orders
about smartness. OK, I'll mention it if I think it's getting too long.
Occasionally the HMI will make the point. Particularly about the
drug officers who are wearing ear-rings and hair on the shoulder. I
slightly regret it, I do wish occasionally they could be a little smarter.
But I go along with what the uniform boys and the Federation, what
they like. In fact, I am pretty liberal in that they want white shirts,
woolly pullies, and anoraks. In a way I have to be a little careful that
what they are wanting is not making us look even more paramilitary
than we were before. This is more my fear than looking untidy or
unkempt. I mean, I hope the people I recruit in the first place have
some pride, personal pride. They have joined a uniform service and
one must assume that they are prepared to wear the uniform as it
should be worn. But undoubtedly there has been a loss of turnout,

the smartness of bearing, and haircuts and headgear. I am philosophical about it.''

''In this county we have managed, because we are still a little bit old-
fashioned in that sense, to maintain, as a general statement, fairly
high, smart appearance. My officers wear white gloves in the summer
months. I didn't introduce it, they were here before, and I suggested
they got rid of them. But they seemed to like it. It softens the image
when all the tourists come here. They push hard for good quality
uniforms so that indicates they like to appear smart. I wouldn't say
that was a major problem. There's just one or two isolated individuals,
it is difficult to smarten them up. But certainly, on the general morality
of the force—yes, that is sloppy. What is happening in the big outside
world is happening in the force. You know, officers are having affairs
with people, they are leaving home, leaving their wives, and this sort
of thing. That really I find upsetting, and a difficult management
issue. I have made it clear on a number of occasions when I can
properly do so, that I find that sort of conduct lowers our standard
in the eyes of the public. And you've got to answer for that. If we
want the privilege of being a police officer, having a slightly higher
status and definitely a higher salary than most others, then we must
accept some of the responsibility that goes with it. Our management
style has not become sloppy, but it is more relaxed in that it is less
formal. But I still think that lines of responsibility are drawn. There
is a desire from grass-roots membership to acknowledge a hierarchy.
It makes them feel a bit comfortable, I think, that they have got a
hierarchy, which they can either blame or get underneath for a bit of
protection.''

''You've got to relate to present-day standards. Well, I don't like
beards anymore than you do—although you are wearing one. I was
brought up in a disciplined service, the RAF, where you didn't wear
a beard, in fact if you had a beard you got it off or you were in trouble.
Although a century ago it was acceptable. When I joined the service,
thirty-two years ago, there was an expectation about appearance.
There was an expectation about extra-marital affairs, about your
general conduct, debt, and what have you. But turn the clock on.
You're got to reflect society's norms really, there's no point the police
service trying to stand as bastions against the norms of society. Now
you get a chief constable wearing a beard. Let's be honest, you are
up against it if you want to be strict. But I take no exception to beards
now ... What I don't like is the untidy one. Now it may be that the
sergeants and inspectors are less likely to take it on board. The public

out there still believe the personal moral standards of policemen should be higher than theirs. Now that's not seen to be the case … It's no good saying we are whiter than white and our officers don't go off and take out somebody else's wife. It would be naïve to say that—we would make fools out of ourselves. The present-day youngsters wouldn't stand for the style of discipline that you read in the old police discipline books … It does no harm if it is relaxed, provided there's still a mutual respect for the rank structure, and a sense of personal discipline and pride in the organization and in the job … The important thing is that sergeants upwards should be setting standards. If you get a drunken chief constable, or a womanizing chief constable, it's not surprising if somebody comes up and says, 'Well, if it's good enough for the chief constable, why shouldn't it be good enough for me?'"

"I am a traditionalist and possibly something of a moralist. I still firmly believe that marriage vows once taken mean a great deal. On a personal note, I deprecate people who are not able to maintain that sort of thing. But they've issued notes of guidance which mean that I must now in my official capacity look upon things of that nature in a different light, and I do so, I hope, very fairly. When I was a young policeman a sexual dalliance might well have been treated as something which was an offence against the discipline code. Now it is not, and cannot be. Even though there are times when the actions of an individual officer once they become headlines would seem to be detrimental to the good image of the force. It is not now one of those things that one does, so one doesn't do it."

While there was a slight majority who were concerned about what they saw as an erosion of discipline standards, a substantial minority (one-third) did not. They regarded the relaxation of militaristic discipline not only as inevitable because of social change, but a welcome move away from authoritarianism.

"I expect the service to manifestly demonstrate signs of discipline, appearance, smartness of deportment, proper recognition of rank without being sycophantic. But we are going through changing times. The notion that the superintendent possessed an extraordinary degree of either intelligence or power is clearly questionable, so we have to adjust. I would like to think that in serious disciplinary matters the service is still as severe and as judgemental about itself as it was hitherto. Perhaps with more objectivity than hitherto. But I would also like to think that there is a proper wind of change going through the organization. I would want a police officer to relate openly and frankly and confidently with members of the public, with the media, with senior officers, and subordinates.''

"There's been a welcome change in thinking. If you had served under some of the old autocrats, blinkered senior officers, that I have served under, you wouldn't have any doubt that thinking has changed. All the people you have recruited today have grown up in a more liberal background. We are all conditioned by the society in which we live, and there has been a tremendous liberalization.''

A small minority (7 per cent) claimed there had not in fact been any change in discipline standards, at any rate in their own experience:

"We've never had any glaring examples of it happening in this force, to be honest. You have to take into account that we are policed, by and large, by the people of this area. We do have imports. We take in a lot of people from Wales, for example, who cannot get into forces because they are full. But, by and large, our people are born and bred in this area. It isn't a nasty area. It doesn't have the extremes some areas have. And I can't honestly recall a situation where there's been a problem of discipline.''

The role of chief constable was generally acknowledged, then, to have changed markedly. In essence, they had changed—with varying degrees of reluctance—from bobbies to bureaucrats. From being *primus inter pares* in a hierarchical organization with firm discipline, but geared to a clear and shared function, they had evolved into professional managers. As the directors of complex organizations their role had more in common with senior administrators in any large modern bureaucracy than with the policemen they managed. Being professional managers they believed they knew what was right for their organization. Consultation was a subtle tactic for managerial control rather than a supplement for limited know-how at the top. In the final analysis, the managers must decide on the basis of professional expertise. This professional perspective carries over into the question of external control of police forces, as the next chapter on the chief constables' views on accountability will show. The single main thread running through the thinking of chief constables about the control of police forces, internal and external, is that when the buck stops, it stops with them. As one county chief succinctly put it: 'We have very good senior command conferences here. We really get at each other, very often we almost come to blows. It's very much a joint approach. I don't mind democracy amongst us provided they recognize the fact when it comes to voting there's only one vote, and that's mine.'

Note

1. For different British perspectives on the applicability of such management theory to policing see Butler, 1984; Weatheritt, 1986; and Bradley, Walker, and Wilkie, 1986. Similar debates have occurred elsewhere. For the USA, see Swanson and Territo, 1982; Geller, 1985; Witham, 1985; Scott, 1986; Fyfe, 1989. For Canada, see Tardif, 1974; Grosman, 1975; O'Reilly and Dostaler, 1983; Hann *et al.*, 1985; MacDonald, 1986; Loree, 1989. For Europe generally, see Fijnaut and Visser, 1985.

11 Who Governs?
The Accountability of Police Forces

All debates about policing issues eventually end up with the question of accountability or control of police forces. The bottom line of any controversy about policing is who governs? Who has the power to determine the policies which will actually be implemented? As policing has become more controversial in the last quarter-century, so police accountability has become an ever more hotly debated topic. By the 1980s, two clearly polarized camps had developed. On the left the view became dominant that the tripartite system of accountability envisaged by the 1962 Report of the Royal Commission on the Police and the 1964 Police Act had been eroded. The local police authorities had been denuded of any significant power. As the legitimate expression of the popular will in particular areas, they ought to be clearly and effectively empowered not only to be equal parties in the triumvirate, but the dominant entity. This followed from a conception of policing as primarily a local service, and a constitutional commitment to local democracy. (Lustgarten, 1986, is the seminal argument supporting this analysis.) The Labour Party clearly espoused a similar line in the 1987 General Election, and remains pledged to reform the structure of accountability in this direction.

On the other hand, the Conservatives have remained fundamentally satisfied with the status quo in terms of basic constitutional structure, and would not wish drastically to reform the 1964 Police Act. However, they do see problems of ensuring that the existing structure works effectively. They have introduced reforms intended to enhance local consultation, and the handling of complaints against the police, in the Police and Criminal Evidence Act 1984 (PACE). They have also tightened the financial scrutiny of police forces by a series of circulars, notably Home Office Circular 114 of 1983, and Circular 106 of 1988. Altogether their strategy has been characterized as the 'transparent stewardship' model of police accountability (Morgan, 1987). The police are stewards of powers delegated from elected representatives, and not immediately controlled by them. However, the manner in which they exercise this stewardship has to be transparent so that it can be evaluated properly.

While the parties of the centre (the Social Democrats and Liberal Democrats) have accepted with Labour that more profound reform of the accountability structure might be needed, they have not committed themselves to specific solutions. Rather, they have tended to argue the case for a major review of the fundamental system, a new Royal Commission on the Police, as a necessary condition of effective change (Alderson, 1986).

This chapter will consider the views of chief constables themselves on these issues, and their experience of the present system.[1] We will examine their views on the accountability of policing policy to local and central government, as well as their assessment of the accountability of individual officers to the public through the complaints system.

Accountability to Local Government

During the 1980s there have been several noted and long-running conflicts between police authorities and chief constables, primarily in the metropolitan areas (e.g. see Loveday, 1985; Okojie, 1985; McLaughlin, 1990). In London, where there is no local police authority, the Greater London Council (GLC) mounted a vigorous yet abortive campaign to secure one. The GLC, together with the other metropolitan authorities, was abolished by the Local Government Act 1985. However, the debate continues about the new Joint Boards which replaced the provincial authorities (Loveday, 1987, 1991).

Despite the much-publicized clashes in a few celebrated cases, nearly half of the chief constables (45 per cent) think their own police authority performs its functions well, and another 35 per cent say quite well. Only 18 per cent feel that their own police authority does its job badly. However, the chief constables' assessment of police authorities in general is less favourable. One-quarter say they do their job badly, and only another quarter say they perform well. A half say they do their job quite well. It is still the case, though, that only a minority of chiefs feel police authorities in general perform their functions badly.

It is clear from the chief constables' comments that their conception of a good police authority is one which acts as a sounding-board for local opinion, but which does not ultimately question the chief's decisions. Police authorities, in general or in particular cases, are criticized either for being political and seeking to direct the police, or apathetic and not supporting them adequately. In the chiefs' view, the good police authority successfully charts the course between the Scylla of political dogmatism and the Charybdis of complacent indifference.

"If you have a good authority, in support, they very adequately fill their role. Because they are, or should be, to a bloke like me a sort of guiding counsel to say, 'Well, are we giving them a square deal? Do you think this is right?' I would love to go to my police authority with this sort of thing about the cautioning procedure we had developed . . . I would love to have the opportunity of going to the police authority and telling them what I have decided to do, as a consensus view of the force. Very rarely do they give you the opportunity of explaining those things, because they've got so much in-fighting amongst themselves. You know, like the House of Commons. Instead of sitting down calmly and saying, 'Yeah, Mr Policeman. Yes. That sounds like a good idea', it's 'We're not so sure. Can we be told about this? It's only a two-page document.'"

"Years ago, the police committee used to start at 11 and finish at 12 for drinks. Now they want to debate, and are more interested in what's going on. This tripartite arrangement is based on the fact that you are a reasonable individual, they [the police authority] are reasonable, and the Home Office is reasonable. And we will work together. I am accountable to the police committee, unless they were making a political decision about an operational matter, which the tripartite set-up obviates happening."

"Here in this county they perform as was intended in 1964. It wouldn't suit Mr Kaufman [then Labour Shadow Home Secretary] but it falls in with the Act. They do a good job. Their one object in life is to get the best service within——shire within the financial constraints imposed by central government. It's unfortunate now that politics has reared its head in some police authorities to the extent it has. I've never experienced it personally."

"It wouldn't be a bad idea if they utilized some of the powers they have now fully. I find it is very difficult to motivate them to be of any practical use to me. They are great ones for making political statements at meetings, but the rest is difficult. I have a Labour-dominated county council, but the Conservatives, with the help of the magistrates, managed to get a Conservative chairman on the police committee ... So I have a difficult time. The contribution they make is very limited. Now, my policy and objectives and strategies document, each year I've taken it in draft form, and got no contribution whatsoever. It's circulated and they have time to think about it. But they come along and make no contribution whatsoever. I try to interest them in the force. I lay on trips around police stations. They are supportive, but not sufficiently critical in a constructive sense, nor do they give me any practical assistance. I suspect I could be comforted by the fact that if I stepped too far out of line it would become obvious by what they say."

"I know, as you do, in the more militant areas of Manchester and Liverpool they take a very active interest in their police authority. There is a very proper role for police authorities today. I think generally, throughout the country, when we get away from those key areas with big problems, they don't use their influence enough. What has horrified me about local government is the lack of knowledge of members of committees. They really are deeply ignorant. My police authority, the level of questioning, the level of appreciation—and I try hard to educate them, I give them lectures and that—but the general level of knowledge and perception about problems is very low, and that's true right across the board. Democracy grindeth exceedingly slowly. They should be more efficient and competent."

Because of the opposed pitfalls of excessive politicization and apathetic indifference, chief constables did not in general prefer Conservative to Labour authorities, even though the main conflicts were with radical Labour ones. Each had characteristic shortcomings. Traditional Labour authorities which were not too politically 'extreme' were often the best, and tended to be financially less parsimonious.

"There has been a tradition in this country when I first came here—an old Conservative county. That sort of style has changed. I suspect before I came here it was almost a doffing the cap situation. But the hung council which we've now had for some six or seven years, if nothing else it stops extremes. We have a very good chairman, who is a socialist chairman. Retired ICI manager, who is interested, questions things, keen to get involved, and to have a wider understanding of policing. And we involve him at every opportunity I can to enhance his learning and information. He's very honest and expects you to be as well. His predecessor, who'd been chairman for fourteen years, a Conservative, was a nice fellow but bloody ineffective. When my predecessor used to go to the police committee, he'd say, 'Well, I'll get the chief constable', instead of being the chairman, and putting his view across. That no longer happens, and within the limitations of the fiscal situation I do reasonably well because I have a supportive committee."

"My police authority here are very good people who don't wear any political colours. If you ask each of them what they stand for, they stand for a set of values, not political colour. The Labour group, old-fashioned socialists, have a little meeting for five minutes. I think they only do it to posture, they never come in with a concerted voice, even though they are the majority. I mean, they said to me, 'You shouldn't privatize, chief.' I want to privatize my canteen cleaning and catering. It's not part of their current flavour of the month. And I said, 'Well, I think it's the best way to do it, the best value for money really.' 'All right, chief, then. You do it.' And that was it. You know I have a very good police authority. So if it ever came to conflict, say over baton rounds, I'd say I don't think it's within your remit, you don't have the knowledge, you don't have the professionalism, the training, or the background to tell me if I should or I shouldn't."

"I don't see any problem with the police authority, but of course I'm living in a relatively moderate county. I've never seen extreme pressure either way, from extreme right or extreme left. Perhaps I sit in rather a little sheltered land. There is a danger. People tend to say, 'Oh, there's likely to be political interference if it's local.' Well, there's likely to be political interference if it's national. Politicians are politicians whether they are local or national, it's a fact of life . . . Your relationship is very much with your chairman. Police authorities, particularly with a caucus provision, tend to become a rubber stamp. The discussions have gone on before the police authority is ever seen to sit in public. I'm having police committee meetings now that sometimes last four or five minutes because everything has been done before we ever set foot in County Hall. So it's nice and easy: I do the job through the chairman. We have an ongoing discussion, quite a bit of chat, trying to keep him in the picture. The public at the end of the day don't see it. It's a relationship thing. A chief constable has to be politically sensitive without being politically involved. He's got to be prepared to relate to his police committee. I've had, since I've been here, five chairmen. To a greater or lesser extent, I've got on with all of them ... The best people I've ever had to work for were old, moderate Labour people. Any suggestion they're not interested in law and order, or the state of society, or catching burglars, it's bloody nonsense! They're as tough as anybody. They're probably about the best to work for. Strangely enough the chief constables who've been mostly in conflict with their police authorities are very often the ones who've been best off for money. I was talking to——— [another county chief constable] today. You've seen him? [R.R.: Not yet.] Meanest bloody police authority in the country. And yet they're always saying how much they support law and order. If you get extremists on any end, either on the Right or the Left, that's where the difficulty arises. You can be in conflict with either of them for different reasons. I've had some odd people on the Right in my time—the hang 'em and flog 'em brigade, trying to get you to make statements about what you'd like to do to people if you had your way, to support them publicly."

As the above quotes imply, most chiefs see good relations with police authorities as a two-sided transaction, a reasonable arrangement for reasonable people, as the common cliché went. In their eyes, the conflicts between authorities and chiefs which had occurred could be as much due to intransigence on the part of the chief as the authority. The chief constable had to be adroit in Machiavellian techniques for 'educating' police authorities to their correct way of thinking, the professional perspective. Ignorance and *naïveté*, not malice, were the most common failings of authority members, and they had to be taught by the chief. Certainly there could be no question of allowing the authority to prevail on any policy matters, but the disagreement should be managed without all-out conflict. This is illustrated by the fact that only 15 per cent of chiefs said they had ever exercised their powers under the Police Act to refuse to give the police authority a report.[2]

"I'm old fashioned. My police authority say I shouldn't waste my time with cannabis, and then heroin. Anyway, the main thing is, I'm a public servant, aren't I, and it is against the law ... I can't remember ever going to them and saying, 'Please, police authority, may I do it?' My relationship with my police authority, which is not unique, is based on not making secrets of things. We meet every six weeks, and there's also subcommittees. There's always a slot on the agenda, which is chief constable's personal report. And I talk to them of our Special Branch, our firearms training policy, selection of firearms.

I take them out on our firearms range. I share information with them. I have an enormously good relationship with my police authority. Not just this one, because I'm now on my third. I had a Conservative police authority when I first came, then a Labour police authority, and now I've got a Joint Board. Entirely different thing. I very often have this conversation with Jim Anderton. I am not hidebound about this business of I'm boss, and they're providers of resources. I treat them always as representatives of my shareholders, the public. If I use them and talk to them and share things with them and seek opinions from them, or want to discuss a new policy, I don't say, 'Well, this is what I'm going to do', I say, 'I propose to do it'. Let me give you an example, which is right up to date. I said at Christmas I'm getting worried about the level of complaints of violence and general intimidation and mayhem in the inner cities on a Friday and Saturday night. And what I propose to do, but I shall need your opinions, is I'm going to give that an uplift in priorities, by putting more policemen on the streets. But I haven't got any money, so, don't make up your minds now, but next time let's talk about it. If you agree in principle now, I'll get the accountants to try and find the money. Then if you agree, we'll do it for three months, measure it, and see. Now the police authority feel involved. It's not a racial matter, really, is it, but they feel involved. There's a little Marxist on it, who is now my best friend. I call him 'little Marxist'. He and I get on basically because, partly, of the fact that he's an avowed Marxist. He and I always go to the town hall together with our wives at Christmas for the annual presentation of Handel's Messiah by the choral society. We've got that kind of relationship. But he says, 'You're very clever, you kick our people from under us all pre-emptively by coming to us all before we ask.' ... There's been a couple of occasions, quite interesting, when I've said to them: 'Look, I want to take you into my confidence on a special job. If anybody talks about this, you'll ruin the whole thing. We've got to trust each other.' And I've walked around sometimes and thought, 'He'll blab, or she'll blab.' But they've swallowed it hook, line, and sinker, and we got on like a house on fire. It's based on this business of how proud I am of the fact that I am a chief constable, and I am an operational man, and you have your business in helping. Now that can be done in a variety of ways. My feeling with them is that we are a partnership and work together. The chairman, vice-chairman, and shadow chairman, I try to keep them, all three of them, addressed of what's going on. They've got a new chairman now who a few weeks ago was invited to go on local TV. And I said to him afterwards,

'I would prefer to brief you before you go. I don't want to tell you, for goodness sake, but you should know certain things.' So on a day to day basis they know what's going on. For example, baton rounds ... I think it's necessary for me to have them ... I said to my police authority: 'First of all I shall have to tell you that we shall disagree. If you understand the whole of my philosophy, you will understand why I go against your wishes' ... And they had a big debate, took it to all community forums, and came back and said, 'We disagree with our chief constable, but, to use his expression, we treat it as an honourable disagreement' ... I go to them every year and say, 'Right, what do you think we should do as a matter of prioritizing things, what should we hit on?' I am one of the leading experts on account-ability, but when it comes to operational matters and control, there are odd occasions where there is room for an honourable disagreement. Because in an old-fashioned way I think I am the professional adviser to the police authority. And if they have fulfilled their most awesome responsibility, and that is the appointment of the chief officer, if they have selected him very carefully, then they have said to themselves on a professional basis, until we have reason otherwise, we trust this man's judgement on professional matters ... That kind of trust, that kind of accountability, wouldn't do tuppence worth of harm in London. You see, they'd chuck Brent, and the policemen who run them will chuck all this left-wingers business. If you look at my police authority in the mucky North, I have as many Marxist and left-wing activists and right-wing nutcases as anybody else. But put them together and you've got a sense of identity and you begin to mould them. If I do my job properly, I'm moulding my police authority, and they're moulding me.''

"At my last police authority meeting I had to argue against the Audit Commission's theory that I could employ more civilians to release police officers for operational work at no extra cost. What my police authority don't understand is that we've civilianized to such an extent now that all the simple mundane jobs where a civilian can come in and take over in a week or two have been civilianized. Now I had to argue like mad, and I've still not convinced them that we've passed the stage where we can buy in civilians at low cost. Now I've got people on my police authority who've been on it since I've been here, and one man in particular never says a word. I've got people who come along who lack the proper status ... These people meet only four times a year with very, very little knowledge and some of them frankly are not very bright. When they come along and take decisions which can be quite traumatic, that is the price of democracy. My police authority have changed somewhat over the years. Not because of the desire to see something happen differently here. They are perfectly happy, I have a good relationship with them. But they read what else is happening in other parts of the world, and I have to answer questions which are totally irrelevant, simply to satisfy them ... It's a question of relating to them. I mean take Manchester, for example. Really Jim Anderton has had two chances, two police authorities, and he's been at odds with both of them. Perhaps they deserve each other. The authority appear quite reasonable to me. I mean even Gabrielle Cox is a very sane person. The difficulties are practical ones that could be overcome differently.''

Thus, the majority of chief constables who saw themselves as enjoying good relations with their own police authorities, attributed much of this to their own efforts and skill at managing the relationship. However, it was recognized that some structures and situations were harder to manage from the chief constable's point of view. Many felt that the Joint Boards which replaced the former unitary metropolitan authorities (after the 1985 Local Government Act) were easier for chiefs to deal with:

"The recent Local Government Act which destroyed the county government in metropolitan terms and introduced the local Joint Boards will perhaps to some extent allay one's fear. Because my experience, and it's limited as yet, it that they are very enthusiastic to have dialogue. Enthusiastic to the point of being ultra-supportive, in saying, 'Are you sure you've got enough money—we're prepared to pay for it.' Which sounds very attractive ... They're still learning and it's certainly an improvement on what one had to put up with in that area before, because it was politically dominated. I think too much is being asked of police authorities frankly, because there's not enough hours in the day to discharge their responsibilities. The Act says they must consult. But if people are not putting themselves forward to be consulted, where on earth do you consult? They control police policy to a greater extent by the fact that they are arbiters of expenditure. Accountability in certain political arenas has become a euphemism of political direction, ideological political direction. That sort of control, it's dangerous I think.''

"If you take the police authority I had in the days of the county council, it was a surfeit of attention from the police authority, in that everything that we did, every minor decision, every aspect of policing, was the subject of constant discussion, formally and informally. If one reflects against that, the new Joint Board's attitude of mind at the moment is 'Get on with your job chief constable, and you report to us. But you are there to row that organization.' It's not just that different people are in charge, I think the involvement of the people who are responsible for policing now is greater within their districts. And their sole concern about the police now is financial and the impact it has on their budgets there. They are very interested in policing but they don't see it as their role currently to be deeply involved in the whys and wherefores of the organization. They see it as being down to me. Whereas the other organization did. And the time available to the current authority, I think, is going to be the determining factor on that. Or the pressure on them from their districts and from elsewhere to become more involved. I'm chasing them currently to be involved and forcing them to be involved. That's the sense of it against their best interests as it were."

"My concern on the accountability role is whether something could be done to take this political part out. I wonder about the Joint Board concept replacing the police authority, as in the metropolitan areas."

Thus most chief constables feel they have good relations with their police authorities, in that they have been successful in developing a relationship in which the authority is not 'political' and accepts their professional perspective. In recent years this has been achieved even in some of the formerly difficult metropolitan areas, as a result of the creation of Joint Boards (Loveday, 1991).

It follows from this basic perspective on the appropriate role of local police authorities that the chief constables overwhelmingly reject the Labour Party commitment to empower police authorities and give them clear control over policy-making. Ninety-five per cent of chiefs rejected the notion that police authorities should control decision-making in the police. This was always justified by the argument that it would result in policing being determined by political rather than professional con-siderations. (The two who did not reject the idea felt that the extent to which they already involved the authority as partners in policy-making meant that a change in the formal situation would make no practical difference.) The chief constables' view is clearly vulnerable to obvious counter-arguments. In a democracy policy is supposed to be formulated by elected representatives not officials, even if the latter are in some sense more expert. This is in fact the principle applied to all other areas of local government, so why should the police be different? The chiefs' justification of their stand grappled with these difficulties in a variety of ways. One tack was to question the truly representative character of local government. The chiefs commonly claimed that they were more in tune with the genuine wishes of the local people than their nominal political representatives. Second, it was often argued that policing was different from other policy areas because it was fundamental to the very existence of the social order, whereas disputes in other policy areas were more mundane. It was as if policing had a sort of sacred character which rendered it too vital to the social fabric to be subject to the rough and tumble of profane party politics. The arguments against giving elected authorities control over police policy are encapsulated by these examples.

"If you've got an authority where there is a good relationship without one being subservient to the other, that by and large you come to an accommodation on priorities, that's one thing. To go down the road suggesting that you should be directed even operationally by politicians, that's not the police I joined! And I certainly would not be happy to be chief constable in that situation, because I wouldn't feel that my profession was worth very much at all. If a politician is going to say one day, 'Well, we should have you dealing with homosexuality in the local toilets', and next day saying, 'There are too many car thefts, get something done!', in direct terms like that, then we are losing sight of it. I'm not sure that is democracy, in any event. [R.R.: Why are the police different from other public services which are controlled by local politicians?] Because at the end of the day politicians, if they controlled the police, could wield far more power in the community than they do controlling the highways authority or something like that ... Are you suggesting seriously that politicians should direct the police into certain areas? You might just get somebody daft enough to say, 'There's too much trouble with these coloured youths, you get in and do some work, chief constable!' And lack the total sensitivity of the situation, the chief constable's professional judgement. Is it by accident that the British police service, still, in spite of everything, has the respect world-wide that it has? Isn't that something to do with the accommodation between the elected members and the people and the police? Our view of fair-play democracy? What benefit are you going to get by suddenly handing over to the politicians? And the people who seem to be shouting for this seem to me a section of the political spectrum who want it for the wrong reasons, that's the problem. Because I think the next thing is, if they can control the police on how they go, it's another means of destabilization if they want."

"Policing would depend on political whim and I'd be against it totally. You would lose the independence of the police which the public values so much. Let's face it, at the end of the day the public belong to all stratas of political thinking—some may be apolitical. Therefore I don't think the policy of policing should be at the whim of whichever party is in power ... I would water down the political influence. It's become too strong in some places, and that's alarmed people, and led to some of the disagreements between some chief officers and their authorities. I've got over the problem here because I've had a lot of political intervention going on. I've managed to find a way round it."

"The proposals [by Labour] are very dangerous. I have seen enough of the intent to control policy that it would worry me if ever that were allowed to be under a new Police Act ... I am worried about the way there has been some hijacking by certain political groups of the local authorities."

"This authority are superb. They have pockets of stone—they don't produce much rate—but hearts of gold. They don't let it go unquestioningly, but if they believe that what I am saying to them is totally sincere and professional they will do their damnedest to assist me. But this [Labour's Manifesto] is wrong. It is coming away from what is the whole strength of the British police service. Their current manifesto says we should jointly enforce the law, which is a bit of an iceberg. I can see me, if that came to pass, sitting down with my authority, and they saying to me, 'Right chief, look, enforcing the law—there is a lot of bloody untaxed vehicles about now. Get out and do something about it!' That is our joint partnership. And I would say, 'No. I've got more important things to do.' And we have a row, and we differ or go down the same road. I believe no matter how loosely it starts—if they said to me, 'Chief! Joint partnership! Go out and preserve tranquillity!' Easy! That's what I do now—it wouldn't stay long that way. People would come along with partisan corners and areas and furrows that they wanted to plough. And they would necessarily, unless the partnership broke down completely, cause me to direct resources to areas I didn't feel were as important. [R.R.: But why should you decide what is important, rather than people elected into office?] Because the people who are voted into office are not professionally fit to decide what those priorities are. How could any local politician decide what resources I should apply to a murder, compared with wilful damage on the estate on which he lives, because he is totally subjective? [R.R.: Perhaps you could advise them about the resources required ...] But I have got to decide at the end of the day in looking at the whole of the county where the emphasis ought to come. Now these people are drawn from the four corners of the county. There are many pressures, conscious or unconscious, party or personal, upon them. And they will speak according to these pressures. I like to think my training and time in the police service has led me to go down an objective professional path which has neither fear nor favour for man or beast. To do what I consider most appropriate for the whole community, not sectors of it. Now if public opinion is totally against it there is a machinery to call me to account, ultimately to send a letter to the Home Secretary. The courts and Parliament are the places that I must answer to.''

"The other chief officers in the county, their roles are absolutely reversed to mine. Their committees draw up a policy for them to implement. As far as I am concerned I get advice on my policy, but the actual way I deal with it is for me, as you well know, under the Police Act. I can see a terrible danger if they said the policy is that you will not use baton rounds, you will not use CS gas. Ken Livingstone would have withdrawn all the police from Brixton because he called them an invading army. My answer is that there are two distinct roles and you can't confuse the two in policing. Because the policeman is really the professional in the tripartite structure. With sensible people—and I'm being critical of chief officers of police as well as others—sensible people operating the system, there are no real problems. [R.R.: The same argument could be extended to other local services. What is special about the police?] The other services do not have the operational responsibility a chief constable has, nor the public face. In terms of policing you really are in a different ball game, which is why, in their wisdom, the Royal Commission said they should be completely different to other chief officers.''

As mentioned in Chapter 8, I asked chief constables specifically how they would react to a situation where they felt the use of plastic bullets was necessary, but their police authority had expressed their opposition to this. Only one chief constable said he would defer to the police authority view (and there were highly unusual circumstances in this area which gave the police authority more influence). One-fifth of the chiefs said it was a situation which would not arise. This included the few who were themselves opposed to plastic bullets, as well as some cases where their authority also approved them. One-half of the chiefs said they would simply ignore the police authority view, while just over a quarter said they would do what they themselves felt right, but would also do their utmost to persuade their authorities to agree. In the final analysis, therefore, this example underlines the overwhelming view that in an operational decision police authority approval is a desirable luxury not a necessity. Actions will be taken as thought to be required by the chief constable, even against the declared views of the authority if this is unavoidable. (This position has, of course, received the blessing of the Court of Appeal—as well as the Home Office—as implied by the judgment in the Northumbria Police Authority case discussed in Chapter 2). The following typifies the characteristic view:

> "At the end of the day we have to carry out our paramount duty to protect life. If there are no means available to you except extreme measures, then any chief constable at the end of the day would do it. It would be inexcusable, at the end of the day, if by unacceptable behaviour on the part of a small group you allow the expectations of society as a whole to be thwarted. You would be flunking out the real issue if you stood aside ... The chief constable, at the end of the day, has to apply those considerations. He would have to face up to the fact that his police authority had made quite clear to him their point of view, and indeed perhaps insisted on a policy of not supplying baton rounds. He would be prepared to justify what he had done, that's really the only way he could tackle it. He would be making that decision, knowing that he would be flying in the face of that authority's wishes."

Given their general agreement with the constitutional status quo, it is hardly surprising that chief constables not only reject Labour's radical reforms overwhelmingly, but also by a clear majority oppose the Liberal–Social Democrat proposal to establish a new Royal Commission to consider the issues. Sixty-eight per cent are against the Royal Commission idea, and only one-quarter support it (with 7 per cent undecided). The majority rejected the Royal Commission idea because it was seen as unnecessary. The present system worked well, and the demand for change only came from unrepresentative minorities.

> "The argument for a Royal Commission assumes there's a controversy. There's a lot of loud noises. But there's no grouse from out there among honourable taxpayers and ratepayers. You go out and talk to them, and they have a view about these loud noise-makers, particularly these politicians, local as well as national. They haven't taken the temperature of Mr Public out there which I do."

> "I don't think actually that anything has changed since 1960. Nothing

has happened since 1960 which might make it feel right to actually move the Constitution. Royal Commissions! They seem to be a British disease. If in doubt have a Royal Commission! At the end of the day, who is actually causing the controversy? That's the intriguing thing about it! So far as I am aware the only people that feel the subject is in any way controversial are a relatively small number of politicians, and a number of media people and academics who feed on those politicians. And they service one another. You've almost got a system, haven't you? The *Daily Mirror* publishes a story, an MP reads that story, asks a question in Parliament. The Home Secretary has to respond, so he instigates some sort of inquiry. The act of setting up the inquiry generates more controversy, which is duly reported on, and the thing feeds on itself. You can get quite ridiculous things, stupid ones, 'Mrs Thatcher and the Queen don't get on!' You can make that run for weeks."

"I don't think we should have another Royal Commission. Nineteen sixty-four solved that. The balance is there. What you've had is two or three, maybe four or five, police authorities that have tried to control the chief constable, have sought to direct the chief constable. What you are looking at in essence is the pursuit of authority or of power. The balance is about right. Provided you're sensible, communication with your police authority will solve many problems. But with the hard Left introducing politics into the hard Left of things—you never satisfy them."

The only exception to the general acceptance of the status quo by the chief constables was with regard to the controversy about the absence of a local police authority for the Metropolitan Police. (Since the 1829 Metropolitan Police Act which established the Met. its police authority has been the Home Secretary.) On this issue most chief constables accepted part of the radical agenda. Sixty per cent thought there should be a local police authority for the Met., along the lines of the present provincial police authorities. Only 20 per cent were against this, with another 20 per cent undecided. Cynics might see this as a sour grapes response. 'If I have to put up with a local police authority, why shouldn't Sir Kenneth Newman or Sir Peter Imbert?'

However, the arguments advanced to support the case for a local police authority in the Met. are consistent with the chief constables' overall views on police authorities. If they are handled and function properly, they can work as a useful sounding-board, and as a means for legitimating policing policy by having the blessing of elected representatives. Why shouldn't the deprived knights of Scotland Yard share these benefits? 'It's a good channel for the flow of local views, so you should have it in London too.' A minority felt, though, that the Met. was a special case and should remain outside the normal structure, because of its particular national as well as local role and responsibilities. The majority view, that it was not satisfactory to have the Home Secretary remain as the Met.'s police authority, reflects a more general opposition to overt national control of policing.

Central Government and Control of Police

On the face of it, chief constables are as much against a police force controlled by central government as by local government. Thus two-thirds said they were opposed to the creation of a national police force, with only one-fifth in favour, and 15 per cent undecided. This is a slightly higher degree of support for a national police force than the *Operational Policing Review* found for all ACPO ranks—13 per cent— and matches their findings for the police service as a whole, 20 per cent (*Operational Policing Review* (1990), 19).

The predominant case against having a national police force was based on the view that there would be a danger of political control, the advantages of local identification would disappear, policies would be uniform throughout the country without being able to adjust styles to local community variations, and there would be less accountability. In addition, some county chiefs feared that their areas would lose resources relative to the cities in a national organization:

"The present system suffers many, many defects. You have forty-three autocratic power centres, all with their own subjective views, as you have found out. And many things could be better if policies were arrived at universally. Having said that, I think on balance we should stay with this local element, local participation. I don't think it is being pessimistic when one says, if you went to a national police force, you do become politicized. You are working for the government of the day. In the miners' strike, if the local socialists were to be translated into the national socialists, then Peter Wright would not have been allowed to police Orgreave. That worries me because I believe we police anything to maintain the law. If a chap wants to picket, he can picket, and if a chap wants to go to work he goes to work. I think we ran the centre line and I don't think there is any partisan view at all. I fear that if we went to a national force."

"I would certainly be against a national police force. Here, large as this area is, whoever sits in this chair, me at the moment, we are identifiable, we are public figures, and we have got to answer for what goes on. But the way things are going, if there's a political will, a national police force will come. Half-way house for a while on a regional basis, until it is shown it doesn't work. There is a momentum. The country has shrunk enormously. Pressure from the media, that if it's done in Milford Haven, why aren't they doing it in Newcastle. The tremendous desire for common standards. This is a small island, why should people be treated differently in Plymouth to Northumbria ... The conflict between central government and local government, where you've got central government of one persuasion, local government of another. Law and order at the centre of the party political stage. We've always been political, that's the nature of our job, but now we're on the party political stage. So the momentum to a national force is there."

"I wouldn't want a national force at any price. Our strength is in the fragmentation of our police service. While some of us have had a tough time with local police committees, most have not, and I wouldn't like to see the problems of the few projected nationally so they became everybody's problem. I don't like the idea of a single Interior Minister having control over the whole police service. We'd lose the tradition we've fought very hard to maintain in terms of local influence and local accountability. You would see an enhancement of the facilities in the inner-city areas to the detriment of the shire counties. This happened with the amalgamation of the forces before."

The latter argument might suggest that opposition to a national force would be concentrated amongst the counties. In fact, however, it is equally prevalent in all types of force.

A minority of chiefs do espouse the national police force idea. They argue it is necessary to achieve efficiency in the fight against sophisticated crime, that it would allow a more rational system for choosing and developing senior officers, and that the loss of accountability argument is a red herring because the extent of central control and uniformity is such that there is already a *de facto* national force. Many chiefs who oppose the idea of a national force would tend to agree about the latter point, but resent it and would like to reverse or at least arrest the momentum of centralization. (In their view, the voluntary co-ordination of the police in the miners' strike, pointed to by many commentators as evidence of an embryonic national force, had as one of its achievements the postponement of the establishment of an overt national force.)

"I'm for the national police force concept. I do not think it is a weapon that the Government can use to oppress the poor and, you know, make everyone subservient. That was adequately dealt with in the Royal Commission. There is an Army that could do that long before we would do it ... As a planning officer over the years I like to look towards cost effectiveness and so on. It does irritate me still, after all this time and the amalgamations, the different way things are done, the different forms. To get an agreement on a national crime force—you know, we tried 20, 25, 30 years ago, we will haven't achieved it. So from a professional, almost mechanical point of view there are things about a national force that I would like to see. It would standardize procedures and policies. It could move manpower to where the workload is, so the inner cities could get more manpower, more resources, and therefore be cost effective professionally. There are other things I'm not so sure about, but they could be got round. There could be inputs by the local councillors just as there used to be. The arguments against nationalization now are precisely arguments that were made when, for example, Norwich and Great Yarmouth, and before that King's Lynn, the separate borough forces, it was suggested they should amalgamate with the county. Now that has all gone by, nobody ever talks about it."

"There's a case for a national force. But in practical terms what is happening is typical of the way British institutions have evolved, empirically and pragmatically. I mean, we are only a spitting distance from a national police force anyway in reality. It's an incremental evolution, not even a conscious one really. It's been a series of reactions to various contingencies which are eventually added up to a police service which is more national in character. But the case for a national police force must be decided on the ultimate question of do the British public want a national police force. I always thought we would get a national police force when there is public pressure to have one."

The previous comments imply that the national police force debate, which has, throughout British police history, aroused so much furore—and still does—is a matter more of form than substance. Many commentators have argued in recent years that the extent of current centralization amounts to a *de facto* national force (Loveday, 1986; Reiner, 1988, 1989). This is recognized but regretted by even the chiefs who baulk at the formalization of a national force.

The pattern of chief constables' careers described in Part II indicates clearly that, as prospective chiefs move up the hierarchy, they increasingly become a cohesive reference group, oriented at least as much to each other and to the Home Office (and its key institutions like the Inspectorate and Bramshill) as to their own forces. The Home Office, to which so many ambitious men owe so much of their careers, will clearly be a potent influence over them. This is clear from the comments made by chiefs about the central bodies of the police world: the Home Office, Her Majesty's Inspectorate of Constabulary (HMI), and the Association of Chief Police Officers (ACPO). These are regarded in a very different way to the local police authorities, who are formally, at least, equal in constitutional theory to the Home Secretary, and certainly supposed to be more significant than ACPO which has no authority in law at all.

Most chief constables view local police authorities *de haut en bas*, as potentially useful avenues of communication with the public, but whose views can in the last analysis be ignored if they conflict with the chief's professional judgement. The central policing institutions are regarded quite differently. The Home Office is seen as a powerful, increasingly interventionist body, which can be disregarded only at the chief's peril. Whereas the local police authorities are given any degree of influence they may enjoy by grace of the chief's concern to cultivate consensus, the Home Office has *power*, based on a variety of sanctions it may wield. The HMI (which consists of former chief constables) and ACPO are not seen as possessing power in the same way. However, as groups of professional peers they have a degree of authority based on respect for expertise and experience, whereas we have seen that police authority members are regarded as lay people who need tutoring in police affairs.

I asked chief constables specifically how much influence these central bodies had on their decision-making. The results are shown in Table 11.1. The Home Office is clearly the paramount power in the field. The overwhelming majority (70 per cent) of chiefs said it had a lot of influence over them, while the rest all rated its influence as fair. The HMI and ACPO are both influential as well, although less so. Just over one-third rated the HMI's influence as a lot, just over a half as fair, and one-tenth as little or none. ACPO appeared the least influential, being seen as a body of peers. Just under one-third rated its influence as a lot, just over one-third as fair, whilst nearly one-third saw it as having little or no influence.

The Home Office is evidently seen by chief constables as the most influential central body in their decision-making. This is despite the fact that chiefs know that the formal status of its circulars is advisory only, and that they have no legal authority to direct any operational decision. Nevertheless most chiefs almost automatically implement the

TABLE 11.1.   *Influence of Central Bodies on Police Decision-Making*

Amount of influence over chief constables	Home Office %	HMI %	ACPO %
A lot	70.0	35.0	32.5
Fair	30.0	52.5	37.5
Little	—	7.5	20.0
None	—	5.0	10.0
TOTAL	100.0	100.0	100.0
N = 40			

advice of its circulars, and take heed of interventions in particular operations. There are two basic reasons for this. First, the Home Office is seen as having available to it a battery of sanctions, formal and informal. Second, it is regarded as the legitimate expression of the popular will, that is, enjoying an electoral mandate.

The formal sanctions available to the Home Office are widely recognized to be blunt instruments, too drastic to be of any real use, even as threats, in relation to everyday issues. The withholding of central government finance or the removal from office of a chief constable are far too extreme sanctions to be contemplated as a means of winning conflicts over routine policy matters.

The more effective sanctions are the informal ones. The bite of these will vary according to the susceptibilities of particular chiefs. The thick-skinned are impervious to nagging, while those who are not interested in any further advancement in the police world will be unconcerned about being in the black books of the Home Office. Thus relatively older chiefs who do not see themselves as going anywhere else in their careers may be the most likely to acquire a measure of independence, although they may also be the keenest on a quiet life and the avoidance of conflict. Even those about to retire may have an interest in the honours which the Home Office can influence. Younger chiefs with ambitions which depend on the Home Office will not necessarily be subservient. The best way to impress is not by being an unfailing yes-man. It may be better to stick your neck out on an issue if you are vindicated by events confirming your judgement. This is a high-risk strategy, but the only way to shine. In any event, the power and influence of the Home Office as a key factor in policy-making is evident. This may be resented by chiefs, or even regarded as illegitimate, but it is an undeniable fact.

"As chief constables we have to be bold enough to make decisions, and I only hope that people don't make decisions at our level based on what their futures are, or whether they get the CBE or a knighthood or whatever ... One doesn't talk about it in terms of control but one would not wish to be too far away from the thinking of the Home Office. I mean, we would all stand and fight our corner to the death if we felt we were right and they were wrong, and they were trying to manipulate us or instruct us. But, on the other hand, one would wish certainly to not be too far out of step with the thinking of the Home Office ... They do have quite considerable influence. The Home Office circulars that accompany legislation are a guide to the enforcement policies that result from new legislation. One is very conscious that they are speaking for the government of the day. I don't think chief constables would want to fly in the face of what the elected government requires. But we took great pains to point out throughout the miners' dispute that the Home Office will never—neither can they—instruct us to do any particular thing. They can certainly give advice, and generally speaking I suspect we would take that advice ... The National Reporting Centre, contrary to what has been suggested, was not government pressure. All it did was to save us having to ring round. I can remember when Charlie McLachlan [late chief constable of Nottinghamshire] grabbed 1,000 men before I knew I was going to get any trouble. And I felt, 'God, I'm not going to be able to get any men from anywhere.' And I was thinking about phoning all the way round. Then they announced the National Reporting Centre was set up. Had that not been set up, I'd have had to ring Devon and Cornwall, and they'd say, 'Charles McLachlan already has mine.' 'Oh, God!' So I ring Bob Bunyard [then chief constable of Essex], and I might get somebody. The NRC cut it short. But it was only moral pressure, that the public, the national interest, must really override local considerations."

"Well, I do whatever the Home Secretary tells me. I do. I accept in the main what the Home Office says. Not always. But it seems to me—there are no figures to prove it—but we are more centralized than we used to be. There does seem to be a greater influence from the Home Office. They really have a very significant influence on how you run your police service, and I don't step outside Home Office circulars. I follow them to the letter. I think they are sensible. And I feel I've got to. I don't want to be sacked by the Home Secretary! So the answer is, yes, a great influence the Home Office."

"Since I've been in ACPO certainly there's been enormous change in the amount of central influence in police forces. Mainly through the money process. And since I've been chief I've noticed the gradual change in that there's more and more central government influence. Part of the problem is that modern-day chief constables are more amenable to accept that sort of central influence than the old style used to be. Part of it is that the modern chief constable arrives, in the main, later to the rank, because there's now only forty-three of them. And his tenure of office is much less, so that turnover is of a higher rate. Whereas, if you go back to the old days, you see this force has only had seven chief constables since 1839, and my predecessor only served four years. Now those chief constables grew up in a style where they managed their force, they wouldn't brook no interference from the Home Office or whatever at all. And they would pass it on down the line. But gradually, as it became a more career-oriented service, and people move around more, there is more acceptance of the central influence than there used to be. There are still the last bastions against change around. You can see them in the country even now. But the vast majority, I think—I wouldn't say they lay back and get raped, but they're inclined that way. My experience was from '51 onwards where we had the old Trenchard style of career policeman. But even the old borough style, who was very aware of local politics and his local watch committee, even he would jib at too much interference from Home Office or HMI. The old style would say, 'Well, it's my force.'"

"The Home Office have a considerable amount of weight because obviously 51 per cent [the central grant for local police finances] is a considerable stick with which to beat one, or the withdrawal of it. [R.R.: Except that surely they'll never really withdraw it?] The possibility is always there, isn't it? One tends to take a lot of notice of it. I mean there is advice and advice. And some advice is really, you know ... Yes you are definitely conscious of the Home Office ... On a major issue you would be either foolhardy or very, very brave to stand out. Because of the threat of withdrawal."

"I think the Home Office is very influential by way of circular. I regard the circulars as almost unwritten law. I think properly so, because it leads to even regulation of police performance, and that's important ... Also the Home Office is an important back-up if you get into dispute with your police authority. Apart from anything it's the fact that the chief hasn't the funds as a private individual to enter into any litigation against the police authority, who would have the funds available to hire the best counsel in the land."

Chiefs are thus well aware that the Home Office can deploy a variety of sanctions, formal and informal, if chief constables proved recalcitrant on an important issue. The knowledge that powers exist often means that they do not have to be used. Apparently voluntary acquiescence may result from the knowledge that coercion is a possible alternative.

> "The National Reporting Centre was terribly misunderstood. It was a co-ordinating body, no one had to tell us what to do. We could have been directed to comply, of course, as you know, under the provisions of the Police Act. But I'd help my colleagues out with manpower if they were in difficulty, to the extent that I was able. And equally I would expect the same support. I don't find any difficulty in doing that. The discretion was given us by law. And if you don't come up with the goods in a reasonable way, there is a compulsion power. [R.R.: The Home Office has never had to exercise it?] No, because most chief constables will respond reasonably and sensibly. If you've got problems yourself which makes it difficult to provide the numbers that you are being asked to produce, then they have enough experience and understanding to understand the dilemma you've got."

However, the relationship between chief constables and Home Office is not primarily one based on the use or potential use of sanctions. It is not a one-dimensional relationship of power, where dominance is the product of success in open conflict (Lukes, 1974). One of the major reasons that chief constables tend to go along with Home Office advice is not fear of sanctions, overt, implied, or anticipated. It is that chief constables by and large accept the authority of the Home Office. They do so not only because they see it as having a legitimacy derived from the electoral process. Even more important, they see it usually as the expression of the consensus of expert professional policing opinion. Much of its policy is the product of consultation and collaboration with HMI and ACPO, acting as the conduits of professional wisdom. Where this consensual process of policy formulation does not occur, Home Office advice is often seen as lacking legitimacy and resented. More commonly it does occur, and is the basis for the acceptance of policies which have been developed co-operatively.

> "The Home Office have influence on policy. They can issue directives for which I don't have any control. And of course I wouldn't dream of not doing what they said should be done. They don't consult as much as they ought to in my view and the view of a lot of other chief constables. If they did perhaps they wouldn't make so many balls-ups

as they sometimes do, and have to go away shamefaced because we have pointed out that something can't work because they over-looked us. So the relationship isn't a bad one. I not infrequently contact individuals of senior rank at the Home Office who are very, very helpful. But sometimes, every now and again, they do something they haven't spoken to ACPO about, and it can present problems. So they influence me by directive not so often. Sometimes by consul-tation. Chief constables are invited to let it be known what their views are, and of course, we always do."

More commonly, circulars from the Home Office are the product of behind-the-scenes discussions, and emerge as expressions of the pro-fessional consensus:

"I largely feel bound by Home Office circulars. Because they are a regurgitation of what we've told them all anyway, through ACPO. So really the Home Office circulars are usually a consensus of views. I haven't had a Home Office circular thrown out here yet. But we don't follow it slavishly. There are certain bits I will pick out."

"We take a good deal of notice of Home Office circulars since they very often arise from close consultation beforehand with ACPO and we've usually agreed. I mean those on public order, for example, have nearly always been seen by me, and discussed with colleagues beforehand. So circulars don't provide too much of a problem ... I'll talk to the Home Office direct and not only through ACPO if I think it appropriate."

"Home Office circulars always have a preface which says, 'In con-sultation with ACPO I am issuing the following advice.' You see they never give directions—that might be a bit euphemistic. But he'd be a foolish chief constable who would fly in the face of Home Office circulars. Most of them are benign, some may be indirectly police directed. Only once did I make it quite clear to the Home Office that I was not supporting a Home Office circular, and that was to do with releasing information to social services *vis-à-vis* foster parents. I can claim to say that eventually they changed the rules, and there's far more sensible information given out to the authorities who have a duty to protect children. I thought it was a ruddy nonsense, if I had intelligence about the criminal propensities of a likely employee in that field, I was bound to tell that this wasn't the right guy or girl to be that ... The Home Office influence is greater now, but it's a joint endeavour anyway. Sometimes we've invited the Home Office to become greater involved. For example, computer systems are not always compatible. And I was very strong, supported by two or three of my senior colleagues, to say the Home Office have got to bang their foot and lean on the Home Secretary to insist that computer development went forward in a disciplined way to ensure compatibility."

However, while the normal mode of policy formulation was consensual, if the relationship broke down it was normally the Home Office that could bring more sanctions to bear. (This is the obverse of the chief constables' typical relationship to their local police authorities.)

"In the main I go along with the Home Office circulars. But, of course, they are usually based after discussions with ACPO anyway, and on the HMI's recommendation, so the three very often hang together. And one goes along with them. I mean, I certainly don't reject the Home Office. Some of the things the Home Office recommend, I can't do. But I always ensure that I've got a good reason why I can't do them: either lack of manpower, or lack of money. If you don't fall in line the HMI will probably, on his next annual inspection, try to twist your arm. But in the main, where forces are not complying with Home Office circulars, it is because they have got good reasons which the Home Office will accept. I don't think the Home Office is that dogmatic. As you know the phraseology of the circulars says we advise or we recommend or the Metropolitan Police adopted this. In the main we go along because it is usually factually correct what they suggest ... Undoubtedly, if they say I'm going to declare your force inefficient and they will recommend we withhold 5 per cent of the grant then obviously I would be under pressure to do something."

"The Home Office advises but you know as well as I do the Home Office circulars are virtually mandatory. I know that ACPO played its part in the negotiations before they came out, and there's a general agreement in the area. For example, the whole multidisciplinary approach to crime in the country, and the developments that came out of that, we took on board ... they are advisory. They can't tell me what to do. If the Home Secretary sent me a letter saying, 'Look I'm disappointed with the way you're policing this air-base because convoys are being attacked *en route*; you're not doing your job properly.' Well, I wouldn't stand it. I'd tell them to go to hell. I'd ignore it totally. But they know that. They know the name of the game as well ... If we don't agree with a circular the argument goes on. In the end I'd have the right to ignore it. But the HMI could come to me and

say, 'You're the only force in the country not doing this. Why not?'
I'd have to argue my case with them. They could then say to me, as
you know, 'I might have to recommend that part of your 51 per cent
grant of your budget gets stopped.' But it's never got to that."

Thus most chiefs interpret Home Office policy advisory circulars as
virtually mandatory. This is partly because they are seen as legitimate,
partly for fear of sanctions. Many chiefs argue (as in the case above)
that this does not extend to operational direction. This does not occur,
and if it did they would resist it.

Yet I was told sufficient stories of such government intervention in
operations to know it is not a rare occurrence. Some important examples
have already been given in Chapter 8 in the discussion of the 1984–5
miners' strike, for example, the proposal to establish a public order
intelligence unit, and the abortive pressure on the Welsh forces to co-
operate with the national mutual aid operation. However, many other
examples were offered to me of specific operational interventions by
central government, usually in important public order conflicts. This
is, of course, a long-standing pattern, especially in labour disputes, as
recent historical work has stressed (Morgan, 1987). The interventions
by the Home Office are certainly not always successful. Usually the
stories I was told concerned attempted Home Office pressure which
was resisted by the chief constable, who was ultimately vindicated by
events. However, although I was only told success stories by chief
constables, the recurrence of attempted Home Office pressure is clear.
It was also indicated that sometimes chief officers will represent as their
independent decision commonly agreed strategies, precisely as a means
of shielding the Government from the opprobrium of possible failure.

"I heard they [the British Movement] were going to come ... to hold
their march in——shire ... I had a message from the Home Office
saying the Home Secretary would like you to know that should you
decide to apply for a ban it will be sympathetically considered. Nudge,
nudge, hint, hint, apply for a ban ... In the end, I got my team round
the table, and we decided that with the intelligence we had, that with
our resources and the time we had to plan, it would be much better
to allow the march to go ahead ... So I made that decision, ignoring
the Home Office ... purely on the professional grounds, that I would
best be able to keep law and order by doing the right thing. OK, if I
was wrong I would have got the blame."

"I have had direct experience of that with the——incident [a controversial public order operation]. Everybody was puzzled and

worried. Mrs Thatcher had tried to make the buggers uncomfortable, and frankly I just spoke to the chief executive and I said, look, I know what I am going to do. You had best stay out of it, so that if I have to be criticized by you I won't be in a position where I say, 'Well, you knew about it, Mr Home Secretary.' Not before the event ... If they have prior knowledge, they are condoning what we might be doing. Now some of the things there, it just might be 85 per cent to 15 per cent in favour of being lawful, but it might just have suited to be 15 per cent unlawful. Now that is the sort of operational risk I have to take, and I'm prepared to stand on my chopping block and not transfer that to the police authority or the Home Secretary or the HMI. [R.R.: How could the operation be seen as unlawful?] ... We took our lawyers' advice on what we thought were the legalities of the law, and it's been proved right. But if I had had to put that to the Home Secretary it would go to another lawyer, who might give me another piece of advice. At the end of the day you have got to make up your mind. So it's quite right that the Home Secretary and the Home Office should be aware of what we were actually going to do. I didn't want it to appear as Maggie Thatcher seeking to appear she was able to control and direct us. I certainly don't think Douglas Hurd [then Home Secretary] would seek that. Yes, I'd speak to them, but I'd say, in much the same terms as to Laurie Byford [then HMI], 'Look, it's better that you don't know. But when it's activated I'll tell you exactly what we're doing.'"

Thus the vaunted independence of the chief constable may be deliberately manipulated to shield the Government from potential embarrassment, should controversial operational decisions, made with its implicit approval, prove to be failures. On the other hand, failures of police operations are often used as the occasion for central government pressure to change policies. Noted examples are the Ripper investigation in Yorkshire, and the urban riots of the early 1980s. Both were the trigger for sweeping changes in procedures for crime investigation and controlling public disorder:

"My hobby horse is the Home Office's growing involvement in operational matters. You are able to demonstrate that sort of view over a period. I mean, we get the Ripper case wrong, and Larry Byford [then HMI] has an inquiry. We end up with the HOLMES computer being imposed upon every policeman. We argue all the time from the particular to the general. You know, we get the policing of industrial disputes wrong, and we get a new industrial relations act. We see a rape interview and the victim mishandled on TV, and we end up with a new chapter of advice from the Home Office on the way to investigate rapes."

"A former Home Secretary indicated that if a chief constable had a riot which might require the use of baton rounds to suppress it, had he not anticipated this, then one must question whether in fact he was doing his job. That was a dictum that was laid down by Willie Whitelaw in 1981."

"One of the things that really disturbs me is the advice and circulars coming from the Home Office. The stream of circulars following Scarman, recommending the need for new forms of consultation, and essentially recommending softly, softly or community policing."

The Home Office is thus seen as a powerful, sometimes authoritative, sometimes resented, force directing the shape of police policy and operations. As has already been mentioned, the other key central police institutions, the Inspectorate and ACPO, are also generally seen as influential, but not to the same extent. Basically, they lack sanctions of their own. The HMI may indirectly enjoy sanctions through its recommendations to the Home Office, but it is the latter which wields them. ACPO has no sanctions other than informal ones, primarily the withholding or bestowing of peer approval. Unlike the Home Office, the HMI and ACPO are not seen as bodies wielding power, but as enjoying a variable amount of authority, depending on the individual chief constable's personal relationship with them.

The HM Inspectorate of Constabulary was established by the 1856 County and Borough Police Act as the medium for Home Office assessment of provincial forces, and a precondition for the payment of the central government contributions to their costs. Almost from the outset the Inspectors have been former chief officers. They are clearly viewed by chief officers as a mediating link with the Home Office, as much a conduit for police views to the Government as vice versa. They are seen as still part of the senior police peer group, rather than external controllers, and their influence is in the first place a personal one. As a former Chief Inspector of Constabulary once put it, the Inspectors 'act as father confessors to the Chief Constables in their region' (St Johnston, 1978, 265). They are 'possessed of no authority of command' and rely on the influence of their character and experience' (ibid. 261–2). This remains basically the case today, although most chief constables perceive the Inspectorate as having become more interventionist and demanding, as the spearhead of the Home Office's growing central role, and in particular of the Financial Management Initiative.

"The Inspectorate of Constabulary has an insatiable appetite for information. If one looks at the growth of the Inspectorate—and I worked there with them twenty years ago—it has grown phenomenally. Even staff officers have staff officers! I hope I am not sounding too cynical, but we have an Inspector of Constabulary coming to us in March, and in preparation for that visit I have had to produce the equal of one man's work for twenty-seven weeks. And that's a tremendous amount of work. The whole of our administration is civilianized, and my number two man has been occupied for twenty-seven weeks producing information for that visit. We hardly ever benefit in real terms. The purpose of the visit, as you know, is to see that we are efficient so we can get the 51 per cent grant."

Generally, however, the HMI is seen not so much as a control, but as a useful senior colleague, and as a means of transmitting police views to officialdom. The relationship is a collegial not a conflictual one.

"The HMI provides advice, helpful advice. As an ex-chief constable he knows the problems of sitting in this chair, and by and large it's very rare I take exception to his advice. And if I did you can come to an accommodation."

"I'm worried about HMI. Their inspections now are very different from the early days. More formal and so on. But I value the particular manager coming along and looking at the force. In effect I stand and look over his shoulder, and see the force through his eyes. That's a good discipline for me. They're milestone events, the formal inspection by HMI, once a year. Also, because they are senior and experienced policemen I know that if I want to go and see somebody about something I can do. There is a drift towards centralization of policing, and they'll play an increasing part in that. They're even defining the system of management adopted by forces. I happen to have been involved in that development for a while, so it's a style I'm comfortable with, but some chief constables are not ... Because I came through a Home Office system I'm influenced by it. Because I've got friends and contacts and so on I've got a few good avenues into the Home Office. So they play a part in influencing me."

"The HMI is influential in that I value his advice. Being a chief constable, I find, in some ways is quite a lonely sort of job. There are not all that many people you can actually talk to about your problems that haven't got some kind of axe to grind. So one really wants sometimes just to have someone to talk to. And I happen to get on very well with my own HMI, and have known him for a number of years. I find him a very easy man to talk to. If I needed that sort of guidance or whatever I wouldn't worry about actually ringing him up. I don't have to ring him up very often. But he rings me up sometimes, and when he comes on his inspection I obviously go round with him. That's not always done but I always do so, and listen to him quite a lot."

"I'm particularly lucky in having an Inspector of Constabulary whom I respect and admire, and therefore if I seek professional guidance I can turn to him. The value of the Inspectorate is on the basis of the individuals in it, not the organization. Because the organization is a very, very small one, and based entirely upon individuals. It could be a lot more effective if it had greater influence within the Home Office. At the moment the Home Office, which is one of the three legs of the tripartite stool, has in my service increased its power enormously. Whenever there has been a dispute between chief constable and police authority the Home Office have intervened by taking that authority unto themselves. The Home Office have now considerably greater powers than when I joined. The Inspectorate in my judgement is not exercising sufficient power within the Home Office. The Home Office should listen far more to the Inspectorate."

The Inspectorate are seen predominantly as a support, not as controllers of the police. This is because they are former chief officers, and thus see the world from the same perspective, understanding the loneliness of the person with whom the buck stops. However, the role of HMI is seen as changing. It has expanded its monitoring and co-ordinating function as the Home Office has tightened its financial scrutiny of forces, and has become the channel for the spread of what is regarded as good practice between forces. A few felt this had not gone far enough:

"I think HMI is broadly speaking a cosmetic exercise ... HMI's visit is all about the feel of the police force ... particularly when the HMI is your predecessor as chief constable. Now as it happens we get on famously well, no problem whatsoever. But a system should be bigger than that. The system should really not allow ex-chiefs to look at their own force."

ACPO has also become a medium for the achievement of the Home Office desire for a more co-ordinated policing system in the absence of formal nationalization. As seen in Chapter 2 it has become more of a professional and indeed operational body, and less of a representative and social association compared to its inception. It remains a completely informal body, unlike the Police Federation, without any statutory or other legal specification of its functions. Nevertheless it is clearly Home Office policy for it to play a pivotal role in supplying the national dimension in policing. To an extent this places it in a position of implicit rivalry with the Metropolitan Police, which has hitherto had a monopoly of acting as the residual national police force.

To most chief constables ACPO is clearly 'their' organization. It is not a power over them, but an arena for the exercise of mutual influence between professional peers. Their criticism is of its looseness and weakness, but not its control. There is, however, a small dissident minority, who see it as a vehicle for ambitious meddlers, rather than the best professionals. These rugged individualists resent the growing power of what is seen as a closed, talking shop. Whereas the inability of ACPO to co-ordinate fully the actions of forty-three individual chiefs is regretted by most, to some it is a source of celebration. The standard favourable view of ACPO is exemplified first by these quotes:

> "The police voice needs to be heard loud and clear to stop bits of stupid legislation coming in. Certainly, over PACE, our voice was not sufficiently put forward ... We are now going forward and firing on about three out of the four cylinders. It is a question of making sure that we in ACPO say to the Home Office and the legislature, 'Look, this is the implications of what you are saying. If you want it, fine, that's the will of Parliament. But don't come to us afterwards and say you're not doing the job, we haven't got the resources.' I think we should strengthen our role in ACPO in the general secretariat. This is under review at the moment. We need in the secretariat not necessarily a retired police officer, but someone who is a good administrator, who can be an assimilator of facts and present and argue logically his case, and can be supported by research elements. As an ACPO committee secretary, I have to go back to my force when I have jobs. I have had to find a chief inspector who is my staff officer, for whom I have no establishment. It is costing my force very substantially in terms of postage, preparation of papers, and the rest of it. We all take it in turn, and nobody queries it because it is part of our overall wider responsibility. But it is a very *ad hoc* situation. I've got to beg and borrow and talk to my treasurer, who's

a fine fellow, and says, 'Yes, fine. We'll try and squeeze a bit here.' So there are no difficulties. But if I had a difficult police authority there might be. It is a very unstructured way in which we work. There is a need to firm up and professionalize the secretariat. You need to have a central secretariat that could feed the committees. Crime Committee is a particularly important committee, which goes into the fundamentals. Jury vetting is a matter which is under discussion, the right of silence, firearms legislation. These have tremendous impact upon society and police resources. And they need to be properly researched ... We are becoming more aware of the need to be seen as one, rather than being out of step. Generally speaking my colleagues follow the advice of ACPO committees, unless a particular chief constable has a problem and wants to see you ... I give numerous TV and radio interviews ... The Hungerford affair, for example. I've only done that because, on the first morning after, I got together with the ACPO president and he said you do it ... I got a message out to all chiefs that any media enquiries were to be referred to me. Yesterday I was asked to go on BBC *Newsnight* to give the police view on the CPS—the DPP was on. I declined to do that on the basis I could see that as unnecessarily controversial. It's a matter of judgement. There are some you won't touch with a barge-pole because you know what they are trying to do is make an awful lot of controversy, and put chief constables in the middle. Baroness Phillips wrote to me the other day and said will you please be a member of a group because I'm very concerned about the number of knives being used, and I need ACPO support. Now I know the Home Office are preparing legislation on that, and I said no because it is a ginger movement, and it's not my role to be part of a ginger group to try and stir up the hornets. But, on the other hand, if the Home Office had turned up and said to us, what do we feel as an association, we'd do it."

"ACPO has quite an influence on me because I sit on five or six committees myself. We debate and distil matters very ponderously and very carefully. For example, ACPO said, 'Look, we think there is a problem in the training of police surgeons. Things have moved at such a pace. We think you ought to get them together, and here is a national syllabus for them.' You look at it and say, 'Christ, yes! When did we last train police surgeons? Get them over to the residential block and let's have a weekend course.' So it does have an influence on me, because it's debated by professionals. It's not mandatory on me at all. But if I wanted to buy a bit of computer kit, I'd make sure it was compatible with what everyone else was buying."

"One would wish that policing could have uniformity, and in that respect we would look towards ACPO to produce a uniform policy. Now, of course, if your own views are opposed to the policy—as, in fact, there is the problem at the moment in the Traffic Committee with drink and drive policies, where one force is clearly out of step with the others. One has still got the freedom to do that. But there is a certain amount of pressure from being a member of an organization, to conform with the uniform view. But problems in some areas can be different so one doesn't necessarily have to make uniformity the rule. But there is always a certain amount of pressure from one's peers. One doesn't want to be a maverick. But having said that we're not in any way controlled by ACPO."

"We've changed in the last ten years or so. ACPO has really come into its own in its modest professional side as distinct from its staff association side. We tend as forty-three chief constables, if we've agreed to fundamental policies—and we do agree on most fundamental issues—to follow that line. But moulded to fit local circumstances. A classic example is an extreme thing—baton rounds. Nobody trains and stocks them if he doesn't perceive he's ever likely to use them, whatever ACPO policy is."

"I agree with us having some common policies. But we are all different, so I don't allow those decisions to be binding on me if they're not right for me and my force. Even though I'm on the Crime Committee and rarely miss a Council meeting. I've always accepted the right of the chief constable to do his own thing, even though he might be out of line with the majority of ACPO. He may be regarded as a bit of an awkward customer! But provided you're not doing it every time, it shouldn't be imposed on all of us. For me ACPO is a valuable way of sharing resources, experience, organizing regional things, and having a professional voice."

The influence of ACPO has grown as chiefs have become more centrally oriented, and less jealous of their autonomy *vis-à-vis* each other and the Government:

"My perception is that there's a bigger change than you'll ever get to perceive in ACPO since I became a member in 1976. Let me share my experience. When I came in, and in this region, notoriously, all the chief constables didn't speak to one another, that's frank. They were old enemies for all sorts of reasons. And certainly deputies and assistants were not allowed to open their mouths at any forum of discussion at the regional meetings. That's altered. There's a much more democratic feel. There are younger, more able chief officers—present company accepted!—who are willing to involve themselves in the goings on of ACPO. My involvement is greater, my neighbours' is, the whole lot is much more involved. They're brighter people. They're not concerned necessarily with their own operational independence, and I am doing this and I am doing that. But there are still some of the other type who do that. I'm not saying there's a new wave and an old wave, but gradually ACPO is changing ... There is a more cohesive approach. ACPO is more involved in putting its view forward in a cohesive way. Before, everybody sort of viewed himself as king in his own territory, there was a tendency towards that. 'I will run my police force exactly as I want and I am not going to come to you. You can do what you like.' There was difficulty, ten years ago, in getting ACPO agreement on any sort of policy at all—almost impossible. You would certainly not get universal agreement from ACPO. Now you get universally agreed policies. For instance, on drunken driving this year there was a Traffic Committee paper. It never happened before. You've got one exception to it, but people are far more ready to accept a cohesive pattern. It is thought also that the Home Office has more influence, and is more responsive now to listening to the problems of policing."

While the majority of chiefs go along with ACPO's greater cohesiveness, a minority of one-fifth express considerable reservations about it, and distance themselves from ACPO. These rugged individualists are illustrated below:

"I've been an active member of ACPO now since 1961, on the CID Committee and a number of the national committees. I don't find ACPOing a very rewarding experience. It tends to be quite a talk shop, and there tends to be a few prima donnas. That's no different from any other organization. I've gone against ACPO policies on many things. For example, on the possession of baton rounds. My colleagues would recognize I've made that decision, it's been made publicly. What they privately think they don't necessarily convey. I have a number of very good friends in ACPO ... Recently we had a very favourable vehicle reclamation scheme, where a chap who has got a slight defect in his vehicle, and the policeman says, 'You go and get it repaired and get the garage to give you a note that you can send to us that it's done. No further action.' And I wanted it four years ago, but ACPO said, 'Hang on! Let's see if for once we can speak with the same voice.' I said, all, right, I'll respect that. And one year goes on, two years go on. It's debated centrally, somebody in the

Home Office says, 'Well, how does this affect the insurance of the vehicle?' All sorts of flab, instead of a robust decision. I don't give a bugger how it affects the insurance. If it's good for our community let's do it. Four years on, ACPO decided it was a good thing. Now that's the way the bureaucratic system works. I've always been called a bit of an independent bugger. But if your experience is it's a good thing for your area, whether it's a good thing for Manchester or Liverpool or the Met. I've no way of knowing. All I know is that I can take the temperature of my own staff. They were anxious to get the thing into being. Our cautioning system—if I went through ACPO channels it would take years. So what I'm prepared to do—if it falls foul I'll finish with egg on my face. I've been around a bit too long perhaps! So I haven't had a rewarding experience persuading them. I should tell the Home Office we're doing this, I shall be advising ACPO to be aware of it. And if they want to watch me make a fool of myself or come in later and pick it up, I'm delighted."

"I've never taken a great interest in being ACPO. I've had my share of committees. And this is controversial—I don't want you to switch this off, but I feel very strongly that many of my colleagues spend far too much time away from their forces. A certain amount of time has to be spent away from the force, but I think there is too much time, unnecessary time, being spent away from forces. In this force I've had perhaps a somewhat closer interest in day-to-day affairs than some of my colleagues. I couldn't leave my force to the extent that many do ... ACPO has very little influence in what I do. We try desperately to all act in accord, but we come apart at the seams. Getting forty-three chief constables to agree to anything is well nigh impossible. ACPO is more like a club than anything else really. We have our committees that deal with things. Occasionally we are able to put a bit of ginger under someone's tail. But generally speaking we are more effective in trying to get the right equipment. When it comes to influencing thoughts on, say, a new Act of Parliament, our influence is very limited."

"ACPO is worth precious little. It's a benevolent sort of association, where the Home Office seeks views sometimes. Whether they get the views of ACPO or whether they get individual views, it's not the view of the service. ACPO is not properly representative. What I worry about is that it depends on activists. I work very hard for the Crime Committee, which is my speciality. But I don't have time for everything else because they need me here, rather than at ACPO committee meetings."

"I find myself increasingly at variance with my colleagues at ACPO. Though I'm secretary of two committees and member of another. The pressures on chief constables now are such that the minute they get a problem half of them want to know what is Joe doing down the road, what has Fred done up there, has anybody ever had this before. Instead of doing what we are paid to do, that is, exercise our judgement and get on with it. As a result of that tendency we end up with an awful lot of so-called policy decisions by ACPO which are honoured more in the breach than the observance. I don't think it's in anyone's interest. If we want a national police force, for God's sake, let's go and have one!"

What emerges from this consideration of the attitude of chief constables to the central institutions of policing is that they defer to them for the most part. The Home Office is seen as having both power and authority, while most chiefs consent to the influence of HMI and ACPO as the expressions of professional consensus. Even though a minority express dissent, central control is universally recognized to be increasing, like it or not. This contrasts with their attitude to local police authorities. While most chiefs seek to cultivate good relations with their authorities, this is seen as a matter of educating them into the professional viewpoint. The local authorities' influence is by grace and favour of the chief constables, the central authorities' is a matter of power and respect. This balance towards the centre was further confirmed by the chief constables' responses to a question directly addressed to it.

The chiefs were asked to imagine that there was a hypothetical riot in their force area. If their secretary came in to tell them that the Home Secretary, the chair of the police authority, and the editor of *The Times* were on the telephone, in what order would they take the calls? Several chiefs argued that the order they gave should not be interpreted as an order of esteem. They considered central and local authorities, and the media as representing public opinion, as all worthy of respect. None the less, the order given, and the reasons for it, are consistent with the overall picture of chief constables' relations with these institutions, so they do reflect a consistent prioritization. Overall, a majority (55 per cent) would answer the Home Secretary first, while 40 per cent would speak to the police authority chair first. (Five per cent said it would depend on specific circumstances.) There is, moreover, a slight tendency for this centralist orientation to be more pronounced among the younger chiefs. Of those aged below 55, 60 per cent would answer the Home Secretary first, and only 33 per cent would speak to the police authority first. Of chiefs aged over 55, a bare majority (52 per cent) put the Home Secretary first, while 44 per cent would answer the police authority first. The precedence given to the Home Secretary by the majority was justified by the argument that the national dimension of policing problems was paramount.

> "No contest. The Home Secretary first. Now, they are the major shareholders. It's not widely stated, but the Home Office and central government pay about 75 per cent of our costs, don't they, if you take the 51 per cent grant and the rate support grant . . . So many of our problems are national problems now, there must be this strong co-ordination."

> "The truth is I would ring the Home Secretary first, and anybody that says different I would find them very difficult to believe . . . All things being equal, if you knew it was on a local subject or something which has raised its head, yes, I would ring the Home Secretary. He is more important in my thinking than the editor of *The Times* or the chairman. He doesn't ring me very often."

> "Very often there can be conflict between local perceived needs and national policies. As a police service we are charged with enforcing the law of the land. The law of the land takes precedence . . . From my point of view the Home Secretary would come first. He is responsible to Parliament."

Overall, then, it seems clear that the line of accountability for chief constables is tilted increasingly towards the centre. Whereas central government is recognized as a significant and legitimate influence over policy and operations, whose wishes can not be ignored with impunity, this is not true of local police authorities. They are regarded, at most, as junior partners in the process of decision-making. Their influence depends very much on the goodwill of the chief constable. While there is room for some autonomy of chief constables in accordance with their assessment of local priorities and needs, this is a very relative autonomy. It is conditioned by their increasing orientation to a national reference group of police colleagues and experts in ACPO, HMI, and the Home Office. Fundamental disagreements are unlikely to occur often within this structure.

Complaints Against the Police

So far we have considered the accountability of chief constables to central or local government in relation to the overall direction of police forces. Another important and much debated aspect of police account- ability is the system for dealing with complaints against individual police officers for specific actions which are claimed to be in breach of the general standards and procedures established by law and the police discipline code.

The adequacy (or inadequacy) of the procedures for handling com- plaints against the police has been a major focus of debate throughout the world in recent decades, and has generated much research and critical comment (Goldsmith, 1988, 1990, 1991; Loveday, 1988; McMahon and Ericson, 1984; Maguire and Corbett, 1989, are some examples of this). A central aspect of this controversy in all countries has been the question whether the investigation and/or adjudication of such complaints should be principally dealt with by the police, as it has been in most countries. Critics have championed instead a variety of forms of independent procedures for dealing with com- plaints against the police, so that justice may both be done and seen to be done.

For the most part professional police opinion has been steadfastly against fully independent systems. The 1976 Police Act introduced an element of independence in the adjudication of complaints in the form of the Police Complaints Board (PCB). While not satisfying critics, the PCB antagonized much police opinion and led to the resignation of Sir Robert Mark. Clamour for a more, or even a fully, independent system continued, gaining influential support, beyond the civil liberties camp, during the early 1980s. Lord Scarman's 1981 Report championed greater independence. In the same year the Police Federation made a complete U-turn and began to campaign for a fully independent system of investigation as well as adjudication (allying itself for this purpose to the National Council for Civil Liberties). Finally in 1984 the Police and Criminal Evidence Act introduced an element of independence in the investigation as well as adjudication of complaints, and the Police Com- plaints Authority (PCA) was set up to supervise the police investigation in the case of serious complaints against the police, such as assault. While this half a loaf of independence failed to satisfy civil libertarians, it seems to have choked the Police Federation, who have repeatedly voted no confidence in the PCA while persisting in their advocacy of a fully independent system.

In this section we will consider the views of chief constables on the complaints system. These views are of particular interest, and offer a contrasting perspective to existing studies of complainants' perspectives and of the views of rank-and-file officers (Maguire and Corbett, 1989). Chief constables' perspectives are important in a number of ways. First, they perform a pivotal role in the adjudication of complaints. They decide guilt, innocence, and the appropriate sanction in most cases where disciplinary hearings take place, and sit alongside two Police Complaints Authority members in those rare instances where the PCA directs that a disciplinary tribunal be held. Second, deputy chief constables have the primary responsibility for complaints investigations, scrutinizing the reports of investigations, and deciding on appropriate action (subject to oversight by the PCA). Almost all chief constables have served as deputy chief constables, and have thus had the crucial experience of carrying the main responsibility for handling complaints within a force. Third, many chief constables have experience of conducting major complaints investigations when they were senior operational officers, and some will have been called on to investigate very serious complaints against other forces while they were chief constables (three were doing so at the time I interviewed them).

In the interviews, I raised two questions directly about the complaints process. The first was a general question asking the chief constables what were the main problems (if any) that they saw in the present system for handling complaints against the police. The second asked them specifically for their views on a completely independent system for investigating complaints.

With regard to the first question, most chief constables (70 per cent) did not see any problems in the present system, while the remaining 30 per cent did raise a variety of issues they saw as problematic. Despite this strong vote of confidence in existing arrangements, only a bare majority (52 per cent) rejected the idea of a completely independent system, the main plank of radical proposals for change. Nearly a third (30 per cent) supported a completely independent system, while 18 per cent were undecided, seeing strong arguments either way. Thus the ACPO position of rejecting a completely independent system, while expressing the majority viewpoint, is the subject of quite widespread internal dissent and debate amongst chief constables.

The characteristic chief constable perspective is the predictably Panglossian one: all is for the best in the best of all possible worlds. In this picture the existing system involves firm but fair investigation and adjudication of complaints against the police. Criticism of the system stems from villains and those with ideological axes to grind. It does not represent an anxiety which is shared by ordinary members of the public, but is the monopoly of unrepresentative yet noisy minorities. This is the view of 38 per cent of chief constables who both believe that there are no problems with the system, and reject the idea of independent investigation of complaints. It represents the modal view of chief constables, although not a majority.

The traditional view claims that the effectiveness and thoroughness of the present system of investigations is attested to on the basis of long personal experience. Independent investigators could not conceivably match the present standard:

"Independent investigation sounds very attractive, but I think it will create more problems than it would solve. It would take a long time to set up a body with the necessary experience and wherewithal to deal with it, because I don't think the people that would staff that would understand the police culture or the police administration. In my experience, when I was at West End Central, and dealt with some pretty hairy discipline inquiries [post-Kray and Richardsons] I was successful in preparing the papers on that because I knew where to look. An outsider wouldn't know where to go, so anyway he'd be shielding those who were wanting shielding. And again, unless you're investigating historical nuances, you've got to run right quickly before anybody has an opportunity to destroy the traces. Policemen are human beings and there's a self-protect factor, but they couldn't pull the wool over *my* eyes. The bad guys will get away with it far easier than they appear to be doing at the moment, if it was an independent investigation. I remember making a point to the Home Secretary when we were talking about the new Complaints Authority. For God's sake we've got to get it right. We're never going to get it completely right, because there's always going to be a certain grouping of critics that are never going to be satisfied. But you've got to get it right, otherwise morale gets damaged and people's faith is lost. My custom here at the moment is as far right as it will ever be. It's not without failures or problems—primarily the new Complaints Authority who are still in a learning process. On a personal level, I've made this point to Cecil Clothier [the first PCA chairman] who I know pretty well: the people that make up the PCA at the moment are too military minded. They can't understand that when you're dealing with a policeman you're not dealing with a lance corporal or rating. They have rights that perhaps the services haven't got. That criticism could be levelled at some of our critics: policemen are entitled to the same precepts of natural justice as the next man.

However I might have made up my mind an officer is as evil as hell, you've still got to go through the sort of process of justice.''

This is the characteristic view of the more traditional chief constables. Their experience convinces 'them that only police officers themselves can successfully investigate other police: criticism of the system comes mainly from those who will never be satisfied, so it is pointless to pay it much heed.

From this perspective, the recent support of the Police Federation for independent investigation is seen as a devious ruse. It is supported by the Federation precisely because it will be *less* effective in rooting out abuses. The present system has the twin virtues of effectively sanctioning the truly deviant police officers, while not applying irrelevant standards to minor peccadilloes. Senior police officers have a nose for the really corrupt copper, while having a more sympathetic understanding of the stresses and strains that generate minor misdemeanours. Outsiders would be defective on both counts, and end up being both ineffective and unjust. As another traditionalist expressed it:

"You are never going to get a complaints system which will satisfy the minority complainers, so therefore you are trying to find something which doesn't exist. That's the starting-point. However, you've got to give something that satisfies the vast majority of people. It's almost impossible to come up with a solution that will satisfy everybody. But when the Federation made their recommendation some years ago that it should be an entirely independent body, they knew and I knew that this was an extremely clever ruse. They knew that the chances of it working are very, very slight ... I mean so many complaints investigations are crime investigations. Now you know we are police officers with an original authority, not from the Government—we get our authority from the Queen. We are the people charged by the community with investigating crime. I am not quite sure how you can have people other than policemen investigating crime. The truth of it is, you can't! So, therefore, do you have a split arrangement, where the police get on investigating crime, with somebody else investigating the system? The *causes célèbres* which cause all the concern are no more than about five or six a year throughout the country. OK, so there are probably another twenty or thirty that cause some concern locally. But you are really talking about taking a steamroller to crack a nut. And at the end of the day you're not going to be successful, because, unless the decision goes

in favour of the complainer, then that person isn't going to be satisfied
... The fact that the Federation are now asking for that independent
system is evidence of the effectiveness of the present system. You ask
any member of the other ranks what they feel like when they are
being investigated, and the lengths that senior officers go to to try
and get to the truth. With one exception—it's no good being dishonest
about it—that of a fellow police officer, investigating a complaint,
where he sees some degree of justification perhaps in a minor assault,
human nature means there will be a tendency for him to more readily
see the police officer's point of view. But in the more serious cases
they are very, very effectively investigated. The problem is satisfying
the public that those investigations are impartial and thorough ...
The Federation realizes the hopelessness of the situation of ever
getting an adequate method of investigation, because at the end of
the day the public do not believe police officers are entitled to the
same protection as the ordinary member of the public. Even genuine
complainers, when it comes down to it, it is their word against the
police ... To be perfectly honest, the Federation are very concerned
with protecting their wrongdoers, as well as those that are only
accused of wrongdoing, it seems at times. I wouldn't like to be too
harsh on them, but if you speak to people in the Federation at a lower
level that nationally you get a different picture. I know that the
chairman and secretary of my own Federation realize the hopelessness
of ever having a fully independent, effective complaints and investigation procedure."

It would be a mistake to conclude that satisfaction with the status
quo and rejection of the idea of an independent system are the prerogative only of the more traditional chiefs. Some of the most progressive chiefs also reject the idea of further change because they
positively support the innovations introduced by the Police and Criminal Evidence Act in 1984. The provision of facilities for informal
resolution of minor complaints, and the mandatory supervision of the
investigations of the most serious cases by the Police Complaints Authority, are welcomed by these chiefs as a system which achieves the
optimal balance between effectiveness and legitimacy, justice being done
and being seen to be done. This perspective is best expressed by one
chief with a reputation as one of the most progressive in the country:

"I don't support any changes, because now we have got conciliation
which is taking away a lot of, I use the word loosely, dross at the
bottom. Not dross for the man who made the complaint, I know, but

we understand the term, you and I, perhaps. The low-level stuff, we are beginning to prune. In terms of independence, I was never unhappy with the policeman's left ball [the Complaints Board], and I am not unhappy with the new Authority. I am only bothered about the perception of it in the eyes of the public. Frankly I don't think the public gives a toss. There is a vociferous pressure group that wants nothing short of independence, knowing they won't get it ... With more serious allegations the PCA does introduce an element of independence ... We had the shooting of——by PC——... we had that case investigation supervised. We saw it at close quarters, and I don't think the PCA could have done anything differently. I have no quarrel with the way it works at all. I think it is admirable. But we were still criticized for being investigating ourselves. I don't know the answer."

Full acceptance of the status quo is thus not necessarily the prerogative of the traditionalists who think independent investigation an anathema. It may be a considered conclusion based on positive support for the attempt by PACE to solve the problems by introducing informal resolution of minor complaints and PCA supervision of the investigation of serious allegations. However, the modernist opponents of change share with the traditionalists the perception that this will not satisfy the 'vociferous minorities' of complainants and anti-police critics. There is also a shared perception of many complaints as 'dross'. In any event the problem of public confidence does not in this view warrant further changes in what is now an acceptable system in itself.

We have seen that the majority (70 per cent) of chief constables saw no problems in the present system. Of the 30 per cent who did, these divided evenly between those who saw the problems as being the failure to satisfy the public, and those seeing problems from a police perspective. The problems identified from a police viewpoint were the burden of complaints investigation for the police in terms of expense and manpower, as well as the damage to morale due to excessive bureaucracy and delays in the system.

Perceiving problems in the system usually but not invariably was associated with support for a fully independent structure. However, a few who perceived problems in the system did not support such a change because they thought independence would make matters worse. Conversely, a few who supported change did so because of concern about public confidence, but did not see this as based on any real defects in the present systems. In addition, there were a number who were undecided about the question of independence. While recognizing the problems of public confidence and the burden of investigations which were posed by the existing systems, they were unsure whether independence would improve or exacerbate matters. Altogether 30 per cent supported a fully independent system, almost but not entirely coinciding with the 30 per cent who felt there were problems in the present system. Another 18 per cent were undecided, but saw some potential advantages in independence.

The reasons for the view that lack of public confidence was a major concern, but would not be alleviated by independence are indicated by the following:

"I have been a deputy chief constable for six years and have been responsible for complaints. One is always conscious of the fact that there is a public perception, at least in the minds of a minority, that you are judges in your own court. But I think any former deputy chief constable would say to you that we are probably harsher judges of our own organization. We don't want people in our organization who let the side down, tarnish their cap badge, and tarnish mine. So we are probably more ruthless than any other organization. We weed people out who don't live up to standards. Where people misinterpret it, is that people sometimes expect officers dealt with where there is no evidence to deal with them, particularly if matters have hit the national press ... But police are entitled to the same degree of treatment in justice as anyone else. There is a sector of the public who don't believe that, for whatever reason I don't know, it may be just to suit their own ends. Now, if you were to go as the Federation suggests to a totally independent system, that is the nub of it—how do you get a totally independent investigative body? I know it happens in some parts of the world, Australia, for example. I am not so sure you would get the quality of investigation we get now. Because, like it or not, the Police Complaints Board before this, and the current Police Complaints Authority, will, in almost every annual report, comment on the quality and depth of police investigations. That is our bread and butter at the end of the day. Well OK—I think there is another thing too. Police officers in trouble, in spite of the Federation advising don't say anything, by and large have a great confidence in one of their own investigating, that they will get a fairer crack than they might from some faceless body. I like to speak from my own experience over a number of years—I can put my hand to my heart here and say to anybody I investigate, it is done in justice, and if he didn't deserve to stay in this force then they don't stay ... An independent body wouldn't have the total confidence of the British police service, so they have got an uphill struggle in the first place . . . The Federation would say that, the amount of criticism they're getting from sections of society saying the police are judge and jury in their own case, let's have a total change. Now I am not sure they are convinced in themselves that it would be better, but certainly it would take away that criticism. My apprehension would be that after two or three years we would still be getting the voices outside saying it is less than just because they are not finding policemen guilty of the offences we feel they are guilty of.''

This view exemplifies the argument of those chief constables who, while recognizing that there is a problem of public confidence because police are perceived as judging themselves, reject the Federation solution of complete independence. They are convinced that independent investigators would be less successful at sustaining allegations, because of the blue curtain of silence which would be an even greater impediment to outsiders who are distrusted by the police in the first place. If this is so, an independent system would be a cosmetic change that would not even bolster public confidence in the long run, when it is seen to be unsuccessful in cracking cases where the public perceives complaints to be justified. The fundamental problem in this view lies not in the failure of the system of investigation, but the public's inability to accept the proper rights of complained-against police officers, and the limits this imposes on the prospects of complaints being sustained.

Those chief constables who support the idea of a move to a fully independent system (30 per cent), as well as those who were undecided (18 per cent), did not believe that such a system would be more effective. Like those who opposed change, they believed that the existing system did investigate and deal with complaints as effectively and fairly as possible (though there were mixed feelings about the Police Complaints Authority). Indeed, many of those who supported independence agreed with those opponents of the idea who argued that an independent system would encounter even more obstacles than police investigators, and would therefore be less effective in practical terms. However, they supported fully independent investigation and adjudication on the grounds that it was necessary in order to achieve public confidence. In other words, it was an innovation with purely symbolic advantages in the battle for public opinion. Operationally it would if anything be less successful than the existing structure. Faith in the intrinsic soundness of the public handling of complaints was universal amongst chief constables. Where there was deep disagreement was in judging the most effective strategy for securing public confidence. Supporters of independence believed in essence that the demands of legitimacy justified sacrificing a measure of effectiveness in dealing with complaints. Some believed that this was also the position of the Police Federation, while the more cynical felt that Federation support for independent investigation was precisely on the grounds of its lesser effectiveness. The following quotes encapsulate these arguments:

"Yes, I would be happy to have the thing entirely independent. I think the principle is, is the scheme acceptable to the general public? If it isn't, there's no good carrying on with it. But we've got to ensure that it's not just a small minority of left-wing councillors and odd-ball media and press criticizing, that the criticisms are founded on fact. I don't honestly think the great majority of the public know what the system is now against what it was before ... The current criticism is emanating from a small group for political reasons, and not based on pure fact, showing that the system isn't working, justice isn't being done, the truth should go. I would be happy to accept a completely independent system. All I am saying is, the present system *is* working ... I have been an investigating officer and would not risk my professional career to support some idiot who had done something wrong. I want him out. I was brought up in the police service and am proud of the police service. I go for policemen far harder than I would go for a criminal, if he is doing wrong I want him out and exposed. Now I may be a bit weak in that I think all investigating officers are like that. But I think most are, because most deputy chief constables who deal with it are my ilk. Our general view is we don't want wrong ones in the service, so we appoint as investigating officers people who we think share those ideals and are determined to get at the truth and who can investigate ... If you are investigating a senior detective officer then your choice of investigators is reduced because you've got to have someone who is as sharp as he is ... I am entirely of the opinion that the present system in honestly and properly done. Whether it is acceptable to the general public is entirely a different matter."

"I still believe that we do our best to sort out a lot of rotten apples. We don't need them. There is evidence since I have been in the force where an allegation was made that a police officer has assaulted someone whilst he was in custody—I can think of three cases where a constable has come forward and given evidence to that effect. So I think the level that is going on in police stations has reduced. Not eliminated—it never will for a number of reasons. Sometimes you might have to hit in response to an attack, it's very difficult to know who is the aggressor. As a rule if you look at our internal disciplinary inquiries it supports my argument that it's not just a whitewash. But I would favour independence in some ways, just to answer our critics. Because they then would say we've really nothing to hide. But quite honestly I don't think they would find out as much about what's happening in the organization as some of our experienced supervisors do, particularly somebody from an outside force. There's absolutely no cover-up or cock-up if you get somebody from an outside force."

All who supported independence were unconvinced of its merits, but felt it essential in public relations terms. A few expressed great exasperation at the various piecemeal changes introduced over recent years. As they perceived an inexorable drive towards an independent system, they would prefer it to be introduced at once to clarify matters.

"What I can't understand is why society, British society, jokes around with this issue. If you don't like the present form of investigation of complaints against policemen, for God's sake get rid of it, but don't wimp about it! I have been away from home, and away from my boss, for the greater part of three years investigating complaints with great application, often in very unpleasant circumstances, doing something that I didn't really want to do, but I did it—perhaps even better because I didn't want to do it. I've never spared anybody and I've never spared myself. By all means get rid of it, and I welcome its release. But please do acknowledge that you cannot then introduce a counterfeit system. What I mean is, if you intend to exchange a very professional approach with something which will not match it, get ready for the problems. Brace yourself for the substitute! Replace though, if you are going to ... Why the hell society and Parliament messes about this, I don't know! Get on with it! Who wants it? Great, do it, don't wimp about it!"

The shared view of chief constables, whatever they thought about the policy question of whether an independent structure should be established, was that it would not be able to surpass the effectiveness of internal police investigations. On the basis of their own experience almost all chiefs felt it was likely to be hopelessly ineffective in practical terms.

"The system as it operates at the moment is no better than the one that was, and it won't get any better. You will never get it right, because at the end of the day you've still got the dissatisfied customer, no matter what you do ... It is useful to have an independent element fitted in, but if you look at the Hong Kong system, the Independent Commission Against Corruption, ... it didn't work. The relationship between them and the Royal Hong Kong police was that they were head-on, physically came to blows, totally opposed to one another, and totally unco-operative ... They didn't trust one another one inch, and the result was that the police officers were interviewed by them, and they said nothing, they said, 'You prove it' ... Unless you change the rules and say police officers must answer or you can comment upon their lack of answering, then if they're silent what can you do? If you did change our protection in law there would be great uproar. There is no doubt at all that the police service could destroy a new system overnight, by superintendents deciding when they're asked to investigate, saying, 'What do you want me to do, you supervise it, you tell me what you want ... I've taken a statement, what do you want me to do now?' The service won't do it because it's a pretty honourable organization, and unless they do it properly somebody is going to shout whitewash ... You end up asking: 'do you trust us or don't you?' We're more ruthless than outsiders ... I had an officer here who, because he was removed from CID duties, decided to take revenge on his detective sergeant. He did this by sending a series of obscene telephone calls to the officer's wife. That matter we detected, it was presented before the magistrates, he went sick, it was heard in his absence, he was convicted. He then suddenly found he was fit again and appealed. He went before the crown court and was convicted on overwhelming evidence, and fined substantially. We had all the psychiatric evidence and all the rest of it and I sacked him, which I presume you would hope I would do. The Home Secretary reinstated him with a caution! I wrote to the Home Secretary and said it amazed me. What standards does he expect from the British police service when he allows people like that man who is a convicted criminal to remain? ... We can be as tough as we like, but outsiders would let us down."

"I honestly believe we are ruthless ... My basic objection to inde-pendence is we will end up with more bad apples still within our barrel than we do now. You have to get up very early in the morning to catch a corrupt, bent police officer. The old adage, it takes one to know one. Bearing in mind my background in A10 [the internal investigations unit set up at Scotland Yard by Robert Mark] and what have you, I know it's no good a solicitor ringing up saying, 'Detective Sergeant So-and-So, we are investigating a complaint. We will come and see you on Friday at two, please have your pocket book, your CID diary, and your case-papers available for us.' By the time you get there they'll be gone! ... Point number two: we are a conservative organization, small 'c'. We are a defensive organization. There will be extra bricks on the ramparts with outsiders, and with a closing of ranks it is going to take a sharp cookie to break through.''

In the same way as chief constables' opinions were divided about an independent system, so too they were in two camps about whether the innovation of the Police Complaints Authority was welcome or not. One group of chief constables felt it got the difficult balance between effectiveness and legitimacy right:

"The Police Complaints Authority have a very pervasive influence in the investigation of complaints now. I still think it is better for police officers to investigate them. But there is an improved perception of the investigation of complaints since the PCA have taken a higher profile. All chief officers don't approve of it, there are quarrels about demarcation, who is doing what. But I think they are seen to be more in control, and that is important. I've never eschewed the idea of an independent element, but what has concerned me has been the investigation. I don't think in practical terms you would get the sort of investigation police officers indulge in ... They are the best trained investigators and interrogators and they get to the bottom of it ... An outside body wouldn't do as well ... They would say, 'We are being blocked', and that would bring more discredit on the police.''

An equal number however felt that the PCA was so anxious about establishing its credibility as an independent body that it acted in a heavy-handed way which damaged police morale and alienated the service:

"I have had personal disagreements with the PCA when I was a deputy chief about my role in the maintenance of discipline and their role ... At a most gentlemanly level, we didn't fall out as some of my colleagues have. But I do fall out with Cecil Clothier's pronunciation as head of the PCA when he said to me, I don't think you as a chief constable sitting in discipline cases should demand the standard of proof that is required in criminal courts. I said, hang on a minute, you are going away from Magna Carta! Let's not move the goal posts unless we do it democratically! We still agree to differ on that. But I shan't do anything! When a man stands in peril in front of me I want it proved beyond all reasonable doubt. Now a particular case, where I was involved, when I had to have a tribunal—much more good would have been achieved if that guy had stood in front of me with just the two of us and no attribution. He wouldn't ever have transgressed again! As it was I knew there wasn't a cat's chance in hell of ever getting him convicted of anything. He walked, and sort of did that [fingers up] to the whole system ... We've been subject to so many changes in the complaints procedure in recent years that it's time to let the blokes at the bottom have a bit of a rest, a bit of stability, poor sods! I believe in rooting out wrongdoers ourselves. I have a philosophy as a chief constable that says that if you do your incompetent best I will support you to the end of the road. Even if I give you the biggest rollicking of your life, it will be with dignity and humanity, because I know with your hand on your heart you're not villainous in what you are doing. If you are middle down the road then I will decide in the circumstances how to deal with you, whether I touch your pocket, give you a good rollicking, or whatever. But if you have been utterly disregarding or villainous then I will sack you or demote you. My Federation know that, my force knows that. I am very uncomplicated—that's where I stand."

It was generally felt that the chief constables were and should remain responsible for police discipline. The PCA was resented for activities which threatened to dilute this with the purpose of demonstrating their strength as an independent watchdog:

"I am not very pleased that my colleagues will not come out publicly and castigate the annual report of the Complaints Authority for the rubbish it is. They categorically claim that they are responsible for police discipline. They aren't at all! They have a responsibility for investigation of complaints against the police, a totally different thing. I mean, in the three and a half years I have been here I have had the unpleasant duty of sacking twenty-two officers. Only three of those cases arose from complaints by members of the public. The other nineteen were the result of internal disciplinary action. One of our problems is that we cannot demonstrate this to the public."

Thus chief constables were unanimously confident about their ability to deal effectively both with complaints and discipline, and to do so with justice to complainants and subordinates alike. The divisions which existed about the desirability of the PCA, or a fully independent system, arose over purely symbolic and strategic questions. What price in effect-iveness was worth paying for greater public confidence and trust?

We know from other research (e.g. Maguire and Corbett, 1989) that the views of complainants, complained-against officers, and the public about the complaints systems are generally negative. By contrast, on the evidence presented above, the one significant party who are happy with the present system are chief constables. They all feel ('know' on the basis of their own experience) that complaints are very thoroughly investigated. They are confident of their ability to judge cases, and assess the moral culpability of officers. If left to them, without problems of proof, they are sure that discipline could be maintained. However, in serious cases (and all accept the justice of the criminal burden of proof for these cases) there are difficulties in achieving this even for internal investigators. This must be even more true for outside inves-tigators, though, who would face tougher, perhaps insuperable prob-lems, penetrating police barriers of secrecy. So the system, with its imperfections, remains the best possible.

The only major problem they see is the apparent failure to command public confidence. Here there is a division in chief constable ranks. They are split between those who feel public confidence must be won by an independent system, even at the price of some loss of effectiveness, and those who regard this as throwing the baby out to preserve the bath water. The latter tend to play down the significance of public dissatisfaction with the system by portraying active complainants as disreputable or 'dross'. However, if investigations are as thorough as the chiefs claim, why do they so rarely result in sustaining allegations, leaving complainants with a sense of grievance, and feeding public suspicion?

There seem to be two main reasons why complaints usually fail to be sustained following an internal investigation, and these are indicated by the views of chief constables described above. First, many cases turn on straightforward conflicts of evidence between the complainant and the officer(s) complained against. In such cases the criminal burden of proof will almost certainly result in the complaint not being sustained. The realization of this, coupled with the intensification of public distrust of the police following a record number of scandals involving abuse of power had led the most progressive of chief officers (notably Sir Peter Imbert) to consider that the burden of proof might have to be changed, and to reconsider the maintenance of the right of silence in the face of disciplinary investigations (Imbert, 1989). It is coming to be realized that the crucial issue is not *who* does the investigating, but the terms on which it is done.

However, a final problem is that many complaints cases are inherently intractable. They are incidents where two rights make a wrong. This was indicated by some chief constables quoted above who frankly admitted that one reason for opposing an independent system was that in some cases only a police officer could fairly assess the stress and provocations a complained-against officer experienced, which generated behaviour which outsiders might condemn but was understandable if not completely to be condoned. It is, of course, this possibility of excessive sympathy to the police viewpoint which generates the critical support for an independent system. However, the complexities of the issue are well brought out in the interviews.

In conclusion, chief constables are fundamentally satisfied with the structure of accountability, although there is some support for reforms such as the establishment of a local police authority for London, or more independence in the complaints system. This is hardly surprising, for as the interviews themselves reveal, the chiefs are very much in the saddle in their local domains. Although ultimately constrained by central government, this is not experienced as restrictive for the most part, but as part of a consensual process of policy-making informed by rational dialogue amongst professional peers.

Notes

1. Those chief constables who have published their views on the accountability debate have tended to argue for a diminution of the extent of the elected element in police authorities at present, in favour of appointed bodies (on the model of Northern Ireland). The leading example is Oliver 1987, though Mark, 1977 and 1978; Anderton, 1981; and McNee, 1983, put similar viewpoints.

2. However, several of these had refused to give reports on a number of occasions, indicating a 'hard core' of chiefs who had difficult relations with their police authority.

Part V

Varieties of Chief Constable:
The Sum of the Parts

12 Barons, Bobbies, Bosses, and Bureaucrats

The previous parts of this book have looked at chief constables' social origins, orientation to work, career paths, occupational and political ideologies, and assessments of the system of accountability. Throughout, the emphasis has been on the views of the group of chief constables as a whole, and the variations which may exist on specific issues. What this macroscopic approach loses sight of is the way that individuals assemble and structure their experiences and reactions into more or less coherent and distinctive total world-views. The purpose of this chapter is to look at the sum of these parts. It will present four case-studies of individual chief constables in some detail, to make sense of their perspectives as a whole. The four have been chosen because they represent what I see as four ideal-typical patterns of chief constable career and style.

Ideal Types of Chief Constable

At one level each individual chief constable is completely unique. However, the common experiences and problems which they encounter tend to generate a common set of responses, which constitute the dominant culture of chief constables that has been presented in previous chapters. Within these overall shared pressures, there are distinctive constellations of particular experiences which can be seen as variations around the central themes. These can be analysed as ideal types in the Weberian sense (Weber, 1949, 84) They are models of logically possible permutations, which are not likely to be encountered in pure form in the real world. But they constitute clear benchmarks for understanding the pressures and processes which structure and generate concrete individual cases.

The main influences on the perspectives of chief constables can be classified, I suggest, into four key dimensions: period, problems, place, and pedigree.

Period

At any one time there is likely to be a dominant set of views, policies, approaches, which are currently fashionable, the flavour of the month, in the chief constable peer group. These may emanate from key institutional influences like the Home Office, and will be spread by HMI and ACPO, as well as informally. They represent the *Zeitgeist* of contemporary chief constable culture. As found in Part III, the current fashion seems to be a sort of (half-resentful) pot-pourri of Scarman spiced with subtle hints of Alderson, which may be labelled post-Scarmanism. This represents a common orienting frame of reference for all chief constables, elements of which are adopted and assembled into individual *bricolages* according to the structuring grids provided by the other dimensions.

Problems

Chief constables' responses to questions are informed by what are seen as the most pressing problems confronting them at that time. These dominant problems will be referred to spontaneously and will implicitly underlie the attitudes exhibited even on questions which do not overtly invoke them. Some of these will be national problems, confronting all chief constables. Important ones which recurred in the interviews were the urban riots and the post-Scarmanist responses to them, the miners' strike, PACE and the CPS, and the Financial Management Initiative. These shared problems underlie the common philosophy of the period.

There will also be particular local problems which are a source of variation in chief constables' responses. Examples would include clashes with local police authorities, particular crime or disorder problems, or local personnel issues and conflict with the Police Federation branch. Such particular problems will colour an individual's responses in distinctive ways. They may be idiosyncratic matters of personality or place, or structured conflicts in specific types of force. For example, the swing to Labour in the 1981 local elections produced the crop of radical police authorities in metropolitan areas which became an important problem confronting a key subgroup of chief constables.

Place

The local area of each chief constable will generate different pressures which affect their perspective. The social and physical ecology, the political structure and culture, the ethnic mix, the economic condition, and many other aspects of the place he is responsible for policing will provide a crucial context for the varying permutations of chief constables' philosophies. These are not merely idiosyncratic, but will fall into distinct clusters of types of place. There will be clear differences, for instance, between the pressures of being chief constable in a large metropolitan force or a relatively small, predominantly rural county force.

Pedigree

The particular social background and career trajectory of each individual chief constable will shape their initial orientation to the job. This pedigree will interact with the pressures of period, place, and problems to generate specific philosophies of policing. Social origin, education, work experience, training, specialization, these and many other personal and career factors will influence the chief constable's perception of his place, problems, and period, and inform his reactions to them.

There are four ideal types of chief constable perspective which I have been able to distinguish based on an elective affinity between congruent elements of period, problems, place, and pedigree. These types, the baron, bobby, boss, and bureaucrat, are outlined below. It must be emphasized that these are ideal types, not real people. They represent tendencies, when all the pressures on a particular chief point in the same direction. Flesh and blood individuals are not likely to fit the totality of a type. First, there are the creative elements of individual interpretation and idiosyncrasy which make people transcend such structuring pressures. Second, in many cases pressures cut across rather than reinforce each other. The result is likely to be a contradictory hybrid, deviating considerably from a pure type. For example, while one type (the baron) may embody the quintessential traditional approach of the rural chief constable, the incumbent chief constable of a county force may well have a pedigree as having been a hard-boiled city detective for most of his earlier career, and having had strong exposure to the national problems underlying the dominant orthodoxy of the period. These contradictory pressures will skew his responses away from the baronial model. Despite those caveats, I suggest the following types do provide useful benchmarks for understanding the range of variation of chief constables' styles and philosophies.

The Baron

The baron is the ideal-typical chief constable of a county (Havenshire). His pedigree is more likely to be middle class than that of other chief constables (though most will be from manual working-class origins as is true of police generally). His background is rural, and much of the attraction of policing initially was that it was an outdoor job. He will have had more military experience than most chief constables, and may have contemplated a military career. (In the past county chiefs were in fact almost invariably military men.) His experience of police work is predominantly operational rather than administrative.

He believes that the police can successfully control crime, and indeed do so reasonably well in his area which is socially stable and harmonious. In his county, order is largely the product of communal self-regulation, and the job of the police is mainly to oil the wheels of this. But he does perceive imminent threats from 'outside' (especially symbolized by the possible incursion of 'coloured' people). There is in the cities a crumbling of authority which he fears is spreading into his area of Havenshire.

His ideal image of society (inside and outside the force) is a paternalistic but hierarchical structure, mediated by norms of deference and *noblesse oblige*. He likes to lead from the front, to be obeyed, but to give his men their say and their due. All is and should be in its place. He is regulated to an extent by the Home Office, and indeed he resents their greater interventionism of recent years. But he controls his local authority and his 'troops', firmly but fairly. The local buck clearly stops with him. However, he fears the signs of politicization which are creeping in even to the Havenshire police authority. Overall, though, he exudes a quiet confidence and satisfaction with his place and career.

The Bobby

The bobby is the ideal-typical chief constable of a small, mixed urban/rural force (Provinshire), centred on a provincial city (Smallville). His pedigree is working class, self-consciously so for he is very much a 'man of the people'. He has no regrets about his lack of higher education, though he is proud of his children's success in this regard. He was attracted to the police as an interesting, varied, people-oriented job.

He also believes that traditional policing is the key to crime control, and vital to social order. It is, however, increasingly hamstrung by political and legal interference and control. He resents attempts at influencing him, whether these emanate from local or central government. The police are seen as the *vox populi*, the representatives of Mr Joe Average, while politicians may be captured by or over-sensitive to minority fashions and interests. He is proud of his own sensitivity to 'average' local opinion, but hostile to professional spokespeople of particular interests, and of minorities perceived as 'strange', or deviant or subversive.

Whilst believing in the tough, no-holds-barred policing of villainy, this should be by traditional methods. He is suspicious of new equipment like shields, plastic bullets, and the like, not on civil libertarian grounds but for what may be called 'macho' objections. Real policemen don't need baton rounds.

He is proud of what he claims as his continuing personal activity as an operational policeman. He relishes 'war' stories, whether of early days on the beat, or (more rarely) recent 'collars' felt from his official car. In a nutshell, he is the bobby on the beat promoted to the top job in the constabulary.

The Boss

The boss is the ideal-typical chief constable—of an earlier vintage—in a metropolitan force area (Gotham City). He has much in common with the pedigree of the bobby but his perspective is given an apocalyptic twist because of seemingly overwhelming problems of crime and disorder in his area.

He is working class and proud of it, though possibly a little resentful about his lack of educational opportunities. He is, however, self-taught, keen to display his scholarly interests and knowledge. He has worked in urban forces throughout, probably in a hard-boiled detective role. He joined the force because of a wish to be a police officer, though the security and career prospects were an added attraction given his humble origins.

The boss recognizes but resents the encroaching grip of central control of policing. He will struggle to contest it, at least on matters of deep interest or principle. His perception of his force area is as an urban jungle, on the edge of breakdown, with the police as the 'new centurions' fighting a losing battle to prevent it tipping over into chaos. In this he is not helped by his local (Labour) authority, who are dominated by political extremists seeking to undermine the police. He is a seasoned campaigner against them, and determined to show who is boss.

He is also the boss of his force, although he controls mainly through authority not power. His men for the most part share his perspective, and are loyal to his leadership. He is not one to suffer criticism gladly, and the troops have to toe the line. Given the pressures of Gotham City the only possible policing tactic is the 'fire-brigade' approach, and the 'community' perspective is the impossible dream of tilters at windmills (mainly found in rural idylls). Reducing crime is not a feasible goal, however. Even the best policing amounts only to a Canute-like holding operation.

The Bureaucrat

The bureaucrat is the very model of a modern chief constable. He is the favoured Home Office flavour for large cities (Conurbville), but also increasingly prevalent in counties. The ideal 'bureaucrat' would combine a mastery of modern managerial approaches with the charismatic image of a traditional bobby or detective. This is to achieve street credibility with rank-and-file police officers, the absence of which has caused problems in some cases.

The pedigree of the bureaucrat is an upwardly mobile working-class background, and he will have a degree and probably extensive experience of research and training. He is very much a believer in, indeed a propagator of, the *Zeitgeist* of the period, the post-Scarman philosophy. He developed this through his immersion in the central institutions of the police world. Paradoxically this attachment to the values of the centre makes him a fervent advocate of the virtues of local consultation.

While recognizing the problems and conflicts which confront the boss, he believes they can be managed through professionalism and diplomacy. Professionalism is the antidote to the Apocalypse-now vision of the boss. Essentially he seeks to generate a planned surrogate for the spontaneous order celebrated by the baron, but this will require surgical skills, the utmost professionalism. Crime and disorder may be increasing, but they have to be viewed in a historical perspective. They were perennial features of British history, and Golden Ageism is a perniciously misleading myth. Alone of all the types, the bureaucrat offers a welcoming embrace to the future. He is aware of the need, however, to connect up with the legitimacy which still accrues to the traditional bobby image, and will assiduously cultivate the aura of whatever operational police experience he had on the street on the way up to the top manager's suite.

As stressed earlier these are ideal types, and no individuals will embody all these elements exactly. None the less, many individuals do approximate closely to these models. The way that individual chief constables experience and respond to the complex of pressures surrounding them will be illustrated by four case-studies, each selected because it comes close to one of the types outlined. These case-studies are intended to illuminate how specific individual chief constables make sense of their lives and the world.

Case One: The Baron

Origins and Orientation

The Baron joined a county force in 1949, at the age of 21. He had previously served in the Fleet Air Arm, after attending a public school. He had entertained the idea of a career in the Navy, but in the end opted for the police service instead. He came from a farming background, and his father had been a professional soldier in the cavalry. This coupled with his own experience in the Fleet Air Arm made him averse 'to be shut up in an office'. The police service was attractive because of its outdoor, quasi-military aspects, what in Chapter 4 was called the 'disciplined body' syndrome.

The Baron spent the first twenty-four years of his service in the county force he had joined, and then went to a combined, largely rural, force as assistant and later deputy chief constable. The three-post rule meant he had to move elsewhere to become a substantive chief constable. At the time of interview he had been chief constable of Havenshire for eight years.

He saw himself as an 'entirely operational man', and had indeed spent much of his career in the CID. ('When I joined, for anybody to be promoted under twelve or fifteen years service was unheard of. My aim was CID, and I got on to that with three years service which was a bit unheard of in those days.') He had not aspired to ACPO rank, because of his commitment to operational work, and had only gone for the ACC post because it was the ACC in charge of crime. He was attracted to policing out of intrinsic interest, and had been completely satisfied. He would without hesitation rejoin if he had his life over: 'I continue to think it's the most fascinating job in the world.' His children had not followed his footsteps, however. His daughter was a designer 'until she produced children', while his son was a estate agent who 'at the age of 34 is earning as much as his father'.

There is a clear congruence between the Baron's rural and military pedigree, his successfully satisfied aspirations to be a detective, and his current place, which he perceives as a relatively problem-free haven of tradition and authority. He is, however, somewhat at odds with his period. He resents styles of policing which he sees being forced upon him from the centre but which he regards as irrelevant to his domain with its comparative absence of the problems of the modern world. As a deferential and disciplined individual he accepts these trends, with some resentment. But as a survivor from an earlier generation he continuously harks back to the Golden Age when his ideas were formed.

Ideology: The Role of the Police

He sees the police mission as a mixture of crime control and a social role: 'It would be a very sad day for us to say, well, our job is solely detection of crime, prevention or detection of offences. We've always fulfilled a social role ... we have a great deal of knowledge about public, about human behaviour ... but I think the problems are mainly resource ones in terms of taking prevention to its ultimate end.' Fashionable talk of a need for 'community policing' is misleading, in this view: it's always been followed. 'In terms of the inevitable changes in reorganization of the force that I've been concerned with, I've very deliberately refused to use the term: in fact, throughout I've used the term traditional policing.'

Scarmanesque comments about the need for sensitive policing, and the priority of tranquillity over law enforcement, amount to a grandmother receiving instruction in the art of egg-sucking. The exercise of discretion is part of the traditional skill in British policing, and problems arise only with the very young, not fully socialised PC.

> "The dangers you speak of [order vs. tranquillity] are rare, they are in the eyes of the junior policeman, who comes from the training school and is told you should do this and do that, and he comes and finds himself even in delightful——shire in the centre of——[large county town], where we've got a fairly substantial coloured community, and sees himself being prevented from doing it the way he was taught in training school ... There isn't anything new about this ... It's no different a situation in essence to when I was a young CID officer and in effect I knew that Bill Bloggs was the author of that particular crime. I was a bloody idiot if I walked into his local

pub on a Saturday night and said, 'Bill, you're nicked.' I picked my
time and place and said, 'OK, Bill!', and that was usually early in the
morning and he was going to work, and he did not have his cronies
about him ... The principle which Scarman was trying to set forward
... I think is the principle that policemen have always used ... The
danger today of saying Scarman says this and Scarman says that,
and the particular circumstances of linking that most usually with a
coloured community, and with a different and somewhat effervescent
and occasionally violent type of personality, is that it gets mis-
interpreted."

Thus the traditional British police officer was well versed in the art
of discreetly adjusting law enforcement to varying circumstances, but
new problems arise in some areas of social change and culturally heterogeneous populations. When Scarman-type changes are introduced
into the policing policies favoured by government, these cause
difficulties for the non-problematic areas where traditional policing had
continued: 'The shortcomings of Scarman were that he looked at the
large conurbations, and thereafter on a political basis it was said we'll
blanket the whole country.' The fundamental police task is the preservation of social stability in the face of conflicting groups in society
and cultural change:

"By nature and rightly so in this country we are a conservative society
and many of the problems we face are the problems of the rapidity
of change. Consciously or otherwise, as change comes along, whilst
society is deciding whether or not it should change—and perhaps it
ought to be cautious about it—and certainly whilst Parliament decides
whether or not we should change, in effect *we* are left to hold the
baby. You can look at many things ... perhaps the easiest, going back,
was the law on things like homosexuality—the law on unlawful sexual
intercourse, where, in my youth and my experience, it was, 'That's
the law'. We would take the matter forward, you get to crown court,
and you'd be set aside—the judges would say there's really no point
in bringing this to us ... It's bloody difficult for the chap on the
ground."

Moral change and ambiguity create enough confusion for the
operational police, but this is exacerbated when the issues become
politicized. When I asked the Baron about the dangers of stop-go
policing arising from Scarmanesque discretion he replied:

"Whether you are being deliberately provocative or not I don't know, the problem is ... the thing we see so often ... The world is much more, our society is—it's much more political ... and in effect we're left as Johnny in the Middle ... The fact is if offences *are* being committed in any sort of number, it's all very well trying to use discretion along the way ... The sad fact is, again, dealing particularly with some of the ethnic communities, the moment you decide you're going to do something, you've got to be able to do it. You can't be beaten half-way."

Criminology

Increasing Crime

To the Baron there was no doubt that crime was increasing in amount. A check-list of reasons was suggested: 'a much more sophisticated society', television, 'a more materialistic society'. The basic problem was the 'change in society' discussed previously. However, what is characteristic of the Baronial conception (as contrasted with the Boss) is the absence of an apocalyptic view of crime and social change. The emphasis is placed on how materialism and affluence lead to a vast increase in relatively minor property crime, which by boosting recorded crime figures unnecessarily exacerbates public concern:

"The fact is, the major areas of crime which we try and grapple with ineffectively ... if I could chop off from the bottom of the crime figures all the—well, they're not tuppenny-halfpenny burglaries any more—but still minor burglaries which are effectively because someone has left the door or window open, if we could chop off the crime which occurs simply because people will leave their damn cars unlocked, we could have a very significant effect on crime figures."

While material affluence thus increases the opportunities for crime, so unemployment creates the personnel, 'the young people who have too much time on their hands,' to take the opportunities.

Can the Police Control Crime?

Although rising crime is related to wider social changes, the Home Office and other researchers are wrong to suggest traditional policing strategies could not cope with it. The problem according to the Baron, is that forces lack the resources to cope.

"First of all, sat here in delightful——, it sounds a bit cheeky to challenge much of the research which is coming out of the Home Office, but I *do* challenge it ... The research was carried out in the situation where the resources were short anyway ... I'm too late, too old in the teeth to change, but I'm quite convinced the crime which concerns us most ... the violence, the vandalism ... The damage which takes place most of all late at night on our streets, and even accepting that today the lonely figure of a policeman wandering down the street won't send them all scattering, none the less we could prevent a good deal of it if in fact the streets were properly manned ... This shouldn't be taken as meaning that I've got some fond idea, particularly as I use the term 'traditional policing' ... that it's going to go back to the years that I knew on the ground, the late thirties and through the forties, 'cos it won't go back to that."

Manpower used in traditional patrols was thus the key to crime control. Detection was also more difficult nowadays because of the more detailed recording processes introduced by PACE, and because suspects were less ready to co-operate with the police. 'The professional criminal says, "Sod it, but I'm not admitting anything." This should be remedied by further change in the rules of criminal procedure, which were 'still something of a game of cricket'. In particular, the 'right of silence' should be abandoned because 'I happen to believe that it's in the interests of society to ensure that the guilty are convicted'.

In general, though, people in——still co-operated with the police, and the formal powers introduced by PACE were not really necessary. 'Outside of the difficult areas and outside of places like the Met. where they had the old Sus Act, we stop people. It's been a practice ever since I've been a policeman. Late at night, purely on the basis of "Can you help us? Where have you been? Have you seen anything?", etc. We haven't really needed a power to do that, and I still don't think we do really.'

Public Order

As with crime, so with public disorder, the Baron was in no doubt that it was increasing. To blame were the same usual suspects, especially the media with their messages of 'explicit violence' which produce a sense of habituation, the feeling that 'there's nothing horrific about it'.

Behind these lay more basic social changes: 'if we move a stage back from TV or whatever, one sees very clearly that many more of the ethnic community, and we're talking basically about coloured people, are becoming part of the general scene ... You have a kernel of an almost totally coloured community in places.'

Although disorder had increased, given the profound nature of social change in the last twenty years, the traditional British approach to policing, discreetly balancing force and social involvement, had been vindicated.

"In the last twenty years we've gone through a social revolution and an industrial revolution with very little loss of life. If you look back at history it's not a bad sort of record ... We should continue to resist the idea of a third force. If you take the metropolitan policeman, if he's one of those poor buggers that's picked up week after week and stuck on to those coaches and taken to those things, that must be a problem for him. If you take people like mine who establish a reputation for themselves, the right sort of reputation, to the effect that I was almost embarrassed by the demand upon them during things like the miners' strike, there is not a problem."

Nevertheless, if the trends elsewhere continued they might be pushed down a confrontational road. For example, it might be necessary to resort to plastic bullets in a life-threatening situation: 'A bloody awful decision to make but at the end of the day if you are talking about life and limb then a senior policeman really has no alternative.' This would not cause a local problem: his authority had been 'very strongly royal blue', though it had recently become a split one.

The Control of Policing

The Baron's conception of the control of the police organization is isomorphic with his view of social control. The ideal is a harmonious but hierarchical order with stable rules, roles, and relationships. Paternalism rules, OK.

The task of the chief who has 'reached this dizzy rank and sits in this chair' is to persuade others, i.e. subordinates and the police authority, to go where he wants. This is best done by personal involvement and concern, by 'leading from the front', not pushing from behind. This is one of the advantages of a relatively small, rural force. 'One of my great delights in——, having served in larger forces, is the fact that I can take a personal interest, occasionally put my grubby finger in, to things I ought to have a personal interest in ... One of my delights is that occasionally, not frequently enough, I can wander into the canteen and just sit and chat to officers ... And it gives me the opportunity to say,

"Look, that bloody complicated memorandum that has changed that procedure ... this is the reason why".'

The police authority is also a body that is to be manipulated to follow his professional lead, a job which is harder with his new split authority than his former 'true blue' one. If the Labour proposals to empower police authorities were enacted, he would have to 'be careful I suppose. In a way I would almost say that it's rubbish that any group of politicians could truly represent all the levels of the local community.' The Home Office on the other hand is 'a fairly strong controlling factor'. This is confirmed by his order of answering the phone in a hypothetical crisis. The Home Secretary first because of 'the need by the Home Secretary to respond to Cabinet or Government'. Then the chairman of the police authority because 'I would need to keep him informed anyway'.

Summary of Baronial Ideology

The Baron's ideal society is a harmonious and hierarchical rural stasis, where all know and accept their place and the rules. This is still largely true of his area, but it is threatened elsewhere, and in a small way even in his own county town, by social change, complexity, and, in particular, multi-culturalism. Ethnic minorities are consistently seen as a problem in themselves.

These factors cause a growth in crime, but this can be contained by traditional policing, both in relation to crime and disorder. But the decline of respect for authority makes this more difficult, as do outside contaminating influences. It is also threatened by politicization which makes the 'piggy in the middle' role of the police harder.

There should be a clear chain of control inside and outside the force. The Home Secretary, responsible to 'Cabinet and Government' ultimately controls the chief constable. (Although the Baron resents the increasing encroachment of uniform centralized policies, violating the operational independence supposedly enshrined in the 1964 Police Act, the Magna Carta of baronial power and constabulary independence.) In turn the chief is in control locally, both of his police authority and of his police officers. *Noblesse oblige*, however, and his rule must be paternalistic not tyrannical. He must be concerned to educate the lay authorities, to provide for the welfare of his troops, and to lead from the front not shove from behind. In this way the Golden Age of knightly virtue may linger a while longer in its rural fastnesses.

Case Two: The Bobby

Origins and Orientation

The essence of the Bobby is that he is a populist, the man of the people, standing firm on their behalf against villains, deviants, and politicos. He is from a working-class background, and proud of it, as he is of his own and his children's mobility from these humble origins. His father 'was a motor mechanic. Working-class background, sir.' His only child, a daughter, is a doctor, a 'registrar anaesthetist'. He was satisfied with his own career: 'It's a fairly rewarding old job really, despite my grumbles'. He had never aspired to great heights: 'You just look for the next job and then you pinch yourself and say, "Well, what the hell am I doing here!"'

Such origins, typical of the police, mean that the police stand for the ordinary people, contrary to the myth that there is one law for the rich and one for the poor:

> "It has never been true, because policemen come not from the rich, and they tend to be as searching when they are dealing with the rich, more so perhaps, than when dealing with the inadequate. There is not that influence. I mean it is no good the Lord Lieutenant walking in here and telling me that he is not going to prosecute somebody. He might go and say that to the Crown Prosecutor and get a different answer, but he wouldn't even come in that door."

He joined the Met. in 1951 at the age of 21, following two years national service. Before that he had been in a grammar school and obtained some school certificate passes, though he had to leave before completing higher school certificate. He had no burning ambition to join the police, despite having had an uncle who was chief constable of a county force. His motives were a mixture of instrumental attractions ('It was a secure job. In those days particularly the idea of having a job that had a pension and was secure was important.') and an intrinsic attraction to 'the uniform' and the 'cops and robbers things, all excitement.'

He served as a uniform PC in London for six and a half years, during which time he married and became a father. He then decided to leave London, 'when there was a great influx of West Indian people. Not to put too fine a point on it, they drove us out. They used to put rubbish in my daughter's pram, they used to accost my wife in the street as she would be coming in, one of the only white girls left in the area. It was a desperately sad thing'. Unable to afford to buy a house elsewhere in London, and with the Met. unwilling to move him, he had transferred to a county force near London, in the area he had grown up in. Shortly after that he became a detective constable, and did six years in CID before promotion to sergeant: 'I lived it, absolutely. Learned more about my trade as a bobby there than probably ever since. There was a detective sergeant there who taught me more about the art of coppering than most people have ever taught me.' He spent most of his operational service in CID (including a period attached to Scotland Yard), with short spells in traffic and administration. He reached ACC in the same county force in 1974, having been on the Senior Command Course the previous year. After that he became deputy chief in another county force in 1976, and did an overseas attachment on behalf of the HMI. Finally in 1980 he was appointed chief constable of his present force—— centring on the port of——.

He is largely satisfied with his current lot. 'I enjoy it here enormously', although 'there are times when I get despondent about the way the service is being treated and I feel like saying, "Sod it, you know what you can do with it! I'm going!"' His main remaining aspiration is:

"I would love to go to the Police College as Commandant ... I think I've got something to offer them. You see to me the police service has lost a great deal of its standards, and the Police College is a place where you can implant some of those standards back ... But I won't get it. First of all, I'm not of that background. They tend not to look at people with essentially very practical backgrounds, though that is very rude to say. I don't think I'm diplomatic enough either, and I would probably rock too many boats."

Ideology: Role of the Police

The Bobby has a broad view of the police function:

"The police serves its community best by policing by consent of his community, by being a part of his community. That doesn't just mean wielding a big stick, and enforcing the law willy-nilly. This is why I find it irritating to get so many circulars from the Home Office which tend to tell us how to suck eggs. I can stand, not I personally, but my force stands on its record here. We have one of the highest detection rates in the country, we've reduced our crime last year by 5 per cent, we have a very low accident level because we enforce the law very toughly on that. But at the same time my force is probably the one organization in the country that raises more for charity than any other ... Policing is essentially a very simple thing. It means getting the community to get on with itself without being too intrusive. When you need to be intrusive, be good, professional, and tough, and get the hell out of there ... The best policeman is everybody's idea of a village policeman, though he may be working in a town. He is the fellow who can turn a blind eye, who can be utterly ruthless when he needs to be, really respected, and yet still he is part of the people he serves. I think I am a village policeman. That is how I view myself."

Present government policy was trying to spread this old wine in new bottles with fancy labels:

"What is happening in terms of nationwide policing is that the Government decides that somewhere, somebody steps out of line, or a new idea is developed. And they try and impose it on everybody. I don't object to people looking at new ideas, but please don't impose it on me! I mean, the flavour of the month is neighbourhood watch. What on earth does that mean! It means what we have been trying to do for 150 years, which is to get our sensible, responsible members of the community to help us do our job. Now I don't need a neighbourhood watch system, with respect to the Home Secretary. Not even with respect! Because here in ——shire they've been watching their neighbours for 150 years, and they still tell us ... The police station is not a fortress. In this part of the world, if granny gets locked in the loo they ring us up. If somebody falls down, or they are worried, they don't ring the social services in the middle of the night, they ring the police, and we still go there ... My authority, to be fair to my police committee who are Labour controlled, it has taken them until last year to introduce consultative committees and lay visitors. They didn't want to do it at all. They believe they have access to us anyway. Now why do I have to have those things imposed upon me by legislation?"

The dangers of Scarmanism lie in the possible creation of no-go areas, though he had succeeded in avoiding that in his area.

"It is a problem, but not here, though it could be. We do have in—— quite a big black community, mostly Asians. We don't operate a no-go system, and I've said, crossing my fingers, there will be no no-go areas here. You have to look after everybody. Within those areas are people who want you there, and generally the people who do not are those in the minority. Scarman looked at just one or two places, and some of my colleagues and our representatives were too quick to agree with everything Scarman said. There were odd spots of difficulty in Toxteth, but Toxteth is a tiny, tiny area with a particular problem. At the end of it policing is policing Joe Average, looking after him not the extremists."

To remain close to the people police forces had to be small and personal. "The Met. is far too big ... One of the great advantages here is that I know everybody. This morning I went to see one of my officer's wives, and I know her. I'm jolly lucky, aren't I? I've got about 1,200 people that I am responsible for, and it's like running a big unruly family. We are coterminous with the county."

Criminology

Increasing Crime

The Bobby thinks crime has increased, and is therefore a greater problem quantitatively, though not qualitatively, in his area. This is not to do with unemployment, a theory to which he objects as a slur on the unemployed. 'I find it very sad when people link unemployment with crime. Because if I was unemployed I wouldn't turn to crime, and a lot of people unemployed don't do that, they are nice people.' Crime is not regarded apocalyptically: 'The things that worry people most these days are the lower levels of crime, in the sense of hooliganism, vandalism, and litter, rather than burglaries or rapes.'

The cause of the increase in crime is the increasing shackles on the police, especially PACE. This has 'the effect of increasing the crime level by reducing our detection rate.'

Can the Police Control Crime?

It follows from the classical deterrence model espoused by the Bobby that the police *could* control crime better if given adequate resources and support for traditional policing:

"It is improper to allow my detectives to carry a case load of 350 crimes per man, and we haven't had an increase in size since 1974. But the Home Office is right really that even saturation policing won't affect some crimes. But what it does do is help the public tranquillity to see the blue uniform ... That's coming back to my philosophy: policing isn't just policemen, but everybody helping us with it. Crime prevention is not about bolts and bars, it's about people."

The quality of policing depends on the traditional skills, but their exercise is increasingly inhibited by new legal controls in PACE and by the Government's concern with cost effectiveness rather than effectiveness:

"The intuitive detective is beginning to disappear. And if you do that you're in trouble because we won the lot by the seat of our pants. There are people in this force who I call thief-takers, useless on paper, but they've got a nose for a thief. Now, don't tell me how, I don't know, but they can pick them like that, there's something wrong with this man. We are not playing cricket in the police service, we are fighting a war, which we are losing, on behalf of the community. Now, when you are fighting a war you've got to be given the tools to do it. If you tie a soldier's hands down behind his back he can't do it. Don't get me wrong. If any of my people were offering gratuitous violence to anybody or they were corrupt, I'd chop their bloody ears off, they wouldn't last two minutes. But you've still got to give them, that sort of cunning old copper, a chance to catch them. And then you get a situation in the Police and Criminal Evidence Act, for instance, where on the taking of intimate samples as they call them, when you've got an indecency or rape of a small child. People have to give their consent in writing before it's taken. In the old days we used to say, 'Mister, look, the doctor is going to take some samples from you.' You don't ask him, you *told* him. You can't do that now. Is that the way to solve these crimes! Our hands are slowly but gradually being tied. It did give us enormous powers, to be fair. Powers to take fingerprints, photographs. A lot of good things. I'm not destroying it completely. But the actual practicality of the thing has been destroyed, the intuitiveness of the detective and the uniform officer, who is very wary now ... What is so objectionable about saying to somebody 'Look, could you just tell where you've come from'? 'Do I look like a thief, officer?', they say. 'Well, if I knew what he looked like, I would not stop you!' ... I know some very well-bred people are villains, and those are the people you need to look at as well as the black lads or the fellow with long hair, though it is a fact that some of these people do identify themselves as likely drug users. The stop and search powers which we enjoyed before we didn't really have ... But it comes back to this business of how you deal with people. You can get away with murder! My good old streetwise bobbies can still do what they used to do. Still chat to people. But now always at the back of their minds they are saying, 'Well, if I get this wrong I'm likely to be disciplined or complained against.' There is a real danger, even in the good people here, of destroying morale.''

The Bobby still relishes his policing role:

"One of my faults is that I do get a bit more involved than I ought to sometimes. But I find it interesting you see, because of my background ... Because we are a tiny force there are occasions when somebody comes in here and says, 'Sir, we've got this problem.' We had a big fraud running here which necessitated getting extradition proceedings from America. I had a good many approaches. So I had my chief superintendent here and said, 'You will really get in it, right in it, because as far as I am concerned there are too many pressures coming from outside which appear to be saying to me, this is a bit sensitive.' Nothing is more likely to get a policeman involved than when people begin saying that to him, you know.''

Public Order

Public order has also got worse. 'There is more hooliganism, street disorder ... The most remarkable people tend to march about the streets and in protest. It is the first thing people do, rather than negotiating ... Responsible, respectable groups of people do it ... There are people who seem to think that violence is a politically acceptable tactic.'

However, the police service was 'in danger of becoming a bit obsessed by it.' Public order had always been a problem, but when he was young the police had been able to cope with violence without the paraphernalia of protective and offensive equipment they now deployed. Present-day officers were less prepared to accept risk, but this was partly because they were now inadequately protected by the courts and society.

"When I was a young bobby working in the East End of London all those years ago, I didn't have the use of water cannons, plastic bullets, CS gas, firearms, and the ultimate things we now have to protect ourselves. At least that's our argument, to protect ourselves—some of the equipment is almost an inducement for people to throw things at us, so you have to use it very, very carefully and sparingly. But we are in that sad situation that our chief officers get pushed by the Federation to buy these things in order to protect people. When I was a young policeman I didn't need that protection, because I was protected by the courts. I worked in a pretty rough, violent area of London, Teddy Boy time, and they were sticking knives into each other and all those sorts of things. But if they touched a policeman, they were going inside. That's the old reaction, the old-fashioned way. They were put inside, a custodial sentence, maybe not for long. Now my policemen are not protected in that way by the courts ... Sadly, now, there's a tremendous amount of assaults on police officers. On a Saturday night in——they expect to get knocked about ... Years ago, we had a whole gang of hooligans who always caused us trouble. And the magistrates used to deal with them very lightly. So next time they caused trouble, we had to put them up for affray, stuck them up before the quarter sessions, they all got a custodial sentence, we were quiet for six months. Not because they were away, but the salutary effect on others. Ultimately the police can do what they like, but if there's no fear it's hard work. At the end of it I mean, being punished, really punished, not patted on the head. Or you are wasting your time."

The Bobby is suspicious of the use of riot control hardware not on civil libertarian but on macho grounds. The British bobby can take it.

"I have said 'over my dead body! We do not have plastic bullets here' ... Interestingly enough my police authority are absolutely delighted by the Government's stance. They take the view that they'll disagree, and get those buggers to pay for it if we use a central store. We get it for nothing! ... I know it's easy sitting here in this nice quiet place and deciding I don't need these things. But we have had situations during the miners' strike here where it was a really nasty situation. One of the questions I ask at promotion boards or at the Senior Command Course Extended Interviews is 'Debate with me that the police service arms itself adequately'. I think it does, in the sense of all the stuff where we arm ourselves which was not used in the past. I think you have to be prepared as a chief constable to accept casualties ... You have to take your Federation with you. They will not agree that you can afford to take casualties. But experience has taught me, I know for a fact, that if you get a bobby hurt when he is unarmed the public immediately come on your side ... Now I am not suggesting you should go to the levels of poor old Blakelock, and you do have to train for that sort of situation. But you have to try and get these people in the Federation to see this is the philosophy of the force, and take them along with you. Remember, they're going to be the senior officers of the future anyway, they're not all militants that the National Federation sometimes appear to be. Not——[the then chairman]. I've got a lot of time for him because we worked together years ago. I just wish he would speak for himself not as a voicepiece for someone else.''

Control of Policing

Just as the Bobby sees the quality of personal relations as the key to police success in controlling crime and disorder, so too is it the way to manage the police force.

> "When I joined the service there was a lot of stupid petty hard discipline. I think you have to build into people a pride and—a dirty word—an *esprit de corps*. You can have very good staff relations if you get off your bum and go and talk to them, find out what's worrying them. It's very difficult for the youngsters, they come in from a different world—I am old fashioned. And you have to teach them discipline. Yet their mums and dads are absolutely delighted by the very balanced young people we manage to turn out ... They want consultations, and that is right. They want to come and talk to the boss.''

As the Bobby thinks of himself and the police force as in tune with the mainstream public he is suspicious of institutional forms of representation such as police authorities. If these simply act as the voice of popular sentiment they are useful sounding-boards, among an array of other contacts. But there is the danger they will become politicized, and argue for narrow, partisan views.

> "I need to be told, you have got it wrong, chief ... I need to listen to this without it being coloured too much by political and party considerations ... I would be a fool not to listen to what they [the police authority] have to say ... but you know, at the end of it, I believe that the British police service has to be independent, not me personally, my office should be independent, so that people can come and talk to me about what they want to talk to me about. Because you can have people there who are determining policy because of a very narrow view of things. We have to police for Joe Average and not for the narrow view. It may be something to do with homosexuality, or obscenity, or whatever it might be, a very narrow view ... I used to debate with Martin Ennals about this whole question of should I have to stand up for election. Well, elected police chiefs are the best way to get corrupt practice that you can ever come across, so I wouldn't agree with that. But it begs the question that I am not accountable,

that I don't listen to what people have to say. I can tell you very easily, and I am sure any chief constable will, that if I get it wrong, by God, it is not just that elected members will tell me, it will be the community who will be on my back in no time. I have to listen to what the press say, I make myself available, like we all do, to anybody, my officers do, we go to consultative committees ... visit schools, we try and keep ourselves at grass roots listening to what people say, and I think in a way we are probably more in touch than some of the elected members. We've got the whole picture ... [R.R.: But you don't have to pay attention.] No, I don't. But that is what *The Commissioner of the Police ex parte Blackburn* said ... you need to maintain an independence of view. I mean, there are people who would say to me you will not under any circumstances investigate any homosexual acts. There is a great bunch of people in this community who think it is filthy and horrible, and want me to investigate it all the time. I can't. So somewhere in the middle we have to settle, don't we? And we have to listen ... I don't think I am unaccountable and arrogant, but I might be to people outside. The difficulty about being a chief constable really is that people place you in impossible positions. They ask you questions, if you fail to answer you are arrogant and unaccountable, if you do answer, you are political. And I think the only answer to that is conscience.''

The extent to which central policing institutions impinge on the Bobby's decisions is also a matter of personal relations.

''In terms of the Home Office, obviously everyone listens to circular letters. But you make your decisions on the basis of who you know, and who actually signed the letter. I am not as impressed with some people in the Home Office who really think they have their feet on the ground, but do not. It's like listening to the local authority, you've got to listen to all shades of opinion. HMI, because you know them personally, it depends who it is really. I sometimes wish they were a little more for the service and less for the Home Office, and the Crown Prosecution Service. But it depends who they are ... ACPO—well, I am a chairman of one committee. And trying to get forty-three bloody-minded autocrats together is pretty difficult ... But you need an association to influence the law-makers not to be so very ridiculous as they are sometimes and look at the practicalities of things, if your objective is to make life better for the community.''

If the Bobby disagrees with central policy he does not find it very difficult to stand against it.

"I stood against the policy in relation to the use of hand-held radars, and against ACPO, very strongly because I was totally opposed to it. I don't find that difficult. During the miners' strike, to a certain extent we stood against some of the things people were trying to get us to do here centrally. 'We will decide, old chaps,' you know, 'we are a bit concerned because you are going to get a lot of pickets, get some aid.' 'Oh, we will cross that bridge when we come to it,' I said. You do get these pressures, from ACPO and the Home Office. I don't object to that, I mean that's their point of view. After all at the end of it if it goes wrong, they will scuttle for cover. The only person who is going to get it in the neck is me. I have to make the decisions, don't I? And I get it wrong sometimes ... It's not really true they hold power over you. One of the best chief constables I worked with was Peter Matthews, who's retired now. Sir Peter, most decorated British policeman. He was outspoken, a tough negotiator, but much respected because of that. To be fair, I don't think people, just because you disagree with them—unless they're going to say, 'This man's an ass!' If you're an ass when you do it, then that's different. One of the things, being a chief constable, you do speak from a position of some security."

Summary of Bobby Ideology

The Bobby is a thoroughgoing populist. He sees the police as standing for ordinary people, against criminals and also against the powerful. The negative side of this is that those who deviate from the norm are seen as outsiders or trouble-makers. The Bobby is unashamedly worried about the advent of black people, for example, though he does 'wish really we were colour blind'.

While recognizing that problems of crime and order are increasing in volume, he is not dramatically concerned, and is aware of the long history of these. 'We sit there with our rose-coloured specs on, but throughout my police service there has been violent behaviour.' Traditional bobbying, relying on the skills and discretion of the old-fashioned police officer, is the answer. This depends on the quality of personal relations with the public which can be achieved by the police. In the same way, management of the police force, and the adequacy of control by political authorities, central or local, is a matter of personal relations. At the end of the day, the Bobby is a localist, and resents

bureaucratic uniformity. He is a champion of constabulary independence, believing that the chief constable is more in touch with
the sentiments of the mainstream local community than any elected
politician. He is a man of the people and for the people, which he sees
as the quintessence of the British police traditions.

Case Three: The Boss

Origins and Orientation

The Boss joined a city police force in 1953, at the age of 21. He grew
up in the area which later became the——Police, and has roots there.
His great uncle had served there towards the end of the nineteenth
century. He comes from a manual working-class background, of which
he is very proud. He is also proud of his and his family's subsequent
achievement. He went to a grammar school, but with some regret left
before taking higher school certificate. He is proud, however, of having
completed a university certificate course in criminology as a young PC,
and achieving a distinction in criminal law.

His attraction to policing was entirely intrinsic. He wanted to be a
policeman 'as long as I can remember', and did his national service in
the Military Police, even though he had to struggle to get in. Before
that he had tried to enter the local police cadets as soon as he left school,
but there were no vacancies. He was ambitious and confident from the
outset of his police career, having come top in all his exams during
training. 'But I would be untruthful if I said now that on joining I felt
I had what it took to become a chief constable.' He is satisfied with his
career achievements, and would certainly rejoin if he had his life over.
'I have been a successful chief constable, in my opinion, and that is not
boasting.' As with the Bobby, he is a populist. He recognizes that those
in authority may not regard him highly. But his confidence derives from
support he receives from the ordinary people in his area, and the rank
and file of the force. He is in tune with these grass-roots constituencies,
rather than political or police élites.

> "If you had to measure it by the reduction in crime, then I would be
> regarded as a total failure I suppose. But I would judge it by trying
> to assess how the public in my police area regard it. And I would say
> that the people, if they were asked, would say that I have met their
> expectations, and that they regard me as a good leader and an effective
> chief constable. I have a huge fan mail from the people out there.

I have not just a mandate from them but a high degree of acclaim. I put my trust in the people out there, and I have done my best for them ... I am sure there are some senior officers who would not look upon me as the brightest star in the police service ... but I have the support of my officers. And the staff associations, in times of great stress and crisis, have never failed to send me the warmest possible message of personal support, and to go public in defence of me and my philosophies and policies."

He remained in the city force he joined right through to the rank of superintendent. He experienced all the varieties of operational work, but mainly uniform patrol. He also did extensive periods in administrative departments, before going on the Senior Command Course. After completing this he became chief superintendent in a nearby county force. He remained there for just under two years, before moving to another county force as assistant chief constable. After a period of attachment to the HMI, he became deputy chief in the same county force. Following a brief sideways move to——as deputy chief, he became their chief constable, and had served there for twelve years at the time of the interview.

The pedigree of the Boss resembles that of the Bobby, but he experienced more of a sense of mission about policing, and a more burning ambition. While succeeding in career mobility terms, he is far less satisfied that he has accomplished his mission, given the more problematic conditions of——. The key thread underlying his responses is this sense of impending apocalypse unless the 'thin blue line' can succeed in its Herculean task, which is made more problematic by stabs in the back from unsupportive authorities.

Ideology: The Role of the Police

The police ideal is 'to serve and protect': 'to create an environment in which the whole community feels confident as a consequence of the police presence to enable them to promote a better quality of life for themselves.' But in practice in——, where

"crime is extremely heavy, crime per head is as great as anywhere in Britain, where there are frequent outbreaks of serious public disorder and many problems endemic in the area which are not faced to the same extent elsewhere ... the chief constable and his officers and even the constables on the beat have to concentrate on the worst excesses that face them: the street crime, the robberies, the thuggery, the scale of drunkenness, the public disorder. The high profile we have to take in that regard out of sheer necessity forces us into a kind of corner, where everyone perceives us to be purely and simply heavy law enforcement officers. ... But we have to be very careful and balance that always with the very necessary duty of assisting the community ... It is an amalgamation of what I call 'sensible policing' which brings all of these elements together."

Could this be described as community policing?

"It's an unfortunate phrase ... John Alderson in Devon and Cornwall was very properly propounding the notion of community policing in the sense in which he understood it ... What I find difficult to do was to convince people that we had been doing it for years, and we are still doing it now. I have as many community officers as anyone has in the quieter shire counties, but the daily round of their duties has to be markedly different ... If I put a community constable out there, not just in the inner city but in my outer divisions and give him a remit to involve himself in the community as community policing is understood, he will turn round and say, 'Well, OK, I will do my best—but I have got a pocket radio here and I am being sent to calls every fifteen minutes' ... It is a great compendium of problems that no one seems to appreciate, and I am unhappy at the rather global view taken of policing in the UK where ideas about policing are articulated without any regard to the very different socio or economic or political factors operating as between one area and other."

This is illustrated by the Scarman Report.

"Lord Scarman never, ever intended that no matter how tense an area, no matter how high the risk of consequential public disorder, that that should influence police officers not to do their job ... We operate here on the very simple basis that we police not just sensitively but sensibly. If, for example, we have to operate a major drugs raid, we do it with no fuss, without prior warning. It is said that we should always consult the people in the community—we have tried that and very often it produces exactly the opposite result. [R.R.: Why?] Forces have mounted to thwart our intentions, and that leads to even greater trouble."

In short, the Boss sees 'sensible' policing, incorporating a social role, as the ideal. However, the pressures of an urban jungle force a more heavy and secretive style to be adopted reluctantly.

Criminology ·

Increasing Crime

"Crime has increased unquestionably. Not just simply the sheer volume of crime, but the public attitude ... There is in many cases too little shame or ignominy attached to crime and the offender: people talk, quite openly, about it being bad luck if they are discovered ... The other thing that worries me is the nature of the crime itself. There can be no doubt that whatever Home Office studies seek to portray, the incidence of violent crime, though as a percentage of the total it is still relatively small, violent crime is now at levels which I would never have regarded as possible. And I joined the police thirty-five years ago, and begun my police life here on the inner city streets of——."

The sources of this lie in a deeper social decay. 'The whole of the changes in society: the freedom of movement, the relaxation of discipline within schools and the home and all our institutions. Add to that the increasing wealth ... the breaking down of many of the old traditional forms of discipline within families and school ... This society of ours is nose-diving rapidly.'

This control theory is widely shared by chief constables. But the Boss places more emphasis on an Apocalypse-now scenario due to authority crumbling.

Can Police Control Crime?

This depends on whether they get firm enough backing.

"Of course, I am completely at odds with the Home Office over this one ... I say to the Home Office, give me as many men as you possibly can and I would make a dramatic impact in——, on the detection of crime in the first instance, and in the longer term the actual commission of crime ... Not simply by increasing the numbers of police officers to engage in traditional forms of policing the streets. I would form that number of police officers into dedicated teams who could target certain kinds of crime, and there will be as a direct consequence a ripple effect which would act as a substantial deterrent ... You only have to think, if I may say so, what we have done here on targeting football hooligans.''

However, the auguries are not good. Far from supporting the police, the Government has undermined them. 'PACE has eroded the capacity of police to successfully investigate crime through processes of interrogation ... But the police service cannot gainsay the right of offenders, suspects to have at their disposal the best support consistent with the proper investigation of offences.' However, the right to silence should be changed, although police legal powers were not the key to crime control in themselves.

In fact, given that crime has increased disproportionately to the number of police and detectives, the clear-up rate has not fallen dramatically. Critics say his is low relative to many other cities. But that is because of his high volume of crime relative to resources, and other forces' more intensive use of prison interviews. 'My detection rate on primary detections is among the highest in the country.'

Like the Bobby, the Boss is keen to be directly involved in operational work, though he seldom can intervene in a standard case. But he is proud of his personal involvement when this becomes possible. 'I have made a number of arrests as chief constable ... Because I stay on the air all the time in my car. The moment I leave my office I am tuned into the control room, I book on a lot like one of my traffic patrols. We have picked up messages on the radio and rushed to the scene and been in a position to grab the offender.'

Public Order

Like crime, public order is a crisis scenario of Apocalypse now.

"The incidence of major public disorder in recent years has been such that it has brought into question the ability of the police successfully to contain it ... That is a matter of historical fact. We are now much more sophisticated and better able to deal with outbreaks of violence whether large or small scale ... I have a highly specialized greatly strengthened tactical aid group, I suppose on a par with the original Metropolitan SPGs ... We have had to alter the whole pattern and concept of daily police operation to take account of this increasingly worrying phenomenon.''

The source of public disorder is the same social and moral decline which produces crime.

"A feeling has grown (but perhaps thankfully it has receded in the last couple of years) that muscle will produce the result people want ... Rent-a-mob! I was talking only at lunchtime today with some local politicians within the Labour Party who were telling me they are sick to death of some of these extremists and anarchists who have attached themselves to legitimate labour protests ... and are designed to create conflict between legitimate protesters and police ... Our police officers now go on duty on the streets of——knowing that the chances are they are going to be assaulted every time they intercede in any situation, and they are. That was certainly not the case when I was a young PC."

While this necessitates a much greater commitment to public order policing, he is against a specialist third force, which would be 'detrimental to the normal patterns of policing in this country.' But plastic bullets *would* be used in a life-threatening situation, although his police authority would not even sanction his purchase of them. 'If in my professional judgement use of baton rounds was justified, I would give that order. I have told them this on many occasions, they are in no doubt whatsoever.'

Control of Policing

Police management must be paternal but firm: 'It would be far better to introduce a policy knowing the men are with you, than from Day One they don't like the idea ... So we have tried to take our officers along here with us all the way along the line.' But 'you have got to have obedience, you have got to have respect ... there is a balance to be struck where you have proper rapport.'

The size of his force prevents his personal contact with all of the rank and file. He is forced to delegate through a bureaucratic structure.

"Twenty-two years ago in a borough force, I had to see the chief constable on the first morning of an investigation which was being conducted at his request while he personally opened the post and slit the letters and at the end of the day signed every bit of correspondence ... The burdens and the policies and the levels of decision-making I have to take are far removed now ... The number one problem is ensuring that *my* basic philosophy and the kind of reasoning which underpins my force policies are communicated to and fully under-stood by the men on the beat.''

His police authority is very active, and the number of meetings he has to attend is disproportionate, 'I have a process of accountability in a public and political sense which is a hundred times greater than in areas where the problems are so much less.'

He is totally opposed to, and very concerned about Labour proposals to empower police authorities to determine police policy.

"I am appalled—it is absolutely outrageous . . . People who are elected to local councils on an average of 20 per cent of the electorate! Why should say a Labour group or even a Conservative group . . . dictate on the basis of a party political doctrine, as has happened frequently here . . . It is wrong for policing to be in any way either directly controlled or substantially influenced by a party political view of the matter. That is why I would much prefer to see the introduction of the Northern Ireland police authority pattern [of appointed not elected members]."

While the local authority should not control the police, and is already too big for its boots, the Home Office has, and should continue to have, an important role and considerable weight in police decision-making. But they do not always 'demonstrate strong enough support of chief constables' for political reasons. They should 'come out of the corner a little more strongly' when chief constables or the police are under attack. But 'from the time I have spent at the Home Office—which I thoroughly enjoyed let me say—I understood the political difficulties of relating to the police service as closely as we might wish, I recognize the reasons why they need to appear to be standing apart so as not to be com-promised'.

He jokingly said he would answer a call from the chair of his authority first in a crisis—but only to say he had to talk to the Home Secretary! This was due to the 'imperative nature of the Home Secretary's responsibility for law and order in this country, and his accountability to Parliament.'

His overall social perspective reflects a sense of growing crisis, especially over race issues.

"On balance we are still a harmonious society, but there are some signs of intolerance as between one section of the community and another . . . What worries me is the polarization of view where the ethnic communities are involved. The difficulties you see occasioned there with the question of education in schools, with the Muslims now wanting schools for their own children with no white children present. The case of Mr Honeyford who expressed his own personal view of the difficulties where you have a mixed communty. These things cannot be ignored. What I feel unhappy about is that every time someone genuinely expresses a point of view, born out of the deepest conviction, in no sense racist, they are accused of being precisely that, expressing a racist point of view. I think if it is not corrected, or if opinions and attitudes don't change, it could lead to very serious discord between ethnic communities in given areas of this country."

Summary of Boss Ideology

The Boss has close local ties. He was born in the city, and worked his way up in that force. He is proud of his working-class background. He is a populist, and feels in touch with his men, and the local people, but not politicians. However, of two evils, the lesser is central government, which has a legitimacy that local government lacks.

But society is becoming more and more an urban jungle, with crime and disorder threatening to get out of hand. The police are forced to get tough. The most serious problems always stem from 'outsiders': rent-a-mob, ethnic minorities, political extremists undermining authority. Crime and disorder are not fundamentally due to local people or factors. The Boss experiences a sense of embattlement against the powers-that-be as social trends are against his views. Politicians, even at the centre, are too politically sensitive to stand for the right, and for the people. So the Boss and his valiant men must struggle against the odds. Not only are they threatened by subversive outsiders, but they are stabbed in the back by élites who should champion the police as the guardians of traditional morality but cravenly betray them. However, the support he receives from Everyman gives the Boss the resolve to continue the struggle.

Case Four: The Bureaucrat

The Bureaucrat is the prototype of the future chief constable. It must be stressed that the word bureaucracy is not used here in any pejorative sense but in its Weberian meaning of a formal organizational structure, in which there is a rational structure of roles and procedures, with selection and promotion governed by demonstrated professional capacity assessed by objective examinations (Weber, 1964; Albrow, 1970). This usage corresponds closely to what is understand as 'professionalism' by many police officers (Reiner, 1978, 202–8).

Origins and Orientation

The Bureaucrat joined a small city police force in 1956 at the age of 19, having already served for three years as a cadet in that same force. He just missed doing national service, and has thus worked in a police environment since leaving grammar school. The city force he entered amalgamated with the surrounding county force during his period there. His father had been a sergeant in the county force.

The Bureaucrat is a beneficiary of the various schemes established during the last thirty years to equip potential high-flyers with the education and skills required for senior command. He was on the Special Course at Bramshill, and promoted sergeant when he went on it after six years' service. He consequently was promoted inspector after another two years. He went to London University as one of the Bramshill Scholars and acquired a good degree in law.

He was promoted to ACPO rank in 1972, becoming ACC in another county force. During this time he was seconded for a couple of years to the directing staff of Bramshill. In 1980 he moved to the Met. as Deputy Assistant Commissioner, and soon after became an Assistant Commissioner. He became chief constable of——, one of the largest provincial forces, in 1985, two years before the interview.

His operational experience was primarily non-specialist: he served in a variety of uniform commands, although he did have short periods in traffic, CID, and administration. However, he has clearly had close involvement with the central institutions of the police world as he moved up, particularly through his numerous periods at Bramshill, and close involvement in the Scarman inquiry while he was at the Met.

He is satisfied overall with his career, and would rejoin. Indeed his son has followed him into the service, and is a PC in the Met. (One of his daughters works in the Foreign Office, the other is a nurse.)

"I've just been talking to a crowd of undergraduates who are on a three-day attachment to the force. They asked me why I joined. I said I came from something of a police tradition because my father and my great uncle had been in the police ... It seemed attractive because of that tradition. It certainly wasn't fast promotions or high status, because the status and money and promotional opportunities now didn't exist then. I was quite well educated at grammar school by the standards of the day, and then I went into the police, which was a little unusual given my background for people in those days ... I had no hesitation in saying the service has been very good to me. I've been very lucky. A lot of being in the right place at the right time."

The Bureaucrat has been at the hub of the development of the dominant police perspective of the period, post-Scarmanism. It is no surprise he shares much of this, for he was instrumental in its development. Paradoxically, however, as a chief officer in tune with the mood of the centre, he is strongly committed to *local* consultation, as a means of restoring to the conurbations the communal spirit which survives unbroken in the shires.

Ideology: The Role of the Police

The Bureaucrat inclines 'solidly' to a broad social conception of the police role, not law enforcement *per se*.

"I remember years ago there was the argument, you may remember, as to who was right, Alderson or Anderton, hard and soft policing. I used to say at the time, there is no such thing as hard or soft policing. There is only good and bad policing, and good policing will have hard and soft elements, according to appropriate circumstances. Soft is the wrong word anyway: it should be accurate and sensitive ... Policing is to do with the *social* causes of crime, interaction with society, prevention, a professional approach. High-profile policing, but certainly not reactive for its own sake ... Wholesome, proactive— not a word I like, but you understand it, towards that rather than purely reactive, à la France or Belgium."

'Community policing' has a clear meaning for him, even though its loose bandying about leads to it

"meaning everything to everybody ... Many see it as a soft option, giving ground to, usually to blacks, but to any group who happen to be pressing upon you ... But there is nothing magical about it. It is policing an area with officers who have a continuum of service in the area, so they build up a reservoir of knowledge of the area, its customs, pressures, sensitivities, and its people, so you have got a bond and bridge, backed up by consultation at all levels. The top level with the chief and his group going through the police committee, all the way down to parish council, local consultative committee, residents' group, and so on. The law is seen not as an end in itself but as a means to an end."

He is thus at one with the Scarman approach and its prioritization of public tranquillity over law enforcement.

"I happened to talk to Lord Scarman a great deal before he wrote his report, and I am not for one minute suggesting he accepted my views, but I know we were at one on this issue, on the difference between law enforcement and social tranquillity. It means just being sure-footed, prioritizing a bit, not bothering too much about petty offences ... Sensitivity so that your drug squad doesn't necessarily go banging in through a front door of a house in Broadwater Farm, when they can simply take the dealer out in a car on the motorway."

The police have always exercised such discretion about law enforcement priorities: 'I remember from Bristol, Professor Banton, you know him, saying once that the police are influenced more by social morality than by the law. That's actually very profound and it still applies. It may turn to difficulties, because people who want that law enforcing will draw comparisons to those who don't.'

Criminology

Increasing Crime

The Bureaucrat believes crime *has* increased, but is aware of the problems with crime statistics, and tries to counter them. 'Oh yes, notwithstanding the British Crime Survey about crimes not reported to the police and that sort of thing. There is undoubtedly more crime about, more violent crime, people fear more.'

The explanation of this is in terms of control theory, but is less moralistic or apocalyptic in tone than it Boss, and less nostalgic than the Baron or the Bobby: 'I wouldn't pretend to have a pat answer. I think it's in the region of a breakdown in social controls, in the family and Church. A more affluent, mobile society. Greater anonymity, so there isn't the fear of sanctions.'

Can Police Control Crime?

The Bureaucrat does not believe the police can control crime by traditional means, more resources for patrol, or CID. He agrees with Home Office research on this: 'I am one of the forty-three chief constables who want more men and money, and yet I know that just throwing manpower and equipment at it without finding new avenues to deploy them is meaningless.' This sceptical view does not arise out of complacency due to lack of problems: 'At the moment, like any big urban area, it's backs to the walls, a quarter million crimes per annum. We've got a job to keep our head above water.'

Increasing the legal powers of the police is not the solution. 'I've never been one to argue for massive increases in police powers. Properly used, we've got most of the ones we need.' Detection rates are not in fact as bad as they appear at first sight. 'If you look at our clear-up rates in the top echelon of crime they have risen ... We still run overall at 30 per cent though, because of the dross at the bottom.' The police *can* control crime, however, by more sophisticated strategies. They should 'put the majority back on conventional patrol, community policing. I would want to use some squads as well: I am not a squad man in general terms, but along with community policing you have got to have the facility of highly targeted, highly briefed specific squads to do a task in hand. We have just started what we call divisional observation teams ... and they are showing quite phenomenal success against the street-robber, housebreaker, and armed robber.'

He himself would not get involved in a specific case, short of a terrorist siege or something with a real international dimension. (Interestingly, not long after this disclaimer, the Bureaucrat arrested a suspect after a short chase *en route* to an official function while in his dinner jacket!)

Public Order

The problem of order is worse, but there is no drama nor any threat of it getting out of hand.

"I think the environment in which we work is more difficult ... but in fact the mechanisms of dealing with it today are easier than three or four years ago because of the equipment we have now got ... A necessary evil, and it makes it easier for us in a human sort of way, it makes it easier for us in human relations terms, because the public perceive the difficulties we have got ... We are now equipped, and we've dealt with three incidents this summer, in which there undoubtedly would have been a full-blooded riot twelve months before, because we were able to get in quickly and stop the riot, indeed stop civil unrest in all its forms.''

The Bureaucrat analyses disorder as having social roots, and not just being a breakdown of controls over evil. 'It has got a lot to do with social frustration. I don't believe that unemployment and social unrest *causes* disorder or crimes, but I do think people are more ready to use it as a justification. A subtle but very real difference ... But in a roundabout and shorthand way, I am I suppose saying that unemployment and social deprivation are very close to causing disorder.'

Whatever the *causes* of disorder, it is imperative to control it. 'In terms of public image ... the worst thing that could happen to us is that we fail to control a riot. Losing out is the worst thing of all.' A 'third force' would be counter-productive and unacceptable 'without a maelstrom.' But tough measures may be needed. He would be prepared to use baton rounds 'if nothing else would suffice'. Public opinion (expressed in local polls) would support him, but he had clashed with his police authority on the issue. He has 'tried to take account of what both the Home Secretary and the chairman of the police committee want, and try and reflect it if I can. When all else fails, I am answerable to the law, the Sovereign ... And that being so I have got to go ahead, closing my ears to what the Home Secretary or the chairman says.'

Control of Police

A consultative, participative style makes management easier. 'I rolled up in this force on a Tuesday ... and I chose to fill it by going along to the Federation office to see them on their ground on my first working day ... I have a good working relationship with them ... I wouldn't necessarily follow everything they said, to reserve the decision in the final analysis to myself, but I want to know the ground on which I tread.' A relaxation from the militaristic style of police management in 'the more rigid society' when he joined was necessary, but also beneficial because it results in 'people who are highly motivated, assuming they are properly trained and led'. The management of a large complex modern force necessarily rules out the personal style of the older chiefs, and necessitates a well-planned and structured system of delegation and specialization. (This he dubs an attack on 'bureaucracy', although it is the essence of the Weberian usage.)

"[A force] with thousands of employees was attempted to be run from one office by——, running it as he had been involved in running a county force of 200 before the war. That mentality is found in quite a lot of forces today. Years ago forces could be run by people who genuinely knew all there was to know. They are still trying to run very large diverse organizations doing it all themselves. It is sheer lunacy ... It doesn't really matter how big the organization is so long as you are structured right and get the authority levels as low as you can."

A consultative approach also works best with the police authority. 'I talk to them about policing, draw them in ... and the result is that (apart from the baton rounds) I reckon I tread forward on a very well-researched path. But you will know alternative styles with other chiefs who keep them at arm's length, and I think that only serves to aggravate them.' But some police authorities also make it impossible because 'they get it so much out of bounds that they fight the chief constable for purely dogmatic, party political reasons.'

He is also strongly influenced by the Home Office, but always tries to involve the local authority too. He is disenchanted with ACPO, because it is dominated by the majority of chief constables of smaller forces, who are seen as hide-bound, and drags on modernization. He favours two-tier entry, Trenchard style. 'I am a member of ACPO ... and it is the best example of life after death that I have ever seen, it is moribund ... ACPO tends to be run by chief constables of smaller forces with time on their hands ... If you average forty-three autocratic bastards like I am then you get the camel-designed-by-a-committee syndrome. I feel sorry that ACPO is as lumbering as it is.'

Summary of Bureaucrat Ideology

The modern force certainly has its share of problems. But these *can* be dealt with by a sophisticated and professional management approach, involving consultation, but with decision-making according to professional and legal criteria in the end. He has a sense of himself as in the vanguard of professionalizing change, in tune with modern Home Office thinking, and post-Scarmanism. He is somewhat disdainful of the majority of his colleagues for acting as brakes on modernization.

He is clear that old methods of policing, and of managing police forces, can no longer work. The way forward is a combination of maximum professionalism with maximum participation. He shares common problems with the Boss but not his pessimistic foreboding about modern social trends. These may make policing more difficult, but it is the police force which must adjust, not vice versa. The Boss, on the other hand, has much more in common with the traditionalists in rural or smaller urban areas, the Baron and the Bobby. He has the misfortune, however, of policing an area which, unlike theirs, has outstripped traditional policing methods. Whereas the first wave of reaction to new problems was the Boss redoubling old approaches, the Bureaucrat is endeavouring to develop new ways to overcome them without losing the virtues of tradition. At present, however, there is no real evidence of any greater success.

Conclusion

The purpose of this chapter has been to allow an insight into the variety of *Weltanschauung* found amongst contemporary chiefs. These tend to be variations around certain central themes of the period, such as the post-Scarmanist philosophy of broad, community-oriented conceptions of the police role, and control theories of crime. However, these are given somewhat different meanings by chiefs of different pedigrees, facing different sorts of problems in different places.

The two varieties of stable traditionalists, the rural version (the Baron) and the small-town version (the Bobby), both see the new directions stemming from the centre as fancy regurgitations of what they were doing anyway. Developed as ways of trying to solve problems they did not face, they resent them as formal straitjackets which might disrupt the delicate spontaneous balances which obtained in their areas.

The Boss shared their traditionalism, but faced a scale of problems they did not. While retaining the confidence of the ordinary public and the police rank and file, these methods did not seem to be making a successful impact on crime and disorder. To the traditionalist this is because the New Centurions of the police have been let down by the political élites.

The Bureaucrat has tried, in league with the Home Office, to develop new ways of achieving the consent to policing (which is seen as existing in more traditional areas) in the turbulent melting-pot of the modern metropolis. This is by a finely tuned balance of professional enforcement and the encouragement of participation as a means of resuscitating consent. At present such strategies remain as much an act of faith as the traditionalism of the Boss. There can be no doubt, however, that the 'bureaucratic' mode is the wave of the future, and will increasingly displace the other approaches as new chief constable appointments are made.

Part VI

Conclusions and Implications: Chief Constables and the Future

13 Back to the Future

The starting-point for this study was the conventional belief that chief constables are the independent and powerful directors and controllers of their forces, the *fons et origo* of local policing policy. The legal doctrine of constabulary independence was outlined in Chapter 2, and it clearly encourages chief officers to regard themselves as accountable to lofty yet abstract principles—the law, their consciences, the dictates of professional wisdom—rather than concrete institutions. British policing is remarkable for 'the high degree of operational autonomy the present system accords to chief constables' (McCabe *et al.*, 1988, 134).

It is not only the Court of Appeal which teaches chief constables to think of themselves in such elevated terms, but the ideology into which they are socialized by the Home Office-designed system of training and promotion. Selectors for the Extended Interviews organized by the Home Office to choose suitable candidates for the Accelerated Promotion Scheme for Graduates (formerly the Graduate Entry Scheme), the Special Course, and the Senior Command Course, are given an information pack which includes a 'Job Description' of a chief officer of police. This tells them: 'His paramount responsibility, since he is subject to no superior executive command, is that of leadership ... He needs, therefore, to have the moral courage to take an action which may be justified only in his belief that it is right.' He cannot rely on any external advice or opinions. The local police authority are relegated to the limited and subordinate role of paying the piper but calling no tunes. It is up to the chief to ensure they are not tone deaf. 'The Police Authority are the suppliers of his material needs. As lay persons they have very little knowledge or judgement of Police requirements ...

Consequently the provisioning of the Force will depend directly on the confidence which the Police Authority have in the advice of their chief officer.' Nor can he lean on internal guidance within his force. 'Since in his professional sphere he will have no critics (at least none that he can hear), he needs to be well balanced ... to counteract the complimentary, if not flattering, aura in which he will find himself.' The chief constable, it seems, is the Lone Ranger, without even a Tonto to help him out.

The official picture, then, is of a lonely man of power, saddled with the momentous existential burden of making decisions of the utmost consequence but able to commune only with the echoes of his own soul. Radical critics of the police do not deny this picture. Rather (following Marx's example with Hegel) they turn it on its head. For professional independence read unaccountable authoritarianism. Chief constables must be penned within a 'constitutional corral' (Uglow, 1988).

The Police Federation, representing the rank-and-file perspective, faces both ways. They are stalwart champions of constabulary independence against external criticism or the radical project of democratic control through the electoral process. However, internally the chief constable is potentially a despot who must be tamed into benevolence. This image is well encapsulated by the cartoon series 'McBoot' which features in their monthly magazine *Police*. The eponymous anti-hero is a snarling tyrant, and the final frame invariably shows him stamping with his outsize hobnail boots on some hapless and prone constable.

The constitutional doctrine of independence lauds unfettered chief constable control over police operations. But the dark side of autonomy is autocracy, glimpsed in different ways by the policed (and their civil libertarian champions), and the rank-and file police. Small wonder that chief constables often refer to themselves jokingly as 'tinpot dictators' and the like.

The motive for this research was this perception of chief constables as the prime movers of local policing policy, and collectively as important influences on national criminal justice policy. If these people do command so much power, who are they? And what do they think? What principles and perspectives underlie their determination of policing policy? The police research literature is replete with studies of canteen cop culture, seen as the key to understanding street-level policing. Nothing, however, was known of top cop culture, presumably the key to understanding suite-level policing. It was my intention to investigate this, but the denouement—their practical subordination to the Home Office—is not what I anticipated at the outset.

In Chapter 2 the history of the office of chief constable, and its present legal status, were reviewed. The professionalization of the chief constables was charted, as their character moved towards the unitary, high-status group of today. This involved a synthesis of the old division between county chiefs, who had distinguished social pedigrees but were not career professionals, and the borough chiefs, who were career police officers but lacked status and power. The key staging-posts in this process were the post-war policy of only recruiting chiefs who had moved all the way up the ranks, and the 1964 Police Act. This ended the constitutional distinctions between county and borough chiefs, and paved the way for the successive amalgamations which have created the large forces of today.

Chapter 2 also demonstrated and discussed the development of the legal doctrine of constabulary independence which underpins the office of chief constable. Finally, it described how recent concern about policing has stimulated a revival of the argument for a direct entry 'officer class' in the police. This, together with a variety of other developments, has prompted a more overt centralization and tighter co-ordination of police forces. It has also reinvigorated the debate about a national police force, which had lain dormant since the 1960 Royal Commission.

Part II on the social origins and career patterns of chief constables showed that many of the proposals to introduce a nationally co-ordinated career, training, and selection structure for chief officers in effect already exist today. Chief constables are predominantly those who were drawn to policing out of intrinsic interest, demonstrated this by joining early, and moved up the hierarchy fast by the standards of their generation. They have usually moved between forces a number of times, and invariably have experienced attachment(s) to national police institutions such as HMI or Bramshill. Almost all have done the Senior Command Course, which the Home Affairs Committee on Higher Police Training recently recommended should be a requirement of chief officer rank. They are high-flying 'cosmopolitans' who orient themselves more to each other as a national police élite than to their forces.

The situation recommended by the Home Affairs Committee largely obtains already in practice. The Home Office is the major informal influence on the careers and selection of chief officers, and has the formal power under the Police Act to veto candidates it deems unsuitable, both before interview by the Police Authority (at the short-listing stage) and afterwards. Small wonder the Home Office rejected the HAC proposal to make ACPO grade officers a nationally employed pool who it would allocate to local forces, when it has considerable power already, which it appears more ready to show nowadays as the recent row over the appointment of a new chief constable for Derbyshire showed.

The bottom line of the analysis of chief constable careers is that they are best understood as a unitary power élite, oriented towards the Home Office, than as forty-three separate powerful individuals. In his classic study, *The Power Élite*, C. Wright Mills suggested three criteria for concluding that a number of élite individuals at the top of different institutions in fact constituted a unitary élite (Mills, 1956, 18–20). The first is a 'psychological similarity and social intermingling', the constitution of the élites by people of similar origin, education, career patterns, and styles of life. 'Considerable traffic of personnel' between institutions, argues Mills, tends to produce a convergence of outlook. The analysis of chief constable biographies in Part II suggests they do satisfy this first ingredient of a unitary élite.

Mills's second criterion is 'structural blending of commanding position and common interest'. Clearly, élite members, drawn from the most ambitious people in their occupations, compete keenly with each other both as individuals and on behalf of their institutions. But the question is whether there are structural differences between the interest of élites in different organizations, over and above personal rivalry. The historical process described in Chapter 2 is one which has diminished, but not eliminated, structural conflicts of interest between types of chief constable. The sharp divide between county and borough chiefs, and between the very large city chiefs and the majority of small borough ones, has disappeared. With the exception of the London forces, differences in the position of chief police officers are now more of degree than kind. Compared to the past, they are moving towards a 'structural blending' of interests.

Finally, Mills asks, is there a 'unity of a more explicit co-ordination' between the élites? Do the factors of common background, career patterns, social intermingling, and shared interest produce a common outlook, and sometimes coalesce into united action? The evidence on the ideology and views on accountability of chief officers produced in Parts III and IV suggest this does happen.

Although there are variations around the common themes (analysed in Part V) there is a dominant ideology amongst chief constables today, which was labelled 'post-Scarmanism'. It sees public tranquillity, rather than law enforcement at all costs, as the traditional path of wisdom for the British police, and regards this as best attained by maximizing the extent of public acceptance and co-operation. The basic roots of crime and disorder lie in a broad erosion of moral and social controls in modern society, which the police can only play a small part in remedying, by alleviating the more visible symptoms. This perspective is one which people at the top of organizations, responsible for all their facets and representing their public face, would have an elective affinity for. But the orthodoxy it now constitutes is the product of propagation from the centre. This is articulated in the resentment expressed in Part III by some more traditional chief constables, who see post-Scarmanism as redundant instruction in the art of egg-sucking.

The clearest police example of 'unity of a more explicit co-ordination' is the national mutual aid operation organized by ACPO through the National Reporting Centre (NRC) during the miners' strike, which was discussed in Chapter 8. The official view, with which most chief constables concur, is that the NRC merely facilitated a completely voluntary process of giving mutual aid, without any central direction, let alone coercion. If this is true, then it is the greatest possible testimony to the commonality of outlook and interest amongst chief constables. They may describe it as common sense, but a unitary élite is precisely one which senses matters in common.

The evidence from chief constables' careers, as well as their views on accountability discussed in Chapter 11, suggests that this dominant ideology does not just develop spontaneously as a reflection of the shared situation and wisdom of chief officers themselves. It is the permeation of a favoured outlook from the Home Office, via the key national policing institutions, the HMI, ACPO, Bramshill, and the Met., which it controls or at least influences heavily. The accounts of chief constables themselves (in Chapter 11) indicate that the majority are inclined to accept Home Office circulars almost automatically, albeit with varying degrees of reluctance. In sum, the evidence from the research suggests that chief constables are fundamentally a unitary national élite, and one which is structured largely by the outlook of the Home Office.

None of this goes without question, however. Chapter 12 emphasized the variations between chief constables, around their common outlook. In the past, the main division between chiefs was the county–borough distinction. This is reproduced nowadays in the difference I indicated between 'barons' and the other types. However, the 'barons' are a diminishing breed. The type I described as a 'boss' is also disappearing. It was the immediate product of the rapid upsurge in crime, disorder, and political conflict which faced urban chiefs in the last two decades, and the outmoded attempt to control these by a straightforward law and order approach.

The key tension between chief constables now—and indeed it is also an internal conflict within each chief—is between the roles of 'bobby' and 'bureaucrat'. How far is the police organization unique, and how far is the job of chief executive in it essentially like being the managing director of any complex bureaucracy? (Chief constables' own views on this were discussed in Chapter 10.)

A combination of the changing exigencies of large police organizations and pressure from the centre, especially emanating from the Financial Management Initiative, has pushed all chief constables in the 'bureaucratic' direction. Willy-nilly, they have all been forced to take up more of the language and style of professional management theory. They have to fit the presentation of their organization and its output into the pattern demanded by the HMI and its matrix of performance indicators. Some chief constables still see and present themselves as primarily 'bobbies', albeit the leading ones. Others, however, have adopted the manner and aspirations of corporate executives, becoming a new species of police yuppy, or spouting the psycho-babble of the management consultant.

There is a limit to the latter process, however. Some unfortunate experiences in recent years have alerted the authorities to the dangers of chief officers losing touch with their rank and file. The ideal model favoured at present is someone who combines intellectual mastery of professional management skills with the operational experience and street credibility to command the confidence of the troops and the public. The most prominent of today's chief officers, such as Sir Peter Imbert and Geoffrey Dear, do succeed in combining these apparently contradictory qualities. So do a number of their colleagues not equally well known as yet. However, clearly people of that calibre are not commonplace.

The problems of recruiting such talent have stimulated a variety of suggested solutions. The favoured police strategy is to redouble efforts to identify potential stars among recruits. The task then is to construct appropriate fast-track careers for them, combining adequate periods of exposure to the full range of policing experiences, as well as training in management skills. Recent ACPO efforts in this direction were pointed out in Chapter 2.

The Government, however, seems increasingly drawn to the concept of an officer class of direct entrants as the panacea for policing problems. Our leaders may have been slow to acknowledge the crisis of confidence in the police but they have been quick to dredge up an outworn solution. In recent months the idea of an officer class for the police, drawn from the armed forces, has been touted increasingly. A Home Office source has been quoted as saying that 'Mrs Thatcher has a bee in her bonnet about it' (*Independent*, 5 Feb. 1990, 1), and with such goading from the top the bandwagon has rapidly gathered pace, gaining the support of some other senior ministers, members of the legal establishment like Sir Frederick Lawton, and influential portions of the press.

The proposal is convenient to many. To defence chiefs worried about cuts flowing from the 'peace dividend', it is handy to be able to point out that they have the boys for other jobs. From the Government's perspective, it is useful to have a scapegoat for the manifest problems of law and order, which in fact owe much to their own social and economic policies.

At the core of the 'officer class' idea lies a simplistic analysis of the source of policing problems. This view was epitomized by an editorial in *the Independent* (26 Jan. 1990) on the 'institutional rot' in the police. 'When fish start to rot, they rot from the head,' it argued. In other words, our policing difficulties stem from poor calibre leadership. (No doubt Mrs Thatcher would be loathe to apply this fishy theory to the country's other problems.) This is an inadequate analysis of the deficiencies of any organization, but it is particularly inappropriate for the police. The constables who deliver policing where it counts, on the streets, have a unique degree of independence and autonomy for the rank and file of an organization. This is not only a product of the peculiarly British constitutional tradition of 'constabulary independence'. It is an inevitable feature of police work, deriving from the nature of the bedrock tasks of policing: dispersed patrol and individual investigation.

The quality of personnel at the bottom of police organizations is a more important ingredient of the quality of policing than the calibre of the top brass. This is one of the major drawbacks of the 'officer class' proposal. By blocking promotion opportunities from the ranks it would reduce the quality and variety of applicants to routine police work, with devastating consequences for the levels of the police organization the public encounter most.

Contrary to the assumptions of the 'officer class' argument, the quality of police officers has been steadily increasing in recent years, due to greater competition for police jobs in a decade of generous police pay and high unemployment. Thirty years ago it was literally unheard of for graduates to enter the police, while now about one-tenth of each year's intake are graduates. There is in addition a virtual mania for education within forces, with considerable numbers studying for degrees and other qualifications in their spare (and sometimes their work) time. This autodidacticism was equally true of those who became chief constables in the past, as Chapter 5 indicated.

The date in Part I suggest a very different picture from the negative one implied by the 'officer class' proponents. Present-day chief constables are a unique generation in the history of British policing. They have all risen from the ranks by dint of meritocratic success, having entered on an equal footing with all other constables. Before the Second World War, as Chapter 2 describes, all county chief constables (and most of those in the largest cities) were direct entrants into senior ranks and came from the 'officer class' backgrounds to which Mrs Thatcher and others now want to return. After the war it became policy that all chiefs should have had professional police experience, working their way up the force hierarchy. But for the first two post-war decades most chiefs were graduates of the short-lived Hendon Police College of the 1930s, started by Lord Trenchard (founder of the RAF and then Metropolitan Commissioner) as a fast track for recruits with suitable social pedigrees.

The next generation of chief constables will probably include many who have benefited from more recent fast-track programmes like the Graduate Entry Scheme and the Special Course at Bramshill. Today's chiefs, however, are in between these eras (apart from a couple of the very youngest who are Special Course alumni). As we have seen, they are pure meritocrats. They come primarily from manual working-class backgrounds. However, they singled themselves out for future success early on, as most went to selective schools (80 per cent were grammar-school boys). The overwhelming majority acquired school-leaving qualifications. Although not one of the chiefs had a degree when he entered the police, a quarter had acquired one during their service, and many had obtained other educational qualifications (such as Diplomas in Management or Criminology). Nearly all have been on the Senior Command Course at Bramshill intended to equip chiefs with the necessary managerial skills.

The overall picture is of a group of men who worked their way up to their élite positions from humble origins by dint of effort and native ability. This combination of relevant police experience and intellectual success in unpropitious circumstances is arguably more indicative of suitability for police management than the possession of a higher social cachet.

Sir Frederick Lawton has argued that the advent of this generation of chiefs coincides with declining public confidence in police evidence, and he calls for a return to an 'officer class' in the hope that this would remedy the growth in police malpractice (*The Times*, 13 June 1990, 17). This is a classic example of the *post hoc ergo propter hoc* logical fallacy. The advent of a meritocratic generation of police chiefs may have coincided with the slump of public confidence in the police. But many things have changed at the same time, notably a spectacular growth in recorded crime and disorder, and a decline in the acceptance of authority in British culture, making the police task immensely harder. In any case, the picture given by police memoirs of the reality of pre-war and early post-war policing, behind the cosy Dixon image, suggests that the absence of scandals then owed more to a deferential working-class culture, and the rose-tinted spectacles of the judiciary, than to an absence of police malpractice. It is a moot point whether police abuse really is more rife now.

The fundamental flaw in the 'officer class' idea is that it gives entirely the wrong signals to the police and the public. British mythology has it that the police are citizens in uniform, but policing is necessarily in tension between its militaristic, forceful elements, and its attempts to gain community consent, a tension which the law quixotically seeks to regulate. The Janus-face of policing was nicely symbolized by Sir Robert Peel's original choice of two Commissioners, one a lawyer and one an Army officer, to lead the embryonic Metropolitan Police in 1829. The resuscitation of an 'officer class' after a decade of controversy about the militarization of policing, and of frail attempts to reinvigorate forms of community policing, would tilt the rudder in the wrong direction entirely.

If there is one outstanding defect in present-day chief constables it is their socially unrepresentative character. As seen above, they are all white, middle aged, conservatively inclined (small 'c') males. This is indicated dramatically by the recent action alleging sex discrimination taken against her force by Alison Halford, Assistant Chief Constable of Merseyside, the most senior police woman in Britain (*Police Review*, 7 Sept. 1990, 1752). The contemporary fulfilment of Sir Robert Peel's principle that the police should be representative of the people would require attention to be paid to the apparent problems facing women and ethnic minority officers in achieving senior rank. Mrs Thatcher's drive to bring in an even more unrepresentative élite from the armed services would be a completely retrograde step, back to the future with a vengeance.

The 'officer class' debate is, however, not the main cloud darkening the sky of the future for chief constables. We have noted in Chapters 2 and 11 the trend towards greater centralization of policing. This is not a new development but the accentuation of a process that goes back to the initial creation of policing on a uniform basis throughout the country, the 1856 County and Borough Police Act. Since then every major piece of legislation concerning the police has imposed greater uniformity on policing. Nor is this just a question of the overt level of formal organization of the police. Historical work, notably Jane

Morgan's important study of the policing of industrial conflict and the labour movement in the first four decades of this century (Morgan, 1987), shows that the Home Office were often closely involved in the day-to-day operations of policing disputes. The 1984–5 miners' strike was far from being a new departure. National labour disputes and other serious public disorders have been a major impetus towards nationalization of policing throughout this century.

Routine crime has also been a stimulus to greater centralization, and to the more efficient co-ordination of the 'war against crime' which it is expected to provide. This was the rationale used by the Royal Commission to justify its advance towards greater control by the Home Office, although it balked at the overt national force advocated in Professor Goodhart's influential dissenting memorandum to the Final Report.

If my conclusions are correct, however, they imply that what the Inns of Court Conservative and Unionist Society, Professor Goodhart, and others forecast in 1962 has come about. Rejecting a *de jure* national police force, we have ended up with the substance of one. But without the structure of accountability for it which the explicit proposals embodied. You cannot have accountability for something that is not supposed to be there.

Arguably, attempts to relocalize control now are like pushing a stream uphill. As 'law and order' has become increasingly politicized it becomes more unlikely that any government would wish to relinquish control over it. The only feasible way for this to be accomplished would be another radical departure from British tradition. The functions of the police would have to be split between more serious crime and disorder, which would become the province of national policing units (as in the 'third force' option for public disorder, which all chief constables currently oppose), and routine patrol and crime investigation, which would be handled by localized and less prestigious police. This solution, found in many countries, is certainly on the agenda of commentators at both ends of the political spectrum.

Short of this functional reallocation, the nationalizing trend cannot really be reversed. Only by recognizing it and accepting it can some accountability over national policies be achieved. Partly this must be to Parliament. But, beyond that, John Alderson's suggestion during the miners' strike should be seriously considered: 'a national (emergency) police committee' comprising the Home Secretary, representatives of local police authorities, ACPO, and arguably the Police Federation (*Guardian*, 13 Sept. 1984, 16). This should not only be an emergency committee, but be responsible for reviewing and formulating national policies and guidelines for policing. (These would also be discussed in Parliament, of course, though detailed work would be done by the committee.)

It is unlikely, however, that such a proposal would be politically feasible, any more than local control, in the present climate. Why should the Government relinquish a position which gives it power without responsibility? The myth of a tripartite structure of governance for essentially local policing, with constabulary independence for operational decisions, is useful for legitimating a system of *de facto* national control.

Recent events described at the end of Chapter 2, however, suggest that there is a developing momentum towards more overt centralization within the existing framework, with a beefed-up Inspectorate and ACPO as its instruments. The main impetus for this now seems to be the advent of European integration, and the need to deal with overseas forces in a co-ordinated way. It could be that this will provide the rationale and legitimation for the final step of constructing a national police force.

For all the recent growth in the power and significance of chief constables which stimulated this study, the outlook for them looks uncertain. They could be caught between the rock of a take-over bid from Dad's Army and the hard place of being nationalized out of existence. What is certain to happen in any event is an accentuation of the trend to tighter central control and bureaucratization.

When I started this research on contemporary chief constables I had to approach forty-three in order to see them all. Had I done it fifty years ago, I would have had to approach 182 chief officers. Twenty-five years ago the number would still have been 121. How long will it be before it is only necessary to contact one?

Appendix A

Introductory Letter from ACPO

8th September, 1986

Dear Sir,

CHIEF CONSTABLES—A SOCIO—LEGAL STUDY

Dr Robert Reiner of Bristol University has been granted a fellowship by Nuffield College to research the role of Chief Constables and his objectives and methods summary is attached.

The President has interviewed Dr Reiner and is of the opinion that, on balance, it would be to the advantage of ACPO to co-operate with this research.

It is, of course, open to each and every Chief Constable to decide for himself whether or not he is willing to be interviewed and Dr Reiner has been made aware of the fact that it is extremely unlikely that every Chief Constable will agree. The President still hopes that this research will, in the end, produce positive results.

Home Office are aware of this project and are supportive.

Yours faithfully,

General Secretary

TO: All Chief Constables

Encl.

Ojectives and Methods

There can be no doubt that chief constables occupy the pivotal position in the system of law-enforcement. They are responsible for the general policy and detailed operational direction and control of policing in their force areas, and are the primary disciplinary authority over their officers. In the last fifteen years the importance of their role has expanded enormously. Amalgamation of smaller police forces into the present forty-three large forces in England and Wales has awesomely enlarged the sphere of their responsibility. At the same time, the growing complexity and volume of the problems faced by police forces, and the increasing sophistication of technology and operational methods employed by them, have made the police management task, especially that of the chief constable, unprecedentedly arduous and demanding. The deepening social tensions of recent years have made chief constables more controversial figures with a higher public profile than ever before. All these changes have made chief constables into an élite group with considerable influence, attracting much public interest, and surrounded by a growing mythology.

However, virtually nothing is known by the public in a systematic and objective way about chief constables. What are their legal powers, and what are the perspectives and character of the people who exercise them? In the last decade, several studies have given us some knowledge of the attitude and practices of rank-and-file police (for example, my own books *The Blue-Coated Worker*, Cambridge University Press, 1978, and *The Politics of the Police*, Wheatsheaf Books, 1985). I would like to gather comparable data, systematically obtained, about the senior command level of police forces. In the absence of such objective and comprehensively researched material, there is a danger that public perceptions and discussions of chief officers will be distorted by the vagaries of media attention to a few prominent figures and incidents. These have been associated with campaigns arguing for enhanced accountability or political control of police forces.

My aim is to fill this vital gap in public knowledge of policing, by gathering some basic information about chief constables. In addition to library research on the legal powers and history of the office of chief constable, I would like to conduct interviews with present-day holders of the office. I have been granted a Fellowship by the Nuffield Foundation for the year 1986–7 to pursue this objective. Specifically, I would like to discover two things: (i) The career patterns and backgrounds of chief constables; (ii) An idea, derived from interviews, of chief constables' philosophies of policing, and their strategies for improving crime control, order-maintenance, and force managerial efficiency. In short, how has the role of chief police officer as manager of a complex and vital organization developed in recent years?

Ideally, I would like to personally interview all forty-three present chief constables in England and Wales, in order to provide a balanced and comprehensive picture of styles and attitudes. The results will be analysed and reported entirely anonymously, with no views being attributed to individuals in any identifiable way, the purpose being to portray the office not the individual incumbent. The interviews will last about one and a half hours, and be based on a standard set of questions which should provide the basis for a discussion which I hope participants will find interesting. I would like to start interviewing in October, and work my way round the country within about five to six months. My report will be submitted for comment and approval to the officers of ACPO before any wider publication. My final goal is a book on chief constables; which will include historical and legal analysis, as well as data on the views of chief constables.

Dr Robert Reiner
Faculty of Law

Appendix B

The Question Schedule

Introduction

[Repeat points in introductory letter]

Section A: Work History

To start with, I wonder whether you would mind telling me some things about your career so far?

1. (a) In which year did you first join a police force, and which constabulary was it?
   (b) Can you recall what attracted you to the police force?
2. Had you previously been employed at all outside the police?
   [If yes, ask 3; if no, go on to 4]
3. (a) What was the last employment you had before you took up work as a policeman?
   (b) When did you have that job?
   (c) For how long did you have it?
   (d) Did you have any other jobs before the police?
       If yes: What were these?
                 When, and for how long did you have each job?
4. Have you ever done military service?
   If yes: Was this national service or war service?
             In which of the forces?
             During which years?
             What rank did you reach?
5. Did you first enter the police force as a cadet?
6. When were you appointed chief constable of X?
7. What was the post you occupied at the time of your appointment to the office of chief constable?
8. What was your immediately preceding post?
9. When were you promoted to the rank of:
   (i) Deputy chief constable
   (ii) Assistant chief constable
   (iii) Chief superintendent

      (iv) Superintendent
      (v) Chief inspector
      (vi) Inspector
      (vii) Sergeant

10.   In what other police forces have you worked, and what posts did you hold? Between what years were these appointments?

11.   In which specialist departments have you worked (i.e. other than territorial uniform divisions)?

12.   What training courses have you been on, other than probationary training?

13.   Have you ever thought seriously about leaving the police, at any time during your career?
      If yes: (a) When and why?
    (b) What would you have done instead?
    (c) What did you do about it?

14.   Did you ever think you would end up as chief constable, when you joined?

15.   Have you any plans for what you might do in the future?

[Section B: The Police Function]

I would like now to discuss your view of what the purposes and priorities of policing are.

1.   Ideas of the police function can roughly be divided into (*a*) a wider 'pro-active' view that they are a public service agency with a broad social control role, perhaps even a responsibility to remedy the social sources of crime; and (*b*) a narrower 'reactive' view, that they should limit themselves to law enforcement and control of public disorder.
    Which of these conceptions do you favour, and why?

2.   What, if anything, does the phrase 'community policing' mean to you?

3.   Lord Scarman suggested there are times when maintenance of public tranquillity might be threatened by the police strictly carrying out their duty to enforce the law. Do you agree?

4.   What problems, if any, does the Scarman approach cause the police?

5.   Is there any danger of the creation of what are, in effect, no-go areas?

6.   Do you agree with the establishment of a new prosecution service independent of the police?

[Section C: Crime and Its Control]

In this section I want to talk about your views of crime, its sources and control.

1.   Do you feel that crime is now a greater problem than when you joined the police?
    What evidence do you have to support your view?
    If greater problem: Why do you think crime has become a greater problem?

2. Are there any features of our society which are likely to aggravate crime problems?

3. Research by the Home Office has suggested that traditional methods of patrol and detection have a limited impact on crime, and that increasing the resources devoted to them would not significantly reduce crime. Do you agree? Why?

4. Are there any legal powers which the police require for effective crime control, but do not have at present?
   If yes: What powers? Should the police have them?

5. Are there any aspects of the procedures designed to safeguard suspects, such as those embodied in the Police and Criminal Evidence Act 1984, which are detrimental to effective crime control by the police?
   If yes: What aspects? Should these procedures be changed? If so, how?

6. If a particular social group disproportionately have criminal records, would it help clear up more offences if they were more often stopped and questioned or searched?

7. Why have clear-up rates fallen over the last twenty-five years? Is this a criticism of police performance in any way?

8. If you were given 500 new recruits tomorrow would it make much difference to your crime control performance? How would you allocate them to maximum effect?

9. Would you yourself ever get involved *directly* in a specific criminal investigation?

Section D: Public Order

I would like to discuss next some issues in the police control of collective public disorder.

1. Is the control of public disorder more difficult for the police now than in the past?
   If yes: Why?

2. Has public disorder become (*a*) more frequent? (*b*) More serious or violent?
   If yes: Why has disorder increased?

3. On what evidence do you base your views?

4. The police response to disorder has become more sophisticated, robust, and forceful in recent years, a trend often described as 'militaristic' policing.
   Why has this occurred?
   Does it cause problems for the police?
   Could the police have taken any steps to avert it?

5. Does the damage done to the public image of the police, or to the psychological approach of the ordinary police officer, by involvement in tough public order situations, justify the creation of a separate 'third force' for public order policing?

6. Suppose during a riot you received information that a building containing

several people was on fire, and that the only tactic that could clear a path for the fire brigade was the deployment of baton rounds;

    (a) Would you sanction their use in this, or any other, situations?

    (b) What would you do if your police authority told you they did not want you to use them?

7. Will the Public Order Act help the police in the task of maintaining order?

Section E: Internal Management

1. In recent years, especially since the Edmund-Davies Report of 1978, the rank and file, as represented by the Police Federation, has gained a more significant consultative role in the determination of force policy.
Is this desirable?
Has it posed any problems for police management?
If yes: In what way?

2. The style of management and discipline in police forces has been said to have relaxed in recent years.
What management problems does this pose, if any?
Are there any benefits?

3. Should the British police be entitled to form an independent trade union, as many Continental forces do?

4. Are there any problems in the present complaints system?

5. Would there be any advantages or problems if the investigation and adjudication of complaints against the police were to be conducted by an entirely independent body?
Would you favour such a system?

6. Has the growth in size of police forces changed the role of chief constables?
In what way?
Has it made the job more difficult?

7. Would you be in favour of a national police service?

8. What are the main management problems facing you as a chief constable?

Section F: The External Environment of the Police Force

1. What do you feel is the role of a local police auathority?

2. How adequately do you feel this role is performed.

    (a) By police authorities in general?

    (b) By your own police authority?

3. The argument is often advanced that police authorities, being democratically elected representatives of local people, should control the policy of the police force. Do you agree?

4. Given the controversy about policing, should there be another Royal Commission on the Police?

5. Should there be a locally elected police authority for London, along the lines of the present provisional authorities?

6. Have you ever had to refuse requests for special reports from your police authority?

7. To what extent do the following bodies influence you in deciding on police innovations, strategy, or other important decisions:
   (i) The Home Office and the Home Secretary
   (ii) HM Inspectorate
   (iii) ACPO

8. You receive a report that a riot is developing in your area. Soon afterwards your secretary informs you that three people are asking for you on the telephone: the Home Secretary, the chair of your police authority, and the editor of *The Times*. In which order would you take the calls? Why?

9. During the 1970s it appeared that some chief constables, as well as the Police Federation, were adopting a much higher profile, frequently expressing views on policing and other social issues.
   Are these developments of which you approve?
   Is there a danger that they could lead to the police no longer being seen as politically impartial?

10. A few years ago a Police Federation spokesman remarked that the police might no longer be able to give equally loyal service regardless of which party was in government.
    Do you agree that it makes a difference to the police which party is in power?
    If yes: In what way?

Section G: Social Perspectives

1. Britain used to be regarded as a remarkably harmonious society. Do you believe it still is one?
   What makes you say this?

2. What are the most important social divisions in our society?
   Are they becoming greater, less great, or remaining the same?

3. Is there any truth in the adage 'there is one law for the rich and one for the poor'?

Section H: Personal Background

Finally, I would like to ask you a little about your background.

1. In what year were you born?
2. Are you married?
3. Have you any children?
   If yes: How many?
   How old is each?
   What do they do?
4. What was the highest educational level you reached?

If degree: What subject was it in?
When and where did you do it?
5. What type of school did you attend?
6. When did you leave school?
7. What sort of work did your father (or guardian) do when you were 18?
Had he been in that kind of work for most of his life?
If no: What were the main jobs he had before then?
8. Overall, are you satisfied with your career in the police service?
Would you rejoin if you had your life over?
9. Finally, are there any comments you would like to make about the interview?
May I thank you for your co-operation.

Appendix C

The History and Structure of the Association of Chief Police Officers

The Association of Chief Police Officers (ACPO) is now regarded by many commentators as the *eminence grise* behind policy-making on policing and criminal justice issues more generally (as was outlined in Chapters 1 and 2). To many chief officers it appears too weak and disorganized a body, as Chapter 11 indicated, and this view seems to be shared by the Government who have encouraged ACPO to upgrade its profile. This Appendix fills in the earlier history of ACPO, and sets out its basic organizational anatomy today.

The History of ACPO

ACPO was formed in 1948, uniting the separate bodies which had existed hitherto for county and borough chief constables. An organization to represent county chiefs dates back to 1858, when they formed the County Chief Constables Club. The urban chiefs followed suit in 1896, when the chief officers of the cities and boroughs established the Chief Constables Association of England and Wales.

Reflecting the sharp divide in social status and power between county and borough chiefs (discussed in Chapter 2), there was little contact between the two bodies representing chief officers until the First World War. Each functioned independently but neither could discuss salaries and other personal issues. The basic business of both organizations was scarcely more then being an 'officers' club' performing primarily social and welfare functions for members. There was negligible involvement in professional and policing matters, either in terms of internal discussion or external policy debates.

The First World War was the catalyst for a more co-ordinated development and upgrading of these associations. A number of conferences were set up towards the end of the war, to facilitate smoother co-operation between the Home Office and police forces. In January 1918 the country was divided into eight districts, with every chief constable in each district acting as delegates. These conferences were regarded as Home Office affairs, and were always attended by officials, one of whom took the chair at each opening meeting. HM Inspectors of Constabulary, the regular link between Home Office and chief officers, also attended.

In 1918 the Central Conference of Chief Constables was also established, to co-ordinate the district conferences. Two representatives from each of the district conferences attended. The objectives of the conference were laid down as: (*a*) To bring the police forces into closer touch with the Home Office; (*b*) To improve contact between government departments and the police executive throughout the country; (*c*) To assist the Home Office in the issue of such instruments as might be required for the guidance of the police. It was subsequently agreed in 1921 that the chief constables' representatives should meet before the conference to discuss the agenda, and the practice of holding such a 'preliminary' meeting was introduced in June 1922, immediately before the conference. The Desborough Committee Report of 1919 (Home Office 1919) and the ensuing Police Act, which were largely responses to the 1918–19 police strikes (Reiner, 1978, 21–5), laid the foundation for more regularized and institutionalized central co-ordination of policing through the newly established Police Department of the Home Office. The setting-up of the Central Conference was an aspect of these wider changes, involving consolidation of the growing links between chief constables and the Home Office which had been set in train by the war.

The Second World War was the stimulus for a further move towards integration, as wartime regulations gave the Home Secretary greater powers over the police. In 1944 the Home Secretary set up a committee to consider postwar reconstruction of the police service. *Inter alia*, it was suggested that the County Chief Constables' Club and the Chief Constables' Association (Cities and Boroughs) of England and Wales should amalgamate, to allow a more co-ordinated input from chief constables into the deliberations about the future of the service. However, at first the county–borough divide remained recalcitrant to bridge-building.

The marriage was, however, forced by the stance taken by Lord Oaksey, chairman of the 1948–9 Committee on Police Conditions of Service (Home Office, 1949). Oaksey insisted on meeting with a single delegation of chief constables, not two separate associations. The product of this shotgun wedding was the Association of Chief Police Officers of England and Wales, constituted in July 1948 as the union of the two previous bodies. The honorary secretary of ACPO was to be a chief constable, and another chief constable acted as honorary secretary to the Central Conference. The chair of the Conference continued to be the Permanent Under-Secretary of State of the Home Office. The Director of Public Prosecutions was also invited regularly, whilst officials of other ministries attended if relevant subjects were on the agenda. Occasionally the Conferences (held two or three times a year) were attended by the Home Secretary.

ACPO was (and remains) an informal body, with its important functions unspecified by any statutory definition or even recognition. However, its role as a policy-developing body has expanded out of all recognition, and its social and quasi-trade-union functions have become more residual. The growth of its business was made explicit in 1968 when ACPO was reconstituted with a central secretariat including a full-time general secretary. Previously the work was undertaken by two serving chief officers and staff from their forces. Until recently the secretariat remained a shoe-string operation. However, as indicated in Chapter 2, it has recently been upgraded, and the new general secretary is for the first time a civilian. The post now has Home Office funding, as a mark of the higher-profile role ACPO is expected to play. In 1970 the scope of ACPO was expanded to bring in the chief officers of the Royal Ulster Constabulary, and it is now the Association of Chief Police Officers of England, Wales, and Northern Ireland.

The formal objectives of ACPO remain as stated at the time of the 1968 reorganization. These are: (*a*) To promote the welfare and efficiency of the police service and safeguard the interests of members of the Association; (*b*) To provide opportunties for discussion and to give advice on matters affecting the police service; (*c*) To provide social amenities for its members. Within this mix the social and representative functions have clearly become subordinated to the policy and operational ones. At the 1967 autumn Conference, the then president warned the members that 'the threat to the independence of chief constables—the right to control their own forces—is likely to come from the Home Office, and is most likely to come through the Inspectorate'. This prophecy has come true, as the earlier chapters indicate, but the upgrading of ACPO which was set in motion by that same Conference has contributed to the process of centralization.

The Structure of ACPO

All chief police officers in England, Wales, and Northern Ireland are members of ACPO. Chief police officers are defined as those holding a substantive rank above that of chief superintendent. This includes Commanders and above in the City and Metropolitan forces in London.

ACPO's rules define five bodies of the Association. These are: (i) the officers of the Association; (ii) the steering committee; (iii) the executive committee; (iv) the Council of the Association; (v) the regions (originally the districts).

The ACPO president acts as chairman, and the general secretary as secretary, of the steering and executive committees, and the Council.

(i) The Officers of the Association

These are the president, who holds office for one year, the vice-president (who usually becomes the next president), the immediate past president, the Commissioner of Police of the Metropolis, the general secretary, the honorary treasurer, and the representative of the assistant Chief Constables. The president and vice-president are elected at the autumn Conference. The election of the vice-president is crucial, for he would normally become president the following year.

(ii) The Steering Committee.

This is comprised of the officers of the Association. It meets when and as required, convened by the president to decide pressing matters. The steering committee has the authority to act for the Association on urgent issues.

(iii) The Executive Committee

In addition to the officers of the Association, the executive committee includes one elected representative chief constable and one assistant chief constable, elected by their peers in each of the seven provincial regions, and four representatives from London region. The representatives are elected for terms of one year, but are eligible for re-election. If a representative cannot attend, he can be replaced by a substitute from the same rank, who has full voting rights. The executive committee can co-opt any members of the Association to advise it.

The role of the executive committee is to act for ACPO on all negotiable matters affecting the pay and conditions of service of members, or of the police service as a whole. It meets at least four times a year.

The committee nominates the president, vice-president, and honorary treasurer at its summer meeting. It also nominates ACPO representatives to the Police Negotiating Board, the Police Advisory Board, and various other outside bodies. It can refer any matters to members of the Association as it deems necessary.

The progress and results of all committees are reported to it by nominated representatives, who also keep the membership informed of all relevant matters. The executive committee also looks at issues submitted to it by regional conferences.

The executive committee has the duty of ensuring that all members of ACPO participate in its business as much as possible, and that there is a proper balance of representation on the various committees.

(iv) The Council of the Association

It is the ACPO Council which is the pivot of its growing role in policy-making. The Council acts for ACPO on all matters of a technical or professional nature. It does this through seven specialist committees which it appoints. Each committee includes a chief constable representative from every region, and a representative of ACPO (Scotland) also sits on each committee. The committees cover Crime and CID issues, Computer Services, Communications, Traffic, General Purposes, Training, and Technical Services.

The ACPO Council's members are the officers of the Association, the City of London Police Commissioner, the Assistant Commissioners of the Met., and all other chief constables in England, Wales and Northern Ireland. The honorary regional secretaries and chairmen, and the honorary secretaries and assistant secretaries of Council committees are members of Council, but without voting rights. There are also three non-voting representatives of ACPO (Scotland). Deputy chiefs may not not attend in the absence of their chiefs.

The appointment of chairmen and secretaries of Council committees are subject to annual review. Committees can appoint subcommittees as required, under the chairmanship of a chief constable member of that specialist Council committee.

The ACPO Council meets four times a year, two of these being the preliminary meetings to the Central Conferences. When convening as the preliminary meeting to Central Conferences, ACPO Council considers the Home Office agenda, about which the various ACPO Council subcommittees will already have made comments. There is also an ACPO Council agenda which is discussed, to decide what matters should be referred to Central Conference.

(v) The Regions

ACPO is divided into eight regions: No. 1, the North West (with six forces including the RUC), No. 2, the North East (consisting of seven forces), No. 3 the Midlands (four forces), No. 4, the East (eight forces), No. 5, the South East (eight forces), No. 6, the South West (five forces), No. 7, Wales (four forces), and No. 8, the Metropolitan Region (the Met. and the City of London forces).

Each region elects its own chairman, honorary secretary, and representatives to the executive committee. Regional conferences meet four times a year and forward resolutions and recommendations through the general secretary for consideration by the executive committee, Council, or Council committees as appropriate.

All ACPO members within a region may attend its meetings. Members of neighbouring regions may be invited to attend on a non-voting basis, as may non-members. Chairmen and honorary secretaries of each region are appointed annually at the meeting prior to the ACPO AGM, as are representatives to the executive committee and Council committees.

Resolutions and recommendations of regional conferences are referred to the ACPO executive committee (if they concern negotiable matters), or the ACPO Council (if they are about professional or technical questions). They are referred through the general secretary. Matters of local concern can also be taken up directly with the Home Office, but a copy must be sent to the ACPO general secretary.

Subordinate conferences may also be held in each region on specialist matters such as crime, traffic, administration, communications, crime prevention, photography and fingerprints, drugs, training, dogs, community liaison, research and development, or statistics. The necessity and frequency of such specialist meetings is decided by the regional conference. The subordinate conferences can send matters on to regional conferences, and thence to the general secretary for the attention of the relevant national committee. From there it could be referred to the Central Conference for a decision.

General Meetings

ACPO has an annual general meeting every autumn, and other general meetings at the discretion of the executive committee and/or the Council. It also arranges joint meetings with representatives of the Home Office and the Local Authority Associations, and with other persons invited by the executive committee and/or the Council.

The Home Office Central Conference of Chief Constables

This now meets twice a year, in May and November. It is attended by the officers of the Association (apart from the two assistant chief constables), and the chairman and honorary secretaries of the seven ACPO Council committees. It is also attended by three representatives from ACPO (Scotland), the chief constable of the RUC, and the City of London Commissioner.

Outside Representation

ACPO representatives sit on, or give evidence to, a host of government, parliamentary, and other committees, working parties, and inquiries. ACPO regulations require such representatives to give the Assocation's official views as laid down by the executive committee and/or the Council. On other occasions, where members express their own views, they are expected to make it clear when these depart from the majority position of ACPO, or to emphaize that the member speaks only as an individual. Members elected or nominated by ACPO to serve on outside bodies or committees are expected to report back and to be prepared to answer questions at the AGM.

As outlined already in Chapter 2, ACPO has over the last few years been dramatically transformed from the social clubs of chief constables out of which it grew. It has clearly become a focal part of the policy-making scene, even though it lacks any clear constitutional basis, and its objective and functioning are governed only by purely internal regulations, scarcely known outside the organization. As it has acquired this higher profile, so it has become a more tightly knit association, a process which is now officially encouraged by the Home Office who are concerned to develop ACPO as the vertebrae of more centrally co-ordinated policing.

Bibliography

ALBROW, M. (1970), *Bureaucracy* (London: Macmillan).

ALDERSON, J. (1979), *Policing Freedom* (Plymouth: Macdonald and Evans).

——(1984), *Law and Disorder* (London: Hamish Hamilton).

——(1986), 'Time for a Royal Commission', *Policing*, 2: 276–82.

——and STEAD, P.J. (1973) (eds.), *The Police We Deserve* (London: Wolf).

ANDERTON, J. (1981), 'The Art and Economics of Policing', paper presented to SSRC Public Policy Study Group Seminar on Central and Local Government Relations, London: Royal Institute of Public Administration, 9 Jan.

BALDWIN, R. (1987), 'Why Accountability?', *British Journal of Criminology*, 27: 97–105.

——and KINSEY, R. (1982), *Police Powers and Politics* (London: Quartet Books).

BANTON, M. (1971), 'The Sociology of the Police', *Police Journal*, 44: 227–43.

——(1973), 'The Sociology of the Police II', *Police Journal*, 46: 341–62.

——(1975), 'The Sociology of the Police III', *Police Journal*, 48: 299–315.

BARITZ, L. (1965), *The Servants of Power* (New York: Wiley).

BAXTER, J., and KOFFMAN, L. (1985) (eds.), *Police: The Constitution and the Community* (Abingdon: Professional Books).

BAYLEY, D. H., and MENDELSOHN, H. A. (1968), *Minorities and the Police* (New York: Free Press).

BENYON, J. (1984) (ed.), *Scarman and After* (Oxford: Pergamon).

——(1985), 'Going Through the Motions: The Political Agenda, the 1981 Riots and the Scarman Enquiry', *Parliamentary Affairs*, 38: 409–22.

——and BOURN, C. (1986) (eds.), *The Police: Powers, Procedures and Proprieties* (Oxford: Pergamon).

BEVAN, V. T., and LIDSTONE, K. (1985), *The Police and Criminal Evidence Act 1984* (London: Butterworth).

BEYNON, H. (1973), *Working for Ford* (London: Penguin).

——and BLACKBURN, R. (1972), *Perceptions of Work* (Cambridge: Cambridge University Press).

BOTTOMLEY, K., and PEASE, K. (1986), *Crime and Punishment: Interpreting the Data* (Milton Keynes: Open University Press).

BOTTOMS, A. E. (1990), 'Crime Prevention: Facing the 1990s', *Policing and Society*, 1: 3–22.

BOWDEN, T. (1978), *Beyond the Limits of the Law* (Harmondsworth: Penguin).

BOX, S. (1981), *Deviance, Reality and Society* (New York: Holt, Rinehart, and Winston).

——(1983), *Deviance, Crime and Mystification* (London: Tavistock).

——(1987), *Recession, Crime and Unemployment* (London: Macmillan).

BRADLEY, D., WALKER, N., and WILKIE, R. (1986), *Managing the Police: Law, Organisation and Democracy* (Brighton: Wheatsheaf).

BRAITHWAITE, J. (1989), *Crime, Shame and Reintegration* (Cambridge: Cambridge University Press).

BROGDEN, M. (1977), 'A Police Authority—The Denial of Conflict', *Sociological Review*, 25: 325–49.

——(1981), 'All Police is Conning Bastards', in B. Fine, A. Hunt, D. McBarnet, and B. Moorhouse (eds.), *Law, State and Society* (London: Croom Helm).

——(1982), *The Police: Autonomy and Consent* (London: Academic Press).

——JEFFERSON, T., and WALKLATE, S. (1988), *Introducing Police Work* (London: Unwin Hyman).

BROWN, J., and HOWES, G. (1975) (eds.), *The Police and the Community* (Farnborough: Saxon House).

BROWN, L., and WILLIS, A. (1985), 'Authoritarianism in British Police Recruits: Importation, Socialisation or Myth?', *Journal of Occupational Psychology*, 58: 97–108.

BUTLER, A. J. P. (1984), *Police Management* (Aldershot: Gower).

CAIN, M. E. (1977), 'An Ironical Departure: The Dilemma of Contemporary Policing', in K. Jones, (ed.), *Yearbook of Social Policy in Britain* (London: Routledge).

——(1979), 'Trends in the Sociology of Police Work', *International Journal of the Sociology of Law*, 7: 143–67.

CAMPBELL, D. (1987), 'Policing: A Power in the Land', *New Statesman*, 8 May: 11–12.

CLARKE, R. V. G. (1983), 'Situational Crime Prevention: Its Theoretical Basis and Practical Scope', in M. Tonry and N. Morris, (eds.), *Crime and Justice: An Annual Review of Research*, iv (Chicago: Chicago University Press).

——and HOUGH, M. (1980) (eds.), *The Effectiveness of Policing* (Farnborough: Gower).

——and MAYHEW, P. (1980) (eds.), *Designing Out Crime* (London: HMSO).

CLAYTON, R., and TOMLINSON, H. (1987), *Civil Actions Against the Police* (London: Sweet and Maxwell).

COCHRANE, R., and BUTLER, A. J. P. (1980), 'The Values of Police Officers, Recruits and Civilians in England', *Journal of Police Science and Administration*, 8: 205–11.

COHEN, B. (1980), 'Leadership Styles of Commanders in the New York City Police Department', *Journal of Police Science and Administration*, 8: 125–38.

COLMAN, A. M., and GORMAN, P. L. (1982), 'Conservatism, Dogmatism and Authoritarianism in Police Officers', *Sociology*, 16: 1–11.

CREWE, I. (1974), 'Studying Élites in Britain', in id. (ed.), *British Political Sociology Yearbook I: Élites in Western Democracy* (London: Croom Helm).

CRITCHLEY, T. A. (1978), *A History of Police in England and Wales*, 2nd edn. (London: Constable).

DIXON, D., BOTTOMLEY, A. K., COLEMAN, C., GILL, M., and WALL, D. (1990), 'Safeguarding the Rights of Suspects in Police Custody', *Policing and Society*, 1: 115–40.

DOWNES, D., and ROCK, P. (1988), *Understanding Deviance*, 2nd edn. (Oxford: Oxford University Press).

ENTER, J. E. (1986), 'The Rise to the Top: An Analysis of Police Chief Career Patterns', *Journal of Police Science and Administration*, 14: 334–46.

FIJNAUT, C., and VISSER, B. (1985) (eds.), *Managing Larger Police Organisations* (Amsterdam: Municipal Police Force).

FINE, B., and MILLAR, R. (1985) (eds.), *Policing the Miners' Strike* (London: Lawrence and Wishart).

FREEMAN, M. D. A. (1985), *The Police and Criminal Evidence Act 1984* (London: Sweet and Maxwell).

FYFE, J. J. (1989) (ed.), *Police Practice in the '90s: Key Management Issues* (Washington DC: International City Management Association).

GEARY, R. (1985), *Policing Industrial Disputes* (Cambridge: Cambridge University Press).

GELLER, W. A. (1985) (ed.), *Police Leadership in America* (New York: Praeger).

GOLDSMITH, A. (1988), 'New Directions in Police Complaints Procedures', *Police Studies*, 11: 60.

——(1990), 'Taking Police Culture Seriously: Police Discretion and the Limits of Law', *Policing and Society*, 1: 91–114.

——(1991) (ed.), *Complaints Against the Police* (Oxford: Oxford University Press).

GOLDTHORPE, J. H., LOCKWOOD, D., BECHHOFER, F., and PLATT, J. (1968), *The Affluent Worker: Industrial Attitudes and Behaviour* (Cambridge: Cambridge University Press).

GOLDTHORPE, J. H., LLEWELLYN, C., PAYNE, C. (1980), *Social Mobility and Class Structure in Modern Britain* (Oxford: Oxford University Press).

GRAEF, R. (1989), *Talking Blues* (London: Collins).

GRIMSHAW, R., and JEFFERSON, T. (1987), *Interpreting Policework* (London: Allen and Unwin).

GROSMAN, B. A. (1975), *Police Command* (Toronto: Macmillan).

HAIN, P. (1979) (ed.), *Policing the Police* (London: Calder).

——(1980) (ed.) *Policing the Police 2* (London: Calder).

HALL, S. (1979), *Drifting into a Law and Order Society* (London: Cobden Trust).

HALSEY, A. H., HEATH, A. F., and RIDGE, J. M. (1980), *Origins and Destinations: Family, Class and Education in Modern Britain* (Oxford: Oxford University Press).

HANN, R. G., McGINNIS, J. H., STENNING, P. C., and FARSON, A. S. (1985), 'Municipal Police Governance and Accountability in Canada: An Empirical Case Study', *Canadian Police College Journal*, 9: 1–85.

HEAL, K., TARLING, R., and BURROWS, J. (1985) (eds.), *Policing Today* (London: HMSO).

HILLYARD, P. (1981), 'From Belfast to Britain', in *Politics and Power 4: Law, Politics and Justice* (London: Routledge).

HIRSCHI, T. (1969), *Causes of Delinquency* (Berkeley: University of California Press).

HIRST, M. (1990), ' "The Chief": A Real Chief's View', *Police*, June: 19.

Home Affairs Committee (1989), *Higher Police Training and the Police Staff College*, House of Commons Paper 110–1 (London: HMSO).

Home Office (1919), *Committee on the Police Service of England, Wales and Scotland, Report* (Chairman: Lord Desborough) (London: HMSO).

——(1949), *Committee on Police Conditions of Service, Report: Parts I and II*, Cmnd. 7674 and 7831 (Chairman: Lord Oaksey) (London: HMSO).

——(1978), *Committee of Inquiry into Police Pay and Negotiating Machinery, Report*, Cmnd. 7283 (Chairman: Lord Edmund-Davies) (London: HMSO).

IMBERT, P. (1989), 'Glasnost at the Yard', *Police Review*, 1 Dec.

IRVING, B., and MCKENZIE, I. (1989), *Police Interrogation* (London: Police Foundation).

JACKSON, B., and MARSDEN, D. (1962), *Education and the Working Class* (Harmondsworth: Penguin).

JEFFERSON, T. (1987), 'Beyond Paramilitarism', *British Journal of Criminology*, 27: 47–53.

——(1990), *The Case Against Paramilitary Policing* (Milton Keynes: Open University Press).

——and GRIMSHAW, R. (1984), *Controlling the Constable* (London: Miller).

JUDGE, T. (1972), *A Man Apart* (London: Barker).

KAKABADSE, A. (1984), 'The Police: A Management Development Survey', *Journal of European Industrial Training*, 8: 3–48.

KETTLE, M. (1980), 'The Politics of Policing and the Policing of Politics', in P. Hain, (ed.), *Policing the Police 2* (London: Calder).

KINSEY, R., LEA, J., and YOUNG, J. (1986), *Losing the Fight Against Crime* (Oxford: Basil Blackwell).

KUYKENDALL, J. L. (1977), 'Police Leadership: An Analysis of Executive Styles', *Criminal Justice Review*, 2: 89–100.

LAMBERT, J. (1986), *Police Powers and Accountability* (London: Croom Helm).

LEIGH, L. (1981), 'The Royal Commission on Criminal Procedure', *Criminal Law Review*, May.

——(1985), *Police Powers in England and Wales*, 2nd edn. (London: Butterworth).

LOREE, D. J. (1989) (ed.), *Research Leaders in Policing* (Ottawa: Canadian Police College).

LOVEDAY, B. (1985), *The Role and Effectiveness of the Merseyside Police Committee* (Liverpool: Merseyside County Council).

——(1986), 'Central Co-ordination, Police Authorities and the Miners' Strike', *Political Quarterly*, 57: 60–73.

LOVEDAY, B. (1987), 'The Joint Boards', *Policing*, 3: 196–213.

——(1988), 'Police Complaints in the USA,' *Policing*, 4: 172–93.

LOVEDAY, B. (1991), 'The New Police Authorities', *Policing and Society* (forthcoming).

LUKES, S. (1974), *Power* (London: Macmillan).

LUSTGARTEN, L. (1986), *The Governance of the Police* (London: Sweet and Maxwell).

McBARNET, D. (1981), *Conviction* (London: Macmillan).

McCABE, S., WALLINGTON, P., ALDERSON, J., GOSTIN, L., and MASON, C. (1988), *The Police, Public Order and Civil Liberties* (London: Routledge).

MacDONALD, V. N. (1986), *A Study of Leadership and Supervision in Policing* (Ottawa: Canadian Police College).

McKENZIE, I., MORGAN, R., and REINER, R. (1990), 'Helping the Police With Their Inquiries', *Criminal Law Review*, Jan.: 22–33.

McLAUGHLIN, E. (1990), '*Community, Policing and Accountability: A Case-Study of Manchester 1981–1988*', Ph.D. Thesis, Faculty of Law: University of Sheffield.

McMAHON, M., and ERICSON, R. (1984), *Policing Reform* (University of Toronto: Centre of Criminology).

McNEE, D. (1979), 'The Queen's Police Keepeth the Peace', *Guardian*, 25 Sept.: 25.

——(1983), *McNee's Law* (London: Collins).

MAGUIRE, M., and CORBETT, C. (1989), 'Patterns and Profiles of Complaints Against the Police,' in R. Morgan and D. Smith (eds.), *Coming to Terms With Policing* (London: Routledge).

MARK, R. (1977), *Policing a Perplexed Society* (London: Allen and Unwin).

——(1978), *In the Office of Constable* (London: Collins).

MARSHALL, G. (1965), *Police and Government* (London: Methuen).

——(1978), 'Police Accountability Revisited', in D. Butler and A. H. Halsey (eds.), *Policy and Politics* (London: Macmillan).

MERTON, R. (1957), 'Patterns of Influence: Local and Cosmopolitan Influentials', in id., *Social Theory and Social Structure*, Ch. 10 (Glencoe: Free Press).

MILLS, C. W. (1956), *The Power Élite* (New York: Oxford University Press).

MORGAN, J. (1987), *Conflict and Order: The Police and Labour Disputes In England and Wales 1900–39* (Oxford: Oxford University Press).

MORGAN, R. (1986), 'Police Consultative Groups: The Implications for Governance of the Police', *Political Quarterly*, 57: 83–7.

——(1987), 'Police Accountability: Developing the Local Infrastructure', *British Journal of Criminology*, 27: 87–96.

——and MAGGS, C. (1985), *Setting the PACE: Police-Community Consultative Arrangements in England and Wales* (University of Bath: Centre for the Study of Social Policy).

——and SWIFT, P. (1987), 'The Future of Police Authorities', *Public Administration*, 65: 259–77.

MORRIS, T. (1985), 'The Case for a Riot Squad', *New Society*, 29 Nov., 363–4.

NORTHAM, G. (1988), *Shooting in the Dark* (London: Faber).

NOTT-BOWER, W. (1926), *Fifty-Two Years A Policeman* (London: Arnold).

OKOJIE, P. (1985), 'Chief Constables and Police Interference: The Case of Anderton and Greater Manchester', in B. Fine and R. Millar (eds.), *Policing the Miners' Strike* (London: Lawrence and Wishart).

OLIVER, I. (1987), *Police, Government and Accountability* (London: Macmillan).

Operational Policing Review, 1990 Joint Consultative Committee of the Police Staff Associations (Surbiton, Surrey: The Police Federation).

O'REILLY, R. R., and DOSTALER, A. (1983), 'Police Manager Development Study II', *Canadian Police College Journal*, 7: 24–51.

PEARSON, G. (1983), *Hooligan* (London: Macmillan).

PIRSLEY, R. D. (1974), 'Leadership and Community Identification Attitudes among Two Categories of Police Chiefs', *Journal of Police Science and Administration*, 2: 414–22.

RAWLINGS, P. (1991), 'Creeping Privatisation? The Police, the Conservative Government and Policing in the late 1980s', in R. Reiner and M. Cross (eds.), *Beyond Law and Order* (London: Macmillan).

REINER, R. (1978), *The Blue-Coated Worker* (Cambridge: Cambridge University Press).

——(1980), 'Fuzzy Thoughts: The Police and Law and Order Politics', *Sociological Review*, 28: 377–413.

——(1981), 'The Politics of Police Power', in *Politics and Power 4: Law, Politics and Justice* (London: Routledge).

——(1982), 'Who Are the Police?', *Political Quarterly*, 53: 165–80.

——(1985), *The Politics of the Police* (Brighton: Wheatsheaf).

——(1988), 'In the Office of Chief Constable', *Current Legal Problems 1988* (London: Stevens), 135–68.

——(1989a), 'Where the Buck Stops: Chief Constables' Views on Police Accountability', in R. Morgan and D. Smith (eds.), *Coming to Terms with Policing* (London: Routledge).

——(1989b), 'The Politics of Police Research', in M. Weatheritt (ed.), *Police Research: Some Future Prospects* (Aldershot: Avebury).

——(1990a), 'Police and Public Order in 1989', in P. Catterall (ed.), *Contemporary Britain: An Annual Review* (Oxford: Basil Blackwell).

——(1990b), 'Pulling Rank on the Police File', *Guardian*, 4 July, 21.

——(1990c), 'Top Cop Class', *Howard Journal of Criminal Justice*, 29: 215–19.

——(1991), 'Chief Constables in England and Wales: A Social Portrait of a Criminal Justice Élite', in id. and M. Cross (eds.), *Beyond Law and Order* (London: Macmillan).

——and CROSS, M. (1991) (eds.), *Beyond Law and Order: Criminal Justice Policy and Politics into the 1990s* (London: Macmillan).

REISS, A. J. (1971), *The Police and the Public* (New Haven: Yale University Press).

ROSE, G. (1979), *A Pictorial History of the Oxford City Police 1869–1968* (Oxford: Oxford University Press).

ROSHIER, B. (1989), *Controlling Crime* (Milton Keynes: Open University Press).

Royal Commission on Police Powers and Procedures (1929), *Report*, Cmnd. 3297 (London: HMSO).

Royal Commission on the Police (1962), *Final Report*, Cmnd. 1728 (London: HMSO).

Royal Commission on Criminal Procedure (1981), *Report*, Cmnd. 8092 (London: HMSO).

ST JOHNSTON, E. (1978), *One Policeman's Story* (Chichester: Barry Rose).

SANDERS, A. (1987), 'Constructing the Case for the Prosecution', *Journal of Law and Society*, 14: 229–53.

—— (1988), 'The Limits to Diversion From Prosecution', *British Journal of Criminology*, 28: 513–32.

—— BRIDGES, L., MULVANEY, A., and CROZIER, G. (1989), *Advice and Assistance at Police Stations and the 24-Hour Duty Solicitor Scheme* (London: Lord Chancellor's Department).

SCARMAN, Lord (1981), *The Brixton Disorders*, Cmnd. 8427 (London: HMSO).

SCOTT, H. (1954), *Scotland Yard* (London: Andre Deutsch).

SCOTT, M. S. (1986), *Managing For Success: A Police Chief's Survival Guide* (Washington, DC: Police Executive Research Forum).

SCRATON, P. (1985), *The State of the Police* (London: Pluto Press).

—— and THOMAS, P. (1985) (eds.), 'The State vs. the People: Lessons From the Coal Dispute', special issue of *Journal of Law and Society*, 12: 3.

SEDLEY, S. (1985), 'The Uniformed Mind', in J. Baxter and L. Koffman (eds.), *Police: The Constitution and the Community* (Abingdon: Professional Books).

SHERR, A. (1989), *Freedom of Protest, Public Order and the Law* (Oxford: Basil Blackwell).

SILLITOE, P. J. (1955), *Cloak Without Dagger* (London: Cassell).

SKOLNICK, J. H. (1969), *The Politics of Protest* (New York: Bantam).

—— and BAYLEY, D. H. (1986), *The New Blue Line* (New York: Free Press).

—— and —— (1988a), 'Theme and Variation in Community Policing', in M. Tonry and N. Morris (eds.) *Crime and Justice*, (Chicago: Chicago University Press), 1–37.

—— and —— (1988b), *Community Policing: Issues and Practices Around the World* (Washington, DC: National Institute of Justice).

SMITH, C. (1981), 'Accountability of Chief Constables in England and Wales', in H. Peers (ed.), *Seaford House Papers 1981*, Seaford House, 85–107.

SMITH, H. (1910), *From Constable to Commissioner* (London: Chatto and Windus).

SMITH, A. T. H. (1987), *Offences against Public Order* (London: Sweet and Maxwell).

STALKER, J. (1988), *Stalker* (London: Harrap).

STANWORTH, P. (1984), 'Élites and Privilege', in P. Abrams and R. Brown (eds.), *UK Society* (London: Weidenfeld and Nicolson).

STEEDMAN, C. (1984), *Policing the Victorian Community* (London: Routledge).

STENNING, P. (1981a), 'The Role of Police Boards and Commissions as Institutions of Municipal Police Governance', in C. D. Shearing (ed.), *Organisational Police Deviance* (Toronto: Butterworth).

——(1981b), *Police Commissions and Boards in Canada* (University of Toronto: Centre of Criminology).

SWANSON, C. R., and TERRITO, L. (1982), 'Police Leadership and Interpersonal Communication Styles' in J. R. Greene (ed.), *Managing Police Work* (Beverly Hills: Sage).

TARDIF, G. (1974), *Police et politique au Quebec* (Montreal: Éditions de l'Aurore).

TAYLOR, I., WALTON, P., and YOUNG, J. (1973), *The New Criminology* (London: Routledge).

THOMPSON, E. P. (1980), 'The State of the Nation', in id., *Writing By Candlelight* (London: Merlin Press), 189–210 (originally published in *New Society*, 8 Nov.–13 Dec. 1979).

THOMSON, B. (1922), *Queer People* (London: Hodder and Stoughton).

TUCK, M. (1989), *Drinking and Disorder: A Study of Non-Metropolitan Violence*, Home Office Research and Planning Unit Study 108 (London: HMSO).

UGLOW, S. (1988), *Policing Liberal Society* (Oxford: Oxford University Press).

VOLD, G. B., and BERNARD, T. J. (1986), *Theoretical Criminology* (New York: Oxford University Press).

WADDINGTON, P. A. J. (1982), 'Conservatism, Dogmatism and Authoritarianism in the Police: A Comment', *Sociology* 16: 592–4.

——(1987), 'Towards Paramilitarism? Dilemmas in Policing Civil Disorder', *British Journal of Criminology*, 27: 37–46.

——(1988), *Arming An Unarmed Police* (London: Police Foundation).

——(1991), *The Strong Arm of the Law* (Oxford: Oxford University Press).

WALL, D. S. (1987), 'Chief Constables: A Changing Élite', In R. Mawby (ed.), *Policing Britain* (Plymouth Polytechnic: Department of Political and Social Sciences).

——(1989), 'The Selection of Chief Constables in England and Wales 1835–1985', M. Phil. Thesis, University of York: Department of Social Policy.

WEATHERITT, M. (1986), *Innovations in Policing* (London: Croom Helm).

WEBER, M. (1949), *The Methodology of the Social Sciences* (Glencoe: Free Press).

——(1964), *The Theory of Economic and Social Organisation* (Glencoe: Free Press).

WESTERGAARD, J., and RESLER, H. (1975), *Class in a Capitalist Society* (London: Heinemann).

WILLIAMS, J. E. HALL (1988) (ed.), *The Role of the Prosecution* (London: Avebury).

WILSON, J. Q. (1968), *Varieties of Police Behaviour* (Cambridge, Mass.: Harvard University Press).

WITHAM, D. C. (1985), *The American Law Enforcement Chief Executive* (Washington, DC: Police Executive Research Forum).

YOUNG, M. (1958), *The Rise of the Meritocracy* (Harmondsworth: Penguin).

ZANDER, M. (1981), 'Royal Commission: No Grounds for Suspicion', *Guardian*, 12 Jan.

—— (1982), 'Police Powers', *Political Quarterly*, 53: 128–43.

—— (1990), *The Police and Criminal Evidence Act 1984*, 2nd edn. (London: Sweet and Maxwell).

Index